Case Studies in Mental Health Treatment

A Cross Section of Journal Articles for Discussion and Evaluation

Edited by

Robert Kalina

Pyrczak Publishing
P.O. Box 39731
Los Angeles, CA 90039

© Copyright 1993 by Pyrczak Publishing. All rights reserved.

ISBN 0–9623744–5–8

Printed in the United States of America.

CONTENTS

INTRODUCTION vii

COGNITIVE THERAPY

1. Changing Mistaken Beliefs through Visualization of Early Recollections — 1

2. Sexual Counseling with a Developmentally Disabled Couple: A Case Study — 7

3. Reducing a Child's Nighttime Fears — 13

4. Treatment of an Adolescent with Bowel Movement Phobia Using Self-Control Therapy — 19

5. "Forbidden Fruit Tastes Especially Sweet." Cognitive-Behavior Therapy with a Kleptomaniac Woman: A Case Report — 27

BEHAVIOR THERAPY AND BEHAVIOR MODIFICATION

6. Behavioral Treatment of Night Bingeing and Rumination in an Adult Case of Bulimia Nervosa — 33

7. Decreasing Junk-Food Consumption Through the Use of Self-Management Procedures: A Case Study — 39

8. Case Report of a Needle Phobia — 45

9. Controlling Extremely Dangerous Aggressive Outbursts when Functional Analysis Fails — 51

10. Linking Descriptive and Experimental Analyses in the Treatment of Bizarre Speech — 59

HUMANISTIC, CLIENT CENTERED, AND GESTALT THERAPY

11. Body Image Changes During Guided Affective Imagery — 71

12. Self and Space — 79

13. The Intruder: A Dream-Work Session with Commentary — 87

14. A Look at the Self-Righteous Defense — 95

15. Grieving the Loss of Narcissistic Entitlement: A Case Study — 103

GROUP AND FAMILY THERAPY

16. A Group Counseling Experience with the Very Old — 115

17. Group and Individual Reactions to the Death of a Member of a University-Affiliated Women's Support Group — 125

18. Multiple Severe Sexual Dysfunctions Resolved in Brief Sex Therapy — 131

19. Childhood Neurotic Disorders with a Sexual Content Need Not Imply Child Sexual Abuse — 135

PSYCHOANALYSIS

20. Pubescence: A Psychoanalytic Study of One Girl's Experience of Puberty — 143

21. The Psychoanalytic Treatment of a Preschool Boy with a Gender Identity Disorder — 155

22. Identity Formation in an Adolescent Girl: Boundaries Between Psychotherapy and Counselling — 167

REHABILITATION

23. Occupational Therapy Intervention for an Adult with Depression and Suicidal Tendencies — 175

24. Extended Inpatient Treatment of a Refractory Heroin Addict: A Multidisciplinary Approach to Patients with a Dual Diagnosis — 181

25. Alcoholic Women's Feminine Self-Concept and Mothering: The Importance of Reinforcing Self-Esteem in Treatment — 189

SPECIALIZED INTERVENTIONS

26. Hypnotherapy for Agoraphobia: A Case Study — 193

27. A Case Analysis in Human Sexuality: Counseling to a Man with Severe Cerebral Palsy — 199

28. Treating Adolescent Satanism in Art Therapy — 209

29. Summoning a Punishing Angel: Treatment of a Depressed Patient with Dissociative Features — 219

HEALTH PSYCHOLOGY AND MEDICINE

30. Therapy for an Anxious Patient Who Believes His Symptoms Are Caused by a Medical Problem — 229

31. Psychotherapy by Telephone: A Therapeutic Tool for Cancer Patients — 235

32. The Longing for Nurturance: A Case of Factitious Cancer — 243

33. Eight Cases of Patients with Unfounded Fear of AIDS — 247

34. Bulimia Nervosa and Acne May Be Related: A Case Report — 253

Notes:

INTRODUCTION

The 34 journal articles in this book—authored by practicing psychotherapists, psychiatrists, psychoanalysts, and counselors—describe the treatment of individual clients. In most cases, the authors discuss a client's psychological problem, the treatment used with the client, and the outcome.

Because this book is designed for use in courses in clinical, counseling, and abnormal psychology, each article is followed by (1) a list of psychological terms for classroom discussion and (2) questions that call for students' opinions on various aspects of the case. Depending on the course objectives, some professors may wish to use the questions as the primary stimulus for classroom discussions, whereas others may prefer to hold general discussions of students' reactions to the articles.

In the table of contents, the articles are grouped into broad categories to assist professors in selecting appropriate articles for class assignments. Because the categories are *not* mutually exclusive, however, many of the articles could have been placed appropriately in more than one category. An illuminating topic for classroom discussion, therefore, is the assignment of the articles to the categories (e.g., Could an article have been appropriately assigned to more than one category? Was it placed in the most appropriate category?).

Objectives

The objectives that guided the development of this book are:

1. To illustrate the use of various types of mental health treatments.

2. To provide in-depth examples of common psychological disorders.

3. To provide case studies written by a number of authors, all of whom provide mental health services. Case studies written from diverse points of view should stimulate lively classroom discussions.

4. To introduce students to case studies in journals as a means of continuing their professional education after completion of their formal schooling.

5. To provide practice in evaluating reports of case studies and, by example, show students how to write case studies for publication in academic journals.

Evaluation Criteria

The last seven questions at the end of each article ask students to evaluate the case study using the following criteria.

1. The demographics of the case are described.

In addition to describing gender and age, the authors should describe other salient characteristics such as race/ethnicity, socioeconomic status, and marital status. Depending upon the nature of the problem and treatment modality, the description of additional characteristics may be desirable.

2. The condition(s) and behavior(s) that necessitated treatment are described in detail.

The description of a condition such as a recent divorce, for example, should contain relevant details such as the length of the marriage, the reasons for divorce, and complications, if any, in the divorce settlement.

"Behavior" refers not only to gross motor behavior but also to verbal and nonverbal expressions of feelings and beliefs.

3. The method of treatment is described in sufficient detail so that it can be replicated.

This is a problematic criterion to apply for two reasons. First, different authors may have made different assumptions about the sophistication and knowledge of their readers; unsophisticated readers who are just beginning their study of psychological treatments may need more detail than seasoned practitioners. Second, describing long-term, intensive treatments in great detail is beyond the scope of the typical journal article; most journal editors expect authors to be as brief as possible while communicating essential facts and themes.

An important ideal in scientific writing is that procedures and outcomes be *operationally defined*; an operational definition is one given in terms of physical steps. In the case of psychological treatments, this ideal requires that all the steps the therapist or counselor followed in the treatment of a client are described in enough detail to enable another practitioner to replicate the entire process without additional information. Given the limitations on journal space, this ideal is, at best, only approximated in most cases. Thus, when applying this criterion, students should ask whether the treatment has been described in such a manner that its essential elements are evident.

4. A rationale is provided for the method of treatment selected.

The author should describe a rationale for using a particular method with a client. This may be based on theory, on previous experiences of the clinician, or on experiences reported in the literature.

5. The client's improvement, if any, is clearly documented.

Documentation may take many forms; direct observations of the client's behavior, self-reports by the client, reports by other individuals who interact with the client, and the client's performance on standardized psychological scales are frequently used. The validity and reliability of the documentation should be considered, especially when relying on self-reports, which may be distorted. In many cases, it is appropriate to utilize more than one type of documentation so that each can serve as a validity check on the other.

6. Follow-up information on the client's improvement, if any, is presented.

Although there are no hard and fast rules on how long the follow-up should last, for many types of problems a minimum of six months is appropriate.

7. The study is appropriate for publication in a journal.

Because there are many thousands of case studies that could be written in the form of articles for consideration by journals each year and because journal space is limited, a case study should have some distinguishing feature(s) that lead to its acceptance for publication. Journal policies differ on this issue. The following statement from the editorial policy of the *Journal of Behavior Therapy and Experimental Psychiatry* provides guidelines on this criterion:

> A case report, to be acceptable, must embody one of the following: (1) a new and original method, target behavior, or population; (2) an apparently advantageous variation of a previous method; (3) an observation of considerable interest; (4) an unusually clear account of the use of an accepted method.

Application of the Criteria

When applying the criteria to the case studies in this book, keep in mind that few authors of case study reports published in journals will be able to meet all of them. This is sometimes due, in part, to physical constraints in the clinical setting (e.g., the client is not available for follow-up). It is also often due to the requirement for brevity imposed by many journals. Thus, in most cases, application of the criteria will require some subjectivity. This subjective element will result in lively classroom discussions, which will enhance learning.

Acknowledgments

I wish to acknowledge the copyright holders who kindly granted permission to reprint the articles; without their cooperation, preparation of this book would have been impossible. Three anonymous reviewers of the first draft of this book provided helpful suggestions. Finally, I wish to thank Holbrook Mahn, Leslie Mahn, and Paula Cizmar for their editorial assistance.

Robert Kalina
Los Angeles, California

Case 1

Changing Mistaken Beliefs through Visualization of Early Recollections*

MaryAnn Lingg

Terry Kottman

There are no chance memories: out of the incalculable number of impressions which meet an individual he chooses to remember only those which he feels, however darkly, to have bearing on his situation. Thus his memories represent his "Story of My Life"; a story he repeats to himself to warm him or comfort him, to keep him concentrated on his goal and to prepare him by means of past experiences so that he will meet the future with an already tested style of action (Adler, 1958, p. 73).

(1) Early recollections are traditionally used in Individual Psychology to facilitate the investigation into a client's life style. While early memories do not determine behavior, they do reflect the client's current self-image, views of the world, and style of interaction with others. When asked to describe specific incidents that took place during the early years of life, the client selects, alters, or imagines events that express the central issues and interests of his or her life (Ackerknecht, 1976; Bruhn & Last, 1982). Gathering early recollections can help the counselor begin to understand the client's struggles, attitudes, hopes, and behaviors (Papanek, 1972). They give the counselor clues about the direction of the client's strivings and the ways the client gains significance. Early recollections indicate the values to which the client ascribes and the dangers the client wishes to avoid (Adler, 1937). Basic mistakes, illuminated by the early recollections, represent the client's basic convictions about self, the world, and others. These ideas, which govern behavior, may or may not be within the client's awareness (Manaster & Corsini, 1982).

(2) Basic mistakes are *basic* because they are the original ideas a child develops to fulfill the needs of belonging and significance. They are considered *mistakes* because they are faulty conclusions drawn from a child's perspective while the child is engaged in the struggle to establish a place in the world. As Dreikurs and Soltz (1964) indicated, "Children are expert observers but make many mistakes in interpreting what they observe. They often draw wrong conclusions and choose mistaken ways in which to find their place" (p. 15).

(3) One of the goals of counseling is to identify basic mistakes and bring them to the client's awareness. It is the counselor's responsibility to discover those early, erroneously developed convictions and to help the client see how those ideas are false and how they can interfere with effective social and personal functioning. Manaster and Corsini (1982) refer to the process of psychotherapy as uncovering the basic mistakes and correcting them.

(4) Sometimes simply talking to the client about mistaken beliefs and bringing them to the client's awareness is enough to bring about changes in the client's self perception. However, at other times, mistaken beliefs and private logic are so ingrained in the client's way of looking at life and self that talking about them does not bring about a change. When this happens the counselor must introduce creative ways of helping the client reexamine basic convictions in order to bring about

---

*Reprinted from *Individual Psychology: The Journal of Adlerian Theory, Research & Practice, 47*, 255-260. Copyright 1991 by the University of Texas Press, 2100 Comal, Austin, Texas 78722. Reprinted with permission.

changes. Early recollections have been used to help the client gain insight into his or her life style. By interpreting an early recollection or series of early recollections to the client, the counselor can hold up a "mirror reflecting the patient's present attitudes and intentions" (Ackerknecht, 1976, p. 54). Since early recollections represent a microcosm of the client's mistaken beliefs and private logic, active interpretation and visualization of early recollections may be an excellent tool for helping the client reconsider mistaken beliefs. It may then be possible for the client to substitute positive convictions for negative beliefs.

The Technique

(5) Before initiating the visualization process, the counselor reviews any previously presented early recollections and asks for any others the client may remember. The counselor is then free to choose the early recollection which best typifies the basic mistake currently under examination.

(6) The counselor begins the visualization process with some basic relaxation techniques such as asking the client to close his or her eyes, take a few deep breaths, and get as comfortable as possible. The counselor then asks the client to visualize the specific incident chosen to represent the particular mistaken belief. It may facilitate the process if the counselor suggests to the client to think of the early recollections as a scene in a play or television show to be watched from the perspective of an audience. The counselor then asks the client to describe the scene as it is unfolding. With eyes still shut, the client is asked to describe the feelings experienced during the interaction. In order to begin to change the mistaken belief, the counselor asks the client to visualize himself or herself as an adult actually entering the scene. The client is asked to visualize the adult self comforting the child self, telling the child self how valuable, important, and lovable he or she is. Then the counselor suggests that the visualized adult begin to help reconsider any mistaken beliefs about what is necessary to achieve significance and belonging.

(7) For instance, in one early recollection, a client was frightened for appropriate reasons, but her father pushed her aside and called her a baby for being fearful. By interpreting this to mean that her father would not accept her feelings, she formulated a mistaken belief which stated that in order to be loved and belong in her family she needed to deny her feelings and be someone other than who she really was. The visualized adult version of her self comforted her child self and reassured her of the appropriateness of her feelings and encouraged her to express those feelings. The adult self also expressed a willingness to accept her as she was, without a need for pretense.

(8) The counselor then asks the client if there is anything else in the visualized interaction that needs to be changed or if there is anything else the child self needs. If the client answers affirmatively, the counselor guides the client through the process of visualizing the adult self making those changes, doing whatever needs to be done in order to help the child self feel comfortable and safe. After bringing the client back to the present, the counselor asks the client to reexamine mistaken beliefs and to consider other more useful ways of gaining a sense of significance and belonging. At this time, the counselor also helps the client change the wording of selected negative self statements.

A Case Study

(9) A 32-year-old female entered counseling after the breakup of a love relationship. The client was experiencing extreme sadness at the disintegration of the relationship and was having difficulty letting go of her investment in the relationship. After establishing rapport with the client, the counselor began to explore her mistaken beliefs. They identified these mistaken beliefs: (a) "it is my responsibility to make and keep others happy"; (b) "I must control others' behavior to feel important"; and (c) "I must hold things together in the family."

(10) For several sessions the client repeatedly stated that she wanted to change her mistaken beliefs, but that she could not change the way she interacted with others. The counselor decided to employ the technique of early recollection visualization as a possible method of helping her get past this impasse. The counselor asked the client to close her eyes, sit comfortably in the chair, take several deep breaths, then recount one of her early recollections and she related this memory:

> I remember one day my mother was supposed to visit an old friend who happened to live on the other side of the city, near an amusement park. My father was going to drop my mother off at her friend's house and take my younger brother and I to the amusement park while my mother visited her friend. Some time before we were getting ready to go, my father was nagging my mother about something and before you knew it, it was a huge argument with my father nitpicking at my mother over anything. This happened quite often. Finally, my mother was so upset that she decided not to visit her

friend. My mother was standing at the front door looking out the window crying. My father was standing in the dining room telling my mother there was no reason to be upset and she should get ready to go out. I was running back and forth between the two of them trying to interpret what the other was saying and trying to smooth things over. I was trying to get my father to stop harassing my mother and trying to get my mother to feel better. I wanted them to stop so things could go as planned.

When the counselor asked about feelings the client replied:

I remember feeling helpless and pulled in two directions. I wanted them to stop arguing because I didn't like my mother to be upset or my father to be angry. I felt responsible for making things better between them and making everyone happy. I wanted things to be OK so we could still go to the park and I felt selfish about that.

(11) The counselor guided the client through the early recollection visualization process described above. The counselor asked the client to visualize herself entering the scene as an adult and encouraged her to hug and comfort her child self. The counselor coached her through a process in which her adult self told the child self that she did not need to always take care of other people nor did she have the power to control others' behavior. The counselor prompted the adult self to tell the child self that she was not responsible for resolving the parental conflict. The counselor also prompted the adult self to hold the child self and reassure her that she was lovable and significant even when she was not taking care of others. When the counselor asked the client if there was anything else she wanted to change in the visualization she replied "I want her to know (child self) that she is really loved." After the adult self told the child self how much she loved her, the counselor brought her out of the visualization.

(12) The counselor and the client processed the early recollection visualization and discussed changes she wished to make in her basic convictions. They talked about how this early recollection illustrated all three of the basic mistakes they had identified. They discussed the client's feelings of sadness and hopelessness in trying to live her life in accordance with these mistaken beliefs. The client said she would like to change her erroneous convictions to the following: (a) "although I can contribute to others' happiness, I do not have the power to make or keep them happy"; (b) "I do not have the power to control others' behavior"; and (c) "it is not my responsibility to hold things together in my family."

(13) After this session, the client reported a release of responsibility from a job that was not hers in the first place: taking care of her parents' relationship and happiness. The client continued to examine her basic mistakes and to look at how these ideas interfered with her present functioning. With the help of the counselor she was also able to relate the basic mistakes highlighted in this early recollection to her continuing investment in the recently ended love relationship. She had experienced difficulty in letting go of the relationship because she believed she was solely responsible for its continuance. She replaced this belief with one that allowed her to stop being responsible for the happiness of others. Thus, she could let go of the illusion that she must control all of her relationships.

(14) A one-month follow-up found the client still experiencing the same release of responsibility and emotional disengagement from the defunct relationship. She reported an increase in her ability to concentrate on other matters and was no longer obsessing about the relationship. She was continuing to redefine her priorities for future relationships and her beliefs about how she could gain a sense of belonging and significance.

Conclusion

(15) Counselors can assist clients in belief reorientation through the use of early recollection visualization. This technique helps clients gain a clearer understanding of their mistaken beliefs and facilitates changes in the ways they gain significance. Early recollection visualization is an action-oriented method which is helpful with clients who have difficulty making a connection between their early decisions and their present behavior. Counselors may recognize this type of client as the one who frequently asks, "Why do I continue to do this?" or who says, "I do not understand why I do the things I do." This technique is also effective with clients who resist examining their mistaken beliefs or persist in negative self-talk. Visualization may also help clients who have a cognitive understanding of their problem but seem to have difficulty changing their feelings and behaviors.

(16) However, counselors should be aware that this technique is not a magical cure. Early recollection visualization is simply one of many therapeutic tools to be used in conjunction with other strategies. It should never be used without a strong counselor-client relationship and an understanding of the client's life-style. Following a visualization, it is imperative that counselors process clients' experiences with them to insure client understanding and well-being.

References

Ackerknecht, L. (1976). New aspects of early recollections (ER) as a diagnostic and therapeutic device. *Individual Psychologist, 13,* 44-54.

Adler, A. (1937). Significance of early recollections. *International Journal of Individual Psychology, 3,* 283-287.

Adler, A. (1958). *What life should mean to you.* New York: Capricorn Books.

Bruhn, A. R., & Last, J. (1982). Earliest childhood memories: Four theoretical perspectives. *Journal of Personality Assessment, 46,* 119-127.

Dreikurs, R., & Soltz, V. (1964). *Children: The challenge.* New York: Hawthorn/Dutton.

Manaster, G., & Corsini, R. (1982). *Individual psychology: Theory and practice.* Itasca, IL: F. E. Peacock.

Papanek, H. (1972). The use of early recollections in psychotherapy. *Individual Psychology, 28,* 169-176.

Terms for Discussion

1. early recollections (paragraphs 1, 4, 5, 7, 10, 11, 12, 15, and 16)

2. self-image (paragraph 1)

3. basic mistakes (paragraphs 1, 2, 3, 4, 5, 12, and 13)

4. mistaken beliefs (paragraphs 6, 7, 8, 9, 10, and 15)

5. visualization process (paragraphs 5, 6, 8, 10, 11, 12, 15, and 16)

6. negative self-talk (paragraph 15)

Questions

7. In your opinion, is the quotation from Adler at the beginning of this article important and appropriate? Explain.

8. In paragraph 1, the authors state that "early memories do not determine behavior." Do you agree?

9. Do you believe that you personally have held mistaken beliefs? If yes, briefly describe some of them and their origin.

10. According to the authors, what should a counselor do before initiation of the visualization process?

11. Does the case report in paragraphs 9 through 14 adequately illustrate the technique described in paragraphs 5 through 8? Explain.

12. In your opinion, do the client's quotations in paragraph 10 reflect the mistaken beliefs identified in paragraph 9? Explain.

13. In your opinion, could the improvement reported in paragraphs 13 and 14 have been coincidental and not the result of the visualization process? Explain.

14. Have the authors convinced you that the visualization technique can assist certain clients with a variety of problems? Explain.

15. Are there other forms of treatment that might have facilitated the client's progress? Explain.

15. Rate the article on the seven criteria described in the introduction to this book on a scale from 5 (highest quality) through 1 (lowest quality). Be prepared to explain your ratings.

Criterion 1: The demographics of the case are described: _____

Criterion 2: The condition(s) and behavior(s) that necessitated treatment are described in detail: _____

Criterion 3: The method of treatment is described in sufficient detail so that it can be replicated without additional information: _____

Criterion 4: A rationale is provided for the method of treatment selected: _____

Criterion 5: The client's improvement, if any, is clearly documented: _____

Criterion 6: Follow-up information on the client's improvement, if any, is presented: _____

Criterion 7: The study is appropriate for publication in a journal: _____

Notes:

Case 2

Sexual Counseling with a Developmentally Disabled Couple: A Case Study*

Deborah I. Frank

ABSTRACT: This article describes the process of sexual counseling with a developmentally disabled couple, illustrating principles and techniques that were unique to this couple's concern. The author asserts that this aspect of a marital relationship should not be denied a couple simply because they are handicapped. Her intent is to help nurses understand some of the issues involved in sexual counseling with developmentally disabled persons, and to motivate nurses to help those who may express concerns.

(1) The principle of normalization suggests that the developmentally disabled have a right to experience a pattern of life as close as possible to the "regular" ways of the culture (Kramer-Monat, 1982). The person's abilities are to be developed to his or her maximum capacity in the areas of independent living, school, employment, and satisfying interpersonal relationships. Satisfying interpersonal relationships may include much more than friendship—the opportunity to marry and have sexual intimacy within that marriage as well.

(2) However, sexual intimacy is one aspect of the mentally retarded person's life that is not often discussed between the nurse and the client. Within institutional or group home settings the goal of staff is often to assist clients to "manage" sexual urges rather than to aid the clients in the appropriate expression of sexual feelings within an intimate relationship.

(3) Furthermore, nurses who recognize the developmentally disabled client's wish to express sexual intimacy may not feel knowledgeable or comfortable enough to provide the counseling needed. The clinical nurse specialist can provide invaluable assistance when this proves to be the case, as demonstrated in the following case illustration.

Case Illustration

(4) A staff member in a group home for the developmentally disabled asked if I would provide sexual counseling to a developmentally disabled couple who had recently married. Both of them were wheelchair bound. Mr. G. had good upper body strength, could independently tend to his own personal car and household tasks, and was able to maintain a part-time job. On the other hand, Mrs. G. was more limited in her ability to function independently. Since her arms lacked strength and fine motor coordination, she needed aid in performing some of her personal care, could only master certain household tasks, and was not employed. Both experienced periodic leg and thigh muscle spasms in addition to having poor voluntary control of their lower limbs.

(5) Mr. G. was able to verbalize in a logical, clear manner, although his thinking was fairly concrete. The house counselor reported that he was able to problem solve and use good judgment in areas that were not too complex. Mrs. G. was described as less mentally capable than her husband. She seemed to have difficulty being realistic when making decisions and at times was impulsive and subject to abrupt mood changes.

(6) The couple had requested sexual counseling because they were unable to have "normal" sexual relationships, which meant, to them, sexual intercourse. The house

---

*Reprinted from *Perspectives in Psychiatric Care*, 27, 1991, pp. 30-34. Copyright 1991 by Nursecom, Inc. Reprinted by permission.

counselors and agency nurse recognized their right to have a satisfying marital sexual relationship, but felt unable to provide adequate guidance in this area. However, they were willing to transport the couple to my office for counseling.

(7) Lack of information about sexual function is often a source of problems for the developmentally disabled (Kempton, 1974). In addition, the couple's physical impairments, possible emotional stress, and environmental constraints could contribute to their sexual concerns. Hence, I planned to focus on these areas in the first counseling session. Although my goal was to assess their concerns during this first meeting, my major focus was to establish rapport and trust with the couple.

Initial Session

(8) Mr. and Mrs. G. were somewhat nervous and embarrassed when we first met. However, they quickly began asking questions—some of which caught me by surprise. They wanted to know how I treated sex problems and if they would have to take off their clothes. I quickly reassured them that this was a "talking" therapy, although I might use pictures and books to clarify what I was saying. This information seemed to reduce their anxiety considerably, which gave me the opportunity to inquire about their concerns.

(9) Both were quite open and expressed genuine worry about their ability to satisfy the other sexually. Mr. G., in particular, was worried about their inability to have intercourse. While he was articulate about how he wished to make love I could not understand specifically why they were having a problem. Thus, the first barrier I encountered was in establishing a common language with the couple so we could understand each other. Using pictures from various books on sexuality (Kaplan, 1975; Masters, Johnson, & Kolodny, 1988), I was able to identify what body parts they were referring to and the problems they were having with sexual positioning.

(10) The physical limitations of Mr. G. made it difficult for him to use the missionary position for sexual intercourse. Mrs. G. also had inner thigh spasms, so that it was sometimes difficult for her to separate her legs. With the use of illustrations showing different sexual positions, the couple was able to discuss positions that would be feasible and comfortable for them. However, they needed much reassurance that these modifications were normal. Also, I encouraged them to experiment using pillows to provide more support for Mrs. G. since she has less muscle strength. Finally, I suggested that they practice the positions with their clothes on during a nonsexual time so that they would not have to focus exclusively on mechanics when they were later having sex.

(11) As we viewed the various pictures, both of them had many questions about other aspects of sexual functioning and reproduction. Mrs. G. was very direct in asking me about my personal experiences. She noticed my baby's picture on the desk, which seemed to elicit many questions about pregnancy and caring for an infant. Aware that she had a hysterectomy, I knew that I should explore her motivations for asking these questions, since they could indicate unresolved feelings about bearing children. However, since I realized that every issue could not be discussed in the first session, I simply answered her questions as honestly as I could.

(12) During this discussion, Mrs. G. asked several times if I would bring my baby to a session. I avoided answering her request, which struck me as inappropriate. However, I felt some ambivalence—while I would ordinarily not bring my child to a therapy session, it also occurred to me that to do so could be of therapeutic value. I decided I should not refuse the request until I had given it some further thought. Because of this request and many other questions the couple had asked related to sex, pregnancy, and my personal life, I found myself feeling rather disorganized at the end of the interview. Yes, I had done much teaching and felt I had established rapport. But I had obtained only sketchy information about the emotional or environmental factors that might also be influencing the couple's sexual satisfaction. In addition, I was unclear as to the implications of Mrs. G.'s interest in having babies. Finally, I had to analyze my own feelings about her request to bring my child to a session and make a decision about how to handle this issue.

Second Session

(13) At the second meeting the couple reported that they had practiced the new positions and had found one that was comfortable to both of them. But Mr. G. quickly added that they had not had intercourse, although both had been very sexually aroused. Attempting to determine the exact nature of the problem, I began to ask very specific questions about how they had proceeded sexually. Mrs. G. provided the critical information when she observed that her husband's penis had a "covering over it that made it hurt when he tried to come inside." Upon further exploration (with the use of illustrations) a plausible reason for their failure to consummate the marriage became apparent. When Mr. G., who had not been circumcised, had an erection, his penile foreskin did not retract. He revealed that he did retract the foreskin manually when he masturbated but

had not done so before attempting vaginal penetration. I suggested that when they were sexually active again he should manually retract the foreskin before penetration.

Environmental Influences

(14) An environmental constraint for Mr. G. was the lack of privacy in having sexual intimacy. The couple did not have their own bedroom and were able to have privacy only once a month. At that time there was extreme pressure on Mr. G. to have an erection and complete sexual intercourse. If he failed to perform, he felt very inadequate and guilty. I stressed that it was quite normal for men to lose their erections when they were under such pressure. We talked about how the couple might obtain privacy on a regular basis. Mrs. G. had several roommates and Mr. G. had one. Both were hesitant to ask their roommates to leave the room so they could be alone, since it was a group home and sharing was clearly one of the norms.

(15) I proposed that Mr. G. might work out an arrangement with his roommate where each of them had the room for privacy at a certain time or on a certain night. Mr. G. responded that his roommate did not have a girlfriend and that he did not wish to make him feel badly about his situation. I pointed out that everyone has privacy needs which could be spent in many ways, such as reading, writing letters, meditating, or being intimate with someone. Still resisting, Mr. G. bluntly stated he would be too embarrassed to talk to his roommate about the arrangement. We explored his reasons for this feeling and then role-played how he might make the request. We practiced several approaches during the session, until Mr. G. felt confident that he could try to approach his roommate.

(16) A similar technique was used to solve the couple's problem of not having an adequate bed. The house had only single beds, which were too small for Mr. and Mrs. G. to be comfortable. The possibility of purchasing a double bed seemed unlikely. However, the couple agreed they could use two single beds if the legs were wired together to insure the beds would not roll apart. Again, we rehearsed how the couple might make this request of the house counselor since the counselor would need to assist them in making the adaptation.

Third Session

(17) I was eager for our third meeting to discover how the couple handled their "assignments." I was somewhat worried that I had been overly optimistic about persons at the house being cooperative and that Mr. and Mrs. G. might be disappointed by the outcome of their assertiveness. They appeared so happy as they entered the office that I knew something had gone well. They were glowing with pleasure because they had been able to achieve "normal" sexual relations. Their happiness helped me realize how meaningful it can be for the developmentally disabled to express themselves sexually. This aspect of a marital relationship should not be denied a couple simply because they are handicapped.

(18) Furthermore, the change in Mr. G.'s confidence level was remarkable. He had not only been effective in his sexual role, but he had experienced positive results from his assertiveness. In fact, the roommate had been pleased by the suggestion that each of them have specific times to have the room for privacy. Thus, the couple had experienced private time together and were feeling very close to each other, as well as proud of their accomplishments.

New Goals

(19) While their sexual relationship was finally satisfying to them, Mrs. G. was quick to announce that she now felt ready for them to have children. I clarified that due to her hysterectomy she could not bear children. Mrs. G. acknowledged that she understood this fact and what it meant to have a hysterectomy. But she continued to insist that she could care for a child. Mr. G. then added that he had had a vasectomy. Mrs. G. also acknowledged that reality, but became more adamant that she could still care for an infant. While I validated her ability to give love to a child, we focused on her ability to care physically for a child.

(20) Mr. G. voiced his doubts about either of them being capable of handling a child at this time. I pointed out that they needed to have a home of their own before even thinking about children. The house did not allow infants, and even if being foster parents was an option, they would need their own apartment. This discussion continued for some time in an emotional and confrontive fashion as the reality of the couple's physical limitations were discussed. At the close of the session, Mrs. G. again requested that I bring my infant to the next meeting. This time I agreed to do so. My decision was partly motivated by the fact that it would give Mrs. G. an enjoyable opportunity to play with an infant. But I also thought it might help Mrs. G. to realize that she could not physically care for a baby. At the close of this meeting I felt emotionally drained and sad. It had been difficult to confront Mrs. G. with the reality of her limitations, knowing that she did have love and affection to offer another person.

Fourth Session

(21) I brought my four-month-old baby to the next session and Mrs. G. held the baby while we talked. Mr. G. reported they were continuing to have satisfying sexual relations and Mrs. G. concurred. He stated he felt very positive about himself and their overall relationship. Mrs. G. disagreed, saying that she did not like it when Mr. G. interrupted her or talked for her. She thought this situation occurred because she was slower to speak or because he did not want to listen to her. Mr. G., defending himself, said he never knew when she was finished speaking, since she paused frequently. I asked the couple how they thought they might solve this problem. Mrs. G. suggested, "I'll tell him when I'm done talking and then he can talk." Her husband agreed that this approach would be helpful. I pointed out to the couple how well they had problem solved, and that they could use this technique at home when other misunderstandings occurred.

(22) Mrs. G. held the baby during the entire discussion, although she required assistance several times to keep the baby on her lap; her arms were not strong enough to control the baby's wiggling movements. Then came the critical time when the baby needed her diaper changed. I asked Mrs. G. if she would like to do that task. Mrs. G. refused, saying that she preferred to hold and rock the baby. I casually commented that diapers came with the fun of holding and rocking, but did not press the issue. Instead, we talked about how she might have contact with infants by volunteering at a day care center, or the nursery at their church. This suggestion was pleasing to the couple as well as realistic to achieve.

(23) We then began reviewing the original concerns the couple had presented and the current status of these problems. Both expressed satisfaction about their sexual relationship. We decided that they might come back for a follow-up meeting within a few weeks, but agreed that their major goals had been accomplished. Toward the end of this session Mrs. G. casually interjected that she wasn't ready to have children. She thought she and her husband needed to work towards getting their own place.

Final Session

(24) I saw this couple again one month later. They continued to express happiness with their sexual relationship. In addition, Mrs. G. was learning to cook and do more household tasks as a step toward obtaining an apartment. She noted that her husband was getting better at listening to her. The house counselor validated the couple's increasing sense of self-confidence and competence in carrying out their responsibilities. Mrs. G. asked for a picture of my baby, but did not say she wanted to have a child herself. I expected this issue would take a while for her to resolve, but at least for the time being her goals were attainable.

Conclusion

(25) This couple illustrated that developmentally disabled persons who are given the chance to develop their potential may be able to experience the satisfaction and pleasures that are inherent within intimate relationships. The need for sex education, problem-solving skills, communication skills, and practice in being assertive were similar to those of many couples who have sexual concerns. However, the counseling included much more validation, redirection, refocusing, and concrete education than it might for a couple with fewer physical and mental limitations. Furthermore, the experience helped me realize that "normalization" is not just an intellectual, theoretical construct. I learned on a very personal level that normalization can indeed improve the quality of life of the developmentally disabled.

References

Kaplan, H. (1975). *The illustrated manual of sex therapy.* New York: Brunner/Mazel.

Kempton, W. (1974). *A teacher's guide to sex education.* Monat, MA: Doxbury.

Masters, W., Johnson, V., & Kolodny, R. (1988). *Human sexuality for nurses.* Boston: Little Brown.

Kramer-Monat, R. (1982). *Sexuality and the mentally retarded: A clinical and therapeutic guidebook.* San Diego, CA: College Hill Press.

Sexual Counseling

Terms for Discussion

1. developmentally disabled (paragraphs 1, 3, 4, 7, 17, and 25)

2. mentally retarded (paragraph 2)

3. impulsive (paragraph 5)

4. abrupt mood change (paragraph 5)

5. anxiety (paragraph 8)

6. role play (paragraph 15)

7. assertiveness (paragraphs 17, 18, and 25)

Questions

8. Do you believe that institutions for the mentally retarded should help them appropriately express sexual feelings rather than "manage" them? (See paragraph 2.) Explain.

9. Comment on the initial counseling session. (See paragraphs 8 through 12.) In your opinion, was it productive? Was the focus correct? Would you have proceeded differently?

10. Was role playing appropriate in this particular case. (See paragraphs 15 and 16.) Why? Why not?

11. Does it surprise you that the counselor felt "emotionally drained and sad" ? (See paragraph 20.)

12. The counselor suggested that this couple could use their problem solving abilities (on their own) when other misunderstandings occurred. (See paragraph 21.) Do you believe that they are likely to have success at this? Explain.

13. Is the fact that the house counselor "validated" the progress of this couple important in establishing that real progress was made? Explain.

14. Are there other forms of treatment that might have facilitated this couple's improvement? Explain.

15. Rate the article on the seven criteria described in the introduction to this book on a scale from 5 (highest quality) through 1 (lowest quality). Be prepared to explain your ratings.

Criterion 1: The demographics of the case are described: _____

Criterion 2: The condition(s) and behavior(s) that necessitated treatment are described in detail: _____

Criterion 3: The method of treatment is described in sufficient detail so that it can be replicated without additional information: _____

Criterion 4: A rationale is provided for the method of treatment selected: _____

Criterion 5: The client's improvement, if any, is clearly documented: _____

Criterion 6: Follow-up information on the client's improvement, if any, is presented: _____

Criterion 7: The study is appropriate for publication in a journal: _____

Case 3

Reducing a Child's Nighttime Fears*

Jon E. Merritt
Portland Public Schools (Oregon)

(1) Nighttime fears have always been a common problem for children and their families. These "monsters," according to a literature review, frequently take the form of strangers or kidnappers who violently attack or hurt the child or members of the family. This may represent a shift away from previously more common fears of the dark or of animals (Orton, 1982; Robinson, Robinson, & Whetsell, 1988). Fears can have a debilitating effect upon the child's growth and day-to-day happiness as well as a disruptive effect on the family's routines and interactions. As exemplified in the case of Paula, a fifth-grade child referred to me several months ago, fears can be stubborn things to dislodge once personal and family patterns have been set and allowed to reinforce themselves (Dollinger, O'Donnell, & Staley, 1984; Moracco & Camilleri, 1983; Sarafino, 1986).

(2) Paula's parents had tried several ways to eliminate or lessen Paula's fears, but none worked. Rewarding her with treats or money worked for only a night or two; Paula soon returned to whining, crying, or procrastinating at bedtime. They tried, with even less success, scolding or telling her that the behavior was not age appropriate. Reasoning with Paula worked, but again only for a very short time. Periodically, Paula's parents simply gave up and let her wander between bedroom and living room and then find her asleep on a couch or in the hall. Everyone, especially Paula, was thoroughly out of patience with this disruption. Paula's parents were puzzled and bereft of ideas, even worrying that Paula might have some serious emotional problems.

(3) In the course of the work in lessening Paula's nighttime fears, I learned a great deal about this issue by analyzing the pieces of information that led to Paula's success. The purpose of this article is to share these ideas with other counselors who may need to help children cope with their fears.

Background Information

(4) Paula, 10 years of age, was referred by her parents because, as they put it, they "couldn't stand it anymore" around bedtime. They described their frustration and anger and their worrying that the continuing friction created by Paula's persistent anxiety would erode their relationship and compound the problem. When asked to describe other aspects of their lives with Paula prior to the current impasse, their answers made it clear that they were caring and competent parents. They disciplined her humanely and consistently and were able to express their love for her, both physically and verbally. There were no early-life traumas, nor did there seem to be any incidents of Paula's being personally attacked or hurt by anyone. Paula's parents, however, revealed several things that seemed to have a direct bearing on Paula's fear of going to bed:

1. The family had moved to a new home 2 months before Paula began to be fearful.
2. Paula's new room faced the backyard, which bordered a park.
3. The house had been burglarized soon after they moved in.
4. Paula's grandmother had recently been mugged, had her purse snatched, and had been knocked down.

---

*Reprinted from *Elementary School Guidance & Counseling*, 25, 1991, pp. 291-295. Copyright 1991 by the American Counseling Association. No further reproduction authorized without written permission.

(5) The parents understood that all of these facts probably had a great deal to do with Paula's behavior, but it was clear in their initial interview that they underestimated the nature of their child's reaction to trauma. They did not realize that fears may generalize to other places or situations beyond the initial fear-producing incident (Dollinger, O'Donnell, & Staley, 1984; Sarafino, 1986), nor did they realize that their own reactions to the fearful behavior, what Hyson (1979) has called "secondary gains," was helping to maintain it. Paula's parents thought that Paula should listen to them and believe what they told her about the slim chances of her fears becoming reality.

(6) Having gathered what seemed to be enough information to begin, I started seeing Paula individually during the latter part of her school day. What follows are the things that were done that seemed to lessen Paula's fears during that time.

Strategies to Lessen Fears and Encourage Control

Involve and Educate Parents

(7) Parents' perceptions of a child's fears are often skewed, usually to the side of dismissing the fears as being short-lived. Fears are not short-lived (Eme & Schmidt, 1978). Parents also underestimate the nature and quantity of their children's fears (Jones & Borgers, 1988), a problem that limits parents' helpfulness in their child's treatment. Parents can and must be appropriately involved in the reduction of their child's fears (Giebenhain & O'Dell, 1984; Duncan, Kraus, & Parks, 1986; Protinsky, 1985; Robinson, Robinson, & Whetsell, 1988). Given these guides and Paula's parents' underestimation of the intensity of her nighttime fears, I asked them to read Edward Sarafino's (1986) book *The Fears of Childhood*. This reading became the focus of twice-monthly consultations in which Paula's parents learned and practiced two responses to Paula's anxious behavior:

1. They responded relatively neutrally and unemotionally to Paula's pleas to stay up. Their responses were limited to acknowledging Paula's fear, with sentences such as "I know you don't want to go," and then following that with polite demands that she follow house rules about bedtime: "But you know bedtime is 9:00 p.m. Goodnight, honey." Then they were to go about their own evening's business and attempt to ignore repeated whining or procrastinating. They reported difficulty in remaining calm and feeling loving toward Paula.

2. Paula's parents rewarded each small effort on her part to "just go to bed" (Paula's words) without all the fuss. They verbally or physically acknowledged her progress in a low-key manner, using affectionate touches, smiles, or words, or went into her room and chatted for a moment after Paula voluntarily went to bed. They did not discuss the fearful thoughts Paula was having unless Paula brought them up, in which case they were again to listen actively with minimal responses. Their role was to support the work that Paula was doing on understanding and taking control of her fears.

Educate the Child

(8) As researchers have noted (Kanfer, Karoly, & Newman, 1975), expectations are powerful determinants in behavior change and are hard to separate from specific interventions. Paula received clear, factual information about the reasons for and the nature of her fears and the assurance that with help and with time, she would overcome them. This happened each week in her individual sessions. I assume that Paula's parents' quiet support and faith in her ability to change her behavior and my reassurance that her knowledge and behavior-change plan would work were important factors leading to the positive outcome. It is hard for a young child to ignore the wishes and expectations of a respected adult.

Allow the Child to Explore and Discuss Fears Through Art

(9) Paula needed to take a thorough look at the images and thoughts that were causing the anxiety and avoidance at bedtime. To that end, she drew in as much detail as possible what she imagined might happen to her. We discussed each picture at length. How is the kidnapper dressed (down to minute details)? How does he get through the fence, through the window? How long does it take? Where are her parents? What happens when she hears the noise? Why would someone kill her or her parents? Were the lights on or off? Are the doors locked?

(10) Gently mingled in with these questions and answers were facts that were directly contradictory to Paula's fears that I had gathered from the police department regarding burglaries and abductions of children. Most burglaries happen during the day. Most house burglars are just a few years older than Paula. The chances of Paula's being abducted from her own bed are so slim that they are almost nonexistent. These facts were discussed often during Paula's weekly visits, frequently in the context of our conversations about her drawings. She said later that having the facts was very important

to her being able to gain control of her fears.

Teach Positive, Competence-Related Self-Affirmation
(11) Paula used a cognitive technique that seems to be effective in fear reduction, that of saying to herself words that helped her lose her fear of being alone in her room (Graziano, Mooney, Huber, & Ignasiak, 1979; Graziano & Mooney, 1982; Kanfer, Karoly, & Newman, 1975). She had no trouble memorizing this affirmation: "I am capable of going to bed alone without being afraid. Nothing bad will happen to me or to my family. I am smart and can figure out what to do in any emergency." She used her sentences each evening when she became aware of intruding fearful thoughts.

Teach Relaxation and Positive Visual Imagery
(12) It was crucial for Paula to have the awareness of and information on fear. A child needs to accept and then put to work that knowledge and the power that comes from it (Hudson & O'Connor, 1981; Protinsky, 1985). The first step in that process was teaching Paula a simple, whole-body relaxation technique and calming visual imagery that she learned readily and used regularly. She chose an image that made her feel relaxed and happy, and she held it in her mind while she lay flat, tensing and relaxing each major muscle group from toes to head. She used it every evening before the negative or fearful thoughts began. Both Paula and her parents reported that the relaxation seemed to "make things go better" around bedtime. Paula's procrastination and whining lessened.

Teach Self-Management
(13) The final piece of the plan was to eliminate Paula's procrastination. I suggested that she "surprise" her parents by simply going to bed with no reminders, no whining, and no foot-dragging. She took the suggestion enthusiastically, fantasizing about her parents' positive reaction after so many weeks of struggling to get her to go to her room. At that point she had been in counseling for 6 weeks, and she felt ready, as she phrased it, to "stop being weird about bedtime." She made a simple chart that helped her monitor the time she went to bed. She rewarded herself with a bright sticker to paste on her chart for each day she was in bed by 9:30. She reached her goal within a week and said that she was quite happy about her parents' surprised and supportive reaction. They celebrated Paula's achievement by going out for dinner.

(14) In a follow-up of this case, Paula told me later that she occasionally baby-sits her little brother, alone in the house, until 8:00 p.m. She reported feeling proud of that.

References

Dollinger, S. J., O'Donnell, J. P., & Staley, A. A. (1984). Lightning-strike disaster: Effects on children's fears and worries. *Journal of Consulting and Clinical Psychology, 52,* 1028-1038.

Duncan, B., Kraus, M. A., & Parks, M. B. (1986). Children's fears and nuclear war: A systems strategy for change. *Youth and Society, 18,* 28-44.

Eme, R., & Schmidt, D. (1978). The stability of children's fears. *Child Development, 49,* 1277-1279.

Giebenhain, J. E., & O'Dell, S. (1984). Evaluation of a parent-training manual for reducing children's fears of the dark. *Journal of Applied Behavioral Analysis, 17,* 121-125.

Graziano, A. M., Mooney, K. C., Huber, C., & Ignasiak, D. (1979). Self-control instruction for children's fear reduction: A multiple case study. *Behavior Therapy and Experimental Psychiatry, 10,* 221-228.

Graziano, A. M., & Mooney, K. C., (1982). Behavioral treatment of "nightfears" in children: Maintenance of improvement at 2½ to 3 year follow-up. *Journal of Counseling and Clinical Psychology, 50,* 598-599.

Hudson, J. O., & O'Connor, C. (1981). The PEACE process: A modified senoi technique for children's nightmares. *The School Counselor, 28,* 347-352.

Hyson, M. C. (1979). Lobster on the sidewalk: Understanding and helping children with fears. *Young Children, 34,* 54-60.

Jones, E. A., & Borgers, S. (1988). Parent perception of children's fears. *Elementary School Guidance & Counseling, 23,* 10-15.

Kanfer, F. H., Karoly, P., & Newman, A. (1975). Reduction of children's fear of the dark by competence related and situational threat-related verbal cues. *Journal of Consulting and Clinical Psychology, 43,* 251-258.

Moracco, J. C., & Camilleri, J. (1983). A study of fears in elementary school children. *Elementary School Guidance & Counseling, 18,* 82-87.

Orton, G. (1982). A comparative study of children's worries. *The Journal of Psychology, 110,* 153-162.

Protinsky, H. (1985). Treatment of children's fears: A strategic utilization approach. *Journal of Marital and Family Therapy, 11,* 95-97.

Robinson, E. H., Robinson, S. L., & Whetsell, M. V. (1988). A study of children's fears. *The Journal of Humanistic Education and Development, 27,* 84-95.

Sarafino, E. (1986). *The fears of childhood.* New York: Human Sciences Press.

Terms for Discussion

1. anxiety (paragraphs 4 and 7)

2. trauma (paragraph 5)

3. generalize (paragraph 5)

4. cognitive technique (paragraph 11)

5. whole body relaxation technique (paragraph 12)

6. visual imagery (paragraph 12)

Questions

7. Speculate on why nighttime fears are a "common problem." (See paragraph 1.)

8. Do you believe that Paula's nighttime fears were a symptom of some underlying serious emotional problems? Explain.

9. Are you surprised that Paula's parents underestimated the nature of Paula's fear and trauma given that they were "caring and competent" parents? Explain. (See paragraphs 4 and 5.)

10. The counselor used six strategies. (See paragraphs 7 through 13.) Do you believe that some were more important than others? Do you believe they were all essential to the course of treatment? Explain.

11. Are there other forms of treatment that might have facilitated Paula's improvement? Explain.

12. Rate the article on the seven criteria described in the introduction to this book on a scale from 5 (highest quality) through 1 (lowest quality). Be prepared to explain your ratings.

Criterion 1: The demographics of the case are described: _____

Criterion 2: The condition(s) and behavior(s) that necessitated treatment are described in detail: _____

Criterion 3: The method of treatment is described in sufficient detail so that it can be replicated without additional information: _____

Criterion 4: A rationale is provided for the method of treatment selected: _____

Criterion 5: The client's improvement, if any, is clearly documented: _____

Criterion 6: Follow-up information on the client's improvement, if any, is presented: _____

Criterion 7: The study is appropriate for publication in a journal: _____

Notes:

Case 4

Treatment of an Adolescent with Bowel Movement Phobia Using Self-Control Therapy*

Andrew R. Eisen
University of Albany, State University of New York

Wendy K. Silverman
Florida International University

SUMMARY: This report describes a self-control treatment of an adolescent with a highly unusual and severely debilitating phobia of having bowel movements in public. The treatment focused predominantly on helping the adolescent to modify his maladaptive thinking and also included role plays, graduated exposure, and homework assignments. Multimethod and multisource assessment data were collected as well as measures of social validity. Treatment gains were maintained at 3 and 6 month follow-up.

(1) Although several behavioral treatment approaches have been used to treat childhood fears and phobias, including systematic desensitization, modeling, and flooding-related procedures, one approach that appears to be most promising, according to recent reviews (Morris & Kratochwill, 1983), is self-control training. In self-control programs, the individual seeking treatment plays the primary role in regulating his own behavior while the therapist acts to facilitate behavior change (Kanfer, 1980). In fear reduction programs, self-control procedures focus on enabling individuals to develop specific cognitive skills and to apply them when confronted with the feared stimulus (Morris & Kratochwill, 1983). Previous studies have employed self-control procedures to help alleviate relatively common child/adolescent fear and anxiety problems such as test anxiety and nighttime fears (Graziano, Mooney, Huber, & Ignasiak, 1979; Leal, Baxter, Martin, & Marx, 1981; Kanfer, Karoly, & Newman, 1975; Genshaft, 1982; Deffenbacher, Mathis, & Michaels, 1979). Despite the tantalizing results from these studies, there are problems with the work conducted to date.

(2) These problems include: (1) the lack of multi-method-multisource assessment procedures. Typically assessment data from only one source (parent or child) and only one method (i.e., self-report) are obtained; (2) the nonsevere nature of the child's problem—generally non-clinical samples have been studied (with the exception of Graziano et al., 1979); and (3) the failure to report systematic follow-up data. Finally, and perhaps most importantly, a major problem with this research is the inclusion of other behavioral techniques such as contingency management and relaxation therapy in the self-control package. It is difficult to ascertain, therefore, how much of the "success" of past studies is due specifically to the cognitive aspects of self-control approaches and how much is due to these other behavioral components.

(3) The following case study reports the use of a self-control approach in a 15-year-old adolescent male with a highly unusual and severely debilitating phobia, namely, a phobia for having bowel movements. The approach was pure in the sense that treatment focused only on helping the client to modify his maladaptive

---
*Journal of Behavior Therapy & Experimental Psychiatry, 22, 1991, pp. 45-51. Copyright 1991 by Pergamon Press Ltd., Oxford, England. Reprinted with permission.

thinking, without including any other behavioral techniques. The study also represents an improvement over those conducted previously in the three areas noted above (i.e., assessment, clinical severity, and follow-up).

Method

Subject
(4) Prior to treatment, the subject was intensely preoccupied with thoughts of having a bowel movement in public and was spending an excessive amount of time toileting to prevent this from occurring. The development of his fear began eight years earlier when the subject experienced a bowel movement in public. Although no subsequent episodes such as this were reported or had occurred, the subject's fear progressively escalated to the point where he remained *housebound* with the exception of attending school. However, while the subject attended school, he was preoccupied there as well with thoughts of a possible accident. This resulted in both a severe deterioration in the youth's academics and peer relationships. For example, he was failing two classes and his advancement to the next grade was questionable. In addition, his phobia prevented him from interacting with his peers, leading to inadequate social relationships.

Assessment
(5) The subject was assessed for anxiety symptomatology, phobias and related problems at the Child Anxiety Program of the Center for Stress and Anxiety Disorders, Albany, New York, using a semi-structured interview specific to assessing and diagnosing anxiety problems in children (The Anxiety Disorders Interview Schedule for Children, ADIS-C, Silverman & Nelles, 1988).

(6) Dependent measures included (1) the mean amount of time the subject spent sitting on the toilet for *each* urge to defecate and (2) the number of hours spent engaged in social outings. Daily ratings of the adolescent's subjective distress and weekly interference ratings completed by his parents were also obtained. In addition, a clinician's rating of distress/interference was taken at pre, post, and followup.

(7) The child self-report measures included the Children's Depression Inventory (CDI) (Kovacs & Beck, 1977), Fear Survey Schedule for Children—Revised (FSSC-R) (Ollendick, 1983), Children's Manifest Anxiety Scale—Revised (CMAS-R) (Reynolds & Richmond, 1978), State-Trait Anxiety Inventory for Children (Trait; STAIC) (Spielberger, 1973), Piers-Harris Self-Concept Scale (Piers & Harris, 1963), Negative Thoughts Questionnaire (Leitenberg, Yost, & Carroll-Wilson, 1986), and the Social Anxiety Scale for Children (SASC) (La Greca, Dando, Wick, Shaw, & Stone, 1988), a ten-item scale that assesses the child's level of social anxiety.

(8) The parent questionnaires included the Child Behavior Checklist (CBCL) (Achenbach, 1978), Child Manifest Anxiety Scale for Parents—Revised (CMAS-R-P) and the Fear Survey Schedule for Parents—Revised (FSSR-P). In addition, the subject's heart rate was measured using a Respironics, Inc. exersentry pulse meter during a behavioral avoidance test.

Procedure
(9) The subject underwent a two week baseline period after both child and parent versions of the ADIS-C and child and parent questionnaires were completed. Relevant thoughts concerning his phobia at home, school, and other activity settings were self-monitored on a daily basis during this time. He recorded these thoughts and the degree of anxiety he experienced on a 1-5 scale (1 = none, 5 = very severe). The subject also self-monitored daily the duration of time he spent sitting on the toilet for each urge to defecate using the stop watch mode of his wristwatch. To check for accuracy, his parents were asked to estimate the duration of time their son spent toileting. In addition, the subject was asked to keep track of the number of hours he engaged in social activities outside of the home. Finally, the subject's parents completed weekly interference ratings (0-4 scale; 0 = none, 4 = very severe) to provide an indication of how much their son's phobia was interfering with his life in terms of social, school, and familial factors.

(10) At the conclusion of baseline, the subject participated in a behavioral avoidance test which enabled concurrent assessment of both fear ratings and heart rate. More importantly, this task provided a direct assessment of the adolescent's fear in the context where his fear usually occurred. Degree of fear was measured via a *Fear Thermometer* made of cardboard that indicated five levels of fear differentiated by color. Each color was made to look increasingly hot (1 = not at all, 5 = very much). Heart rate was measured continuously using a Respironics Inc. exersentry pulse meter. The physiological assessment consisted of four periods: adaptation (10 min), resting baseline (5 min), behavioral avoidance test (BAT) (10 min), post BAT baseline (5 min). Average heart rate for each period was calculated by averaging across the initial 15 sec of each phase and then multiplied by 4 to reflect beats per minute (bpm).

Change scores were computed by subtracting the post BAT baseline from the average heart rate for each phase.

(11) At baseline, the subject was completely avoiding car trips. This was due to his perception of an increased likelihood of experiencing a bowel movement since a restroom was not in close proximity. For this reason, the BAT consisted of a 10 min car trip. Once the BAT was completed, the subject underwent a post BAT baseline phase in the same clinic room as the initial baseline period.

Treatment

(12) Treatment consisted of a 14-week program with an emphasis on the following components: an awareness of cognitive activities when scared, use of self-talk, imagery, role plays, a graduated sequence of imaginal and *in vivo* exposures to relevant fear provoking situations (based on fear hierarchy) and homework assignments. The therapist acted as a coping model by using these general strategies and the subject incorporated this information in the form of a plan for coping with his fear. Throughout treatment, the subject continued to self-monitor on a daily basis the duration of time for each urge to defecate, relevant thoughts and the degree of anxiety experienced, and the number of hours engaged in social activities. In addition, the subject's parents continued to complete weekly interference ratings.

(13) At the end of treatment and at 3 and 6 month follow-ups, the subject and his parents completed the assessment questionnaires. The subject also participated in the BAT at posttest and 6 month follow-up as well.

Results

(14) The results at post-treatment and follow-up indicate considerable improvement in almost all areas. Specifically, Figure 1 reveals a substantial decrease in the amount of time the subject spent sitting on the toilet from baseline to the end of treatment. This decrement was maintained at 3 and 6 month follow-ups. Figure 2 indicates improvements in the *social index*, i.e., the amount of time involved in activities outside of the home with the exception of school. A major reason for the improvement observed in the social index is because during the seventh week of treatment the subject took a part-time job (15 hours/week) and joined his high school ski club.

(15) The subject also demonstrated a considerable reduction in his self-reported anxiety ratings (see Figure 3). His parents simultaneously documented a decrease in how much their son's phobia interfered with aspects of his life (see Figure 4).

(16) These treatment gains were maintained at follow-up. The subject's school performance improved remarkably and he advanced successfully to the next academic level.

(17) Additional areas of improvement were indicated by the subject's and parents' scores on a number of questionnaires completed pre and post treatment and at follow-up. These results are presented in Table 1. Specifically, the child self-report measures of anxiety [CMAS-R, STAIC (trait), Negative Thoughts Questionnaire, and the Social Anxiety Scale] indicated considerable decrements in the adolescent's anxiety level with continued reductions at 6 month follow-up. Although improvements in the adolescent's level of depression (CDI) and fear (FSSC-R) were not evident at post-test, decrements in those two indices were noticeable at 6 month follow-up. In addition, the Piers-Harris Self-Concept Scale indicated an improvement in the adolescent's self-concept at post-test which continued at follow-up.

(18) There were improvements noted on several of the parent self-report measures as well. For example, on the CBCL the parents rated their son's internalizing and externalizing behaviors as reduced at post-test (from 66 to 61 and 60 to 57, respectively) and at 6 month follow-up (61 and 57, respectively). The parents' report of their son's total behavior problems on the CBCL was also reduced at post-test (from 62 to 56) with continued improvement at 6 month follow-up (50). In addition, the parents' report of their son's anxiety (CMAS-P-R) and fear (FSS-P-R) were both reduced at post-test (from 17 to 10 and 116 to 110, respectively) and maintained at 6 month follow-up (11 and 98, respectively).

(19) For the physiological assessment, the subject experienced a decrement in average heart rate from pre-test (82.4 bpm) to 6 month follow-up (68.8 bpm). His change score during the BAT indicated a decrement in heart rate acceleration from pre-test (12 bpm) to 6 month follow-up (4 bpm). Finally, the subject experienced a reduction in his fear ratings during the BAT from pre-test (3.5) to 6 month follow-up (1.0). In addition, a clinician's rating of distress/interference based on a 0-8 scale (0 = none, 8 = very severely disabling) indicated improvement from pre- to post-test which was maintained at follow-up (pre = 7; post-test = 1; 6 month follow-up = 1).

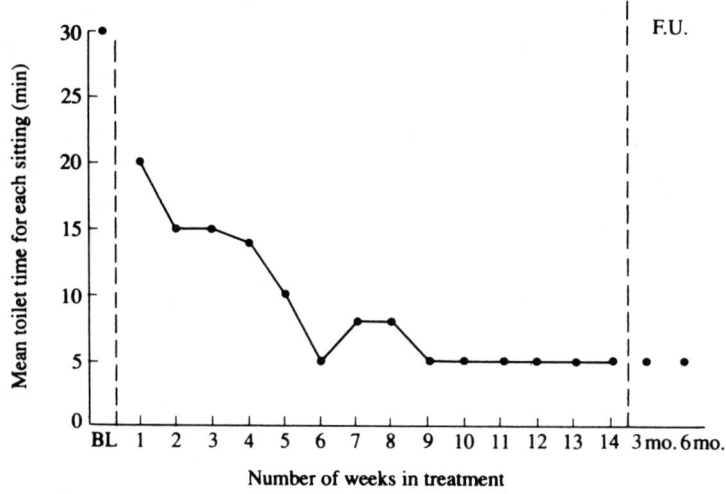

Figure 1. Mean toileting for each sitting (min) (weekly mean). Baseline is averaged over two weeks.

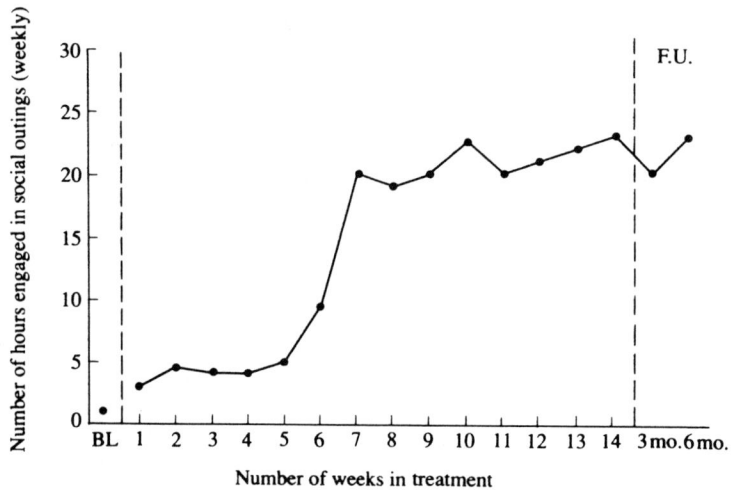

Figure 2. Number of hours engaged in social outings (weekly). Baseline is averaged over two weeks.

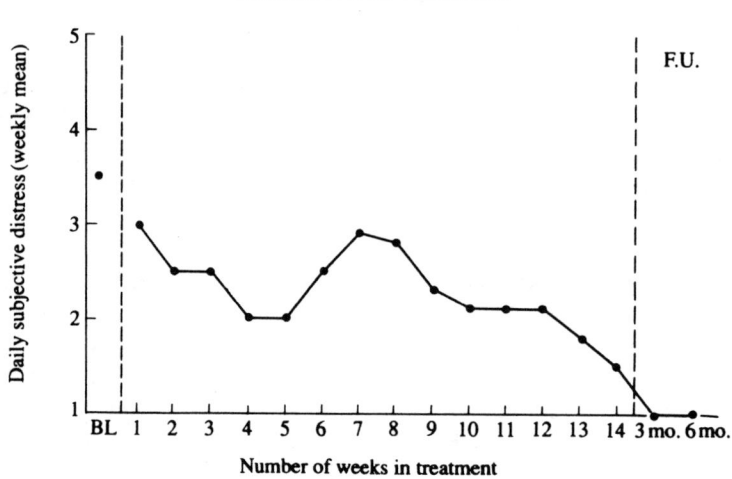

Figure 3. Daily subjective distress (weekly mean). Baseline is averaged over two weeks.

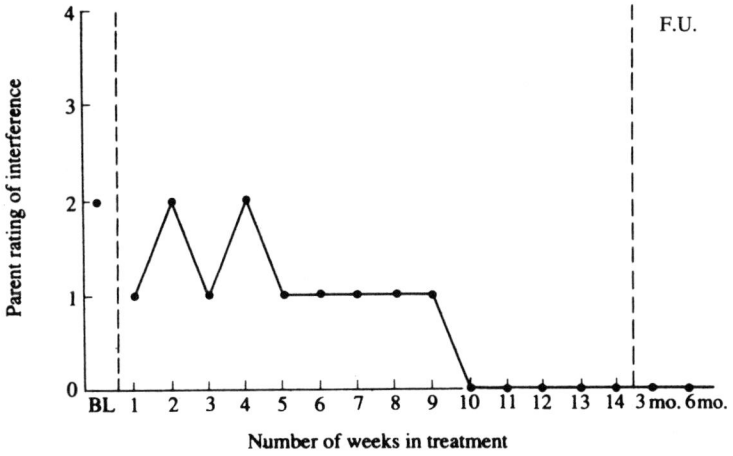

Figure 4. Parent rating of interference (weekly). Baseline is averaged over two weeks.

Table 1
Pre- and Post-Treatment Scores on Child Self-Report Measures

Measure	Pre	Post	3 Months	6 Months
Children's Depression Inventory	8	8	6	5
Fear Survey Schedule (C)-R	104	103	94	90
Children's Manifest Anxiety Scale-R	12	6	6	3
STAIC 2 (Trait)	40	26	26	25
Piers-Harris Self-Concept Scale	53	57	69	67
Negative Thoughts Questionnaire	35	30	29	21
Social Anxiety Scale	10	7	6	5

Discussion

(20) This case provides further evidence for the effectiveness and applicability of self-control procedures with a clinically severe phobia. The study is an improvement over past studies since it makes use of a multimethod-multisource assessment procedure, incorporates systematic follow-up data at 3 and 6 months and focuses on the training of self-regulatory skills, without the use of external reinforcement. Although it is difficult to draw firm conclusions with an AB design, the decrements in toileting and anxiety coupled with increased socialization maintained at 6-month follow-up, suggests the self-control package was effective for this highly unusual phobia in a 15-year-old male adolescent. Before generalizability issues can be addressed, it would be important to examine this treatment package with younger children and with different types of phobias. In addition, future research is warranted comparing self-control procedures to behavioral interventions under controlled conditions. Such work is currently being conducted at our clinic.

References

Achenbach, T. (1978). The child behavior profile: I. Boys aged 6-11. *Journal of Consulting and Clinical Psychology, 46*, 478-488.

Deffenbacher, J. L., Mathis, H., & Michaels, A. C. (1979). Two self-control procedures in the reduction of targeted and non-targeted anxieties. *Journal of Consulting Psychology, 26*, 120-127.

Genshaft, J. L. (1982). The use of cognitive behavior therapy for reducing math anxiety. *School Psychology Review, 11*, 32-34.

Graziano, A. M., Mooney, K. C., Huber, C., & Ignasiak, D. (1979). Self-control instructions for children's fear reduction. *Journal of Behavior Therapy and Experimental Psychiatry, 10*, 221-227.

Kanfer, F. H., Karoly, P., & Newman, A. (1975). A reduction of children's fear of the dark by confidence-related and situational threat-related verbal cues. *Journal of Consulting and Clinical Psychology, 43*, 251-258.

Kanfer, F. H. (1980). Self-management methods. In F. H. Kanfer and A. P. Goldstein (Eds.), *Helping people change* (2nd ed.). New York: Pergamon Press.

Kovacs, M., & Beck, A. T. (1977). An empirical-clinical approach toward a definition of childhood depression. In J. G. Schultebrandt & A. Raskin (Eds.), *Depression in children: Diagnosis, treatment, and conceptual models*. New York: Raven Press.

La Greca, A. M., Dando, S. K., Wick, P., Shaw, & Stone, W. L. (1988). The development of the social anxiety scale for children (SASC): Reliability and concurrent validity. *Journal of Clinical Child Psychology, 17*, 84-91.

Leal, L. L., Baxter, E. G., Martin, J., & Marx, R. W. (1981). Cognitive modification and systematic desensitization with test anxious high school students. *Journal of Counseling Psychology, 28,* 525-528.

Leitenberg, H., Yost, L. W., & Carroll-Wilson, M. (1986). Negative cognitive errors in children: Questionnaire development, normative data, and comparisons between children with and without self-reported symptoms of depression, low self-esteem, and evaluation anxiety. *Journal of Consulting and Clinical Psychology, 54,* 528-536.

Morris, R. J., & Kratochwill, T. R. (1983). *Treating children's fears and phobias: A behavioral approach.* New York: Pergamon Press.

Ollendick, T. H. (1983). Reliability and validity of the revised fear survey schedule for children (FSSC-R). *Behaviour Research and Therapy, 21,* 685-692.

Piers, E. V., & Harris, D. B. (1963). *The Piers-Harris Self-Concept Scale.* Unpublished manuscript, Pennsylvania State University.

Reynolds, C. R., & Richmond, B. 0. (1978). What I think and feel: A revised measure of children's manifest anxiety. *Journal of Abnormal Child Psychology, 6,* 271-280.

Silverman, W. K., & Nelles, W. B. (1988). The Anxiety Disorders Interview Schedule for Children. *Journal of the American Academy of Child and Adolescent Psychiatry, 27,* 1772-1778.

Spielberger, C. D. (1973). *Manual for the state-trait anxiety inventory for children.* Palo Alto, CA: Consulting Psychologists Press.

Terms for Discussion

1. phobia (paragraphs 1, 3, 4, 9, and 20)

2. self-control training (paragraphs 1 and 20)

3. cognitive skills (paragraph 1)

4. multimethod-multisource assessment (paragraphs 2 and 20)

5. self-report measures (paragraphs 2, 7, and 15)

6. dependent measures (paragraph 6)

7. baseline (paragraphs 9, 10, 11, and 14)

8. self-monitor (paragraphs 9 and 12)

9. self-talk (paragraph 12)

10. imagery (paragraph 12)

11. role plays (paragraph 12)

12. fear hierarchy (paragraph 12)

13. AB design (paragraph 20)

Questions for Discussion

14. In paragraph 1, the authors mention several behavioral treatment approaches that have been used to treat fears and phobias, including self-control programs. Does this case report convince you that one is superior to the others? Explain.

15. In your opinion, how important are multimethod-multisource assessment procedures in a case report of this type? Explain.

16. If you were the therapist, would you have explored the psychodynamics underlying the problem more fully than was apparently done in this case? Why? Why not?

17. Comment on the adequacy of the assessment procedures. Were they comprehensive? Were all needed? Explain.

18. How important are the four figures to your understanding of the results? Would it have been sufficient for the authors to have just described the results in the body of the text? Why? Why not?

19. In the last paragraph, the authors note that "it is difficult to draw firm conclusions with an AB design." Speculate on why this is? Is there a better design?

20. Are there other forms of treatment other than the behavioral approaches described in paragraph 1 that might have been used to facilitate the improvement of the client? Explain.

21. Rate the article on the seven criteria described in the introduction to this book on a scale from 5 (highest quality) through 1 (lowest quality). Be prepared to explain your ratings.

Criterion 1: The demographics of the case are described: _____

Criterion 2: The condition(s) and behavior(s) that necessitated treatment are described in detail: _____

Criterion 3: The method of treatment is described in sufficient detail so that it can be replicated without additional information: _____

Criterion 4: A rationale is provided for the method of treatment selected: _____

Criterion 5: The client's improvement, if any, is clearly documented: _____

Criterion 6: Follow-up information on the client's improvement, if any, is presented: _____

Criterion 7: The study is appropriate for publication in a journal: _____

Notes:

Case 5

"Forbidden Fruit Tastes Especially Sweet." Cognitive-Behavior Therapy with a Kleptomaniac Woman—A Case Report*

Dieter Schwartz
Psychotherapist in Private Practice

Burkhard Hoellen
Psychotherapeutische Beratungsstelle der Arbeiterwohlfahrt
Germany

ABSTRACT. This case study deals with a 42-year-old married woman who has already been sentenced once for theft and again awaits court trial at the beginning of her therapy. A psychiatric evaluation attested to her "compulsive stealing," i.e., kleptomania. Besides difficult to control compulsion to steal, the client is suffering from depressions, feelings of guilt and anxiety. Her sexual life is very problematic. The underlying cognitions for her compulsive stealing are detected and disputed, whereby Izard's Differential Emotions Theory and criminological findings are concurrent with a cognitive-behavioral analysis. Therapy was successfully terminated after 39 sessions within 16 months.

Case History

(1) The client has been married for more than 15 years and has a grown-up son. For a few years now the client has had a part-time job. Her husband is an executive, the family owns a house and is financially well off.

(2) Two years before she consulted us for the first time, the client had been caught for shoplifting (total value of the stolen items: less than DM 40,-). For this a court had fined her. Because of a new act of shoplifting she has now to face another court trial. In the first trial she did not say a word to her defense; however, the court did not investigate possible psychological motives for her offense. She remained silent when the presiding judge questioned her about her reasons for stealing the items. To us she explained she had preferred a "normal" sentencing rather than talking about "her compulsion to steal."

(3) In a psychiatric evaluation established because of the new charge and our intervention it was attested that in the client's case a "genuine compulsive stealing in the sense of kleptomania might be present, respectively might not be excluded."

Course Of The Therapy

Problem Structuring

(4) When at the beginning of her therapy (May 84) the client was asked about her problem she answered that the "temptation" to steal was still so strong that "here above all she needed help." She said that her problem was the "compulsion to steal and to get caught again" so that the solution of this problem "would settle many others." We agreed upon the client having at least two problems:

Problem No. 1—the "compulsion—the temptation to steal something"
Problem No. 2—the current trial and its possi-

---

*Psychotherapy in Private Practice, 8, 1991, pp. 19-25. Copyright 1991 by The Haworth Press, Inc. Reprinted with permission.

ble consequences ("No, I don't intend to go to prison, I would rather commit suicide. At least I am not a criminal, am I?")

(5) Referring to this question (and to our hypothesis that our client's self-esteem very likely was under great stress) we then established what she was thinking about herself. Result: "How can I do something like that?" "What kind of person am I?" "I think it terrible that I do that." (Often catastrophizing or globally damning cognitions appear in the form of rhetorical questions, Schwartz, 1987.)

(6) Due to these cognitions she was "depressed for hours," felt, she "could have cried out loud from pain" and often could not find sleep all night long. (Problem No. 3—depressions and feeling of guilt as consequence of her negative self-image.) The client added voluntarily: "Besides I am afraid. I mean, you see, we live in the country, we built our house there, my parents live nearby . . . ." (Problem No. 4—being afraid of what "other people" might think "if all would come to the public.")

Goal Setting and Phase of Motivation

(7) After having determined the client's essential problem areas which were partly outlined according to the A-B-C formula of RET, again the question of the sequence of handling the problems had to be discussed. As was to be expected the client intended to begin with problem No. 1, since with its solution "everything else would be settled." We agreed with her in as much as her other problems would have been less prominent if "nothing had happened at all."

(8) We asked the client what in her opinion would presumably be different if she were no longer afraid of other people learning of her situation, if she did not feel such a great pain, had no depressions and no feeling of guilt but her problem No. 1 (the "compulsion") still remained unchanged. Answer: "I would feel relieved."

(9) Here, however, the client discovered two obstacles on the way to reach this aim:

1. She believed that someone in her situation simply had to feel the way she did.
2. She even considered her feeling of guilt and her depressions as an effective brake for her "compulsion" ("Otherwise everything would turn into a routine").

(10) Obstacle 1 could be eliminated when the client accepted our suggestion just to try if she could slightly change her feelings of guilt, depressions and anxiety into concern and discontent (Kessler & Hoellen, 1982). With regard to obstacle 2 we asked the client if her feeling of guilt, her depressions and fears had until then effectively prevented her from stealing. We made the paradox proposal of helping her get an even stronger feeling of guilt as a kind of "brake" for "protecting (her) from her compulsion" in the future.

(11) Reaction of the client, repeatedly and thoughtfully: "No, this will not do me any good . . . ."

(12) After that we could agree on the aim for the first therapy stage—the reducing of her depressions, of her feelings of guilt and anxiety.

Cognitive Restructuring and Disputation

(13) During the following sessions we disputed the cognitions responsible for the client's inappropriate feelings. Her most important self-harming thoughts: "My life is ruined, how *awful* it had to come to this"; "I am an unbearable person"; "It would be *terrible* if my parents and other people knew about this." Her extreme depending on the judgment of other people, especially her parents, led to great fears of the client. We asked her to imagine her son having her problem. What would she be thinking of him? How would she react if he opened his heart to her? Would she condemn him as being a totally wretched person? Would she reject him? The client denied both. Then we asked her if she had any hints for her parents reacting differently towards their daughter (i.e., towards the client). The client denied this as well. So she finally realized that her situation did not have to come to such a bad end as she assumed, even if her parents should learn about her problem. Besides this disputation of her distorted perception we also disputed her self-damning cognitions.

(14) Here again the "role reversal" helped her. She came to the insight that similar "wrong-doings" by her son, although displeasing for her, could not make her see her son as an entirely "unbearable person."

(15) Transferring these insights to herself now the client began disputing the self-harming parts of her beliefs:

a. Does shoplifting, juridically and morally a damnable action, convert her into a worthless *person*?
b. Does hell break loose when other people learn about my "condemnable actions"? Am I completely dependent on the judgement of others?

c. Is it true that *I can't stand* the possibly painful difficulties that the court trial might bring about?

(16) In connection with these disputations we had the client describe her feelings when she was committing the shoplifting. Apart from fear (of getting caught with all its consequences, including the following depressions and the feeling of guilt) she also admitted feeling a "prickling sensation."

(17) Following Izard's Differential Emotions Theory indicating the emotion profile of anxiety containing besides fear as the second strongest emotion also the positive emotion "interest-excitement," this comes as no surprise (Izard, 1981). Criminologists are aware of the fact that kleptomaniacs acting in the heat of passion "abreact unfulfilled desires by acts of grabbing" (Plack, 1974).

(18) Here we therefore decided to examine the client's sexual life in a few sessions. It turned out that until then the client had rarely experienced intensive sexual tensions in her married life. Apart from this she had not had intercourse with a man other than her husband, not even before marriage. Neither had she ever masturbated nor did she know exactly whether she ever had an orgasm. Asked if there was something really exciting in her life at all, the client answered: "No, nothing."

(19) Then we asked the client: "Assume you could take away whatever you like, in any store and no one in the world (including yourself) would come up with the idea that shoplifting is illegal, would you still feel the prickling sensations?" Answer: "Well, it would be gone then. This is only logical. It is exactly what you say that one is not allowed to do. Forbidden fruit tastes especially sweet."

(20) After that we disputed the client's cognitions: "I *should* not steal. It is highly damnable, terrible dangerous and leads into the complete catastrophe."

(21) As an alternative to not being allowed she worked out to say in the future instead of: "I must not . . ." simply "I do not want to, it leads me to too much trouble." From then on the client also regularly used this new way of thinking at home: she imagined walking through a supermarket and at an "opportune place" getting the idea of "What about pocketing this?" Now, however, she imagined a vivid and detailed scene how she resisted the "compulsion" by means of her new philosophy.

(22) Parallel to this we began to focus the therapy on her married and sexual life. Within the frame of the bibliotherapy she read with great interest the section about sexual and love-making problems in the self-help book of one of the authors (Schwartz, 1987). She said that much of what was described in the book applied to her as well. In particular she behaved sexually very passively towards her husband and hardly ever took the initiative neither in approaching her husband nor concerning the kind and way of lovemaking. She was fully aware of her longing to have sexual contacts more often but until then, however, had avoided speaking with her husband about it. Thoughts like: "My husband is not interested in me, anyway"; "What if he refuses?" prevented her from being more active and from talking to her husband about her sexual problems. Thereupon we agreed on concrete steps she was to carry out for improving her situation:

1. Speak with her husband about her problem in the sexual sphere.
2. Take the initiative for having sexual contacts at a predetermined number of times.
3. Talk about her desires concerning the kind and way of lovemaking.

(23) We disputed the client's fear of "being turned down" (fear of being rejected by her husband) and her various assumptions referring to her husband's not being interested in her. By this she realized that her husband's not being in the mood for lovemaking did not mean that he rejected her as a person. She herself loved her husband and yet, was not always "in the right mood." To her surprise her husband's reactions were very positive and already after another few therapy sessions the client had succeeded in making her matrimonial sexual life more interesting and satisfying for her.

(24) At the end of the therapy (after 39 sessions in 16 months) the client reported to have a satisfying sexual life and a noticeably better relationship with her husband; besides, she could now go out shopping in supermarkets without greatly suffering from her "compulsion," i.e., not having "to pocket" something. In follow-up sessions 3 and 5 years (May 89) after termination, the client indicated that treatment gains were being maintained without exception. In the court trial (Dec 84) the client was sentenced again because according to current German law and the practice of psychiatric evaluations "kleptomania" only leads to a restricted criminal responsibility which implements only a somewhat lenient sentence (a suspended sentence of 9 months).

Discussion of the Therapeutic Methods

(25) The question concerning the success of the therapy has to be answered considering various aspects. From the viewpoint of the public institutions (e.g., the courts) and according to the client's opinion right at the start of the therapy, the success meant that she learned to resist her "compulsion" to commit shoplifting.

(26) According to the client's opinion at the end of the therapy and even 5 years later the improvement of her married and sexual life gained considerably more importance. Similar to this it cannot be clearly defined by the course of the therapy what played a more important part in the success concerning the client's "compulsion" —was it the cognitive restructuring or the change in her sexual life? In the criminological-oriented as well as in the therapeutical-oriented literature (cf. Plack, 1979) a causal significance is attributed to the factor "banished sexuality" concerning "kleptomania." The present authors are in basic agreement with that notion.

(27) It is to be noted, however, that the client came to her own rescue in the actual tempting situations in supermarkets particularly by means of the cognitive-restructuring, i.e., by compensating the "bad aftertaste of the sweet, forbidden fruit" with discovering new highlights in her (sexual) life.

References

Izard, C. E. (1981). *Human emotions.* New York: Plenum Press.

Kessler, B., & Hoellen, B. (1982). *Rational-emotive therapie in der klinischen praxis.* Weinheim: Beltz.

Plack, A. (1979). *Plaedoyer fuer die abschaffung des strafrechts.* Muenchen: P. List Verlag.

Schwartz, D. (1987). *Gefuehle erkennen und positiv beeinflussen.* Landsberg: Verlag mvg.

Terms for Discussion

1. compulsion (paragraphs 4, 25, and 26)

2. self-esteem (paragraph 5)

3. catastrophizing (paragraph 5)

4. depression (paragraphs 6, 8, 9, 10, 12, and 16)

5. feelings of guilt (paragraphs 6, 8, 9, 10, 12, and 16)

6. anxiety (paragraphs 10, 12, and 17)

7. cognitive restructuring (paragraphs 13, 26, and 27)

8. role reversal (paragraph 14)

9. interest-excitement (paragraph 17)

10. bibliotherapy (paragraph 22)

Questions

11. Does it surprise you that depression was associated with kleptomania? Explain.

12. Do you agree with the therapists' decision to handle problem No. 1 first? (See paragraphs 4 and 7.) Explain.

13. What is your opinion on the paradoxical proposal mentioned in paragraph 10?

14. How would you answer the question posed by the authors in paragraph 26?

15. Are there other types of treatment that might have facilitated the client's improvement? Explain.

16. Rate the article on the seven criteria described in the introduction to this book on a scale from 5 (highest quality) through 1 (lowest quality). Be prepared to explain your ratings.

Criterion 1: The demographics of the case are described: _____

Criterion 2: The condition(s) and behavior(s) that necessitated treatment are described in detail: _____

Criterion 3: The method of treatment is described in sufficient detail so that it can be replicated without additional information: _____

Criterion 4: A rationale is provided for the method of treatment selected: _____

Criterion 5: The client's improvement, if any, is clearly documented: _____

Criterion 6: Follow-up information on the client's improvement, if any, is presented: _____

Criterion 7: The study is appropriate for publication in a journal: _____

Notes:

Case 6

Behavioral Treatment of Night Bingeing and Rumination in an Adult Case of Bulimia Nervosa*

Donald A. Williamson, Olga D. Lawson, Sandra M. Bennett and Lisa Hinz
Louisiana State University

SUMMARY: A 24-year-old female, diagnosed as bulimia nervosa with night bingeing and rumination, was treated by individual and group behavior therapy. A changing criterion design progressively adjusted the criterion for reinforcement as the treatment obtained diminution of night bingeing. Night bingeing was finally eliminated, without evidence of recurrence at 3 month and 2 year follow-ups. Rumination was regarded as a collateral behavior and diminished in tandem with reduction of night bingeing. Other improvements in bulimia nervosa were observed over the course of treatment.

(1) Uncontrollable binge eating at night was first identified by Stunkard, Grace, & Wolff (1955) as an eating problem which was especially intractable. Stunkard (1976) further described this syndrome, noting that it combined wakening during the night, binge eating, and lack of appetite in the morning. Such people usually cannot sleep if bingeing is prevented. There have been few reports of either behavioral or non-behavioral treatment of this problem. Such strategies as have been reported, have generally involved rather elaborate response prevention measures. For example, Coates (1978) unsuccessfully attempted to control night eating in an adult male by teaching self-control, and eventually had to resort to locking all food away from the subject at night.

(2) Another recently identified eating problem among adult bulimics is chronic rumination, which consists of voluntary regurgitation of partially digested food into the mouth where it is subsequently rechewed and reswallowed or else expectorated (Larocca & Della-Fera, 1986, p. 209). Rumination in infants has long been recognized as a significant health problem and there have been many reports of successful treatment by behavioral approaches (Williamson, Prather, Heffer, & Kelley, 1988). While there is some controversy concerning the clinical significance of chronic rumination in adults (Levine, Wingate, Pfeffer, & Butcher, 1983), most authorities have noted that it is most commonly observed in patients diagnosed as bulimia nervosa (Blinder, 1986; Fairburn & Cooper, 1984). Reports on the treatment of this eating problem have been limited to two uncontrolled case studies (Larocca & Della-Fera, 1986) and a brief report on seven patients by Fairburn and Cooper (1984).

(3) This paper describes the treatment of an interesting case who presented both night bingeing and chronic rumination. Treatment focused primarily upon night bingeing since rumination was strongly associated with it. A changing criterion design (Kazdin, 1982) was used to evaluate the efficacy of a contingency management intervention directly to reduce night bingeing.

Method

Subject
(4) The subject, Doreen, was a 24-year-old white professional woman who had referred herself for outpatient treatment of an eating disorder. Clinical interviews and psychological testing met the diagnostic criteria for buli-

---

*Reprinted from the *Journal of Behavior Therapy and Experimental Psychiatry*, 20, 1989, pp. 73-77. Copyright 1989 by Pergamon Press Ltd., England. Reprinted with permission.

mia nervosa (American Psychiatric Association, 1987; Russell, 1979). Doreen reported bingeing every night and ruminating about every other night, and several times a week during the day. She also "purged" by self-induced vomiting about once a month. She was preoccupied with body size and shape. Night bingeing typically occurred after sleeping 1-3 hours. She was usually unable to return to sleep unless she ate. Night binges were quite varied, depending upon availability of food. This was sometimes very unusual, e.g., uncooked fish sticks or large amounts of sugar on bread. She had often tried to prevent this night bingeing without success, finding that her efforts only led to increased anxiety and insomnia.

(5) Rumination was described as regurgitating and re-swallowing ingested foods. Periods of rumination typically lasted from a few minutes to over twenty minutes. Doreen felt very guilty about her bingeing, purging, and rumination, stating that she felt it a terrible secret to be kept from friends and relatives.

(6) Doreen's eating disorder had begun at approximately 17, when she binged and "purged" on a daily basis. Rumination was initiated to help reduce the vomiting. Over the course of several years, the vomiting had been greatly reduced in frequency, but had not been eliminated. She believed that she now used rumination as a replacement for vomiting for "purging."

(7) Psychological testing indicated no significant personality disturbance. Doreen's profile on the Minnesota Multiphasic Personality Inventory was within normal limits. Her score on the Beck Depression Inventory was 6. She reported considerable anxiety in social situations, especially when dating. She was very self-conscious about her appearance and body size, and was quite unassertive in most social situations, including those that were work-related.

(8) A moderately severe case of bulimia nervosa was indicated by a self-reported average of 9 binges and 8 episodes of rumination per week, and by a score of 90 on the Bulimia Test (Smith & Thelen, 1984) and 27 on the Eating Attitudes Test (Garner & Garfinkel, 1979). Doreen's height was 5 feet 5 in., and her weight of 132 lbs was within the normal range for her height and build. Despite being statistically normal, she felt that she was "fat" and was highly motivated to lose weight. Her dissatisfaction with body size was the primary motivation for the extreme methods she used to produce weight loss. She believed that if she lost weight, she would be less self-conscious with men. Night bingeing was her main concern, because after the reduction in vomiting, it had led to small increases in weight. The behavioral analysis indicated that if night bingeing could be eliminated, her concern with her body size would be reduced, and she would be less likely to engage in vomiting and rumination. The treatment plan was based upon this formulation.

Treatment

(9) After 5 weeks of baseline recording of bingeing and rumination, Doreen was referred for individual and group therapy. Over the course of 27 weeks, she had 15 individual therapy sessions and 18 group therapy sessions.

(10) *Group therapy.* In a closed group of six bulimics, two upper level graduate students in clinical psychology served as co-therapists. Each session lasted 1.5–2 hrs. and involved exposure to the eating of foods with prevention of vomiting responses, as well as cognitive restructuring to modify irrational beliefs concerning weight, dieting, and body size. Foods were introduced in a hierarchical manner so that those that were least feared were first consumed, and more feared foods introduced over the treatment period. Larger amounts of foods were then gradually introduced. The group met over a 23 week period. During the first month, it met twice a week, gradually diminishing to once a month by the end of the period.

(11) *Contingency management.* This therapy focused upon reducing the frequency of night bingeing by using contingency management procedures. The target aimed at was nights without bingeing after going to sleep. Since rumination was highly correlated with night bingeing, it was hypothesized that it would be indirectly modified by successful treatment of night bingeing.

(12) Treatment required establishing a very strong reinforcement contingency. Doreen reported that she was very fond of wearing jewelry and would miss it if deprived of it. She agreed to bring to the therapist all her jewelry, which would be returned to her contingent upon successful attainment of weekly treatment goals. These goals involved using a changing criterion design whereby the number of nights a week without night bingeing was gradually increased from 2 during the first two weeks of treatment to 7 at the end of treatment. After completion of this intervention, she was followed for 8 weeks with no contingency in place. After this period, she was assessed at 3 month and 2 year follow-ups.

(13) *Evaluation of treatment outcome.* Assessment of the frequency of binges and rumination used the self-monitoring procedure described by Williamson, Kelley,

Cavell, and Prather (1987). Self-monitored data were collected continuously throughout baseline and treatment. During follow-up, Doreen recorded her eating behavior for two-week periods. At baseline, mid-treatment (after 11 weeks of treatment), end of treatment, and at 3 month and 2 year follow-up, some initial measures were repeated: weight, Beck Depression Inventory (BDI), the Bulimia Test and the Eating Attitudes Test (see above).

Results

(14) Figure 1 illustrates changes in night bingeing over the course of treatment and follow-up. During the five weeks of baseline, the subject averaged 1.6 nights per week without bingeing. There was considerable variability, however, from week to week. During the first two weeks of treatment, the criterion for reinforcement by access to jewelry was two nights without bingeing. When this criterion was met, the criterion was changed to three nights without bingeing. This criterion being achieved on two consecutive weeks, it was changed to four nights per week. At this point, a slight regression was observed. The criterion was met in the third and fourth weeks of this phase and was then changed to five nights per week. Again, a slight regression was observed and three weeks were required before the criterion for reinforcement was achieved.

(15) After two successful weeks, the criterion was changed to six nights, which was achieved for the next two weeks. The final criterion, seven nights without night bingeing, implied cessation of the behavior. This criterion was met in the third week of this phase and was maintained for three consecutive weeks. At this point, Doreen had earned all of her jewelry, and the contingency management program was dropped. She was then seen for eight weeks of individual therapy without a contingency management program. Initially there were a few lapses. During the last four weeks, however, night bingeing ceased. Follow-up data collected at 3 months and 2 years following treatment showed that she never reported recurrence of night bingeing.

(16) Table 1 summarizes the results of more general changes in eating behavior, weight, and rumination. Each dependent variable was assessed at baseline, mid-treatment, post treatment (week 24), and at 3 month and 2 year follow-up. Doreen's weight gradually increased from 132 lbs at baseline to 139 lbs at 3 month follow-up. At two year follow-up, her weight had decreased to 134 lbs. Scores of the BDI showed that she was never significantly depressed throughout the course of treatment or follow-up. Scores of the Bulimia Test and the Eating Attitudes Test showed substantial improvement during treatment and especially at 2 year follow-up. Frequency of binges were somewhat reduced at mid-treatment and had reached zero at the end of treatment and throughout follow-up. Rumination also decreased in frequency during treatment and was reportedly eliminated at the end of treatment and at follow-up. Anecdotal reports by Doreen at 2 year follow-up suggested substantial improvement. She never woke at night with urges to binge, and other aspects of her life, e.g., social anxiety and assertion, had improved. She reported very little concern about body size and weight. She noted having been

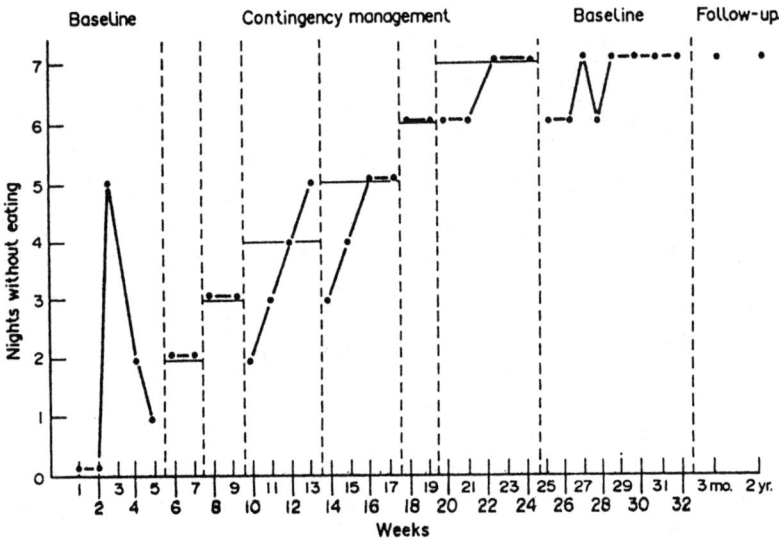

Figure 1. Changes in night bingeing as a function of changes in the reinforcement contingency.

Table 1

Treatment outcome	Baseline	Mid Treatment	Post Treatment	Three Month Follow-up	Two Year Follow-up
Weight	132	135	138	139	134
BDI	6	1	4	0	0
Bulimia Test	90	76	83	63	53
Eating Attitudes Test	27	16	16	14	10
Binges/week	9	7	0	0	0
Ruminations/week	8	4	0	0	0

pleasantly surprised to find that she could maintain a normal weight level without dieting, purging, or ruminating.

Discussion

(17) This single case study is the first successful application of behavior therapy to an adult case of night bingeing and rumination. A changing criterion design was used to expand the effects of a contingency management program for reinforcing nights without bingeing. Reinforcement of progressively increasing restraint from night bingeing apparently resulted in its complete elimination. But since the patient also had cognitive-behavioral group therapy for bulimia, the possible contribution of the latter must be recognized.

(18) As shown in Table 1, the treatment program was successful in reducing the general eating disorder and the rumination in addition to the binge eating that was the object of treatment. Since rumination was noted as highly correlated with night bingeing it was expected to diminish by modifying night bingeing, and in fact rumination declined as night bingeing was eliminated. The finding that rumination could be treated as a collateral behavior (Hayes, Nelson, & Jarrett, 1986) is of significance since others have found it to be highly resistant to treatment (Larocca & Della-Fera, 1986). Our findings are consistent with the brief report by Fairburn and Cooper (1984) that ruminators who regained control over eating stopped ruminating. Future studies should attempt to replicate this finding more extensively in order to evaluate its generality.

References

American Psychiatric Association (1987). *Diagnostic and statistical manual of mental disorders* (3rd Ed.—revised). Washington, DC: Author.

Blinder, B. J. (1986). Rumination: A benign disorder? *International Journal of Eating Disorders, 5,* 385-386.

Coates, T. J. (1978). Successive self-management strategies toward coping with night eating. *Journal of Behavior Therapy and Experimental Psychiatry, 9,* 181-183.

Fairburn, C. G., & Cooper, P. J. (1984). Rumination in bulimia nervosa. *British Medical Journal, 288,* 826-827.

Garner, D. M., & Garfinkel, P. E. (1979). The eating attitudes test: An index of the symptoms of anorexia. *Psychological Medicine, 9,* 273-279.

Hayes, S. C., Nelson, R. O., & Jarrett, R. B. (1986). Evaluating the quality of behavioral assessment. In R. O. Nelson & S. C. Hayes (Eds.), *Conceptual foundations of behavioral assessment* (pp. 463-503). New York: Guilford Press.

Kazdin, A. E. (1982). Single-case experimental designs. In P. C. Kendall & J. N. Butcher (Eds.), *Handbook of research methods in clinical psychology* (pp. 461-490). New York: John Wiley & Sons.

Larocca, F. E., & Della-Fera, M. A. (1986). Rumination: Its significance in adults with bulimia nervosa. *Psychosomatics, 27,* 209-212.

Levine, D. F., Wingate, D. L., Pfeffer, J. M., & Butcher, P. (1983). Habitual rumination: A benign disorder. *British Medical Journal, 287,* 255-256.

Russell, G. (1979). Bulimia nervosa: An ominous variant of anorexia nervosa. *Psychological Medicine, 9,* 429-448.

Smith, M. C., & Thelen, M. H. (1984). Development and validation of a test for bulimia. *Journal of Consulting and Clinical Psychology, 52,* 863-872.

Stunkard, A. J. (1976). *The pain of obesity.* Palo Alto, CA: Bull Press.

Stunkard, A. J., Grace, W. J., & Wolff, H. G. (1955). The night-eating syndrome: A pattern of food intake among certain obese patients. *American Journal of Medicine, 19,* 78-86.

Williamson, D. A., Kelley, M. L., Cavell, T. A., & Prather, R. C. (1987). Eating and eliminating disorders. In C. L. Frame & J. L. Matson (Eds.), *Handbook of assessment in childhood psychopathology: Applied issues in differential diagnosis and treatment evaluation.* New York: Plenum.

Williamson, D. A., Prather, R. C., Heffer, R. W., & Kelley, M. L. (1988). Eating disorders. In J. L. Matson (Ed.), *Treating childhood and adolescent psychopathology.* New York: Plenum,

Terms for Discussion

1. syndrome ((paragraph 1)

2. bulimia nervosa (paragraphs 2, 4, and 8)

3. changing criterion design (paragraphs 3, 12, and 17)

4. contingency management intervention (paragraphs 3, 11, 12, and 15)

5. baseline (paragraphs 9, 13, 14, and 16)

6. cognitive restructuring (paragraph 10)

7. self-monitoring (paragraph 13)

8. criterion for reinforcement (paragraph 14)

9. dependent variable (paragraph 16)

Questions

10. Does the reported association between bulimia nervosa and rumination make sense? Explain.

11. Given the information about Doreen in paragraphs 4 through 6, would you have expected to find a personality disturbance indicated by the Minnesota Multiphasic Personality Inventory? (Also see paragraph 7.)

12. In your opinion, was the initial baseline of five weeks of sufficient duration? Explain.

13. Are there advantages and disadvantages to using self-monitoring to collect data? Explain.

14. What are the advantages, if any, of using a changing criterion design?

15. The authors note that cognitive-behavioral group therapy was used in conjunction with contingency management. (See paragraph 17.) In your opinion, could the group therapy have been the primary agent of change in this case?

16. Are there other types of treatment that might have facilitated Doreen's improvement? Explain.

17. Rate the article on the seven criteria described in the introduction to this book on a scale from 5 (highest quality) through 1 (lowest quality). Be prepared to explain your ratings.

Criterion 1: The demographics of the case are described: _____

Criterion 2: The condition(s) and behavior(s) that necessitated treatment are described in detail: _____

Criterion 3: The method of treatment is described in sufficient detail so that it can be replicated without additional information: _____

Criterion 4: A rationale is provided for the method of treatment selected: _____

Criterion 5: The client's improvement, if any, is clearly documented: _____

Criterion 6: Follow-up information on the client's improvement, if any, is presented: _____

Criterion 7: The study is appropriate for publication in a journal: _____

Case 7

Decreasing Junk-Food Consumption Through the Use of Self-Management Procedures: A Case Study*

J. Regis McNamara
Ohio University

Joseph P. Green
Ohio University

SUMMARY: By using a self-management program, a 25-yr.-old white male was able to decrease the amount of junk food and beverage consumed while increasing the amount of healthier food and beverage ingested during evening snacks. This change was evident at 6 wk. and at a 6-mo. follow-up. Factors contributing to this success were discussed.

(1) "You are what you eat" is a common nutritional saying. Yet despite the importance of diet to good health, large numbers of individuals consume foods which are felt to have inadequate or deleterious nutritional value for them. Excessive consumption of foods which are high in saturated fats, sugar, and salt are frequently characterized as "bad" food, while foods which are high in fiber content such as whole grain bread and cereals as well as fruits, vegetables, fish, and nuts are viewed as "good" food (Friedman & DiMatteo, 1989).

(2) There have been a number of attempts to change the eating habits of people from less desirable to more desirable types of food. Using mass media and community education, the Three Community Study (Maccoby, Farquhar, Wood, & Alexander, 1977) showed that diets could be somewhat modified through community-wide health promotion efforts. Smaller scale interventions using a variety of labeling and prompting strategies have been successful in increasing the sale of low calorie and low fat items in cafeterias (Dubbert, Johnson, Schlundt, & Montague, 1984; Mayer, Heins, Vogel, Morrison, Lankester, & Jacobs, 1986) as well as increasing the sales of salads, a low-fat, high-fiber menu selection (Wagner & Winett, 1988) at a fast-food restaurant.

(3) One class of "bad" foods which has not received much attention in terms of dietary modification is junk food. Although a variety of junk foods have been identified as eaten regularly by Americans (Lasky, 1977; Perl, 1980), very few behavioral studies have been done to decrease this type of food consumption. Intervention studies have shown that both monetary reward and aversive conditioning are effective in temporarily suppressing consumption of junk foods (Hazer, Aeschleman, & Robertson, 1985; Clapham & Abramson, 1985). The present study extends previous work by using a self-management perspective to intervene with this problem.

---

*Reproduced with permission of the authors and publisher from McNamara, J. R. & Green, J. P. "Decreasing junk-food consumption through the use of self-management procedures: A case study." *Psychological Reports, 69,* 1991, pp. 19-22. Copyright 1991 by Psychological Reports.

History

(4) J, a 25-yr.-old white male, who stands 6 ft. 3 in. tall and weighs 185 lbs., as part of a self-management exercise in a graduate behavioral course (McNamara, 1986), expressed concern over the large amounts of junk food he consumed late at night while watching television. Although not experiencing any negative physical side effects from such eating, J desired to decrease the amount of junk food and beverages consumed for preventive health reasons. J's father had recently undergone heart surgery, and this event motivated J to adopt a healthier diet. Specifically, J wanted to decrease the amount of junk food and beverages consumed while increasing the amount of fruit and fruit juices consumed when resting in a plush easy chair watching television late at night.

Program Overview

(5) The elements of the program were broadly derived from research and practice in self-management (cf. Karoly & Kanfer, 1982). Self-monitoring of junk food (chips, pretzels, popcorn, and candy) and junk beverage (soda pop) along with acceptable foods (fruit) and beverages (fruit juices) was initiated during baseline and continued over the next six weeks and then at follow-up. To facilitate recording all food was to be consumed out of a designated bowl and glass. When refills were needed, J had to go to the kitchen to make the refills. Getting J to recognize triggers that occasion consumption of junk food (e.g., sitting in the TV chair) and increasing self-awareness about this eating behavior (e.g., recognizing the amount of food placed in mouth) were identified as important initial steps in the process of establishing better self-control. The ultimate goal was to have J decrease the amount of junk food and beverage ingested while trying to have him increase the relative amounts of more acceptable food and beverage consumed.

Behavioral Intervention

(6) From Week 1 until Week 6 J was instructed to try to consume equal amounts of acceptable and junk food. The acceptable food and beverage was to be consumed first, however. The use of this Premack type of approach (Danaher, 1974) was intended to increase the amount and reinforcement value of the acceptable food and beverage consumed. Second, it was believed that junk food intake would decline because J would become satiated earlier with acceptable food.

(7) From Weeks 3 through 6, junk food and beverage bowls were placed on a table at the other side of the television room away from J's chair. To access the junk food, after consuming the acceptable food, he had to walk over to the table, acquire a small amount of the food (e.g., a handful of chips), and return to his chair before eating. Finally, during Weeks 5 and 6, J allowed himself to eat only during commercials.

Results And Discussion

(8) Inspection of Table I indicates that the six-week self-management program resulted in the accomplishment of both goals. J's intake of junk food decreased considerably from 14 bowls of food consumed per week during baseline to 1 1/2 bowls per week at Week 6, while soda pop consumed went from 104 ounces at baseline to just 16 ounces consumed per week at termination. Also, J increased his consumption of fruit and fruit juices. A 6-mo. follow-up probe for 1 wk. showed that J was once again consuming junk food and beverages at levels that were just somewhat higher than at the close of the program but much lower than at baseline. That is, he was consuming 2 bowls of junk food and 24 ounces of soda pop, while fruit and fruit juices were at 2 bowls and 32 ounces, respectively. Although weight reduction was not an objective goal, J lost 4 pounds during the 6-wk. treatment period.

(9) J was able to achieve his objectives during the time the program was in effect. Although some slippage in eating behavior occurred at follow-up, he did not return to his old eating habits of excessive junk-food consumption while watching TV at night. J was glad to have adopted a healthier snacking diet at the end of the program, and this sense of accomplishment coupled with the new dietary preferences and self-control were sufficient to maintain relatively low consumption of junk food at a short-term follow-up. Having met his goal of reducing the consumption of junk food, J reported an enhanced sense of personal competence in controlling undesirable behaviors. Thus, self-efficacy (Bandura, 1982) was increased.

(10) In the present program the following factors were present: a commitment to change, external support and structure to support the change, and, finally, a well developed self-management strategy to help engineer the change. Once the course ended all of these elements were removed simultaneously with only minimal relapse noted. Follow-up treatments have been used somewhat successfully in reducing relapse problems in weight control (Sarafino, 1990). Their use in changing snack preference where weight is not a problem is unclear and may not be needed if sufficient decreases occur initially coupled with a sense of accomplishment and self-control.

Table 1
Consumption of Food and Beverage

	Food (Bowls)			Beverage (Ounces)	
Week	*Junk*	*Acceptable*	*Week*	*Junk*	*Acceptable*
Baseline	14.0	.3	Baseline	104	2
1	6.0	6.5	1	66	48
2	3.0	2.3	2	24	29
3	5.5	3.0	3	41	60
4	5.5	2.3	4	16	40
5	3.0	2.3	5	16	32
6	1.5	1.5	6	16	16

(11) The present case demonstrated how dietary preferences for junk food can be altered by using self-management techniques. Short-term follow-up indicated that most of the change was maintained. Such maintenance was surprising given the encouragement on TV to buy and eat junk food visible to the client every night. Although long-term modification of eating habits is believed to be a difficult and complex task (cf. Wadden & Brownell, 1984), short-term modification of junk-food snacking may be more easily accomplished within a self-management framework.

References

Bandura, A. (1982). Self-efficacy, mechanism in human agency. *American Psychologist, 37*, 122-147.

Clapham, K., & Abramson, E. E. (1985). Aversive conditioning of junk food consumption: A multiple baseline study. *Addictive Behaviors, 10*, 437-440.

Danaher, B. G. (1974). Theoretical foundations and clinical applications of the Premack principle: Review and critique. *Behavior Therapy, 5*, 307-324.

Dubbert, P. M., Johnson, W. G., Schlundt, D. G., & Montague. N. W. (1984). The influence of caloric information on cafeteria food choice. *Journal of Applied Behavior Analysis, 17*, 82-85.

Friedman, H. S., & Dimatteo, M. R. (1989). *Health psychology*. Englewood Cliffs, NJ: Prentice-Hall.

Hazer, J. T., Aeschleman, S. R., & Robertson, R. B. (1985). Decreasing junk food consumption: A comparison of self-perception theory and reinforcement theory. *Motivation and Emotion, 9*, 87-99.

Karoly, P., & Kanfer, F. H. (Eds.) (1982). *Self-management and behavior change: From theory to practice*. New York: Pergamon.

Lasky, M. S. (1977). *The complete junk food book*. New York: McGraw-Hill.

Maccoby, N., Farquhar, J. W., Wood, P. D., & Alexander, J. (1977). Reducing the risk of cardiovascular disease: Effects of a community-based campaign on knowledge and behavior. *Journal of Community Health, 3*, 110-114.

Mayer, J. A., Heins, J. M., Vogel, J. M., Morrison, D. C., Lankester, L. V., & Jacobs, A. L. (1986). Promoting, low-fat entree choices in public cafeterias. *Journal of Applied Behavior Analysis, 19*, 397-402.

McNamara, J. R. (1986.) Personal therapy in the training of behavior therapists. *Psychotherapy, 23*, 370-374.

Perl, I. (1980). *Junk food, fast food, health food: What America eats and why*. New York: Houghton Mifflin.

Sarafino, E. P. (1990). *Health psychology: Biopsychosocial interactions*. New York: Wiley.

Wadden, T. A., & Brownell, D. K. (1984). The development and modification of dietary practice in individuals, groups, and large populations. In J. D. Matarazzo, S. Weiss, J. A. Herd, N. E. Miller, & S. M. Weiss (Eds.), *Behavioral health*. New York: Wiley. Pp. 608-631.

Wagner, J. L., & Winett, R. A. (1988). Promoting one low-fat, high fiber selection in a fast-food restaurant. *Journal of Applied Behavior Analysis, 21*, 179-185.

Terms for Discussion

1. aversive conditioning (paragraph 3)

2. self-management (paragraphs 3, 4, 5, and 8)

3. self-monitoring (paragraph 5)

4. self-control (paragraphs 5, 9, and 10)

5. baseline (paragraph 5)

6. reinforcement value (paragraph 6)

7. self-efficacy (paragraph 9)

Questions

8. Is it likely that the self-monitoring was less than perfectly accurate? Explain.

9. The goals in paragraph 5 are stated in general terms (e.g., decrease amount of junk food). Would it have been desirable to have established more specific goals such as "consume no more than 1 ounce of junk food"? Why? Why not?

10. In your opinion, is the increase in the number of bowls of acceptable food of practical significance? Explain.

11. In paragraph 11, the authors suggest that the self-management program altered J's preferences for junk food. In your opinion, how likely is it that the changes were coincidental with the program and not a result of the program?

12. Are there any other types of treatment that might have facilitated J's improvement. Explain.

13. Rate the article on the seven criteria described in the introduction to this book on a scale from 5 (highest quality) through 1 (lowest quality). Be prepared to explain your ratings.

Criterion 1: The demographics of the case are described: _____

Criterion 2: The condition(s) and behavior(s) that necessitated treatment are described in detail: _____

Criterion 3: The method of treatment is described in sufficient detail so that it can be replicated without additional information: _____

Criterion 4: A rationale is provided for the method of treatment selected: _____

Criterion 5: The client's improvement, if any, is clearly documented: _____

Criterion 6: Follow-up information on the client's improvement, if any, is presented: _____

Criterion 7: The study is appropriate for publication in a journal: _____

Notes:

Case 8

Case Report of a Needle Phobia*

Everett H. Ellinwood
Duke University

James G. Hamilton
Duke University

(1) Blood-injury phobia is defined in the psychiatric literature as a fear of exposure to blood, injury, pain, needles, or deformities.[1] In other phobias, exposure to the phobic cue usually causes tachycardia. In contrast, blood-injury phobia victims typically experience a diphasic cardiovascular response of an initial tachycardia, followed by bradycardia, hypotension, shock, vertigo, syncope, diaphoresis, nausea, and occasionally even coma, asystole, and death.[1,2] The concept of needle phobia is important for health care professionals to understand, since patients fearful of needles often avoid medical and dental treatment. Here a case of severe needle phobia in an otherwise nonphobic physician and his physiological response to having blood drawn is reported.

Case Report

(2) J.G.H. was a 39-year-old, male emergency department and family physician with extensive experience treating surgical wounds, suturing lacerations, and drawing blood. His medical history revealed, however, a life long involuntary fear of receiving injections or having blood drawn. He had had a strong sense of dread, with near fainting and diaphoresis, when using needles on others at the start of his medical training. His fear of others having needle procedures had been self-extinguished by first observing and then performing lancet heel sticks on neonates, and later inserting intravenous lines and drawing blood from adults. He remained very fearful of having needle procedures himself. His history revealed multiple episodes over a 19-year period of avoiding or refusing needle procedures such as having blood drawn for routine tests during physical examinations and having a scalp laceration sutured after an automobile accident.

(3) The subject's family history was strongly positive for needle phobia. The subject's father had an aversion to any needle procedure. Two of his father's first cousins fainted or almost fainted when they had blood drawn or received injections. The subject's mother experienced near syncope on any needle encounter. She reported an episode of fainting at the sight of an intravenous needle in a relative's foot in the hospital. She also noted that during a minor surgical procedure her pulse rate on a cardiac monitor dropped from 70 beats per minute to about 50 beats per minute on insertion of an intravenous needle. The subject's brother, an internist and emergency medicine physician, reported great anxiety and near syncope on having his blood drawn. The subject's maternal grandmother refused to have injections and instead always requested oral medication from her family physician. A maternal uncle, a family physician, reported that he experienced near syncope, diaphoresis, palpitations, and tachycardia with any needle procedure, and that his five offspring, two of whom are physicians, are all deathly afraid of having needle procedures. No other blood injury phobias were discovered during research of the family history.

(4) A treatment program of behavioral desensitization using a hierarchy of increasingly phobic stimuli was agreed upon, following standard exposure therapy for phobias as previously described.[1,3-5] Initially, for an hour each day for a month, the subject practiced fantasy rehearsal imaging of sticking a needle into his forearm

---

*Reprinted from *The Journal of Family Practice*, *32*, 1991, pp. 420-422. Copyright 1991 by Appleton and Lange. Reprinted by permission of Appleton and Lange.

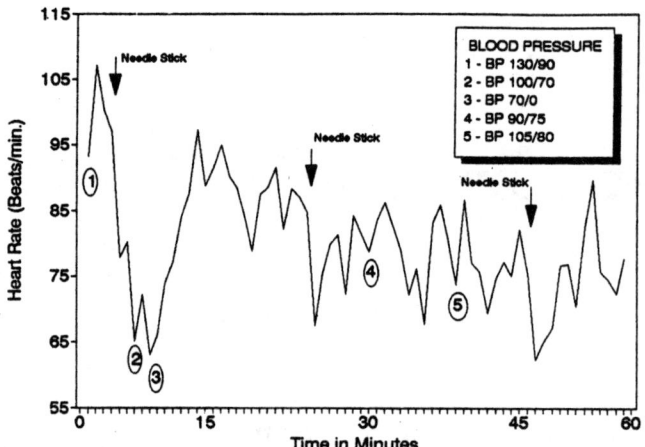

Figure 1. Cardiovascular response to venipuncture in a patient with needle phobia. Heart rate and blood pressure plunge with needle insertions, as is evident in this computer-generated graph.

veins, using a broken cotton swab, an alcohol pad, and a tourniquet. He then progressed to barely breaking the epidermal surface with a 30-gauge needle, and was eventually able to insert the needle into his forearm musculature up to the needle hub. After approximately another month's practice, he was able to self-cannulate a forearm flexor vein with a small butterfly needle long enough to withdraw a 10-mL sample of blood.

(5) After 3 months of treatment, the subject was able to agree to having blood drawn from the antecubital fossa. Before venipuncture, while attached to a cardiac monitor, his heart maintained a rate of 98 beats per minute with a prominent sinus arrhythmia for over 1 hour. His blood pressure remained at his normal 130/90 mm Hg. Immediately upon needle insertion, he experienced severe anxiety, near syncope, pallor, and diaphoresis. His blood pressure plunged to a low of 70/0 mm Hg, and his pulse rate fell to a low of 63 beats per minute. As illustrated in Figure 1, the pulse rate dropped markedly during each of the three venipunctures in this session. Also, computer analysis revealed that each pulse rate drop with venipuncture coincided with a loss of the sinus arrythmia otherwise present throughout the experiment. A moderate decrease in pulse to approximately 70 beats per minute persisted for over 3 hours after venipuncture. Although the catechol (epinephrine and norepinephrine) levels were well within normal range, the corticosteroid and antidiuretic hormone levels during the needle challenge were clearly elevated (Table 1).

(6) Another blood drawing was performed for a medical examination over 1½ years after this initial experiment. On cannulation of a dorsal hand vein while recumbent, J.G.H.'s blood pressure immediately fell from his baseline to 84/56 mm Hg, and his pulse slowed to 58 beats per minute.

Discussion

(7) These data are consistent with an unconditioned physiological response to an isolated needle phobia. The cardiovascular response of bradycardia and hypotension, often termed vasomotor, vasodepressor, or vasovagal syncope, was dramatically sudden in this subject, with an onset directly coincident with needle insertion. The bradycardic response was particularly evident in that not only did the subject respond with bradycardia during each of the three blood withdrawals, he also partially responded on occasions when taking another blood sample was even discussed. Furthermore, as was evidenced during a later blood drawing, this reflex persisted even after 1½ years and after extensive treatment. J.G.H.'s sinus arrhythmia is interesting in light of a previous report of sinus arrhythmia with bradycardia among subjects exposed to emotional stimuli.[6] Whether those with needle phobia usually experience sinus arrhythmia with needle challenge is unknown.

(8) The subject's unremarkable epinephrine and norepinephrine response is in line with similar findings during blood testing in another victim of vasomotor

Table 1. Stress Hormone Levels During Venipuncture in a Patient with Needle Phobia

Hormones	Subject Values	Normal Values
Antidiuretic hormone	11.80 pg/mL	0.5-1.5 pg/mL
Corticotropin releasing factor		<10.0 pg/mL
Total	4.96 pg/mL	
Free	<2.00 pg/mL	
Corticotropin	6.3 pmol/L	0.4-2.4 pmol/L*
Cortisol	673 nmol/L	83-359 nmol/L*
Norepinephrine	170.0 pg/mL	200-500.0 pg/mL
Epinephrine	37.00 pg/mL	10-90.0 pg/mL
Dopamine	29.00 pg/mL	10-35.0 pg/mL
ß-Endorphin	6.15 pmol/L	5-25 pmol/L

*Normal afternoon levels.

syncope.[7] On the other hand, his cortisol response was high, compared with that of several other previously reported subjects with fear of needles.[8] The normal values for corticosteroids given in Table 1 are those for afternoon levels, the time of day during which the blood for this experiment was drawn.

(9) The subject's dramatically high level of antidiuretic hormone (ADH), a hormone that conserves intravascular fluid volume, is logical during an episode of cardiovascular depression. The hypotension and bradycardia during blood drawing in the subject surely causes a decreased cerebral perfusion, and the pituitary, in turn, can be expected to secrete more antidiuretic hormone in response to a perceived decreased blood volume. An increased antidiuretic hormone level has previously been reported in a subject undergoing venipuncture.[9] Interestingly, an increased level of renin, which also conserves intravascular volume, has also been reported in a vasomotor syncope victim.[7] One can hypothesize that an exaggerated antidiuretic hormone secretion in patients with needle phobia, as in the present subject, contributes to learning the fear of needles observed in needle phobia, since intravenous antidiuretic hormone administration in experimental animals greatly enhances avoidance learning.[10] Antidiuretic hormone has also been suggested as a cause of pallor and nausea in vasomotor syncope.[11]

(10) Previous case studies indicate a strong familial tendency in blood-injury and need phobia.[3,4,12] The heritability of blood-injury phobia as determined by twin studies, including fear of injections, wounds, blood, and pain, is 0.48.[13] Therefore, although at this time a role for learned behavior is undefined, the finding in the present study of a strong personal and family medical history of isolated needle phobia, along with definitive electrocardiographic and biochemical changes, is compatible with a distinct, genetically influenced disorder.

(11) The trait of needle phobia may have evolved among *Homo sapiens* because of its selective value in the avoidance of puncture injuries from tree limbs, shrubs, and weapons. Most violent deaths throughout human history and prehistory have been due to cutting, stabbing, and piercing injuries from axes, spears, knives, swords, and arrows. An adverse cardiovascular reflex with fainting might have been of selective value in learning to avoid previously encountered situations during which one's skin was punctured. Marks[1,5] has suggested that bradycardia in response to blood-injury cues might have evolved in situations where mobility and fainting produced less risk of further injury than a "fight-or-flight" type of response. As with most genetic traits, multiple factors probably interacted to evolve the complex reflex underlying needle phobia.

(12) The incidence of needle phobia among the general US population can be estimated at well over 4%[14]; probably over 10 million Americans suffer from needle phobia. The sample of patients usually seen in the family physician's office, however, almost surely contains a much smaller percentage of needle phobia, since those with this disorder tend to remove themselves from the patient population. This potential avoidance of health care in such a large number of people underscores the importance of this condition and its challenge for medical management and treatment.

References

1. Marks I. Blood-injury phobia: a review. *Am J Psychiatry* 1988; 145:1207-13.

2. Graham DT, Kabler JD, Lunsford JL Jr. Vasovagal fainting: a diphasic response. *Psychosom Med* 1961; 23:493-507.

3. Hsu LKG. Novel symptom emergence after behavior therapy in a case of hypodermic injection phobia. *Am J Psychiatry* 1978;.135: 238-9.

4. Yulc W, Fernando P. Blood phobia—beware. *Behav Res Ther* 1980; 18:587-90.

5. Marks, IM. *Fears, phobias, and rituals: panic, anxiety and their disorders.* New York: Oxford University Press, 1987.

6. Carruthers M, Taggart P. Vagotonicity of violence: biochemical and cardiac responses to violent films and television programmes. *Br Med J* 1973; 3:384-9.

7. Goldstein DS, Spanarkel M, Pitterman A, et al. Circulatory control mechanisms in vasodepressor syncope. *Am Heart J* 1982; 104: 1071-5.

8. Rose RM, Hurst MW. Plasma cortisol and growth hormone responses to intravenous catheterization. *J Human Stress* 1975; 1:22-36.

9. Noble RL, Taylor NBG. Antidiuretic substances in human urine after hemorrhage, fainting, dehydration and acceleration. *J Physiol* (Lond) 1953; 122:220-37.

10. van Wimersma Greidanus TB, Bohus B, de Wied D. The role of vasopressin in memory processes. *Prog Brain Res* 1975; 42:135-41.

11. Weissler AM, Warren JV. Syncope: pathophysiology and differential diagnosis. In: Hurst JW. *The Heart*, 6th ed. New York: McGraw-Hill, 1986:509.12.

12. Öst L-G, Hugdahl K. Acquisition of blood and dental phobia and anxiety response patterns in clinical patients. *Behav Res Ther* 1985; 23:27-34.

13. Torgersen S. The nature and origin of common phobic fears. *Br J Psychiatry* 1979; 134:343-51.

14. Kleinknecht RA. Vasovagal syncope and blood/injury fear. *Behav Res Ther* 1987; 25:175-8.

Terms for Discussion

1. phobia (paragraphs 1, 3, 7, 9, and 12)

2. self-extinguished fear (paragraph 2)

3. behavioral desensitization (paragraph 4)

4. exposure therapy (paragraph 4)

5. unconditioned physiological response (paragraph 7)

6. avoidance learning (paragraph 9)

7. reflex (paragraph 11)

Questions

8. Given the subject's phobia, does his choice of a profession seem odd? Explain.

9. Do you agree that the subject is probably having an unconditioned physiological response to needle procedures? (See paragraph 7.)

10. Do you believe that this subject has a genetically influenced disorder? Explain.

11. Have the authors convinced you that needle phobia is an important problem that deserves more attention and research?

12. Are there other forms of treatment that might have facilitated this subject's improvement? Explain.

13. Rate the article on the seven criteria described in the introduction to this book on a scale from 5 (highest quality) through 1 (lowest quality). Be prepared to explain your ratings.

Criterion 1: The demographics of the case are described: _____

Criterion 2: The condition(s) and behavior(s) that necessitated treatment are described in detail: _____

Criterion 3: The method of treatment is described in sufficient detail so that it can be replicated without additional information: _____

Criterion 4: A rationale is provided for the method of treatment selected: _____

Criterion 5: The client's improvement, if any, is clearly documented: _____

Criterion 6: Follow-up information on the client's improvement, if any, is presented: _____

Criterion 7: The study is appropriate for publication in a journal: _____

Notes:

Case 9

Controlling Extremely Dangerous Aggressive Outbursts when Functional Analysis Fails*

Jason R. Dura
Bowling Green State University

SUMMARY: This article describes and illustrates a treatment program aimed at addressing intermittent extremely aggressive behavior in an 11-year-old girl who was blind, multiply handicapped, and profoundly mentally retarded. In the month preceding treatment she had injured a peer, a paid careprovider, and her mother. Functional analysis produced no clear antecedents to aggression. Punishment was used to introduce a superordinate contingency. Differential reinforcement of alternative behavior combined with contingent restraint reduced, then eliminated aggression. Follow-up at an age equivalent of 4 years, 6 months indicated a continued absence of aggression. Results are discussed in regards to the balance between research methodology, agency policy, right to effective treatment, and social validity.

(1) Controlling aggressive behavior remains one of the most elusive goals in behavior modification. Controlling aggressive behavior in individuals with mental retardation and multiple physical handicaps is complicated by the presence of physical disability and the need for multiple trials in learning. Isolated therapeutic techniques derived from behavior analytic theory have generally not been effective in controlling aggressive behavior in individuals who are blind and have severe or profound mental retardation (Altmeyer, Williams, & Sams, 1985; Barton & Lagrow, 1983; Luiselli, 1988; Sisson, Van Hasselt, & Hersen, 1987). In contrast, combinations of behaviorally derived methods appear to hold promise (Altmeyer, et al., 1985; Sisson, et al., 1987).

(2) In the case of aggression displayed by individuals who are blind and have severe or profound mental retardation, punishment appears to be a necessary component of effective programming. A thorough review of the literature produced no empirical evidence for cessation of low-rate aggression in individuals with severe or profound mental retardation and visual handicaps unless reinforcement techniques were combined with punishment. Similarly, in reviewing literature on treating aggression in persons who were deaf and blind Sisson, et al. (1987) reported no study in which aggression was eliminated without some form of punishment as a programming component.

(3) Multiple studies have demonstrated the efficacy of combined treatment "packages" in the control of aggressive responding (Luiselli, Myles, Evans, & Boyce, 1985). For example, differential reinforcement of other behavior (DRO) was shown to control aggressive behavior when combined with non-exclusionary time-out in a 15-year-old blind girl with mild to moderate mental retardation (Luiselli, et al., 1985). Similarly, aggressive biting of self and others was eliminated in a 16-year-old girl who was blind and severely mentally retarded using differential reinforcement of other behavior combined with time-out and the contingent application of an aversive gustatory stimulus (Altmeyer, et al., 1985).

(4) Reinforcement procedures combined with either isolation time-out or physical restraint appear to have been

---

*Reproduced with permission of author and publisher from Dura, J. "Controlling extremely dangerous aggressive outbursts when functional analysis fails." *Psychological Reports, 69*, 1991, pp. 451-459. Copyright 1991 by Psychological Reports.

the most consistently successful treatment approaches with persons with sensory handicaps and mental retardation. Luiselli and Greenidge (1982) reported the successful combination of differential reinforcement of other behavior and isolation time-out in the elimination of high-rate aggression in a 12-year-old who had maternal rubella syndrome. A stepwise treatment procedure was required to eliminate aggression completely, with time-out moving through three stages before reaching isolation time-out at which point aggression ceased. Similar results were produced in the treatment of aggression in a 15-year-old child with partial vision, hearing loss, and mental retardation (Luiselli, Myles, & Littman-Quinn, 1983), a 7-year-old girl and a 7-year-old boy with mental retardation (Luiselli, Suskin, & Slocumb, 1984), and a 13-year-old girl with mental retardation, hearing impairment, and retinitis pigmentosa (Luiselli, 1990).

(5) As the above cases illustrate, multiple treatment techniques were necessary to eliminate aggression. While most studies achieved complete elimination of the aggressive behavior, the frequency of aggression during baseline was inversely related to the length of time necessary to control the behavior. For example, the treatment package utilized by Altmeyer, et al. (1985) reduced the frequency of biting massively in the first month, but required several additional months to eliminate biting completely. This time limitation carries with it the risk of serious injury to both residents and staff when a single aggressive incident is capable of producing severe or permanent damage.

(6) Ideally, programming aimed at eliminating aggression evolves from functional analysis which provides clear evidence of causal relationships between antecedent variables and the target behavior (i.e., aggression). However, in practice, functional analysis does not always provide clear directions for programming (Haynes & O'Brien, 1990). When this occurs, treatment may still be guided by the contingency rules if a superordinate contingency is imposed. Punishment provides such a superordinate contingency.

(7) In an effort to accelerate the control of aggressive responding, a treatment method was created which utilized a common antecedent to aggression (high demands; Carr & Newsom, 1985) in a controlled setting to promote aggression and to provide for frequent and safe consequation. The program allowed for and, to some extent, encouraged aggression in a safe setting so that aggressive behavior might be treated safely, and more rapidly. This was hypothesized to reduce highly dangerous aggressive behavior more quickly, safely, and humanely. Single-case designs offer empirical evaluation of treatment effects with single individuals and have been supported as appropriate for evaluating outcome with individuals who have multiple handicaps (Van Hasselt & Hersen, 1981). The present study evaluated consequenting aggression in a controlled setting using a single-case experimental design.

Method

Subject

(8) The subject was an 11-year-old girl who was blind, nonambulatory, profoundly mentally retarded, and had many autistic characteristics. On her most recent psychological evaluation, Ruth (a pseudonym) earned a raw score of 23 on the Bayley Test of Infant Development–Mental Scale, showing age equivalent functioning at the 2-month level. Adaptive behavior as measured using the Vineland Adaptive Behavior Scale was at the 7-month level over-all. Her medical diagnoses included hydrocephaly which was shunted, porencephalic cyst, optic atrophy, and seizures which were controlled with medication. Ruth had right-sided hemiplegia and her right arm was less developed than her left and showed limited functional use. She lived in a large residential setting and attended school during the day.

(9) Aggression was emitted intermittently during training and play. Functional analysis did not indicate a clear pattern of antecedents. Aggression occurred early, middle, and late during interactions with no clear pattern apparent. Aggression was present and absent during play, instructional tasks, meals, hygiene tasks, and with familiar and unfamiliar people. Scratching eyes was the most dangerous aggressive behavior and accounted for the majority of injuries inflicted. Ruth pinched skin, scratched eyes, and pulled hair using her left hand. When attempts were made to remove her hand, she would sometimes attempt to bite. There was constant concern for the safety of residents and staff, and her parent had recently been injured during a home visit; while aggression was infrequent, the risk of serious injury from aggression was constant. Spontaneous exploration of her environment was prohibited due to danger to peers. Scratching eyes was blocked during baseline and thus not observed.

Setting

(10) Baseline and treatment occurred during play sessions on a 4 x 6-ft. mat covered with a nonabrasive material. Play sessions lasted 15 minutes (M = 15.49 min.). Play sessions occurred in a public living area. Nearby a large sign was hung which explained the rationale for programming as well as the procedure. To

participate in programming staff had to volunteer and receive specific safety training. Multiple toys were provided which Ruth had previously been observed playing with independently. Play sessions never ended with punishment. Following punishment Ruth and the trainer returned to play and remained in play for at least one minute with no aggression prior to the session's end. Aggression proximate to the normal ending of the play sessions caused variation in the length of early sessions.

Procedure

(11) The first phase of the study was a modified baseline period. Traditional baseline was not possible due to the risk of injury so a modified baseline was attempted in which staff engaged Ruth in play and counted the frequency of aggressive behaviors. Play (touching any toy) was reinforced with tactile stimulation and verbal praise (differential reinforcement of alternative behavior [DRA]). Ruth responded to tactile stimulation and verbal praise by smiling and cooing. During modified baseline, attempts at eye scratching were blocked because risk of permanent damage to staff was high, so this behavior was not observed. When attacked, staff volunteers were instructed to free themselves of Ruth's grasp after each incident and remove themselves from her presence for one minute. Staff were asked to disengage from the child to avoid inflating the rate of aggression during baseline due to the situation's escalation.

(12) In the second phase differential reinforcement of other behavior was provided with verbal praise and tactile stimulation given for touching toys as in Phase 1. Aggression (hair pulling, pinching, biting, or touching others' faces—a prelude to eye scratching) was consequented with a warning, i.e., "no pull," "no bite," or "no touch," and redirection to play. If Ruth did not respond to the verbal warning and redirection to play (aggression continued), then 60 seconds of graduated restraint was instituted. Throughout the restraint procedure, Ruth lay face down on a mat with the staff member on hands and knees over her holding Ruth's arms to her sides with her legs secured between the staff member's foot and knee. At all times, the staff members bore their own weight. The release criterion was 10 seconds of no struggling after a 60-second minimum of restraint. The restraint was graduated in that as Ruth stopped struggling the restraint was eased.

(13) The third phase of the study was a modified version of the second phase. Toy touching was reinforced with tactile stimulation and praise and aggression was first consequented with a verbal warning and redirection. Continued aggression was consequented with graduated restraint but the length of graduated restraint was increased to 5 minutes. Length of restraint was increased in an effort to speed cessation of aggression due to continued safety concerns. If Ruth immediately removed her hand from the staff member in response to the warning, no consequence other than the warning was provided. This contingency was maintained until the cessation of formal data collection when aggression and warnings had been absent for two months.

Results

(14) The data on aggressive behavior are presented in Fig. 1. During modified baseline, the rate of aggression was low but baseline was stopped and treatment instituted after three play sessions over three days when a staff member was injured when bitten while trying to free herself of the child's grasp. For this reason no baseline data are available.

(15) Aggression during Phase 1 was variable and showed no clear indication of reduction prior to the initiation of Phase 2. Introduction of extended manual restraint in Phase 2 preceded a marked decline in aggression. Aggression varied from 1 to 0 occurrences per session after Session 50 and then gradually disappeared by Session 85.

(16) Reliability of data recording of aggression was provided by volunteer staff's supervisor observing and cosigning records. Aggressive behaviors were infrequent (no more than 8 occurred in any one session) and dramatic so confirmatory counts were readily available. Also, play sessions occurred in a public living area.

(17) Generalization across people and then people and settings followed the cessation of data collection after two months without aggression. First, all unit staff were instructed in use of the warnings and restraint procedure. Staff currently involved in programming introduced new staff, and aggression remained absent. After this point any staff were allowed to interact with Ruth. As aggression continued to be absent, isolation from peers was targeted for removal. To test Ruth's safety with generally defenseless peers, a staff volunteer lay on an adjacent mat and Ruth's boundary markers were removed. Ruth was observed to crawl to the adjacent mat and touch the staff member without attempting aggression. Boundary markers were then removed permanently. (Staff continue to be in close proximity during peer interactions as a safety precaution.) Ruth's volunteer and her family were informed of her cessation of aggression and were instructed in the warning and restraint procedure. Follow-up at an age equivalent of 4

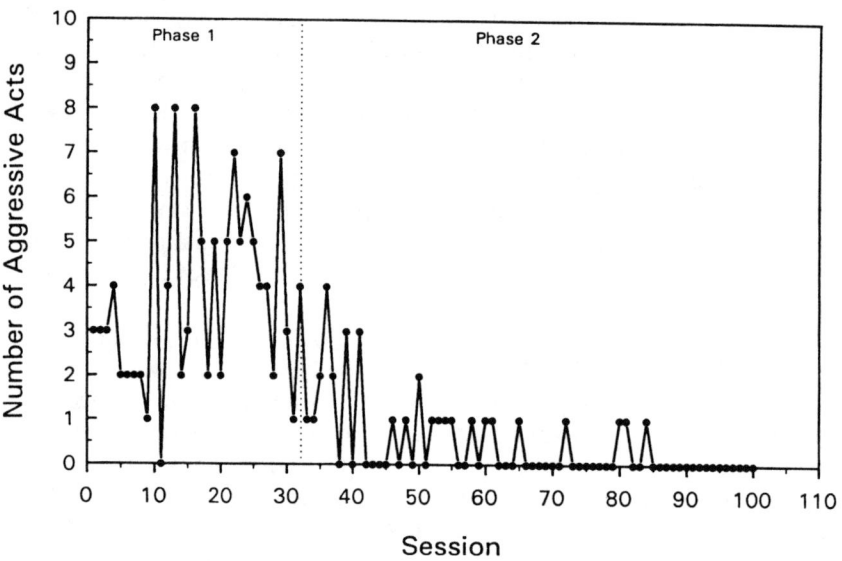

FIG. 1. Acts of aggression by session across Phase 1 and Phase 2.

years, 6 months found the subject to be integrated with peers and family. The subject readily accepts physical contact and engages in simple interactive play. No further problems with aggression have occurred.

Discussion

(18) Results support the use of the combination of differential reinforcement of alternative behavior and a mild aversive consequence as effective in reducing, then eliminating extremely dangerous aggression. At the conclusion of formal data collection, the subject responded to warnings by placing her hand on her lap. Also, when her spontaneous exploration brought her hand in contact with another's neck, she responded by immediately returning her hand to her lap without receiving a warning. Follow-up at an age equivalent of 4 years, 6 months found the subject fully integrated with peers and family. No further problems with aggression were reported, and instead a pattern of continued safe interaction was described.

(19) The combination of reinforcement of play, warning, redirection, and manual restraint to consequent aggression in Phase 2 effectively reduced and then eliminated aggression. The frequency of aggression decreased smoothly until the occurrence of aggression became inconsistent and then disappeared. The reduction of aggression, when aggression was paired with restraint, suggests restraint served as a punisher in the present study. Specifically noting this effect is important, given that prior research has demonstrated restraint may serve as a potent reinforcer as well (Favell, McGimsey, & Jones, 1978; Favell, McGimsey, Jones, & Cannon, 1981).

(20) Manual restraint has a number of advantages. It provides control of the movements of a potentially dangerous individual, is immediate in that transfer to a specified "time-out" area is not necessary, (if sustained) may allow a deceleration of sympathetic nervous arousal, and guards the safety of the aggressive individual as well as potential targets. This is especially true for planned use of restraint. Hill and Spreat (1987) reviewed 8684 restraint implementations over 12 months in an ICF-MR and found planned use of restraint was significantly less dangerous than emergency restraint. While the nature of injuries incurred was consistently minor across types of restraint, the cost associated with injuries was not. In the present study the safe-guarding role of planned manual restraint was confirmed through 150 + aggressive attempts without injury to the girl or staff.

(21) There is considerable ongoing controversy regarding the use of punishment in managing the behavior of individuals with handicaps. The decision to use an aversive restraint in the present case followed extensive attempts at differential reinforcement of alternative behavior. Although interactive play had increased, aggression had continued. At the time of intervention the subject was physically isolated to ensure the safety of peers. This was of considerable concern and judged only acceptable as an interim procedure. Spontaneous exploration of the environment and interaction with peers provides multiple learning and social opportunities (Simmons & Davidson, 1985). Continued isolation could have seriously compromised habilitation. Furthermore, physical handicaps and adaptive limitations required the subject be provided considerable assistance

with daily living tasks. Each interaction brought with it the risk for permanent injury to the child and staff. The child had injured her mother's eye on their most recent contact, and the mother indicated future contact with herself and siblings would depend on cessation of aggression. In a meeting of the interdisciplinary treatment team the necessity of using punishment was assessed. The subject's parent reviewed the treatment plan and provided consent.

(22) In retrospect, prior to the addition of restraint as a formalized punishment procedure, only the illusion of nonaversive intervention was present. Brief restraint was being used, as is the common practice, as a crisis intervention method. In the absence of effective programming, intermittent brief restraint during aggressive outbursts would have continued. In real terms then restraint as a programming component simply involved the addition of a predetermined duration for restraint and a release criterion.

(23) The current intervention is not presented as a treatment of choice except in similarly extreme cases. Individuals with verbal abilities may be taught a variety of conflict resolution strategies that were not possible in the present case. The literature discussed in the introduction was purposely focused on individuals with multiple physical and sensory handicaps, severe or profound mental retardation, and imminently dangerous aggression.

(24) In practice the implementation of treatment in accordance with strict experimental methodology is not always possible. The present case diverged from ideal experimental procedure at three junctures. First, traditional baseline was attempted but was stopped when a staff member was injured while trying to escape the child's grasp. While traditional baseline would have been ideal for methodological concerns, the risk of additional injury was deemed too great to justify additional baseline.

(25) Second, the rule of least restrictive intervention guided the decision on duration of manual restraint in Phase 1. One minute of restraint was felt the least restrictive amount of time with possible efficacy. Only after aggression did not decrease was a more extensive duration of restraint implemented. It is possible that total treatment time would have been significantly shorter had five minutes been the original restraint time length.

(26) Finally, no reversal phase was attempted. Noonan and Bickel (1981) review the ethical concerns involved in traditional reversal designs. The high risk of permanent injury associated with aggression in the present case made any risk of additional aggression unacceptable. Even in the baseline condition with staff instructed in defensive techniques, an injury had occurred.

(27) The decision to prompt the occurrence of aggression was not without precedent. Matson and Ollendick (1976) described the use of prompting in the successful elimination of infrequent biting in nine children. In their study a functional analysis indicated the type of situation in which biting was likely to occur and this type of situation was then arranged intermittently throughout the day. Matson and Ollendick (1976) did not detail the rationale *per se* but appeared to be emphasizing a desire to increase the rate of aggression, subsequent delivery of the consequence, and thereby decrease the length of treatment.

(28) Social validity standards encourage judging programming efforts relative to expected outcome (Wolf, 1976). However, programming must be designed in the absence of specific outcome data. The literature may be instructive, but it provides no guarantees. The current case supports the addition of an additional standard to guide programming decisions. Compare the content of programming to expectations regarding outcome in the absence of effective treatment. At the time of intervention, safety concerns required Ruth be totally isolated from peers. Family visits had ceased following Ruth injuring her mother's eye, and Ruth's mother indicated there would be no further contact between Ruth and her family until the danger of aggression ceased. Complete social isolation had occurred, and for safety reasons had to continue. Failure to provide effective treatment would have required continued isolation.

References

Altmeyer, B. K., Williams, D. E., & Sams, V. (1985). Treatment of severe self-injurious and aggressive biting. *Journal of Behavior Therapy & Experimental Psychiatry, 16,* 159-167.

Barton, L. E., & Lagrow, S. J. (1983). Reducing self-injuries and aggressive behavior in deaf-blind persons through overcorrection. *Journal of Visual Impairment & Blindness, 77,* 421-424.

Carr, E. G., & Newsom, C. (1985). Demand-related tantrums: Conceptualization and treatment. *Behavior Modification, 9,* 403-426.

Favell, J. E., McGimsey, J. F., & Jones, M. L. (1978). The use of physical restraint in the treatment of self-injury and as a positive reinforcement. *Journal of Applied Behavioral Analysis, 11,* 225-241.

Favell, J. E., McGimsey, J. F., Jones, M. L., & Cannon, P. R. (1981). Physical restraint as a positive reinforcement. *American Journal of Mental Deficiency, 85,* 425-432.

Haynes, S. N., & O'Brien, W. H. (1990). Functional analysis in behavior therapy. *Clinical Psychology Review, 10,* 649-668.

Hill, J., & Spreat, S. (1987). Staff injury rates associated with the implementation of contingent restraint. *Mental Retardation. 25,* 141-145.

Luiselli, J. K. (1988). Positive reinforcement interventions in the classroom. *Journal of Visual Impairment & Blindness, 22,* 17-20.

Luiselli, J. K. (1990). Case study: Reinforcement control of assaultive behavior in sensory impaired child. *Behavioral Residential Treatment, 5,* 45-53.

Luiselli, J. K., & Greenidge, A. (1982). Behavioral treatment of high-rate aggression in a rubella child. *Journal of Behavior Therapy and Experimental Psychiatry, 13,* 153-157.

Luiselli, J. K., Myles, E., Evans, T. P., & Boyce, D. A. (1985). Reinforcement control of severe dysfunctional behavior of blind, multihandicapped students. *American Journal of Mental Deficiency, 90,* 328-334.

Luiselli, J. K., Suskin, L., & Slocumb, P. L. (1984). Application of immobilization time-out in management programming with developmentally disabled children. *Child & Family Behavior Therapy, 6,* 1-15.

Matson, J. L., & Ollendick, T. H. (1976). Elimination of low frequency biting. *Behavior Therapy, 7,* 410-412.

Noonan, J. M., & Bickel, W. K. (1981). The ethics of experimental design. *Mental Retardation, 19,* 271-274.

Simmons, J. N., & Davidson, I. F. (1985). Perspectives on intervention with young blind children. *Child Care, Health and Development, 11,* 183-193.

Sisson, L. A., Van Hasselt, V. B., & Hersen, M. (1987). Psychological approaches with deaf-blind persons: Strategies and issues in research and treatment. *Clinical Psychology Review, 7,* 303-328.

Van Hasselt, V. B., & Hersen, M. (1981). Applications of single-case designs to research with visually impaired individuals. *Journal of Visual Impairment & Blindness, 75,* 359-362.

Wolf, M. M. (1976). Social validity: The case for subjective measurement of how applied behavior analysis is finding its heart. *Journal of Applied Behavior Analysis, 11,* 203-214.

Terms for Discussion

1. behavior modification (paragraph 1)

2. differential reinforcement (paragraphs 3, 4, 11, 12, and 21)

3. time-out (paragraphs 3, 4, and 20)

4. functional analysis (paragraphs 6 and 9)

5. superordinate contingency (paragraph 6)

6. baseline (paragraphs 10, 11, and 14)

7. reliability of data (paragraph 16)

8. reversal phase (paragraph 26)

Questions

9. In paragraph 7, the author states that the program allowed for and, to some extent, encouraged aggression. Does this seem like a good idea? (Also see paragraph 27.)

10. Speculate on why the play sessions were never allowed to end with punishment. (See paragraph 10.)

11. What is your opinion on the selection of "restraint" as a form of punishment for use with Ruth? Are there other punishments that might be more effective? Does it surprise you that in some cases restraint may also serve as a reinforcer? (See paragraph 19.)

12. In your opinion, did the author take adequate safeguards to protect the safety of others both during the course of this study and afterwards? Explain.

13. The author notes that there is controversy regarding the use of punishment in managing the behavior of individuals with handicaps. In general, what is your opinion on this controversy? What is your opinion in Ruth's case?

14. In paragraphs 24 through 26, the author describes the ways in which this study diverges from an ideal experiment. In your opinion, is this study worthwhile despite these weaknesses? Explain.

15. Rate the article on the seven criteria described in the introduction to this book on a scale from 5 (highest quality) through 1 (lowest quality). Be prepared to explain your ratings.

Criterion 1: The demographics of the case are described: _____

Criterion 2: The condition(s) and behavior(s) that necessitated treatment are described in detail: _____

Criterion 3: The method of treatment is described in sufficient detail so that it can be replicated without additional information: _____

Criterion 4: A rationale is provided for the method of treatment selected: _____

Criterion 5: The client's improvement, if any, is clearly documented: _____

Criterion 6: Follow-up information on the client's improvement, if any, is presented: _____

Criterion 7: The study is appropriate for publication in a journal: _____

Notes:

Case 10

Linking Descriptive and Experimental Analyses in the Treatment of Bizarre Speech*

F. Charles Mace
University of Pennsylvania

Joseph S. Lalli
Lehigh University

ABSTRACT: Descriptive and experimental methods were used to analyze the environmental determinants of an adult's bizarre speech. A descriptive analysis of behavior under natural conditions indicated that bizarre vocalizations occurred most often in the presence of task-related demands and in the absence of adult attention. Further, bizarre speech occurring during tasks was followed frequently by the cessation of task demands by staff or the subject's voluntary disengagement from task-related activities; bizarre speech observed during noninteractional periods (i.e., in the absence of adult attention) was frequently followed by staff attention. The escape and attention hypotheses were tested under analogue conditions. Results of the experimental analysis supported only the attention hypothesis; that is, bizarre speech appeared to function as an attention-producing behavior. The functional analysis data were used to select two different yet functionally equivalent treatments. The first treatment provided the subject with noncontingent scheduled attention. The second intervention taught the subject social language skills in the form of initiation and expansion statements. Both interventions were effective in suppressing maladapted speech. Advantages of linking descriptive and experimental analyses are discussed.

(1) A behavior problem that has received little attention in the functional analysis literature, but that is common in developmentally disabled and psychiatric populations, is bizarre or maladapted speech. Whereas psychodynamic and organic theories view bizarre vocalizations as symptoms of an underlying disorder, behavior analysts consider these behaviors to be successful operants (Burns, Heiby, & Tharp, 1983; Layng & Andronis, 1984; Skinner, 1957). Accordingly, bizarre comments may function as veiled mands shaped and maintained by positive and negative reinforcement contingencies.

(2) We have found only two studies that experimentally analyzed the reinforcement contingencies maintaining bizarre vocalizations. Mace, Webb, Sharkey, Mattson, and Rosen (1988) assessed the bizarre comments of a woman diagnosed with schizophrenia during three analogue conditions. Maladapted statements occurred most often when the therapist temporarily discontinued task demands and were relatively frequent when the therapist provided indulgent attention contingent on bizarre comments. Similarly, Durand and Crimmins (1987) varied levels of task demands and adult attention and found the maladapted vocalizations of a 9-year-old boy

---

*Reprinted from *Journal of Applied Behavior Analysis*, 24, 1991, pp. 553-562. Copyright 1991 by the Society for the Experimental Analysis of Behavior. Reprinted with permission.

with autism to correlate with the presence and absence of task demands.

(3) Methods used to analyze the function of aberrant behavior have varied considerably. Most studies have used an experimental approach in which the variables hypothesized to control the target behavior are manipulated by the experimenter under well-controlled analogue conditions. Using experimental methods, some researchers have alternately introduced and withdrawn antecedent stimulus conditions that may occasion aberrant behavior and inferred the operant function based on the pattern of responses observed (e.g., Carr & Newsom, 1985). Others have arranged varying consequences for the problem behavior, permitting a more direct inference regarding the reinforcement contingencies maintaining the aberrant behavior (e.g., Iwata, Dorsey, Slifer, Bauman, & Richman, 1982).

(4) Descriptive analysis represents an alternative approach for assessing the function of maladapted behavior. A descriptive analysis assesses behavior-environment interactions in the natural settings in which maladapted behavior occurs without manipulating variables suspected to influence the target behavior. The resulting data are by nature correlational rather than experimental and are only suggestive of functional relationships operating in the subject's natural environment. Descriptive data provide an empirical basis for formulating hypotheses to test later via experimental analysis (Bijou, Peterson, & Ault, 1968; Mace & Belfiore, 1990; Mace, Lalli, & Pinter-Lalli, 1991).

(5) Given the respective advantages of descriptive and experimental analyses, combining these approaches may improve the validity of a functional analysis. The present study illustrates this combination to identify contingencies maintaining the bizarre statements of a 46-year-old man with moderate mental retardation (Experiment 1). The descriptive analysis provided an empirical basis for formulating hypotheses tested subsequently in an experimental analysis during analogue conditions. These findings were used to develop two different yet functionally equivalent interventions to reduce bizarre vocalization (Experiment 2).

EXPERIMENT I

Method

Subject and Setting
(6) The subject in this investigation was Mitch, a 46-year-old man with moderate mental retardation. He had grand mal seizures controlled to a frequency of one per week with 500 mg of tegretol twice daily and 250 mg of mysoline thrice daily. Mitch's psychiatrist also prescribed 100 mg of mellaril twice daily to treat "delusional and hallucinatory" speech. Although Mitch was observed occasionally to speak in complete sentences using a large vocabulary, he rarely initiated conversations with others, nor did he expand on conversations initiated by staff or other clients. Rather, Mitch was observed frequently to make bizarre or unusual statements. These vocalizations included self-talk, statements unrelated to the topic being discussed, and mumbling. Bizarre comments were often accompanied by unusual gestures or body movements (e.g., slapping the floor with both hands and saying "I've got to put out that fire.").

(7) All analysis sessions were conducted in the university-affiliated group home where Mitch resided with five other clients who had moderate or severe mental retardation. Observations during the descriptive analysis and generalization phases of the study were obtained in several different rooms of the group home with zero to two staff and zero to five clients present as Mitch moved about freely. Experimental analysis sessions were conducted in the home's large eat-in kitchen with a large oval table and eight chairs.

Procedures
(8) *Descriptive analysis.* Two independent data collectors observed Mitch in an unobtrusive manner during naturally occurring situations at the group home. Observation sessions were 30 to 60 min in duration and were conducted at random times between the hours of 3:00 p.m. and 9:00 p.m. The observation system permitted data to be collected concurrently on naturally occurring antecedent events, bizarre speech, and naturally occurring events subsequent to aberrant speech. On the basis of informal observations and available functional analysis research, four antecedent and five subsequent event categories were recorded. The antecedent event categories were (a) interaction, (b) no interaction, (c) task, and (d) alone. Subsequent event categories were (a) social disapproval, (b) positive interaction, (c) tangible reinforcement, (d) task disengagement, and (e) no staff/client response. Operational definitions for bizarre speech and the antecedent and subsequent event categories are available from the authors upon request.

(9) Concurrent data on the target behavior and naturally occurring environmental events were obtained using a continuous 10-s partial-interval recording procedure (Mace et al., 1991). Antecedent event categories were

scored throughout the entire observation session because each occurrence of these events was a potential antecedent to aberrant speech. Subsequent event categories were scored immediately following each instance of aberrant speech and for the next three 10-s intervals.

(10) *Experimental analysis.* Analysis of the descriptive data suggested two viable hypotheses regarding the function of Mitch's bizarre speech. Hypothesis 1 was that Mitch's maladapted vocalizations were positively reinforced by staff attention, usually in the form of socially disapproving comments. According to Hypothesis 2, bizarre comments were negatively reinforced by staff discontinuation of instruction or Mitch's voluntary disengagement from the task. The validity of these two hypotheses were tested experimentally during four analogue conditions. Bizarre vocalizations were measured using a continuous 5-s partial-interval recording procedure. Integrity measures for the independent variables were measured on an occurrence and nonoccurrence basis using a continuous 5-s interval recording procedure. The percentage of correct applications of each independent variable according to the procedure and schedule exceeded 85% in all cases. The analogue conditions described below were presented during 15-min sessions according to a randomized multielement arrangement, with two conditions per day separated by a 10-min free period.

(11) In the first condition, no demand-social disapproval, the experimenter instructed another client in a food preparation task using prompts and praise for correct responses. Mitch was free to move around the kitchen but generally stood at a distance of 1 to 3 m from the experimenter. The experimenter did not look at or speak to Mitch unless Mitch emitted a vocalization. The experimenter made eye contact with Mitch and responded positively to each of Mitch's appropriate vocalizations (e.g., "Thanks for telling me, Mitch," or "I had a good day today; thanks for asking."). Contingent on bizarre vocalizations, the experimenter provided a disapproving comment on a variable-ratio (VR) 2 schedule (e.g., "Mitch, stop talking like that. You know your mother's not here."). This condition, including the schedules of reinforcement, was designed to test the attention hypothesis.

(12) The second condition, no demand-interaction, consisted of one-to-one discussion between Mitch and the experimenter while both were seated facing each other at the kitchen table. The experimenter initiated conversation by directing a question to Mitch (e.g., "What did you do at work today?"). The experimenter responded to each appropriate vocal response by asking a follow-up question related to the topic of Mitch's statement. All bizarre vocalizations were ignored by the experimenter. Each time the conversation paused for 15 s, the experimenter directed a statement to Mitch to continue the discussion (e.g., "I stopped at Pete's today for a cup of coffee."). Because this condition provided Mitch with noncontingent attention without task related demands, bizarre speech was expected to occur infrequently.

(13) The third condition, task disengagement, represented naturally occurring situations in which Mitch was engaged in a household task, and occurrences of bizarre vocal responses were followed by the experimenter's discontinuation of instructions for task performance. The experimenter presented Mitch with one household task per session. Tasks were selected that required an instructor's assistance to complete (e.g., meal preparation). Instruction consisted of a least-to-most intrusive prompt hierarchy (i.e., vocal, gestural, model, physical) with an interprompt interval of 10 s. The experimenter provided descriptive praise contingent on correct responses to each prompt. To test the escape function of bizarre speech, the experimenter backed away two steps from the subject and discontinued instruction for 30 s, contingent on occurrences of bizarre speech. A VR 2 schedule, approximating the schedule observed during the descriptive analysis, was followed. After the 30-s escape interval, the experimenter resumed task instruction. The experimenter responded to each of Mitch's appropriate vocalizations as in the first condition.

(14) The fourth condition, task-social disapproval plus disengagement, was designed to approximate situations in which bizarre vocalizations were followed by the experimenter's disapproving comment and discontinuation of the task. In addition, this condition permitted comparisons to the other conditions while varying only one variable at a time. Procedures in this condition were identical to the third condition with the following exception. Immediately following a bizarre vocalization, the experimenter provided a disapproving comment (VR 4 schedule) and then began the 30-s escape interval (VR 2 schedule). Again, the consequences and schedules applied to bizarre speech paralleled those observed during the descriptive analysis.

Interobserver Agreement

(15) A second independent observer collected data on the relevant dependent and independent variables during a minimum of 30% of the sessions per condition

and experimental phase. Total, occurrence, and nonoccurrence agreements were calculated on an interval-by-interval basis according to Page and Iwata (1986). Mean interobserver agreement values were 81% or higher for all observational categories during the descriptive analysis and were 90% or higher for all measures during the experimental analysis.

Results

(16) Figure 1 presents three different analyses of the descriptive data collected under natural conditions. The upper panel reflects the probability of observing bizarre speech within 20 s following the occurrence of a given antecedent event. This measure, for each session in which a minimum of 2 min of the antecedent condition was observed, was calculated by dividing the number of intervals scored with bizarre speech and a given antecedent by the number of intervals scored with a given antecedent. This analysis indicated that bizarre speech was observed with moderate frequency subsequent to task conditions and when social interaction was unavailable (i.e., the alone and no interaction conditions). By contrast, virtually no bizarre speech was observed when Mitch was interacting with staff in the absence of task-related demands (i.e., the interaction condition).

(17) The middle panel of Figure 1 shows the distribution of subsequent events given the occurrence of bizarre speech during a task. The measure was calculated by dividing the number of intervals jointly scored task and bizarre speech that were followed within two intervals by a given subsequent event by the number of intervals jointly scored task and bizarre speech. Jointly scored is defined as the antecedent event occurring within the same or preceding two intervals. The objective of this analysis was to determine whether disengagement from task-related activities naturally followed bizarre speech either as a result of staff discontinuing instruction or Mitch's voluntary disengagement from the task, a relation that would be expected to occur if bizarre vocalizations were negatively reinforced by escape from task-related demands. Results of this analysis showed that Mitch frequently disengaged himself from his assigned task following maladapted comments. However, staff attention in the form of positive interaction and social disapproval was observed intermittently to follow bizarre speech during task conditions.

(18) Finally, the lower panel of Figure 1 presents the distribution of subsequent events given the occurrence of bizarre speech during no demand–no interaction conditions. Calculation of this measure was the same as that used for the task condition, except that the relevant antecedent and subsequent event categories were

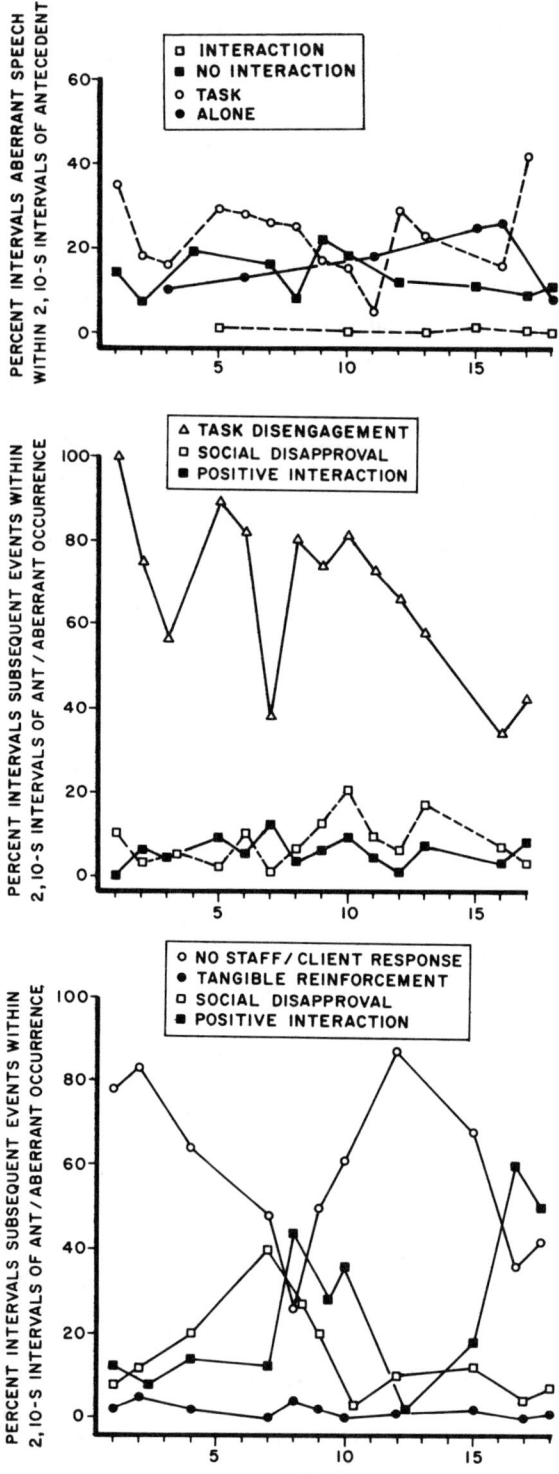

Figure 1. Results of the descriptive analysis of bizarre speech observed in Mitch's natural environment. The upper panel shows percentage of intervals with aberrant speech scored during four antecedent environmental events. The middle panel depicts percentage of intervals with subsequent events observed within 20 s of aberrant speech occurring during a task. The lower panel shows percentage of intervals with subsequent events observed within 20 s of aberrant speech during no demand–no interaction situations.

substituted. This analysis indicated that, when Mitch was not interacting with others, the majority of his bizarre vocalizations received no response by staff or other clients. However, approximately 50% of the intervals jointly scored no demand–no interaction and bizarre speech were followed by attention either in the form of social disapproval or positive interactions. Together, these direct analyses provided an empirical basis for two hypotheses concerning the function of Mitch's bizarre vocalizations: (a) bizarre speech was negatively reinforced by escape from task-related demands, and (b) bizarre speech was positively reinforced by the attention of others.

EXPERIMENT 2

Method

Subject, Setting, and Measurement
(19) The subject, setting, and the definition and measurement of bizarre speech for this portion of the study were identical to Experiment 1.

Procedure
(20) *Intervention 1: Scheduled attention.* The first intervention provided response-independent attention (i.e., scheduled comments) and attention for appropriate vocalizations, and required staff to discontinue attention that had been contingent on Mitch's bizarre vocalizations (i.e., extinction). The experimenter instructed another resident in a food preparation task as described in the no demand–social disapproval condition. However, in the course of providing instruction to Mitch's coresident, the experimenter directed a comment to Mitch on a variable-time schedule (VT 90 s, VT 60 s, or VT 30 s, in different experimental phases). Examples of experimenter comments were "Mitch, Ellen's doing a great job cooking the spaghetti," and "Mitch, I heard that you guys are going bowling tonight." The experimenter ignored all bizarre vocalizations.

(21) *Intervention 2: Initiation and expansion training.* The effectiveness of scheduled attention provided further support for the attention hypothesis and suggested that other interventions that provided Mitch with attention would also be effective. The second intervention was designed to teach Mitch a socially appropriate response that would function equivalently to bizarre speech (i.e., evoke staff attention). Carr and Durand (1985) demonstrated that clients successfully acquired socially appropriate responses and substituted these responses for maladapted behaviors when the behaviors were functionally equivalent (i.e., produced the same consequences).

(22) Conversation initiation and expansion skills were taught separately and sequentially using procedures taken directly from Haring, Roger, Lee, Breen, and Gaylord-Ross (1986). Training was conducted in the kitchen while the experimenter was instructing a coresident in a food preparation task. Sessions were 20 min in duration and occurred three to four times per week. Briefly, training entailed providing vocal prompts to initiate or expand on conversations every 90 s. If Mitch did not respond appropriately to the prompt, the trainer provided a verbal model of the skill; this was repeated until Mitch emitted the target response. Initiations consisted of any statement that began a conversation or changed its topic. Expansions referred to contextually appropriate statements or questions that added new information to the conversation. (Detailed training procedures and operational definitions are available in Haring et al., 1986, or upon request from the authors.) Both conversation skills were measured using a continuous 10-s partial-interval recording procedure.

(23) The effects of initiation and expansion training on Mitch's conversation skills were evaluated during a five-phase sequence. Conditions during the no demand phase were identical to the no demand–social disapproval condition, except bizarre vocalizations were ignored. The no demand–prompts to converse phase added experimenter vocal prompts for Mitch to initiate or expand conversation every 90 s. Initiation training procedures continued until Mitch responded correctly during three consecutive sessions to a minimum of 75% of the prompts to initiate. During initiation maintenance and expansion training, initiation prompts were discontinued while holding other aspects of the training sessions constant. Expansion training continued until Mitch responded correctly to 75% of the prompts across three consecutive sessions. Finally, during the generalization phase, Mitch's initiation and expansion skills were assessed across different staff, locations of the group home, and times of the day. One of three staff (other than the original trainer) met with Mitch in a different location in the group home at a randomly determined time between 3:00 p.m. and 9:00 p.m. Generalization sessions were initiated with the staff member saying "Mitch, how was your day today?" The staff person replied appropriately to each of Mitch's initiation and expansion statements and provided no further prompts.

Interobserver Agreement
(24) Interobserver agreement data were collected for bizarre speech, initiations, and expansions, as well as for the correct application of each independent variable in the experimental analysis and conversation skills

training phases. Agreement data were obtained for a minimum of 30% of the sessions distributed equally across experimental conditions and phases and were analyzed in the manner described in Experiment 1. Mean interobserver agreement values were 82% or higher for all measures.

Experimental Design

(25) The effectiveness of scheduled attention was evaluated using a modified reversal design with the no demand–social disapproval condition of the experimental analysis serving as the initial baseline. The sequence of phases was A/B1/A/B1/B2/B3/B1/A/B1/A, where A is no demand-social disapproval and B1, B2, and B3 are scheduled attention at VT 90 s, VT 30 s, and VT 60 s, respectively.

(26) A multiple baseline design across initiation and expansion skills was used to assess the effects of the training procedure on Mitch's conversation. Subsequent to training, Mitch independently initiated or expanded on conversations such that it was not possible to evaluate the effects of the training procedure on bizarre speech with a reversal design.

Results

(27) The results of the experimental analysis appear in Figure 2. Experimental manipulation of the consequences of Mitch's bizarre speech resulted in high levels of maladapted vocalizations only during the no demand–social disapproval condition. The other three conditions, which supplied noncontingent attention in the form of positive interaction or task instruction, resulted in little or no occurrences of bizarre speech. Considered collectively, the results of the descriptive and experimental analyses indicated that Mitch's bizarre speech occurred as a function of the attention this behavior evoked from others at the group home. Experiment 2 evaluated the effectiveness of two treatments for Mitch's bizarre speech derived from the descriptive and experimental analyses.

(28) Figure 2 also presents the results of the evaluation of the two analyses-derived interventions. The no demand–social approval condition of the experimental analysis served as the initial baseline. Providing attention on a VT 90-s schedule independent of bizarre vocalizations resulted in a sharp decrease in the target behavior to near zero levels. When scheduled attention was discontinued and social approval for bizarre speech was reinstated, maladapted speech returned to pretreatment levels. However, the first replication of the VT 90-s scheduled attention condition failed to recapture the initial treatment effect. Bizarre speech decreased to near zero rates, once again, when the rate of response-independent attention was increased to a VT 30-s schedule and was later thinned to VT 60-s and VT 90-s schedules in successive phases.

(29) Evaluation of the effects of conversation initiation and expansion training began with a high level of bizarre speech (M = 42.5% intervals) during the no demand phase (see Figure 2). Introduction of prompts (no demand–prompts to converse phase) reduced bizarre vocalizations apparently because it provided Mitch with a form of regular attention functionally equivalent to the scheduled attention condition. Low levels of bizarre speech were maintained during and subsequent to initiation and expansion training (i.e., during the initiation maintenance and generalization phases). That is, following conversation training, experimenter-initiated attention was discontinued without a resumption of bizarre speech.

(30) With the introduction of conversation training, Mitch's independent initiations and expansions per training session increased from zero to two and zero to six to seven and 20, respectively. Both skills were maintained or increased when all experimenter prompts were discontinued and no other experimenter-initiated attention was supplied. In addtion, initiations and expansions were generalized to other staff members.

Discussion

(31) We presented a methodology for linking descriptive and experimental analyses of bizarre speech. The descriptive analysis involved repeated direct observations of client behavior during uncontrolled natural situations. Concurrent data on bizarre speech and environmental events antecedent and subsequent to the target response were analyzed using simple conditional percentages to reflect the likelihood of bizarre vocalizations occurring under different environmental circumstances. Two plausible hypotheses regarding the function of Mitch's bizarre vocalizations emerged from the descriptive analysis. First, bizarre comments may have been negatively reinforced by the discontinuation of task-related demands. Second, such comments may have been positively reinforced by the attention of others. When these hypotheses were tested using traditional experimental methods (e.g., Carr, Newsom, & Binkoff, 1980; Iwata et al., 1982), bizarre speech was found to be functionally related to attention and not to Mitch's escape from task-related demands.

(32) We believe this case illustrates some of the benefits

Treatment of Bizarre Speech

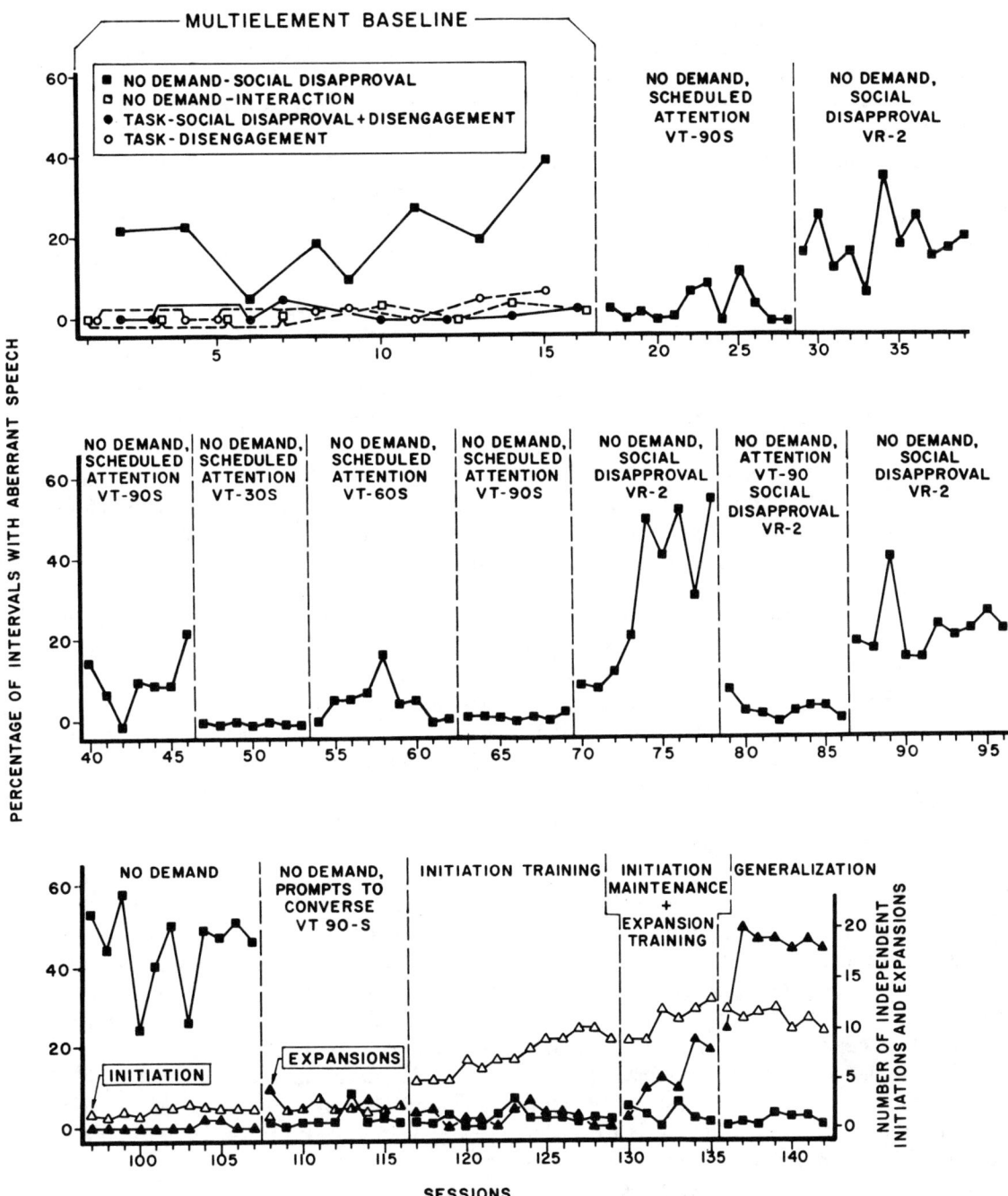

Figure 2. Percentage of intervals with aberrant speech during experimental analogue conditions (i.e., multielement baseline), analysis-derived treatment conditions (i.e., scheduled attention and conversation training), and baseline conditions (i.e., no demand–social disapproval, no demand). The number of independent initiation and expansion statements are presented during the last five phases in which the effects of the conversation training intervention were evaluated.

of combining descriptive and experimental approaches to functional analysis. Had our intervention been developed on the basis of the descriptive analysis alone, treatment during task conditions may have consisted of increased reinforcement for task completion, reduction of task difficulty, penalties for dawdling, or even guided compliance. These treatments were not only unnecessary, but their implementation could have been counterproductive inasmuch as inadvertent attention may have been supplied for inappropriate behavior.

(33) However, the descriptive analysis contributed importantly to the design and interpretation of the experimental analysis. First, repeated observations under natural conditions indicated (a) the type of demand and no-demand situations that Mitch normally encountered, (b) common forms of attention and escape that accompanied bizarre speech, and (c) an estimate of the natural schedule for escape and attention. This information permitted the design of experimental analogue conditions similar to Mitch's normal environment, a factor that should enhance the generality of the experimental analysis. The finding that Mitch's bizarre speech was maintained by attention required a small degree of inference to natural conditions. Second, to the extent that the descriptive analysis narrows the scope of plausible hypotheses, the experimental analysis can test fewer hypotheses with greater precision. With two hypotheses to test, we were able to design four experimental conditions that differed minimally except for the variable under study.

(34) This study also illustrated that pretreatment analysis of the function of maladapted behavior can give rise to multiple treatment approaches that may prove effective. Knowing that Mitch's bizarre speech was positively reinforced by the attentive reactions of others suggested that, in addition to ignoring bizarre comments, increasing the rate of noncontingent attention would decrease this problem behavior. This treatment objective was accomplished via two distinct interventions. First, scheduled attention supplied the same class of reinforcers that maintained bizarre speech, but did so independently of the target behavior. Although response-independent reinforcement is an effective response-reduction procedure, scheduled attention had practical limitations that did not augur well for its long-term adoption. The effectiveness of scheduled attention appeared to depend on reliable implementation by the group-home staff, who have numerous competing responsibilities. Moreover, this intervention would require training other service providers and dozens in the community in order to achieve generality of the treatment effect.

(35) Training Mitch to initiate and expand on conversation circumvented some of the practical problems encountered with scheduled attention. First, Mitch was able to prompt staff to attend to him by initiating and maintaining interaction. Second, Mitch could regulate the amount and timing of attention he received and thereby maintain a level of attention sufficient to discourage high levels of bizarre speech. Finally, Mitch's skill at prompting conversation seemed better suited to community settings in which continuity of programming varies. Indeed, following initiation and expansion training, Mitch prompted interaction so readily that a reversal design to demonstrate the effects of training on bizarre speech was not possible without ignoring Mitch's prompts.

(36) Combining descriptive and experimental analyses may be impeded by practical constraints indigenous to many applied settings. One obvious constraint is the additional time involved in conducting two analyses (i.e., number of sessions). Another obstacle to performing the descriptive portion of this methodology is the spatial proximity of the natural and treatment environments. Many outpatient and acute-care inpatient facilities do not have the resources to conduct observations in relevant community settings. Settings most amenable to this approach are those in which the natural and treatment environments are the same (e.g., classrooms, residential and vocational programs).

(37) The availability of less time-consuming methods to assess the operant function of aberrant behavior (e.g., Cooper, Wacker, Sasso, Reamers, & Donn, 1990; Durand & Crimmins, 1988) may limit the applicability of the present methodology to certain situations. However, this approach may lead to effective treatment for particularly challenging cases to the extent that a combination of descriptive and experimental methods may yield more information about the reinforcement contingencies maintaining problem behavior in a client's natural environment.

(38) Finally, the contributions of the functional analysis of aberrant behavior extend beyond treatment development to the advancement of a scientific understanding of the nature of behavior disorders. Traditional accounts of the etiology of behaviors such as bizarre speech continue to dominate the psychological literature (Layng & Andronis, 1984). Although experimental evidence for the behavioral basis of some behavior disorders is growing (e.g., aggression, self-injury), behavior analysis of bizarre speech has remained largely theoretical (Burns et al., 1983; Layng & Andronis, 1984). The methodology described here seems well suited to the task of

identifying complex contingencies maintaining behavior attributed to psychotic, delusional, or other unobservable processes.

References

Bijou, S. W., Peterson, R. F., & Ault, M. H. (1968). A method to integrate descriptive and experimental field studies at the level of data and empirical concepts. *Journal of Applied Behavior Analysis, 1,* 177-210.

Burns, C. E. S., Heiby, E. M., & Tharp, R. G. (1983). A verbal behavior analysis of auditory hallucinations. *The Behavior Analyst, 6,* 133-143.

Carr, E. G., & Durand, V. M. (1985). Reducing behavior problems through functional communication training. *Journal of Applied Behavior Analysis, 18,* 111-126.

Carr, E. G., & Newsom, C. (1985). Demand-related tantrums. *Behavior Modification, 9,* 403-426.

Carr, E. G., & Newsom, C., & Binkoff, J. (1980). Escape as a factor in the aggressive behavior of two retarded children. *Journal of Applied Behavior Analysis, 13,* 101-117.

Cooper, L., Wacker, D., Sasso, G., Reimers, T., & Donn, L. (1990). Using parents as therapists to assess the appropriate behavior of their children through a functional analysis: Application to a tertiary diagnostic clinic. *Journal of Applied Behavior Analysis, 23,* 285-296.

Durand, V. M., & Crimmins, D. B. (1987). Assessment and treatment of psychotic speech in an autistic child. *Journal of Autism and Developmental Disorders, 17,* 17-28.

Durand, V. M., & Crimmins, D. B. (1988). Identifying the variables maintaining self-injurious behavior. *Journal of Autism and Developmental Disorders, 18,* 99-117.

Haring, T. G., Roger, B., Lee, M., Breen, C., & Gaylord-Ross, R. (1986). Teaching social language to moderately handicapped students. *Journal of Applied Behavior Analysis, 19,* 159-171.

Iwata, B. A., Dorsey, M., Slifer, K., Bauman, K., & Richman, G. S. (1982). Toward a functional analysis of self-injury. *Analysis and Intervention in Developmental Disabilities, 2,* 3-20.

Layng, T. V. J., & Andronis, P. T. (1984). Toward a functional analysis of delusional speech and hallucinatory behavior. *The Behavior Analyst, 7,* 139-156.

Mace, F. C., & Belfiore, P. (1990). Behavioral momentum in the treatment of escape-motivated stereotypy. *Journal of Applied Behavior Analysis, 23,* 507-514.

Mace, F. C., Lalli, J. S., & Pinter-Lalli, E. (1991). Functional analysis and treatment of aberrant behavior. *Research in Developmental Disabilities, 12,* 155-180.

Mace, F. C., Webb, M. E., Sharkey, R. W., Mattson, D. M., & Rosen, H. S. (1988). Functional analysis and treatment of bizarre speech. *Journal of Behavior Therapy and Experimental Psychiatry, 19,* 714-721.

Page, T. J., & Iwata, B. A. (1986). Interobserver agreement: History, theory and current methods. In A. Poling & R. W. Fuqua (Eds.), *Research in applied behavior analysis* (pp. 99-126). New York: Plenum Press.

Skinner, B. F. (1957). *Verbal behavior.* Englewood Cliffs, NJ: Prentice-Hall.

Terms for Discussion

1. functional analysis (paragraphs 1, 5, 8, and 38)

2. operants (paragraphs 1 and 3)

3. mands (paragraph 1)

4. reinforcement contingencies (paragraphs 1, 2, 3, 5, and 37)

5. analogue conditions (paragraphs 2, 5, 10, and 33)

6. partial-interval recording (paragraphs 9, 10, and 22)

7. variable-ratio (VR) schedule (paragraphs 11, 13, and 14)

8. noncontingent attention (paragraphs 12 and 34)

9. variable-time (VT) schedule (paragraphs 20, 25, and 28)

10. reversal design (paragraphs 25, 26, and 35)

11. multiple baseline design (paragraph 26)

Questions

12. In the first and last paragraphs, the authors mention the issue of whether bizarre speech is a symptom of an underlying disorder or is a behavior maintained by complex contingencies. What is your opinion on this issue as it applies to Mitch's case?

13. Do you agree that, when possible, a descriptive analysis should precede an experimental analysis? Explain.

14. The authors mention that operational definitions are available from the authors upon request. (See paragraph 8.) Would these be of interest to you if you were conducting a similar case study? Explain.

15. What is your opinion of the authors' decision to use a variable-ratio schedule? (See paragraphs 11, 13, and 14.)

16. In your opinion, is the rate of interobserver agreement described in paragraphs 15 and 24 adequate? Explain.

17. What does the upper panel of Figure 1 suggest to you?

18. The authors used a variable-time schedule in Experiment 2. Do you believe that this was a good choice? Explain.

19. If you did not have time to conduct both a descriptive and experimental analysis in a case like Mitch's, which one would you choose? (See paragraph 36.) Explain.

20. Are there other types of treatment that might have facilitated Mitch's improvement? Explain.

21. Rate the article on the seven criteria described in the introduction to this book on a scale from 5 (highest quality) through 1 (lowest quality). Be prepared to explain your ratings.

Criterion 1: The demographics of the case are described: _____

Criterion 2: The condition(s) and behavior(s) that necessitated treatment are described in detail: _____

Criterion 3: The method of treatment is described in sufficient detail so that it can be replicated without additional information: _____

Criterion 4: A rationale is provided for the method of treatment selected: _____

Criterion 5: The client's improvement, if any, is clearly documented: _____

Criterion 6: Follow-up information on the client's improvement, if any, is presented: _____

Criterion 7: The study is appropriate for publication in a journal: _____

Notes:

Case 11

Body Image Changes During Guided Affective Imagery*

Stephen J. Rojcewicz, Jr.
Saint Elizabeth Hospital, Washington, DC

ABSTRACT: An unusual body experience, the sensation of his whole body expanding to four or five times its normal size, occurred spontaneously in a forty-two year old attorney after five months of psychotherapy, using the technique of Guided Affective Imagery. Having entered therapy with the complaint of the absence of feelings, the attorney was able, through guided affective imagery, to experience emotions, with complex richness and variety. The use of guided affective imagery emphasizes the point that the potential for growth lies basically within the patient. The therapeutic use of imagery builds upon the view that the dream or daydreams is not merely a wish-fulfillment, but a trial act, an attempt to deal with the dynamics and issues, a beginning of therapeutic action. His body image experience expresses the meanings he is living, his increasing awareness of a rich emotional life, and the enlargement of his ego, his own personal growth.

The Case Description

(1) An unusual body experience, the sensation of his whole body expanding to four or five times its normal size, occurred spontaneously in a forty-two year old attorney after five months of psychotherapy, using the technique of guided affective imagery. The body experience, long forgotten, had occurred originally at age ten.

(2) The patient, an attorney with advanced degrees, entered psychotherapy with a chief complaint of being unable to experience any emotions. He had been married twice and was currently separated from his wife. He states that any feelings he did have were given him by his wife, whom he described as a lively, over-emotional person. She provided him with feelings by telling him that he felt such-and-such; otherwise, he was aware of no feelings whatsoever.

(3) After several months of therapy of a traditional, insight-oriented approach, the patient continued to complain of an absence of feelings. He apparently had little overt emotional life: his only promising activity was woodworking class, where he was carving a cherry-wood tree trunk. He was encouraged to continue this activity, in the hope that he could express or become aware of feelings through woodworking or creativity. Ostensibly, however, he continued without feelings.

(4) In a few months, guided affective imagery was introduced. This technique was developed by Leuner in Germany and has connections to other psychiatric techniques employing active imagery. It consists in having the patient vividly imagine himself in certain scenes. The therapist can suggest certain details, actions or outcomes, which the patient then visualizes through his imagination (Kosbab, 1974; Leuner, 1969). The technique provides an opportunity for a patient otherwise inhibited, to develop a fantasy production related to his problem, to experience the affects involved, and to allow the emotional responses to run their full course. The method gives the patient the opportunity to examine situations associated with original childhood fears and anxieties that are often central to adult psychopathology, and to work on the roots of the conflict (Leuner, 1977). It can lead to the resolution of neurotic conflicts on a symbolic level. It has been used successfully in patients with neuroses, borderline states, psychosomatic disturbances, and in the training of psychotherapists. In addition, the use of imagery can be particularly effective in

---

*Reprinted from *The Humanistic Psychologist*, 18, 1990, pp. 270-278. Copyright 1990 by Division 32 of the American Psychological Association. Reprinted with permission.

resolving impasses in therapy (Klagsbrun & Brown, 1984).

(5) Guided affective imagery bears a strong resemblance to a technique developed in France in the 1930's through the 1960's by Robert Desoille, and called "le Rêve Éveillé Dirigé" (directed daydream) (Desoille, 1955). Desoille claimed to have used it successfully in the treatment of patients with a wide variety of neurotic and characterological problems. The patient is instructed to experience a daydream usually with the theme of a journey of ascent or descent. The therapist focuses this material into a dramatization or symbolization of core issues or conflicts, and assists the patient to overcome these conflicts through symbolization in the daydream. For example, if the patient is paralyzed in the presence of a monster representing an authority figure, he is instructed to place the monster in another environment and watch its metamorphosis, or to touch the monster with a magic wand. The monster changes into a non-frightening figure that the patient can fully confront. The daydream is followed by a thorough discussion of the material produced, in order to re-educate the patient. Desoille saw his technique as based on Pavlovian theory: it created a new conditioned reflex to replace a previously conditioned, self-defeating, neurotic response.

(6) In the first session of guided affective imagery, this patient was asked to imagine certain standard scenes (a meadow, river, forest, mountain and cave) and to describe what happened. There was a vivid richness to his imagery—a marked contrast to the description of his everyday life as dull and lacking feelings. He spontaneously elaborated on the scenes with great and often fantastic detail. However, if someone approached him in the imaginary scene, cloudiness and obscurity developed. There was also a sharp differentiation of his visual field—the right side was dark, in shadow, and the left side was bright and sunny; adventurous happenings occurred on the left side of the visual field.

(7) The second session began with the same split of the visual field into a right half in shadow and a left half in sunshine. The patient was instructed to go on a journey. He began walking with a woman (who resembled a relative who was usually happy) and with a child (who resembled his sister). The woman led him to a farm where a family gathering was taking place. He then entered a car, saw himself standing in front of a rainbow, and walked toward the light. He crossed a desert finally reaching an ocean. Seeing the sun set in the ocean, he experienced a spontaneous feeling—he was happy. He then climbed on a surfboard, and guided by porpoises (he made a phonic association to "purposes"), he crossed the ocean to reach an island. His wife was there and embraced him, and again he felt happy. They walked together on the beach, but both were distant. His wife left. Lots of activity occurred but he felt bored. He left the island by flying through the air, and descended into a cyclone. There were birds sitting in metal nests, and a large powerful waterfall nearby. He enjoyed the scenery, but wondered, "what am I doing?" and became aware of a feeling of loneliness. In this session, therefore, he was able to experience and acknowledge several emotions.

(8) Subsequent sessions continued to show the rich detail and multiple, changing images described above, with the patient experiencing and acknowledging various emotions that matched the scenes being described, e.g., sadness, anxiety, irritation. A prominent early theme was his wife's providing him with emotions. By the third session of guided affective imagery, a particular figure appeared, who was associated with the patient's being able to have his own, not his wife's emotions. This figure was usually standing, raising both arms, often bare-chested, and having a helmet and wings: it was described by the patient as resembling Mercury.

(9) After approximately four months of guided affective imagery, the patient made several breakthroughs in expressing emotions through this technique. In one session, he began with the image of his mother wearing a mask. When she removed the mask, she turned away, obscuring her face but giving him a brief flash of an old, wrinkled face. Finally the face turned into a monster head: hairy, wolfish and resembling a pig. The patient was given instructions to overfeed the monster, to give it more food than anyone could possibly eat. By this means the monster became tired and sleepy; the monster's face resolved, then the head turned away. It was now a pretty cartoon face looking at the patient. The patient then acknowledged how irritated he had been at all the masks his mother had presented to him. He became sad, and nearly cried. He was instructed to tell his mother how sad he had been. He shouted it mentally and described a sense of relief and feeling well.

(10) The image of his mother in a mask began the next session. She was standing staring out of a window. She turned, and the side of her face away from the patient was dark and distorted, while the side of her face towards the patient was pretty. He was instructed to tell her what he feels about her. He began, "Mother, I want to talk to you. Won't you listen to me?" But he could not continue. He stated that he cannot tell her face, he cannot even bear to look at her face, because of the rotten flesh. He was instructed to ask her, "Are you turning into this rotten face so that I would be prevented from talking

to you?" With this, the rottenness disappeared; she had a sweet face, but it was a mask. "When I want to talk to you, why do you show me this face?" he asked. He moved closer to her, and added, "I want you to listen to me." He lost sight of the scene, which was flooded by light. He noticed that his mother was now a skeleton. "Why did you turn into a skeleton? I feel left out. It's another way not to pay attention to me," he said. His mother reappeared, dressed in a long 1890's dress. Her face was normal and she seemed thirty years old; he seemed eight or nine. She kissed him on the cheek, and he felt put off. He told her that he wants her to listen to him and that he has written a poem, "I'm going back home to Nebraska." She turned away, looking bored. A man appeared, and she talked to him, interrupting the poem. He was then instructed to tell her how angry he is. Although he did so, she seemed to humor him, to laugh at him. The man hugged him and he felt good. At this point, his body seemed distorted, and shaped like a large round balloon. He told his mother how happy he was when his father gave him a hug, how sad when she ignored him. The mother told the father that the boy doesn't know what he wants. He knocked the cigarette holder from her hands, and she slapped him, telling him to go. He responded by saying that he wants her to love him, he wants her to listen. The room then filled with smoke, and the scene ended.

(11) In the next session, he imagined a scene that had occurred in reality three years previously. He had been expressing some genuine feelings to his wife. She turned it into an argument, with crying and screaming. He withdrew emotionally, no longer expressed the feelings, and went to sleep. He had a sudden recognition that this pattern had gone on for years, and had been a major inhibiting factor in his ability to acknowledge and express feelings. At this point, he spontaneously experienced a swelling sensation, as if his head had swelled four or five times its normal size; this was accompanied by an awareness of breathing. With each inspiration, he had the sensation that the top of his head was expanding. It was a good sensation, a powerful feeling that left him with an impression of strength and potency.

(12) This spontaneous body sensation continued to occur, but with variation. In the next session, he was enjoying an image of conversational give-and-take with people. Then occurred the sensation of the swelling of his whole body. This was described as a pleasant but very unusual sensation. He could also feel a pulse in his skin, then a throbbing in his arm. There was an aura, midway between smelling and hearing, that he had experienced before. He had a sudden memory of Nebraska, when he was a boy of ten, and was alone in his house, looking out windows or staring at the ceiling. The sensation of his body expanding had first occurred at this time. He then experienced a whole series of memories: of his aunt's house, his toys and belongings, etc. He remembered, with affect, incidents of being scolded by his mother, and being punished by having to stay inside.

(13) Several sessions later, he had a spontaneous image of a large, comfortable chair in a warm room with wood paneling. A woman, similar to Whistler's mother, is there. The next room is an old room filled with images he had previously discussed. There is a chest, partly open, showing a manuscript. He could not read the title, however. He was asked to hold it up to a mirror. He was then able to read the title, "Songs of Life." He immediately described the hair on the back of his neck as standing up, and his skin as tingling all over. "I can cry for joy," he said. Further association showed that the woman represented the therapist and the book represented the story of the patient's life. Rather than the dusty, dry life he thought he had, he now saw himself as holding a treasure.

(14) In subsequent sessions of guided affective imagery, he was able to confront his father and his mother with long repressed resentments and feelings, and to tell his wife to listen to him, rather than impose her feelings upon him. When he told his father that he loved him, something that he had not been able to do in real life, he again experienced the sensation of his whole body, and especially his head, expanding, with a corresponding pleasant, exalted feeling.

(15) The next six months were spent in exploration of the darker side of his personality, with images such as a volcano, a cave, an unkempt garden surrounded by a brick wall. The unfolding of these scenes brought back many memories of his father's not showing any emotions, and of his mother's (and later his wife's) jealousy of his attention to other people, e.g., he had a memory of his first date and first kiss: he was powerfully affected, feeling as if he were about to start an unknown adventure. However, the next day his mother told him not to spend any more time with that girl, and he obeyed. The interpretation was made that these themes were the major inhibitions that led to his seeming lack of emotions: identification with his father, feeling no emotions, and not experiencing any emotions that would have made his mother jealous.

(16) After approximately eighteen months of therapy, he accepted a position in another state. The last month of therapy was devoted to the issue of his moving. His last visual image was of constructing a home in the new

state. He described in vivid detail the grounds and his house. His wife, mother and father visit, in scenes of emotional reconciliation. Finally, the therapist visits. Sitting on the floor is the table that he had made from the cherry tree trunk. He described it as the first creative thing he had ever made purely from his own imagination, and that its creation was a milestone in getting in touch with his own creativity. In his image the therapist is moving around, nodding approvingly.,

Discussion

(17) The use of guided affective imagery was a major element in making this patient aware that he had feelings, which came as a revealing and encouraging enlightenment. The therapist's "guiding" in the guided affective imagery, such as instructing the patient to overfeed the monster or to stay in a situation and tell his parents and wife about his reactions, allowed him to face emotional issues directly. He now saw that he could confront important people in his life without catastrophe to himself or to them, and he thus had a corrective emotional experience. He had permission to experience sadness, to become actively involved with people, and to tell them directly about his feelings. Rather than have no feelings whatever, he now had a rich emotional life, and was able to improve greatly his interpersonal relations in the real world.

(18) The sensation of his body expanding to a size four or five times larger than normal, or of his head expanding in a similar manner, with an accompanying pleasant, warm sensation, occurred seven or eight times in therapy. Related experiences have been described in normal people while falling asleep, and in patients with schizophrenia and with epilepsy (Lukianowicz, 1967). The sensation of enlargement of a part of the body, such as the head or extremities, has been described in cases of inner ear disease (Schilder, 1970) and in drug intoxication (Jaspers, 1963), including normal volunteers taking phencyclidine (Luby et al., 1959).

(19) In 1936 at the Fourteenth Psychoanalytic Congress in Marienbad, Otto Isakower described a phenomenon that, despite some major differences, bears much resemblance to what this patient experienced (Isakower, 1938). The Isakower phenomenon is the experiencing of an external object that comes nearer and nearer, and grows to a gigantic size. It is accompanied by multiple sensations in various sensory organs (auditory, visual, tactile, etc.) that are often amorphous, with a blurring of distinction between different regions of the body. In many cases there are distinct sensations of floating, sinking or giddiness, or a general feeling of warmth and comfort. The phenomenon occurs in both psychiatric patients and normal subjects, and had often been previously experienced in childhood by these subjects, although long forgotten. It is significant that the body experience of this patient had originally occurred during childhood. As pointed out by Barolin (1961), the technique of guided affective imagery makes it likely that the patient will reexperience vividly important childhood events, and even undergo age regression.

(20) Waugaman (1986) has recently discovered that a similar phenomenon had been mentioned by Sigmund Freud, decades prior to Isakower's description. Freud alludes to this phenomenon in a brief footnote to "A childhood recollection from *Dichtung und Wahrheit*" written in 1917 (Freud, 1968).

(21) Isakower viewed this phenomenon as a generalized regression to very primitive, primary bodily experiences. The psychoanalytic literature has viewed it as a regression from the primal scene experience by re-creation of the mother's breast (Fink, 1967), as a memory trace of the infantile experience of the early separation between self and external object (Spitz, 1955) and as a defense against Oedipal conflict (Richards, 1985).

(22) The major similarities between the Isakower phenomenon and the body experience of this patient are the sense of enlargement, the multiple amorphous sensations involved with a blurring of boundaries (the patient described a sensation midway between smelling and hearing), and a generalized feeling of warmth and comfort. The major distinction, of course, is that the patient's enlargement was of internal body, not of an external object.

(23) A contemporary novelist, the Nobel Prize winner Saul Bellow, has described a body sensation of one of his major characters that resembles in some ways the sensation of this patient. Henderson has a sudden revelation of empathy with an African king and experiences great joy: "I was swayed, I thrilled when I hear this .... My heart was moved to such an extent, that I felt my face stretch until it must have been as long as a city block. I was blazing with fever and mental excitement because of the loftiness of our conversation, and I saw things not double or triple merely, but in countless outlines of wavering color: gold, red, green, umber, and so on, all flowing concentrically around each object." (Bellow, 1950, p. 215).

(24) For this patient, the bodily sensation of becoming larger occurred when he demonstrated that somehow he could now rely on himself—relying on inner resources as a relief from boredom at age ten in the original instance, and finally being able to tell his father that he

loved him and becoming self-assertive with his wife, during the course of guided affective imagery.

(25) For years he had learned to suppress his emotions, and with them, the full awareness of his interpersonal relations and the richness and nuances of his life. He had prevented the pain of being hurt because of his father's lack of emotion, but at the cost of being neither hurt nor fulfilled, achieving neither genuine solitude nor authentic "being-with" another person. He had not acknowledged any emotion that would have made his mother jealous, but at the price of all emotions, the repudiation of adventure and the inhibition of mutual human relations. He had accepted feeling from his wife, but at the penalty of true passion, an affective life of his own.

(26) With therapy, especially the guided affective imagery and his unique bodily experiences, he recaptured his own emotional life. He became confident in himself, his emotions, his capacity for genuine human experience.

(27) In itself, the use of guided affective imagery emphasizes the point that the potential for growth lies basically within the patient. As Van den Berg (1972) has pointed out, the therapeutic use of dreams or daydreams builds upon the view of Ludwig Binswanger, the Swiss existentialist psychiatrist, that the dream or daydream is not merely a wish-fulfillment, but a trial act, an attempt to deal with the dynamics and issues, a beginning of therapeutic action (Binswanger, 1963). The patient's daydreams revealed to himself the growing strength of his imagination, his ability to face painful situations by relying on himself, his increasing awareness of a rich emotional life.

(28) It was fitting, then, that the body image experience of an expanded body and expanded head expresses the meanings the patient is now living—his increasing awareness of a rich emotional life, and the enlargement of his ego, his own personal growth.

References

Barolin, G. (1961). Spontane altersregression im symboldrama und ihre klinische bedeutung. *Zeitschrift für Psychotherapie und medizinische Psychologie, 11*, 77-99.

Bellow, S. (1950). *Henderson the rain king.* New York: Viking Press.

Binswanger, L. (1963). Dream and existence. In J. Needleman (Ed. and Trans.), *Being-in-the-world: Selected papers of Ludwig Binswanger* (pp. 222-248). New York: Basic Books. (original work published 1930).

Desoille, R. (1955). *Introduction a une psychothérapie rationelle.* Paris: L'Arche.

Fink, G. (1967). Analysis of the Isakower phenomenon. *Journal of the American Psychoanalytic Association, 15*, 281-293.

Freud, S. (1968). A childhood recollection from Dichtung und Wahreit. *Standard edition of the complete psychological works of Sigmund Freud* (pp. 145-156). London: Hogarth Press. (J. Strachey, Ed. and Trans.). (Original work published 1917).

Isakower, O. (1938). A contribution to the patho-psychology of phenomena associated with falling asleep. *International Journal of Psycho-Analysis, 19*, 331-345. (Original work published 1936).

Jaspers, K. (1963). *General psychopathology* (J. Hoenig & M. W. Hamilton, Trans.). Manchester: Manchester University Press. (Original work published, 7th edition, 1959).

Klagsbrun, J., & Brown, D. (1984). Getting the picture: The use of imagery to clarify the therapeutic impasses. *Psychotherapy, 21*, 254-259.

Kosbab, F.P. (1974). Imagery techniques in psychiatry. *Archives of General Psychiatry, 31*, 283-290.

Leuner, H. (1969). Guided affective imagery. *American Journal of Psychotherapy, 23*, 4-22.

Leuner, H. (1977). Guided affective imagery: An account of its development. *Journal of Mental Imagery, 1*, 73-92.

Luby, E. D., Cohen, B. D., Rosenbaum, G., Gottlieb, J. S., & Kelley, R. (1959). Study of a new schizophrenomimetic drug—Sernyl. *AMA Archives of Neurology and Psychiatry, 81*, 363-369.

Lukianowicz, N. (1967). Body image disturbance in psychiatric disorders. *British Journal of Psychiatry, 113*, 31-47.

Richards, A. D. (1985). Isakower-like experience on the couch: A contribution to the psychoanalytic understanding of regressive ego phenomena. *Psychoanalytic Quarterly, 54*, 415-434.

Schilder, P. (1970). *The image and appearance of the human body.* New York: International Universities Press. (Original work published 1935).

Spitz, R. A. (1955). The primal cavity: A contribution to the genesis of perception and its role for psychoanalytic theory. *Psychoanalytic Study of the Child, 10*, 215-240.

Van den Berg, J. H. (1972). *A different existence.* Pittsburgh: Duquesne University Press.

Waugaman, R. (1986). A footnote in Freud's work and the Isakower phenomenon. *Psychoanalytic Quarterly, 55*, 310-312.

Terms for Discussion

1. guided affective imagery (throughout article)

2. insight-oriented therapy (paragraph 3)

3. neurotic conflicts (paragraphs 4 and 5)

4. borderline states (paragraph 4)

5. psychosomatic disturbances (paragraph 4)

6. impasses in therapy (paragraph 4)

7. characterological problems (paragraph 5)

Questions

8. What is your interpretation of the patient's split visual field? Is it of significance? (See paragraphs 6 and 7.)

9. Do you believe that the patient's sensation that the top of his head was expanding is important? Explain.

10. Do you agree with the author that "guided affective imagery was a major element in making this patient aware that he had feelings"? (See paragraph 17.)

11. In your opinion, would it be important to know more about how and why this patient had learned to suppress his emotions or are the revelations through guided affective imagery sufficient? Explain.

12. Has the author convinced you of the value of guided affective imagery for use with this patient? Has he convinced you, by example, that it might be of value for use with other patients with other problems?

13. Are there other types of treatment that might have facilitated the patient's improvement? Explain.

14. Rate the article on the seven criteria described in the introduction to this book on a scale from 5 (highest quality) through 1 (lowest quality). Be prepared to explain your ratings.

Criterion 1: The demographics of the case are described: _____

Criterion 2: The condition(s) and behavior(s) that necessitated treatment are described in detail: _____

Criterion 3: The method of treatment is described in sufficient detail so that it can be replicated without additional information: _____

Criterion 4: A rationale is provided for the method of treatment selected: _____

Criterion 5: The client's improvement, if any, is clearly documented: _____

Criterion 6: Follow-up information on the client's improvement, if any, is presented: _____

Criterion 7: The study is appropriate for publication in a journal: _____

Notes:

Case 12

Self and Space*

Kaisa Puhakka
West Georgia College

ABSTRACT: Seemingly incomparable, self and space are seen as related, both psychologically and ontologically. The experience of self as expansive space has distinct psychological benefits, which are explored through a clinical vignette. Next, the issue of the "reality" of self is taken up. It is argued that the ontological status of self is indeterminate, which means that it is open to being that which it is considered to be. The powerful effect of such considerations on the being of self and its life experience are explored both through various philosophical conceptions of self (e.g., as extensionless point, intentional consciousness, or limitless space) and through the self-fulfilling prophecies which conceptions of self generate in people's lives. Lastly, it is proposed that the consideration of self as space can open the door to a rich, expanded, connected, harmonious living.

(1) Our uneducated intuition tells us that space is vast and "out there." The same intuition tells us that our selves are very small and "in here." In fact the self which we most intimately know and consider to be the enjoyer of our perceptions and feelings, the agent of our actions in the world, the center of our private worlds—this self seems not only very small but highly elusive; it defies all attempts to capture it and turn it into an object of observation. How could there then be any comparison between self and space? The notion that there should be a connection between the two sounds odd, even ludicrous. But that is precisely what is proposed in this article. The reader is invited to consider that self and space are not only connected but are very much of a kind.

(2) The idea that there is a kinship between self and space is not new. In Hindu and Buddhist literature, the self, understood as consciousness, is often described through spatial metaphors. In general people with a mystical bent, regardless of background, have tended to appreciate the close and intimate connection between self and space or to even consider self as space. This is understandable, for the experience of Oneness of All, the dawnings of mystical insight, is not likely to be had by a person who considers his or her self to be very small.

(3) But this article is not about mysticism. The consideration of self as space is quite compatible with life in the mundane world. In the following pages I shall try to persuade by arguments and illustrate by examples that the consideration of self as space is not only eminently reasonable but it also opens up the possibility of a drastic enhancement of one's way of being in the world and enjoyment of life.

(4) The question as to whether the self is "really" space will have to be addressed as well. For the ontological predilections that we harbor, often unawares, tend to have a far greater power to compel belief and action than do practical considerations. The application of Husserl's epoche to our naturalistic attitude regarding self and space is the first step toward dislodging and bringing into awareness the hidden assumptions and thus freeing up the consideration of alternative possibilities. But beyond this, the realization that none of these possibilities are *ontologically compelling* allows one to freely consider that self is space and to truly enjoy the practical benefits of doing so.

Experiencing Self as Space

(5) Let us return to our uneducated intuition and its claim that self and space are distinct and indeed incomparable. This claim rests on two dichotomies. One is that space is infinitely vast and unbounded whereas self is very small, perhaps infinitesimally small, and bounded. The other is that space is "out there" and self is "in

---

*Reprinted from *The Humanistic Psychologist, 18,* 1990, pp. 259-270. Copyright 1990 by Division 32 of the American Psychological Association. Reprinted with permission.

here." Taking up the unbounded and infinite vs. bounded and finite dichotomy first, one can easily see that space has no boundaries. There is no particular point or line where space ends and something else begins. The objects that exist in space do not constitute such points or lines; space pervades the objects, extending through them and beyond them uninterrupted. Now what of the self and its boundaries? Psychoanalysts and depth psychologists talk about the "boundaries of self" or "ego boundaries," but when one searches for these within one's awareness, they are nowhere to be found. One becomes aware of the body's boundaries, or more precisely, of the sensations of temperature and air currents and other tactile sensations which impinge upon the skin that is taken to be the boundary of the body. But one's awareness moves through these sensations without ever encountering a point or a line that marks the boundary of the self. The psychoanalytic and depth psychological boundaries are theoretical constructs. As such, they can be tremendously valuable in the context of theory and also of clinical practice. But when it comes to real, as opposed to theoretical, boundaries, we find that none exist for the self, any more than exist for space.

(6) The "in here" vs. "out there" dichotomy likewise has no basis in direct experience and observation. When one contemplates the vastness of space from a hilltop on a starry night, habitual ways of thinking may incline one to consider the vastness to be "out there," as opposed to "in here." But just how far down toward the "in here" does the vastness extend from "out there"? If one were to fix a point as far in space as possible and then trace the course from that point to one's self, would one be able to spot the exact location where the "out there" becomes the "in here"? The answer to this question can be readily found by performing the experiment. My own experiment tells me there is no such point. No gap or discontinuity is found between "in here" and "out there," between self and space.

(7) If all that has been said above is true and even fairly obvious, then why is it that we often feel so small? Why is it that it is so much *easier* to contemplate the vastness and even infinitude of space than it is to consider one's self to be space, let alone vast or infinite? Before attempting to answer these questions, let us consider the various ways in which people experience themselves as space.

(8) A noisy cocktail party is the shy person's nightmare. Unable to engage herself in any of the conversations and goings on which zoom by her, around her, through her, she feels unbearably constricted, suffocated. In the worst case, she may feel transparent, even invisible, as though she is not there; people look through her and talk past her. There is in her experience no space that she feels is hers and with the experience of no space, she feels lost, nearly vanished.

(9) A very different kind of experience was had by the person whom I once watched, unbeknownst to himself, walking alone on the hills of the Black Forest in Germany. Walking briskly on a narrow footpath amidst the trees, the young man hummed to himself. Momentarily he paused to listen to a distant bird call, then let out a whistle in answer. Walking slowly now, he stretched his arms out and his hands gently brushed the tree trunks and bushes he passed by. Then he crossed his arms behind his back, arched slightly backward and looked up at the sky above. In this manner, he continued to walk until he passed out of my sight. But I caught a glimpse of his face and the fullness of life in his smile. His was the look of a king in his realm.

(10) Many a person has had the experience of walking alone in a park or a forest and having that expansive feeling of at once belonging to, owning, and being one with all the life forms around. In such moments one feels magnanimous and free, and one feels oneself to be vast. But there are many other times when one feels "shrunken," feels one's space to be invaded or intruded upon. Such "spatial" experiences of expanding and shrinking are common and intimately familiar to people. Ordinarily, however, they are attributed to something "out there" that impacts on the person. The peaceful harmony of nature is believed to give the person an expanded feeling, whereas big crowds and nasty, aggressive people are believed to make the person feel shrunken. But this leaves the self's state precariously up to the circumstances surrounding the person. And it need not be so.

Expanding One's Self-Space
(11) The "in here" vs. "out there" distinction, as already discussed, has no basis in a person's immediate experience. There are no compelling reasons, therefore, to wait for something "out there," i.e., something other than oneself to rescue one from one's shrunken state. There is no need to take a trip abroad or even to a park to free one's self from its too narrow and cramped up bounds. It can be accomplished right here, "in here" as well as anywhere. The following story of Joe, a psychotherapy patient, illustrates how it can be done.

(12) Joe had made good progress in his one and a half years of psychotherapy. Much less withdrawn and oblivious to the rest of the world outside his computer work than before, he felt he could assert himself with his boss and, to some extent even with his family. But even

Self and Space

though he could now be assertive when necessary, he still felt vaguely uncomfortable just being around people. He told me that one of his very favorite things in life was to go to the public library and browse around. He would pick up a book, walk over to the large reading room and sit down at one of the long tables. There were seldom other people in the room, and Joe especially looked forward to the times when he had the place all to himself. At such times, he said, he would be in a festive mood and feel as though he owned the place. It was a moment when everything in his life was "just right." But when another person walked into the room, the magic of the moment was broken. Joe found himself hoping that the person would not come to his table, found himself even cussing at the person and having mean, aggressive thoughts about the person.

(13) A mild-mannered and rational individual, Joe related the story with considerable embarrassment. He noted that he could not understand why he felt this way as there was plenty of room for himself and the other person in the reading room, and the other person obviously had no ill intentions toward him. I asked him if he felt as though his own space shrunk when the other person entered the room, and Joe nodded eagerly and said that that's exactly how he felt. A brief discussion then ensued in which Joe's sense of his self and of his space and the various situations in which he felt big and in which he felt small were explored. I asked if he was interested in doing an experiment to explore all this further. He readily agreed, and we proceeded as follows.

(14) Joe was instructed to get in touch with and observe his space right now as he was sitting in the chair and tell me whether or not it extends outward beyond his skin and if it does how far outward it extends. He could keep his eyes open or closed, whichever seemed to work best for him. Joe closed his eyes and after a few seconds indicated that his space extends about two feet in all directions around his head. I then asked him to expand his space two more feet outward. In about twenty seconds, he said, with a faint smile on his face, that he had done so. He was next asked to expand his space to ten feet around him and not to let the wall behind his back stop him but to move through it and other objects, as necessary. After about one minute, he nodded his head to indicate he had done it. I asked him if he had included me in his space, since I was well within the ten-foot radius of his space. With a voice that conveyed surprise and disbelief at my question, he said that he had not. He showed me how, in expanding his space, he had bent his space so it went around where I was sitting. I asked him to expand his space now ten feet in all directions, not bending it but letting me be included. After only thirty seconds, he opened his eyes, looked at me, then around the room, and again at me, and burst out: "This is amazing!" He said he felt very relaxed and comfortable and then proceeded to describe feelings of warmth and affection toward me he had never felt before. Warmth and affection indeed surrounded me, and extended through me back to him.

(15) Next week Joe told me that he had been practicing expanding his space all week long. He narrated an incident during the week which occurred when he took his family to an aquarium exhibit. They were standing in front of a display when another couple strolled up. Joe said that he took this opportunity to expand his space and include these people in it. He did not feel any of the usual irritation, tension, and being intruded upon. All of a sudden, he found himself turning to the couple and starting up a conversation with them—something he said he would not in his wildest imagination have thought of doing in the past. He said his relationship with his wife also felt completely different nowadays.

(16) One day, three months later, I checked with Joe whether he still remembered our experiment. He shook his head with a smile and said, "how could I forget! I still do it every day." We seemed to have addressed the core problem in Joe's life, namely, that he had been too big for the cramped up space he thought the world "out there," particularly the human world, granted him. His anger and frustration at others whom he thought responsible for his predicament had made him all the more convinced that he, and others, would be better off with him being caged up in a very small space. But now he was coming out, in full splendor and being as big as he could. What was more, he was finding out that other people around him were none the worse for it.

The Ontological Question: Is Self Really Space?

(17) Was Joe's experience one of "being" space or of "having" space? Was he, himself, expanding, or was he just having more personal space? Joe's experience as described above, including the instructions given to him to "expand his space," is quite ambiguous regarding this distinction. There are both linguistic and philosophical problems here that are beyond the scope of this article. Thus language forces us into a dualistic mode of expression whenever we talk about someone doing or acting upon something, even if the doer and the object are one and the same. Joe could have been instructed to "expand himself" instead of "expand his space," but the distinction between the one who expands and the one who is expanded would still have been implied by the language used. The choice of words used in the instructions given to Joe was based on clinical considerations, namely, that

"self" had ideational content such as grandiosity and inferiority for him, whereas "space" was free of such content yet experientially real for Joe. The philosophical problems concern the distinction between "being" and "having"; whether there might be several rather than just one mode of "having"; and whether some of these modes are closer to "being" than others, and thus, whether the distinction between being and having is a matter of degree.

(18) Fortunately, it is not necessary for the purpose of this paper to have answers for all these questions or a solution to the linguistic problem. Being space and having space are both possibilities for the self to consider. Joe's experience had a unity to it which is not conveyed by the linguistic expression but to which the immediate transformation of his self-experience attests. The power of this transformation also suggests that more was involved than just the space around Joe; he, himself, was centrally and intimately involved. This points to Joe's experience as being one in which he considered himself to be, not just have, space.

(19) The transformative power that the experiment had on Joe's life had to do with Joe's ability to embrace the notion of his space as being unqualifiedly real as well as his willingness to consider himself to be his space. The consideration that he or his space extends out beyond his body and that he can have himself extend further out is not just an intriguing idea, nor a meaningful symbol, nor even a metaphor for self-experience. The intellectual in us may shudder at such naiveté. But an authentic consideration demands an unreserved giving of oneself to the possibility being considered. Though such an attitude is naive in being unquestioning and unreflective, it is very different from the naiveté of the naturalistic attitude. The latter is constrained by the assumptions and prejudices that are unquestioningly accepted, whereas the former is completely open to the possibilities at hand.

(20) Not everybody is likely to be as open and willing as Joe to consider his or her self to be space. What gets in the way of being completely open to the possibility that self is space is the nagging feeling that it just might be something else, even if we don't at this point know what it "really is."

(21) The feeling that the self "really is" something, and that we should know what it is before venturing out with our own considerations is deeply ingrained. I submit, however, that the self is nothing before it is considered to be something, that indeed it is what it is considered to be. This statement could easily be misunderstood as an endorsement of a frivolous and arbitrary relativism in matters ontological. But nothing of the kind is intended here. I am calling attention to the self's unique capacity to consider itself to be something. The self represents the extreme case of the phenomenon of self-fulfilling prophecy in human affairs. The knowledge of a prediction of future behavior influences the way humans behave, individually and in groups. And as every psycho- therapist knows, the way people consider their selves to be influences their self-experience. But much of the time, the considerations that are being modified in psychotherapy are rather superficial and only concern a person's self-image, not the self behind the image.

(22) But is there a self behind the self-image, beholding the image and bestowing it with value and significance? And is there a self behind this self too? Would there be an endless reflexive spiral, as appears in a mirror reflected within a mirror? If one attempts to answer these questions by thought and inference, one may indeed get caught up in such an endless spiral. But this would prove nothing about the self, only about the nature of thought and inference. The way to find the answer is not to think but to observe directly. One will find that no endless reflexive spiral presents itself within the field of awareness. What one does find is awareness that extends beyond the images one has of oneself or the values and significance attached to them. Within that awareness, there is the capacity to consider the self not in terms of ideas and images but as a real existent (i.e., the "I", apart from the ideas and images that I and others may have of me). Considerations of existence are our deepest ontological concern and they have more powerful transformative effects on our lives than other considerations do. The spatiality of self is such an ontological consideration.

(23) Individuals and traditions who have pondered deeply on the self and undertaken a direct experiential investigation of its nature and dimensions frequently conclude that the self is best described in spatial terms. To mention just a few examples, the Hindu classic *Yoga Vasistha* claims that space, understood in the infinite or absolute sense, consciousness, and creation are "mere words and they indicate the same truth, even as synonyms do" (Venkatesananda, 1984, p. 291). The Buddhist Nirvana or Voidness is described—in so far as it can be described at all—as analogous to space. Thus Long-chen-pa, a fourteenth century Tibetan Buddhist Master described "the foundational sphere of the Clear Light of Voidness within everyone's mind-stream" as being "as all-pervasive as is space" (Berzin, et al., 1979, p. 40). Among contemporary Tibetan Lamas, Tarthang Tulku (1977) is most notable in expounding the view that self and space are coextensive and more

Self and Space

fundamental than our ordinary understanding of time (Puhakka, 1980). Among Westerners, Hartshorne (1983) and Merrell-Wolff (1944/1983) have seen the intimate connection, if not identity, between self and space.

(24) The intimate connection between emotional well being and the experience of spatiality has not escaped the notice of psychologists either (Kruger, 1979; Levin, 1985). According to Levin (1985), ordinary experience is confined and closed off to a small, solidified space. The egocentric, ego-logically constituted space of our lived experience is the very source of our neurotic suffering or pathology. Levin defines pathology (neurosis) as "getting stuck in a space which is frozen into a dualistically polarized, and hence deeply conflicted, structure that is inimical to change, growth and in general a meaningful, creative existence" (1985, p. 341). Whereas, according to Levin,

> When we get deeply in touch with our bodily felt sense of *motility*, when we can feel the *depth* of its melodic arc *(arche)*, we will find ourselves suddenly *released* into a space of much greater openness, greater richness, and greater emotional hospitality, than our customary experience, to whose claustrophobia we tend to become habituated, would ever give us reason to believe possible. (p. 343)

(25) When Joe understood and agreed to follow the instruction to expand his space, he was, momentarily at least willing to let go of any frozen, confined notion of his "ego." He was also "moving" himself outward, thus being in touch with what Levin calls a sense of "motility." However, this sense of motility perhaps should not be characterized as "bodily" (in the sense of physical) any more than it should be characterized as "mental" (in the sense of ideational process or content). The space clearly extended beyond the boundaries of Joe's physical body, hence the experience was not just a "bodily felt sense" even if the expansive movement incorporates the body as well. But the crucial element in Joe's experience was not a sensation or a feeling at all but an act of intention or of will: in considering himself to be space, Joe was, in a sense, creating space that for him did not exist before.

(26) Let us now return to the ontological question. Even if it appears feasible, and even desirable, to consider the self to be space, is it *necessary* to consider it so? Could the self just as well be considered to be something other than space? Of course it can. There is a venerable tradition, starting from Descartes, of considering self to be an extension point: a self that does not extend but only intends. The world of objects as well as meanings and values presents itself to the self which, as intentionality, is always a consciousness of something or other. This is the fundamental dictum of Husserlian phenomenological analysis. And it can be readily confirmed in one's immediate experience. Thus when an object, say a lamp on my desk, presents itself to my awareness, there may be, momentarily, in my field of awareness nothing but the lamp; I am not aware of myself apart from the lamp.

(27) But when, in the next moment, I intend to turn the lamp on, this moment of awareness is different from the earlier moment in that I am aware of myself, so to speak, extending to the lamp. In situations of this type, it is not correct to describe one's self as being confined within the boundaries of one's body. Much less would it be correct to say that one's self is an extensionless point. Merleau-Ponty (1945/1962) has shown that even within the confines of the body, one's experience has a spatial character, consisting of directly experienced relationships, directionalities that are irreducible to objects or points in space. His example of how a person immediately and unreflectively knows to scratch the spot on one's body where a mosquito stung illustrates how there is, within bodily space, "a knowledge of place which is reducible to a sort of coexistence with that place" (1945/1962 p. 105). Yet when one's attention is absorbed by an object, such as the lamp in the earlier example, it appears perfectly reasonable to say that the self is an extensionless point, a pure intentionality.

(28) What the self ultimately is, is thus not written in stone. More than any other thing of the world, it defies attempts to pin it down ontologically. Self as the thinker of our thoughts, the enjoyer of our perceptions and feelings, the agent of our actions eludes our attempts to capture it in any of the ontological categories into which we fit the objects of thoughts, feelings and actions. Thus even when we have our ontological maps otherwise well drawn up (e.g. reality is "process" or it is "static;" rocks and trees are "physical" things, whereas thoughts, feelings and images are "mental" things) our selves don't easily find a place on such maps. That the self's nature is not a "given" (even though its existence is beyond doubt) leaves us in a unique and existentially primordial predicament which Heidegger had described as the "uncanniness of Dasein": the intimate encounter with "the nothing and nowhere" of one's existence, of "not being at home" in the sense of not being able to accept the reassurances of the public self of "they-self" (Heidegger, 1927/1962, pp. 233, 321). But its capacity to defy being determined shows the self's ontological power: it is capable of determining its own being by its own consideration. Its capacity to consider itself is prior to any ontological determination of its nature. Because of this

state of affairs, the exercise of this capacity has a sort of ontological necessity about it: in a fundamental sense, as long as we are alive as humans, we cannot even in our most cynical or unreflective moments remain indifferent to our existence in the world. No one has understood this better than Heidegger who chose the term "care" to designate the fundamental ontological aspect of Dasein (Heidegger, 1927/1962 pp. 225-273).

Conclusion

(29) The consideration of self as space is an act of free choice. There is nothing that compels our selves to be space or that ontologically forces such a consideration upon us. But we cannot escape the predicament that, as long as we live, our selves are considered to be something or other, by ourselves or by others. The necessity for self-consideration arises out of the freedom from being already determined. Thus we have no choice about considering the self; the choice only concerns what the self is considered to be. Within this freedom, the self can be space, can be expansive and include other living and nonliving things in it, if it considers itself to be so. Unique in this respect among all phenomena, the self has the ontological capacity to be what it considers itself to be.

(30) The self is our doorway to experience. How one considers one's self to be, so will one's experience be. We could also say that the self defines the horizons of our experience. The self as an extensionless point opens up to its particular intentional object; the self as space embraces vast stretches and pervades many things. Our survival as species has depended on the ability to perceive and respond to intentional objects displayed to the extensionless self with clarity and sharpness, and our successful functioning as members of a fast-moving technological society continues to depend on such an ability. We exercise this ability unreflectively and habitually. But we also have the ability to consider the self to be space. Phenomenological reflection upon ordinary, "embodied" experience reveals the spatiality and potential unboundedness of such an experience. We can reach and embody ever more, becoming, through intimacy with others and with the world at large, the "ecological body," the "transpersonal body" (Aanstoos, 1989) and, as suggested in the beginning of this article, even the embodiment of the stars and heavens beyond.

(31) As Levin observes, "psychic pathology is always played out, always mirrored, in the agonies of space" (1985, p. 343). But our ecstatic, creative living is also mirrored and played out in space. The active consideration of self as space transforms ordinary embodied experience by turning its potential openness into an actuality. It can open up a way of embracing and being embraced by the world that is fearless and generous. The vastness and greatness of one's own being magnifies rather than diminishes the being of others. Through the ages, mystics and men and women of wisdom have known this. But the example presented here and other examples that we may recall from our own exalted moments of vastness show that one need not be a mystic or practice spiritual austerities to walk through the doorway of an expanded self to a rich, connected, harmonious living.

References

Aanstoos, C. M. (1989). *The body, eros, and postmodernity.* Paper presented to the Human Science Research Conference, Arhus, Denmark, August.

Berzin, A., Sherpa Tulku, & Kapstein, M. (1979). *The four-themed precious garland: An introduction to Dzog-Ch'en, the great completeness.* India: The Library of Tibetan Works and Archives.

Hartshorne, C. (1980). Mysticism and rationalistic metaphysics. In R. Woods (Ed.), *Understanding mysticism* (pp. 415-421). Garden City, NY: Doubleday.

Heidegger, M. (1962). *Being and time* (Macquarrie and Robinson, Trans.). New York: Harper & Row. (Original work published 1927)

Kruger, D. (1979). *Introduction to phenomenological psychology.* Pittsburgh: Duquesne University Press.

Levin, D. M. (1985). *The body's recollection of being.* Boston: Routledge & Kegan Paul.

Merrell-Wolff, F. (1983). *Pathways through to space.* New York: Julian Press. (Original work published 1944)

Merleau-Ponty, M. (1962). *Phenomenology of perception* (C. Smith, Trans.). New York: Humanities Press. (Original work published 1945)

Puhakka, K. (1980). Beyond outer and inner space. In R. H. Moon & S. Randall (Eds.), *Dimensions of thought: Current explorations in time, space, and knowledge* (pp. 97-120). Berkeley, CA: Dharma Publishing.

Tarthang Tulku. (1977). *Time, space, and knowledge.* Berkeley, CA: Dharma Publishing.

Venkatesananda, S.(1984). *The concise Yoga Vasistha.* Albany: State University of New York Press.

Terms for Discussion

1. ontological (paragraphs 4, 22, 26, 28, and 29)

2. psychoanalyst (paragraph 5)

3. ego (paragraphs 5, 24, and 25)

4. self-image (paragraphs 21 and 22)

5. phenomenological analysis (paragraphs 26 and 30)

Questions

6. Has the author convinced you in paragraphs 5 through 10 that self can be experienced as space? Explain.

7. Is knowing more about Joe's previous psychotherapy (see paragraph 12) important to understanding the main themes of this article and to understanding Joe's case? Explain.

8. Joe was withdrawn and oblivious to the rest of the world. (See paragraph 12.) In your opinion, would learning to expand one's self-space be of therapeutic value if used with clients with other types of problems? Explain.

9. The author notes in paragraph 20 that "not everybody is likely to be as open and willing as Joe to consider his or her self to be space." How open are you to this idea?

10. What are your opinions on the ideas expressed in paragraph 21?

11. Do you agree with the author's conclusion? (See paragraphs 29 through 31.)

12. Are there other types of treatment that might have facilitated Joe's improvement? Explain.

13. Rate the article on the seven criteria described in the introduction to this book on a scale from 5 (highest quality) through 1 (lowest quality). Be prepared to explain your ratings.

Criterion 1: The demographics of the case are described: _____

Criterion 2: The condition(s) and behavior(s) that necessitated treatment are described in detail: _____

Criterion 3: The method of treatment is described in sufficient detail so that it can be replicated without additional information: _____

Criterion 4: A rationale is provided for the method of treatment selected: _____

Criterion 5: The client's improvement, if any, is clearly documented: _____

Criterion 6: Follow-up information on the client's improvement, if any, is presented: _____

Criterion 7: The study is appropriate for publication in a journal: _____

Case 13

The Intruder: A Dream-Work Session with Commentary*

Daphna Amram

(1) The following is a transcription of a recorded session with a client who has been in long-term therapy with me. To this transcription I have added a commentary in which I have tried to give a flavor of the thinking processes of a Gestalt therapist "in action." As a trainer of Gestalt therapists I think it most important that theory not remain the sole preserve of learned articles but be constantly integrated with and related to therapy in practice. I hope the following article contributes toward this goal.

(2) THERAPIST: What would you like to work on today? *[This question is asked of the client for three reasons: firstly, it directs the client's awareness to what he wants from the therapeutic session; secondly, in becoming aware of what he wants to work on the client takes responsibility for his needs at that particular moment; and, thirdly, if the client's field is confused or dull this question allows him to focus on clearing his emotional field in the process of which something will naturally become figural and of interest.]*

(3) CLIENT: I have a dream I'd like to work on. *[The client is clear about what he wants to work on.]*

(4) THERAPIST: Tell me the dream in the present tense. *[Asking the client to retell the dream in the present tense is most important in Gestalt therapy enabling him to actually experience which is to make contact with the existential reality of his dream.]*

(5) CLIENT: In my dream I go back to the neighborhood in which I grew up as a boy and I'm showing some people around. I start off at the top of the street where there was a great big park; in one section of the park there were swings, merry-go-rounds, slippery dip and so on, but now as I show these people around, the park has shrunk and that section of the park with the swings has disappeared—the whole park has just shrunk. Then suddenly I find myself at the bottom of the street and I look across and see these double-story houses which weren't there when I lived in the neighborhood. *[The client's dream begins with a description of a childhood playground which then shrinks away. A possible interpretation is that a childhood full of play has now disappeared; the child's world has been projected and alienated. While the therapist gains direction from this projection, the interpretation is bracketed for the therapy process has its own dynamic of unfolding, which the therapist does not wish to preempt. Note is taken of a possible polarity split between that which is represented by the top of the street and that which is represented by the bottom of the street.]* I go into the courtyard to investigate and I look up at these houses and I see a maid sweeping the steps. I don't want her to see me—I don't belong here so I walk out and as I walk out I notice an enormous looking house—more like a castle. *[The content of this polarity split becomes more focused: at the beginning of the dream the client is in familiar surroundings at the top of the street. At the bottom of the street however he appears as a stranger in unfamiliar surroundings.]* The corner of it faces the street and it's made out of stone, a yellowish ochre stone. The stones on the right hand side are all smooth and the stones on the left hand side are all rough and at the top there's a turret. Then there's a switch again and I find myself in the Gestalt group. I'm drawing the castle and as I begin to draw I realize that the turret is taking up the whole piece of paper so I screw it up and throw the piece of paper away. I take another piece of paper and start again and as I'm drawing the left hand side of the castle—suddenly—like magic—I'm not

---

*Reprinted from *The Gestalt Journal*, 14, 1991, p. 61-72. Copyright 1991 by Daphna Amram. Reprinted with permission.

aware of me doing it, the castle that I'm drawing with my left hand becomes writing in black and blue but I can't read what I've written... and that's the end of the dream.

(6) THERAPIST: How do you feel now? *[The awareness and contacting of feelings in the here and now is crucial in the healing process. After telling the dream therefore the client is asked to become aware of his feelings for in reliving the dream, unaware and alienated feelings may surface and be contacted.]*

(7) CLIENT: Well, I feel like I've got energy.

(8) THERAPIST: Where do you experience the energy? *[By asking the client where in his body a particular feeling is located he becomes aware of the nexus between psyche and soma. There may also be meaning in the actual physical location of feelings. It is thus important to check whether the location of a particular feeling is appropriate. Awareness of the physical location of feelings also makes for a sharper figure preventing the client from being flooded or confused by diffuse feelings.]*

(9) CLIENT: In my chest . . . . Well, energy and also a bit of anxiety. *[Anxiety is an interruption of the client's energy and indicates he can neither support himself nor find the necessary environmental support to contact or confront a perceived threat.]*

(10) THERAPIST: Go to your chest, identify with your anxiety and tell me about your existence at this moment as P's anxiety. *[The meaning of the anxiety or avoidance for the client can be brought into awareness through the technique of identification. Identifying with the interruption paradoxically brings the client into contact with that which he has avoided or alienated from himself. Clearing up the interruptions to gestalt formation will allow this client's energy to flow unimpeded, "filling" those holes in his personality which he has anxiously avoided contacting.]*

(11) CLIENT: Well [laughing], it's partly being conscious of having to speak loudly into the microphone . . . .

(12) THERAPIST: Make contact with the microphone and say that directly.

(13) CLIENT: Yeah. I'm not just speaking to D. I have to speak to you . . . . I have to speak louder to you than I do to D. I feel like you're sort of an intruder. *[The client here makes clear what he has alienated although its meaning for him is not as yet clear. By identifying the microphone as the cause of his anxiety the client indicates he is projecting into the environment (the microphone). By asking the client to make contact with the object of his projection its meaning becomes clear and we must now deal with this content, that is, with feelings of intrusion.]*

(14) THERAPIST: Is there any place in your dream where you experience yourself as being an intruder? *[Noting that feelings of intrusion also appeared in the client's dream with which he began the session, he is asked whether he is aware of a connection between the intruder in his present reality (the microphone) and being an intruder in his dream. At this point it is important to return to the client's internal world (his dream projection) rather than staying in the external world (his projection onto the microphone). For it is the dream that is calling him to solve a conflict, to resolve unfinished business, deal with "the intruder" and close that particular gestalt. The projection onto the microphone however pushes the client away from dealing with the issue in his internal world for it is not the microphone that has meaning for the client—it is a mere symbol, a projection of the dream projection. Thus directing the client to find the intruder "inside", in his dream, helps him get back to the internal conflict which he wishes to resolve.]*

(15) CLIENT: When I see the double-story houses and go into the courtyard I see the woman cleaning the steps and I feel that I don't belong here. I don't want to be seen. I better leave. *[One side of the polarity is here diagnosed as "not belonging" (the dream intruder). Whether this need not to belong, to remain unseen and anonymous, is a true or "as if" need of the client's will become clear as the session progresses. The other side of the polarity as yet dimly formulated by the client can be assumed (by the dialectic of opposites) to be the need to belong, to be familiar, to have his "presence felt."]*

(16) THERAPIST: And when you say it now you still experience yourself as being an intruder?

(17) CLIENT: I feel a bit sad when I said that.

(18) THERAPIST: Where do you experience the sadness?

(19) CLIENT: In my eyes and throat . . . a lot of the time I do feel like an intruder. *[The client here identifies the dream projection as reflecting his existential reality. We are now back in the "external" world after having shuttled from the client's internal world (dream)*

The Intruder

to his external world (microphone), back to his internal world (dream intruder) and here once again to his external world. With each shift the client's awareness has been sufficiently supported to enable him to reach to recognition of his being an intruder and expressing the sadness that this awareness brings with it. (What exactly "being an intruder" was for the client is not yet apparent.)]

(20) THERAPIST: Say that again. *[Asking the client to repeat a sentence is an important technique for oftentimes he will make hesitant contact with a feeling that is meaningful yet unfamiliar. By repeating key sentences such feelings may become more figural and the field less blurred.]*

(21) CLIENT: A lot of the time I *do* feel like an intruder—that I don't belong to the places I go. *[Here the client indicates that the meaning of intruding for him is not belonging which indicates a deep unsatisfied need—the client's need to belong.]*

(22) THERAPIST: Stay with the sense of being an intruder now and not belonging. *[The client is here directed to his present reality. Where, in the here and now, does he feel he does not belong.]*

(23) CLIENT: Well being in this country I feel like I don't belong. When I was in . . . I felt like I didn't belong. When I'm in . . . even though I was born there I still feel like I don't belong. Just a sense of . . . no sense of . . . I feel this sort of . . . I feel this sort of . . . I have to move on because I don't belong here.

(24) THERAPIST: And when you say it now how do you feel? *[While in the process of dealing with the content issues, it remains of prime importance for the client to be in constant contact with his feelings. If therapist and client can achieve this then a major step forward has been taken in the therapeutic work for contact and awareness of feelings has per se both healing qualities and the power to support the client. Feelings have an integrative function. Calling attention to his feelings whenever there is a change of content helps the client develop a skill of creating for himself an integrated sense of wholeness.]*

(25) CLIENT: Well, it takes the energy out of me. I feel I'm at the mercy of . . . . If I felt comfortable in a place then I wouldn't keep moving on. *[The client here identities his need for a place of comfort.]*

(26) THERAPIST: O.K. So be the place now. Identify with the place and then develop a dialogue between the intruder in you and the place you intrude upon. *[The technique therefore is to ask the client to identify with the alienated need ("Be the place of comfort now") and then have him make contact with the "intruder" (a projection he has already "reowned"). In polarity work of this nature it is important that the therapist correctly identify the two poles of the dialectical process. In asking the client to identify himself as the place of comfort he is again directed away from external places (the countries he enumerates and upon which he projects) towards the place within himself that he keeps avoiding, moving away from, fearful of investing himself in. What is that place, not in physical terms but in terms of feelings, thoughts and behavior?]*

(27) CLIENT: I'm an intruder . . . . I intrude into you . . . uh . . . and . . . .

(28) THERAPIST: What's happening?

(29) CLIENT: Well I'm sort of . . . a bit confused. I'm not sure of being an intruder that feels self concious about intruding or—I don't know—an intruder that wants to intrude. I'm confused about what to be . . . . *[Confusion of the field is the means whereby the client avoids making contact with the two needs that are in conflict and leaving himself with no support avoids taking responsibility both for his need to belong and his need not to belong (although he does identify more with his need not to belong, that is, with the intruder). We know this to be the case for he does not actualize either need in his life. When he doesn't belong he feels sad—this is not what he really wants; and the "comfort" of belonging eludes him. So he remains in limbo and this is his distress.]*

(30) THERAPIST: Try both of them. *[The process of contacting and supporting both needs is begun.]*

(31) CLIENT: I intrude into you and I feel really uncomfortable and self conscious. I feel that I shouldn't intrude and even though I do intrude I know I'll leave you after a short time because the feeling of discomfort will continue to grow till I have to leave. *[The client begins by identifying with the need not to belong ("I shouldn't intrude"). It is clear at this point of the therapeutic process that the need not to belong is a false need based on an introjection. We know it constitutes an introjection and is not the result of identification or assimilation on the part of the client by the discomfort the client associates with this need. It fails to give him a sense of wholeness or satisfaction. Moreover, the client in his behavior has never made any attempt to intrude. On the contrary, he is constantly moving away.*

The Intruder

He has thus taken responsibility for the environment, for it is not the client that intrudes upon the environment but rather the environment that intrudes upon the client. Instead of saying "I shouldn't intrude" (I shouldn't belong) which is an introjection the client needs to be able to give back responsibility to where it belongs in the environment and say "You shouldn't intrude upon me."]

(32) THERAPIST: What do you feel now? *[The client's growing discomfort indicates he is approaching something he would rather avoid. Recognizing such feelings however paradoxically brings him closer to that which he is avoiding. Hence the importance of contacting feelings at each step of the therapeutic process.]*

(33) CLIENT: Well I feel growing discomfort . . . like a felling of being less and less able to breathe and that if I don't leave then I'll stop breathing.

(34) THERAPIST: Do you feel that now?

(35) CLIENT: I feel more sad thinking about it and talking about it. And even though I don't feel the panic to that extent now there's going to come a point where I'm going to start panicking and have to leave and I don't want to have to feel all the time that I have to leave.

(36) THERAPIST: Do you want to try the other part or stay with this? *[Giving the client the responsibility to choose the direction he wishes to take is respectful of the need to deal with what is figural for him at this point.]*

(37) CLIENT: I'll try the other part. *[Without direction from the therapist the client chooses to identify with the other side of the polarity—the part that needs to belong.]* I intrude and that's what I want to do. I'm not concerned about whom I intrude upon, where I intrude upon. I'm only interested in myself . . . . I feel strong as an intruder. It gives me a sense of power. When I intrude . . . well . . . people will . . . well, I make my presence felt. *[Client shows discomfort].*

(38) THERAPIST: What do you experience now?

(39) CLIENT: Uh . . . well . . . what came to mind was the work we did last session.

(40) THERAPIST: And how do you feel when you reconnect with your work last session? *[A change of content occurs and so his awareness is directed to how this shift affects his feelings.]*

(41) CLIENT: Uh . . . dizzy . . . dizzy and uncertain. Dizzy about making the connection. Uncertain about where to go from here. *[His dizziness and uncertainty indicate avoidance.]* Maybe I can start off by . . . uh . . . being the one intruded upon—I feel intruded upon . . . . Just like the self-conscious intruder was saying he doesn't feel comfortable in any place, I don't feel like inside me there's any place where I feel at ease . . . . I want to get out of my body . . . . I want to get the intruder out of me and at the same time . . . . *[At this point the client has come to an awareness, after identifying with the place intruded upon, that the meaning of this place is in fact his own body. He also recognizes the introjection ("I want to get the intruder out of me"). The next step for the therapist is to create a situation in which the client can make contact with the introjecter. This constitutes the real unfinished business for the gestalt can only come to closure when the issues are dealt with in the "appropriate" context.]*

(42) THERAPIST: Who has intruded on you?

(43) CLIENT: My father.

(44) THERAPIST: Talk to him. Tell him "Get out of my body." *[Here we have the technique of inviting significant others with which the client has unfinished business into "the empty chair." The client is invited to have a direct and open dialogue which will help him integrate the experience.*

The therapist also uses the technique of "feeding a sentence" to the client. This sentence is focused on because of the therapist's awareness of its significance. It is important to stress here that the sentence is not imposed upon the client but is in fact a sentence the client himself used earlier indicating an introjection ("I want to get out of my body"). In feeding him this sentence the client is asked to project the introject.

Instead of "I want me out" which has been his guiding principle—forcing himself out of every society he enters—he is asked to give back the responsibility for the intruding to the person who intruded upon him. This sentence thus carries important healing and integrative qualities.]

(45) CLIENT: I want you to get out of my body.

(46) THERAPIST: Say it again.

(47) CLIENT: *[louder]* I want you to get out of my body.

(48) THERAPIST: Say it again.

ruder

NT: *[louder still]* I want you to get out of my

PIST: How do you feel? *[It is important to nt's feelings after he has made contact.]*

Stuck. I want to pull you out of me, rip tomach and throat but it feels like you've my stomach and I can't see any way of ithout hurting myself. I can't . . . . Oh te the two. *[The client's difficulty indi- confluence. His boundaries have be- d with those of his father that we have n differentiating his boundaries from der." Here the question that follows f allying with you?"]*

sk him: Is that what he wanted, to as one and not two separate peo- of allying with you?

want to be so much a part of me f me?

don't really know what you're et stuck . . . . *[The client is impasse, a point at which he avoids doing so getting the se is really telling us that he thing differently but that he and making contact with the oices.]*

(54) THERAPIST: What do you experience now?

(55) CLIENT: All the energy I felt at the beginning is gone. Whatever I do I can't get him out . . . .

(56) THERAPIST: Say that to him.

(57) CLIENT: Whatever I try I end up in the same place I can't get you out. . . you're just stronger than I am . . . . I don't know what to do [tearful]. *[Re-establishing contact with the father. The contact of dialogue per se works toward differentiation of self and other and consequently the breaking up of confluence for it requires the awareness and recognition of otherness.]*

(58) THERAPIST: I'm aware we're coming close to the end of the session and I want to share with you something I'm aware of right now. You tell you father: "You are a permanent intruder in my body." And when you tell me that you move from one place to another never allowing yourself to settle anywhere I have a sense you

are doing it for your father. You are of your own will moving away, taking the role of not being an intruder anywhere. Instead of letting go of your father you let go of places. *[It is not as threatening for the client to let go of places as it is to let go of his father. His father is his identity (confluence) and as long as he still feels a child he needs to hold on to him. The threat is to let go of his father and face the anonymity and aloneness within. The client "plays" as if he were a stranger, as if he did not belong, yet he in fact belongs (unawares) to his father.]*

(59) CLIENT: Yeah. Part of my going from place to place is to get away from him . . . . But . . . going away doesn't help . . . . I take him with me. *[The client expresses an inability to project the introject.]*

(60) THERAPIST: So what in this intruding of your father's is so important to you that you take it with you wherever you go? What's the meaning for you in letting go of places but maintaining your father inside you, so close and so permanent? *[The client is made aware of the difference between what he does in the external world and what he does in his internal world.]*

(61) CLIENT: I don't know.

(62) THERAPIST: Can you imagine in your fantasy what would happen if you let go of your father and maintained a place for yourself? *[Gestalt therapy is existential, experiential and experimental. The client is here asked to experiment in fantasy with "what would happen if . . .?"]*

(63) CLIENT: [laughing] I might be happy. There'd be room for other people.

(64) THERAPIST: So by keeping your father you're preventing yourself from being happy and making room for other people.

(65) CLIENT: It's hard for me to accept that I should have to suffer by doing that . . . . Perhaps it has something to do with a fear of growing up . . . . *[The experiment lends the client to an awareness of the need fulfilled by maintaining confluence. It is this continuing need that keeps the client stuck and constitutes unfinished business to be dealt with in a later session.]*

(66) THERAPIST: So how do you want to close this session for today?

(67) CLIENT: Well, just to say I haven't yet given up on growing up. *[The unfinished business is reflected in*

the client's holding on to a childhood that has long since passed, yet which remains an unclosed gestalt. We are thus faced with another conflict: The client's need to remain a child versus his need to grow up. The conflict cannot be dealt with as long as he identifies with neither side of the polarity. In summary, the client's true need is to belong. His "as if need" is not to belong to be a stranger, anonymous and distant (that this is a false need is indicated by the client's sadness and discomfort when contacting this apparent need).

Related to his existential need to belong are a further two needs: The need to remain a child the meaning of which in this context is belonging just to the family; and, the need to be grown up (to let go of the confluent relationship with his father rather than letting go of places) and belong not only to the family but to others as well.

If the unfinished business of childhood is adequately dealt with, the grown up will emerge naturally.]

Terms for Discussion

1. Gestalt (throughout article)

2. projection (paragraphs 5, 13, 14, 19, 26, and 59)

3. anxiety (paragraphs 9, 10, and 13)

4. identification (paragraph 10)

5. polarity work (paragraphs 26 and 37)

6. introjection (paragraphs 31 and 59)

7. impasse (paragraph 53)

Questions

8. Overall, has the author given you the "flavor of the thinking of a Gestalt therapist"? (See paragraph 1.)

9. Comment on the author's commentary in paragraph 8. What is your opinion of the main ideas?

10. The author mentions and illustrates a number of specific techniques. Do you believe that some are more important than others? Are some appropriate for use in other forms of therapy? Explain.

11. The author mentions that Gestalt therapy is "existential." (See paragraph 61.) What is your understanding of that term as it relates to the content of this article?

12. What is your opinion on the last sentence of the article?

The Intruder

13. Are there other types of treatment that might have helped this client in the session described? Explain.

14. Rate the article on the seven criteria described in the introduction to this book on a scale from 5 (highest quality) through 1 (lowest quality). Be prepared to explain your ratings. Note that the criteria should be applied in light of the author's stated purpose. (See paragraph 1.) Thus, some of the criteria may not be applicable.

Criterion 1: The demographics of the case are described: _____

Criterion 2: The condition(s) and behavior(s) that necessitated treatment are described in detail: _____

Criterion 3: The method of treatment is described in sufficient detail so that it can be replicated without additional information: _____

Criterion 4: A rationale is provided for the method of treatment selected: _____

Criterion 5: The client's improvement, if any, is clearly documented: _____

Criterion 6: Follow-up information on the client's improvement, if any, is presented: _____

Criterion 7: The study is appropriate for publication in a journal: _____

Notes:

Case 14

A Look at the Self-Righteous Defense*

David E. Stewart, Jr.
Psychotherapist in Private Practice

SUMMARY: This paper focuses on a 29-year-old, self-righteous woman named Sally and her work in therapy. There is an examination of what has made Sally self-righteous and what actual behaviors she exhibits. The paper concludes with a discussion of the types of interventions that have seemed to work well for her.

(1) What is self-righteousness? Who is the self-righteous patient? How does this person act? How did the self-righteous person get to be this way? How can such often frustrating behavior be understood and best responded to in the therapy setting?

(2) It is too easy to define self-righteousness as the act of disagreeing with the therapist. There is a certain hint of the need to define right versus wrong in the very label, self-righteous. It is tempting to see any person who does not recognize that the therapist is right as wrong or sinful (Peck, 1983). In many cases this leads to designating a person as self-righteous simply because she or he believes (in the therapist's opinion, wrongly) that she or he is right. This, in itself, seems pretty self-righteous. It also suggests (erroneously) that the struggle to prove who is right and who is wrong will lead anywhere productive in the therapy process.

(3) It might be fairer and more useful to come up with a broader behavioral definition for self-righteousness than "she disagrees with me," or "he doesn't see the truth of what I am showing him (yet) because he is too . . . ." At least this definition should describe what objective qualities one would expect to find in a self-righteous person separate from that person's acceptance or rejection of the therapist or the therapist's treatments. If the therapist relies on the subjective assessment of whether the person is agreeing or disagreeing with the truth (as perceived by the therapist), the person will likely experience the therapist as one more person who is trying to force some outside set of feelings or values on that person against her or his will. Such force will probably duplicate some of the original experience of the person which has led her or him to be self-righteous in the first place. Such force will probably be met with a forceful reaction of equal size.

(4) At this point a dictionary definition might be helpful. *The Unabridged Random House Dictionary* (1966) defines self-righteous as "Confident of one's own righteousness [morally just, right], especially when smugly moralistic and intolerant of the opinions and behavior of others" (p. 1295). This definition is a mixed bag. There are positive *and* negative components in it.

(5) But, there are positive and negative components to self-righteousness, too. To see self-righteousness as purely negative (or positive for that matter) misses the point. The weighing of the "positive" versus the "negative" only exaggerates the struggle between right and wrong which the person seeking therapy usually already feels. Such behavior described in the above definition, even the "smug moralism and intolerance," can serve a useful, protective purpose on the one hand. It can also serve a self-limiting, and therefore, harmful purpose on the other.

(6) "Confident of one's own righteousness" sounds great. "Smugly moralistic and intolerant" doesn't sound so good. Both the affirming and critical aspects of self-righteousness are represented. The self-righteous person who feels right, feels positive. She or he *knows* what is just. There is a certain amount of self-affirmation in this kind of knowing.

---
*Reprinted from *Psychotherapy Patient*, 7, 1991, pp. 45-55. Copyright 1991 by The Haworth Press. All rights reserved. Reprinted with permission.

Self-Righteous Defense

(7) And yet, who can describe the expression of a person's self-righteous feelings and thoughts as wholly positive. Such expression is usually filled with critical judgments and comparative assessments of others. Such evaluations make the speaker look "good'" and the others look "bad." When one is "right," the others are "wrong." There is the implication that the speaker is better than the ones spoken about.

(8) [An aside: when the therapist disagrees about the content of the self-righteous person's evaluation, the feelings generated can be negative in a second sense. Whereas in the first case, the person is set against the "opinions and behavior of others," in the second case she or he is set against the therapist as well. When the therapist disagrees, she or he may also become yet another target of the self-righteous person's defenses.

(9) There is a problem when this second type of conflict is set up between the therapist and the self-righteous person. It is not just that the person seeking therapy and the therapist disagree, per se. Conflict and disagreement are often a healthy part of therapy. The problem is that a secondary disagreement and the attendant conflicts may actually distract the person seeking to understand her or his more basic, lifelong self-righteous attitudes and behavior from these original and more emotionally powerful targets.]

(10) So, what is self-righteousness? It is the confident belief in a person's own rightness or moral just-ness. It is a sense of virtue or ethical purity associated with the person herself or himself. It is expressed outwardly in that person's behavior in her or his smug ("I'm better than you") moralizing and in intolerance of the opinions and behavior of others. This outward expression can be focused on specific individuals or on less specific groups of people. The sense of superiority can be supported by actual, objective data as in the case of someone with a high IQ score feeling "better than" because she or he is smarter than those with lower scores. It can just as easily be focused on less objective differences. The self-righteous person can actually be discernibly (by someone else) right or not. It is the apparent belief in her or his rightness and her or his subsequent attitudes and actions which count.

(11) Who is this person and how does she or he act? To discuss this, it may be useful to look at a particular case. This is the case of Sally. She is a 29-year-old, single female. She lives with two of her four brothers (one older, one younger). Her only sister (younger) also lived with her until her recent marriage. She has two other brothers (both older) who live in other parts of the United States.

(12) Sally works as a registered nurse in private practice with a group of physicians and other nurses. She had served as head nurse in her previous job but now is content (?) to just be one of the staff. While both of the brothers who live with her work and earn a living, the arrangement is clearly one in which she takes care of them. She sees herself as "providing a family" for them since their parents are overseas working as missionaries in another part of the world. Sally sees herself as "the only family any of her brothers has" and she was supporting her sister completely until her recent marriage.

(13) Because of her parents' missionary work, Sally has had a lot of religious training. Most of it has been of the same conservative, Protestant type that her parents teach in their overseas work. She has recently been very distressed by her own questioning of her childhood beliefs. She has *always* believed that "God was looking out for her." This meant that He was her protector and provider in the absence of her parents. At the same time she has believed that He is out to get her for her past sins. This apparent conflict did not bother her until she ran into difficulty at her last job. That was when she entered therapy.

(14) She had been hired to be the head nurse in a small general medical practice. After one year of frustration with the head physician's lack of interest in "quality patient care" she found herself being criticized for spending too much time with individual patients and not seeing enough different people. Not only did two of the three other doctors side against her, she began to sense that many of the nonmedical staff saw her as inefficient and not a team player. She was eventually demoted to work as a staff nurse with the only physician who seemed to her to be "on her side."

(15) She began her therapy with a strong sense of moral indignation at what she considered the mercenary priorities of most of the people with whom she worked. She felt morally superior and described her response to the treatment she received as "moving more and more away from working cooperatively with the other staff," except the one doctor with whom she was allied in attitude and work habits.

(16) Sally tried to work harder after her demotion. She said she wanted to prove to the others that her ideas about how to treat patients were right. She tried to

Self-Righteous Defense

ignore her feelings of anger about how she was being treated by most of her fellow workers. She also ignored the advice of her friends that much of what she was dealing with was not her fault. She did not make much progress in her attempt to change things at work. After 6 months both she and the physician she worked for were let go.

(17) This led her into a deep depression. Her system for seeing the world came into question. Her beliefs that people were all basically good, and that, if she would treat people the way she wanted to be treated, they would like her and agree with her both failed. She began to alternate between her original belief that she was better than her co-workers and a fear that she was much, much worse.

(18) She also found herself less able to hold on to her belief in a benevolent God who was watching out for her. She began to feel more and more that He was sending her various hardships as punishment. Sally sometimes felt she was still right but she began to question her right to claim to be so in the face of her own apparent failures. Finally, her failure to convert her fellow workers to her work ethic, her loss of job, and her doubts and feelings of disbelief began to feel to her like further evidence that she was no longer right but wrong.

(19) Sally seemed to be self-righteous in her belief that she was morally and, sometimes, medically superior to her colleagues in her last practice. Her confidence in her actual medical abilities seemed to rest on a feeling that she was better in comparison to the other medical personnel. Likewise she felt superior in her spiritual training to several of the secretarial staff who had talked with her about their religious beliefs and experiences. She said she felt that hers were more sophisticated and mature.

(20) In spite of her own conflicts about her religious beliefs (and the frustration these conflicts caused her in a religious system that required certainty), Sally maintained her feeling of "better than" through a profession of confidence in her faith in the very beliefs about which she felt the strongest conflicts. Only in the privacy of her therapy did she begin to feel the discordance of her actions toward her fellow employees at work. She seemed to be able to feel self-confident in public about beliefs she herself doubted. And, she seemed to be able to turn that self-confidence against the others at her office in the form of intolerance with regard to both their medical skills and their religious beliefs. Other than that, she was not able to express any anger toward those people even when her treatment might have warranted it. More direct anger did not fit into her "acceptable belief system." She had to be "bigger than they were."

(21) Clearly, Sally had been acting in a self-righteous manner toward her fellow employees at her previous job. In addition to her fellow workers, she spoke often of feeling better than most of the patients. Many of them did not receive her assistance graciously or follow her directions the way she had intended. Recently she has even said that she feels better than the rest of her family because she has done more for them than they have for her and she has gone through so much being in therapy.

(22) There is an interesting balance to the almost arrogant feeling of her superiority and moralizing. Alongside her smugness is a kind and gentle side. In addition, she is likely to follow some statement about her being so great with an equally forceful statement about her total lack of value or worth. For instance, immediately after she said she felt better than anyone else in her family she said, "I don't deserve to be the one who gets any help in therapy." She went on to cite examples of the needs that three of her brothers had as "greater and more deserving" than any of her needs.

(23) In fact, many of her feelings of "better than" are closely related to situations in which she seems to be scared that she is inadequate, wrong, sinful, or bad. It is tempting to guess that the self-righteousness may be no more than a mask for the fear of or actual feeling that she is somehow grossly at fault or unworthy. "I am better" may be the only way she can try to balance her belief that "I am no good." Finkelhor and Browne (1985), in their discussion of the results of the specific trauma of child abuse, see stigmatization or feeling bad as one of the usual results. Al Pesso (1988) sees such guilt and shame resulting from the damage to the ego whatever the type of abuse or trauma.

(24) As the course of our work has progressed this has seemed more and more likely. Specifically, Sally has been able to see that she had gotten herself into a pattern at her previous job and in her family of working so hard because she believed she "had to be twice as good as anyone else to just be considered as OK." This, in turn, left her feeling she had done more than anyone else so maybe she was better.

(25) It has taken Sally a long time to begin to see some of the roots of her overwork. At her last job and in providing so much for her various family members she

was actually feeling bad about herself and trying to make up for what she took as the truth of her inadequacy. She had been so effective at achieving what she set out to that she almost forgot how bad she often felt about herself and how she had historically used this to motivate herself to do more.

(26) Now she is beginning to make the connection. Her present job is still in nursing but Sally is not caught up in any need to overachieve. She is not working late for free or giving up her days off the way she was inclined to in her previous position. She has begun to charge her brothers a reasonable amount of rent and has given up some of her position in the family as the one who will fix everything. Most recently, she suggested that her younger brother seek counseling for some of the personal problems about which he had consulted her.

(27) Not surprisingly, the place she has had the most difficulty has been in dealing with the earliest experiences in which she had these feelings of being bad. Not only does she still feel at fault for some of what happened to her, she also feels wrong for "dwelling on these things from the past." She feels self-indulgent for reliving (and relieving) the pain that she still feels.

(28) While her early-school-age time was filled with many traumatic experiences, they may be gathered together under the heading of Going Away To School. When she was just six, her parents sent her some 700 miles away to boarding school. It was the common practice of the missionary group to which her parents belonged, and all of her brothers and her sister were sent away at the same age. The children were allowed home for a visit at Christmas and during summer vacation. Sally also lived with her family one year in the United States when her parents were stateside.

(29) Sally has remembered several cases of physical abuse at school and has also recounted a general style of living that tended to ignore her individual needs in favor of group discipline and orderliness. The most powerful memory she had of her being sent off to school is the original event itself. She can remember what she wore, who else went with her (and who didn't). She can remember the trip and she can remember the first night (and the several nights after that) when she cried herself to sleep.

(30) What was interesting was that she was originally surprised that she had any feelings left about her being sent off to school at all. She said that it had happened. She said that it didn't feel right. She did not seem to have any sense that such an event in her past might be linked to feelings which she still had, either of her pain or her unworthiness.

(31) As she has worked with this period in her life in therapy, the picture has gotten clearer. A 6-year-old girl was suddenly separated from her parents for no understandable (to her) reason. Whenever she asked, she was told to be quiet and go back to her seat or room. She was punished for crying (for feeling her pain) and she was rewarded for her ability to function efficiently and without adult assistance. This had a deep effect on her sense of herself as wrong. What she said and did were all criticized and how she felt was either punished or ignored.

(32) At the same time she was presented with a picture of a God who saw everything (including her situation). She was taught that this God was in control of everything and so her fate seemed to come from Him. He rewarded the righteous and punished the evil. She had been punished; therefore she had been bad and must make amends. She would have to "be twice as good to be considered OK."

(33) It is a powerful combination. She felt bad. When she was not comforted or relieved from her pain and separation from her family she began to feel she was at fault, she was bad. Her everyday experience at school, as well as being sent off to school at her tender age in the first place, underlined her feelings of badness. The logic of the religious system endorsed by both her parents and the school to which they sent her added the final straw. She must *be* bad.

(34) It does not seem necessary to argue whether she developed *all* of her sense of badness out of her experiences at school. Nor is it necessary to link *all* of her self-righteousness to her reaction to the pain of these events. It seems clear that she gained a strong sense of something being wrong with her from the trauma of being sent to school at too young an age. And, she reacted to her sense of being bad by trying to be extra good to create some type of defense against how bad she felt she was.

(35) The way to work in such a situation has already been hinted at in the discussion of the definition of the term self-righteous itself. That is, it is important for the therapist to try to steer away from secondary, polarizing conflicts with the person in therapy. "Right" versus "Wrong" or "Good" versus "Bad" arguments are not always avoidable but they are seldom productive for the person's actual therapy. Such arguments tend to merely reproduce the original feelings and dilemmas as they

Self-Righteous Defense

distract everyone's attention into a conflict that usually lacks a useful resolution.

(36) To avoid this, what has worked well with Sally is to take the tact of affirming what she feels as right, even when *she* is not so sure. It is, after all, what she feels. For one thing, she probably has worked harder or studied better or done her daily nursing tasks more diligently than her fellows. She has made it her business to do so. More importantly, she definitely *feels* she has.

(37) Affirming her feelings has been important in helping her create a sense of the reality and validity of what she, herself, feels. In one sense it is a replacement for some of what she didn't get as a child. So much of what she learned at boarding school was to look to others for cues as to how to feel. Few people seemed interested in how *she* felt. Ultimately she became unclear who she was.

(38) [This was clearly reflected in her difficulty in integrating her more mature religious feelings with her earlier, younger ideas. Her lack of confidence in her own feelings has made her unsure of even her most innocent doubts. By affirming the feelings she has for both sets of conflicting ideas, she could begin to gain permission to have both the old and new ideas as she needed them. Neither set has to be right or wrong.]

(39) Trust is difficult to develop after serious trauma (Finkelhor & Browne, 1985). Affirmation of her feelings has been a great key to opening the door for some increased trust between Sally and her therapist. Trust of some of what her therapist said has led to an increase of trust in herself as well. That was necessary for her to begin to look at what she had been doing and feeling. She has now begun to be able to look more trustingly at herself and see the way (and some of why) she has worked so hard on the one hand, and how she has felt so resentful and how she has needed to isolate herself on the other.

(40) Distrust may also manifest itself in isolation and an aversion to intimate relationships (Finkelhor & Browne, 1985). The affirming of her feelings has given her a relationship (with the therapist) in which to begin to feel some of what she felt when these events happened. Remember, she was alone, cut off from her parents and not given much empathetic response from the adults designated to care for her. Her solution (to try to be better or, at least, act like she felt better than anyone else around her) was forged when she felt most alone. It is a role she must play by herself. [It is ironic how well her self-righteousness has helped her keep others away so that the solo position is maintained.]

(41) Perhaps being self-righteous is more than just acting to compensate for a sense of badness or inadequacy. There are certainly more aspects of Sally's background which may have played an important part in the development of her self-righteous attitude as a defense. The above understanding of her self-righteousness has been helpful in opening new paths for her to explore. The idea that her self-righteousness may have its roots in the traumas associated with her going to boarding school at age six, has offered her and her therapist a way to relate to the defenses this particular person uses without getting ensnared (too often) in them.

(42) The affirmation of her feelings has begun a process in which she is beginning to identify who she is by looking at how *she* feels (not her parents, her brothers, her sister, her fellow workers, even her therapist). As she has gained some confidence in her feelings, she has begun to feel capable of wrestling with some of her religious questions, even when she still feels "the old ways" may be right. She has opened the door to trust her own feelings and the expression of feelings from a few others in her life. And finally, she is considering what she might be able to reasonably *get* out of having personal relationships with other people.

(43) From Sally's case, it seems that a self-righteous person may be worried about being "right" (and quick to assert that that is the case) because she or he is actually convinced of being "wrong" or "bad." The situation may have gotten that way because the child was traumatized at an early age when loss or punishment meant (to the child) that "*I* must have done something wrong." The prevailing religious or cultural value system may have reinforced premature conclusions. Self-righteousness defends some type of self-hate.

(44) In this case, the intervention that has given the most to the person *and* her therapist has been that of firm affirmation. She has not always appreciated the therapist stopping to note that she seems to feel sad as she describes some painful event, or affirm that some incident sounds like it made her mad. She has often tried to fool herself by saying that something "didn't really matter; ain't no big thing." She has persisted and she is seeing herself as a person with many new and unsettling feelings. Her frustration is sometimes less. Every now and again she likes whom she sees, just as she is.

References

Finkelhor, D., & Browne, A. (1985). The traumatic impact of child sexual abuse: A conceptualization. *American Journal of Orthopsychiatry, 55*(4), 530-541.

Peck, M. S. (1983). *People of the lie.* New York: Simon and Schuster.

Pesso, A. (1988). *Abuse.* Franklin, N.H.: PS Press.

The Unabridged Random House Dictionary. (1966). New York: Random House.

Terms for Discussion

1. self-righteousness (throughout article)

2. depression (paragraph 17)

3. direct anger (paragraph 20)

4. ego (paragraph 23)

Questions

5. In your opinion, does the author adequately answer the five questions posed in the first paragraph of the article? Explain.

6. The author discusses the positive and negative connotations of "self-righteousness." (See paragraphs 4 through 10.) Before you read the article, did you believe that the connotation was primarily positive or negative? Has the article changed your opinion? Explain.

7. Sally is a 29-year-old, single female who lives with an older and a younger brother. Do you believe that the dynamics of this household/family relationship are adequately described by the author? Explain.

8. In what areas did Sally feel superior to her colleagues?

9. Sally expressed little direct anger at her colleagues. In your opinion, is this consistent with the diagnosis of self-righteousness? Explain.

10. The author suggests that, in this case, self-righteousness may be a mask for feeling at fault or unworthy. Do you believe that this may frequently be true of self-righteous people? Explain.

11. In your opinion, do Sally's experiences during her early-school-age time justify the author's use of consistent affirmation of Sally's feelings? Explain.

12. The author does not describe Sally's romantic relationships or the lack of them, although paragraph 40 might imply that she had none. Would more information on this have been helpful to you in understanding Sally's case? Explain.

13. Sally's therapy is apparently still in progress. (See paragraph 14.) Based on the information in the article, what is your prognosis for her recovery?

14. If you have known a self-righteous person, briefly describe some of his or her behaviors (including verbalizations) that illustrate this trait.

15. The author uses the term "defense" in the title. What is a defense mechanism? Is self-righteousness an example of one?

16. Are there any other types of treatment that might have facilitated Sally's improvement? Explain.

17. Rate the article on the seven criteria described in the introduction to this book on a scale from 5 (highest quality) through 1 (lowest quality). Be prepared to explain your ratings.

Criterion 1: The demographics of the case are described: _____

Criterion 2: The condition(s) and behavior(s) that necessitated treatment are described in detail: _____

Criterion 3: The method of treatment is described in sufficient detail so that it can be replicated without additional information: _____

Criterion 4: A rationale is provided for the method of treatment selected: _____

Criterion 5: The client's improvement, if any, is clearly documented: _____

Criterion 6: Follow-up information on the client's improvement, if any, is presented: _____

Criterion 7: The study is appropriate for publication in a journal: _____

Notes:

Case 15

Grieving the Loss of Narcissistic Entitlement: A Case Study*

Elaine Neuman Kulp
DuPage Counseling and Referral Services, Inc.
Illinois Benedictine College

ABSTRACT: The child deprived of a sufficient and constant supply of emotional sustenance draws upon his or her imagination for relief from emotional pain and anxiety. This "fantasy bond" is addictive in its capacity to provide some repeatable internal gratification. Often the satisfaction achieved through this fantasy becomes preferred to seeking real satisfactions from other individuals. The realities of a relationship, with its inherent limitations, often intrude on the fantasy bond whose limitations are in the control of the one doing the fantasy work.

The child who experiences early narcissistic injury attempts to recover these losses later in life by reworking the impaired attachment with the original primary caretaker in other significant relationships or in attachments to significant ideals or institutions during adolescence and adulthood. But the injured child also draws upon his or her imagination creating fantasized attachments for relief from emotional pain and anxiety.

The therapist needs to support mourning work for these earliest narcissistic injuries and losses, thus facilitating the client's ability to cope with the vicissitudes of relationships in a healthier and more adaptive manner.

The Nature and Function of the Fantasy Bond

(1) The child deprived of a sufficient and constant supply of emotional sustenance draws upon his or her imagination for relief from emotional pain and anxiety. When the primary caretaker is unable to provide healthy selfobject functions—sustained emotional responses appropriate to the child's developmental needs—the child may resort to an imaginary connection, referred to as a "fantasy bond" (Firestone, 1988), to partially supply the needed emotional fuel for the development of the healthy, separate self. The fantasy serves as the resource for the selfobject experience, partially gratifying unfulfilled intrapsychic needs deficient in the archaic child-caretaker bond:

> Selfobject experiences can be the function not only of objects, but also of symbolism or ideas representing objects. Like other selfobject experiences, they serve by performing the specific function of providing a self-evoking and self-sustaining experience to the potential and to the emerged self. (Wolf, 1988, p. 53)

The fantasy bond is addictive in its capacity to provide some repeatable internal gratification. Firestone defined the fantasy bond thus:

> an illusion of connection with another person, formed originally with the mother as a compensation for what was missing in the infant's early environment. Later, this self-parenting process or fusion is transferred to significant others in adult associations. The term is not meant to describe bonding as positive attachment. (1988, p. 4)

Often the satisfaction achieved through a fantasy bond becomes preferred to seeking real satisfactions from other individuals. The realities of a relationship, with its accompanying limitations, often intrude on the fantasy bond whose limitations are in the control of the one doing the fantasy work.

(2) The child who experiences such early narcissistic injury—deprivation of appropriate, ongoing emotional

---

*Reprinted from *Journal of College Student Psychotherapy*, 5, 1991, pp. 45-65. Copyright 1991 by The Hayworth Press. All rights reserved. Reprinted with permission.

interactions needed to develop a healthy, separate self—attempts to recover from these losses later in life. The child attempts to rework the impaired attachment with the original primary caretaker in relationships or in attachments to significant ideals or institutions in adolescence and in adulthood. The child's natural entitlement during the healthy narcissistic phase of development (Mahler, Pine, & Berman, 1975) to receive sustained and supportive responses is sabotaged by the primary caretaker's inability to provide such responses. This results in the formation of defenses to cope with the ongoing disappointment and failure to receive appropriate empathic responses.

(3) The narcissistically vulnerable college student may view the other (person, ideal, institution) in an unrealistic and fantasy-bound manner, wishing and hoping that the other will magically identify, and satisfy his or her needs. When the partner is unable to meet these needs, the wounded adult-child feels rage and rejection. This rekindles the original and often repressed rage and feelings of loss that the child experienced with the inadequate caretaker.

(4) This emotionally vulnerable college student needs to engage in a grieving process in response to the deprivation of these early narcissistic supplies to which he or she was entitled, and that were necessary for healthy psychological development. I consider the student's capacity to grieve and to use the grieving process as an appropriate intervention for repairing early injury. Facilitating the grief process enables the client to begin making more appropriate and meaningful choices. I emphasize the need to consider the client's existential perspective and its impact on his or her interpretations and consequent affective responses.

Clinical Work With "David" Over a One-Year Period

(5) "David" is a sensitive, psychologically intuitive twenty-two year-old college student who communicates a sense of loneliness and appears quite vulnerable to emotional injury. He has repeatedly demonstrated an ability to make some successful adaptations to a chaotic family dynamic, where expectations change abruptly, and without warning. David can intellectualize his anger toward family members, particularly his stepfather, and yet has difficulty dealing with anger on an affective level. His mother, now deceased, seemed to encourage a symbiotic, dependent relationship between herself and David, which extended to his relationship with his maternal grandmother, with whom he is now struggling to establish appropriate boundaries to avert the exhaustive time demands that she continues to make on David. The death of David's mother, when he was 20, left him without his primary protector in the family dynamic. His stepfather's immature and inappropriate coping mechanisms after the death of his wife left David emotionally unprotected, vulnerable, and drawn into a parental role with an immature and very needy father figure. David struggles against the financial manipulation and dependence he feels in his relationship with his stepfather. David's primary area of self-satisfaction has come from academics and from activities that do not place a heavy demand on interpersonal social skills.

The Fantasy Bond With "David"

(6) David attached to an external institution (college) and tried to embody that institution with the magical power to fill the void and ease the hurt. When this did not happen, a sense of helplessness and hopelessness emerged. Thus, shortly after he began college, his energy diminished, a problem compounded by his mother's death, and he became suicidal, seriously considering carbon monoxide poisoning.

(7) David acts out life's ultimate victim position. He observes himself to be outside the mainstream of life, while he looks through the metaphorical window of the candy shop. Life means pain and suffering, as a consequence of the narcissistically wounding aggressors in his history. He feels entitled to compensation on a financial level, the only reward he feels he is owed. I tried to help David integrate and tolerate his psychic pain in order to move away from it, rather than to project it outwardly or defend against it with a depressive stance.

(8) David announced early in therapy that it was hard for him to terminate with his previous therapists, but that he knew he could survive that experience. He needed to assure himself and perhaps to inform me of this vulnerability. He seemed most anxious in his silence when I told him I would be gone for a few weeks in November for my son's surgery. I did not feel that David could handle being confronted with my observation of the meaning of his silence—that he would have experienced such confrontation as an injury. But any sense he might have had of me as an "eternally available therapist" was confronted in that moment. He never commented on or questioned any aspect of my absence.

(9) David repeatedly expressed envy of the vitality and energy he witnessed in his friends. On several occasions, he sat "on the side lines" observing a friend interact with others with confidence and vitality, leaving

him literally and psychologically immobilized, even unable to acknowledge being in the same room as the object of his envy. He continues to be mystified by the "good fortune" of others, their "ideal" childhoods, and their "perpetual support" from warm and consistent parents. He is conscious of feeling far behind his peers in terms of achievement of life goals and in his lacking zest for life.

Nature and History of Early Injuries

Where was the deprivation?
(10) David's biological parents divorced when he was two, and his mother remarried when he turned four. He has recently discovered that his mother was seeing his stepfather while still married to his biological father. This substantiates the chaotic and inappropriate kind of energy David's mom directed toward him, both encouraging helpless, symbiotic behavior and squashing attempts to separate on a physical or psychological level. David does not communicate a sense of owning his body or being comfortable in his physical self; he appears awkward and very self-conscious.

(11) His mother's remarriage left David vulnerable to a man who operated with extreme unpredictability:

David: *He [stepfather] has a terrible temper. One bad day at work and he will not talk to anyone for two weeks. . . . He didn't like the way the coach coached a basketball game when I was in junior high so he threw things, screamed and yelled constantly, and didn't talk to the family for two weeks.*
T: *So anything could provoke him?*
David: *Right—you walked on glass.*
T: *That must have been so exhausting.*
David: *It was. He would go for two weeks and all of a sudden he got tired of this, and it was back to normal, so you never knew when it was going to be OK, when would he start screaming again, or how to react to his screaming.*
T: *So no middle of the road, just extremes.*
David: *Right, right, and he didn't know how to express emotions, like love, or anything so the only way he knew to express it was to get mad so if you were five minutes late (a little thing), instead of saying, "I was really worried about you," or whatever, he had to get really angry so there was nothing we could do.*
T: *Must have felt like you were living on the edge.*
David: *Yeah, when I was younger, I had to wait until 5:30 or 6:00 to see what kind of mood he was in before I would bring friends over because if he was in a bad mood there was just no way.*

T: *Did he drink?*
David: *No, not at all. I think he got it from his parents. I know his dad pushed his brother down a staircase when he was young; his mother just took it and wound up in a mental institution.*
T: *Was he physically abusive with you:*
David: *No, he never hit us.*
T: *Did you live in fear that he would?*
David: *No, but we always lived in fear that he would leave because my mom was a secretary and only made $6,000.*
T: *It's so hard though. Here's someone that you are dependent on who is also scaring the life out of you.*
David: *It was hard because he wasn't our father. We were four years old and trying to pretend he was our father.*
T: *What did you call him?*
David: *Bill. At age four, they asked us what we wanted to do and at the time I still had a real father; I didn't know my real father would vanish.*

Indicators of Narcissistic Disturbances

(12) Certain behavioral and affective characteristics, some described by Miller (1981), get reinforced in narcissistically disturbed individuals and form the core of their style of adaptation. Mahler et al. (1975) described the rapprochement subphase of the separation-individuation process (occurring approximately between the ages of 15 and 24 months) as healthy if the child is capable of tolerating the growing awareness that he or she exists as a separate person from the mother (the primary caretaker). The child ideally has permission to renegotiate his or her relationship in terms of emerging needs for both separateness and reconnection with the mother.

(13) The college student who did not receive sustained emotional responses appropriate for his or her developmental needs during the rapprochement subphase, is prone to remain fixated at an earlier developmental phase. A college student who experienced inadequate nurturing during the rapprochement subphase may display certain "markers," enumerated and discussed later in this article, which indicate that the individual experienced narcissistic injury during the early developmental phases of the first three years of life. Individuals whose cognitive, affective, and behavioral stances reflect a predominance of these symptoms, in relationship to others, also may be vulnerable to enacting the core defense structure of the fantasy bond (Firestone, 1986).

(14) When the child evolves toward object constancy

(Mahler, et al. 1975), he or she reaches the phase of development during which the child can tolerate a more integrated and realistic internal representation of both self and other: "When the issues of rapprochement are well-handled, the child achieves an internalized source of comfort and love. With this internalization, the other is seen more and more as a person in his or her own right rather than as a narcissistically cathected part of the child's self" (Johnson, 1987, p. 33). Johnson, like Miller, viewed the psychopathology that forms in adults as resulting from deficits in the formation of self structure. Therapeutic intervention seeks to provide new experiences with which to challenge the initial deficits. When the client internalizes the new experiences, this acknowledges and strengthens the individual's sense of separate self—"real self."

Markers for Movement in Therapy

Clinging behavior (fear of abandonment).
(15) David's primary symbolic connections with significant caretakers involve monetary dependency and control. He is getting stronger in his wish to seek financial autonomy that he associates with psychological freedom. He previously needed to get this limited symbolic assurance of his worth and meaning from his stepfather by challenging the limits of what the stepfather gives him to sustain his college education. David continues to try to find ways to extend his college time, wanting to change majors (accounting from business management), which would mean extending his undergraduate work to more than five years.

(16) When David's mother died, his one sustaining relationship—albeit one marked by mutual clinging and neediness—disappeared. He was not encouraged to build the skills needed to form relationships outside the family arena. Thus, interactions with others leave David feeling uncomfortably on stage and extremely vulnerable. He shared how he dropped a class in business: he walked out when the professor insisted he meet a new student and then introduce him to the class. Being without the basic skills that would help him to form attachments to peers, he avoids any risk of injury by creating a life structure in which he minimizes social contact with others. David expends a great deal of energy repressing his needs for interpersonal attachment. While he cognitively laments this plight, he appears somewhat intractable and steadfastly avoids the mechanics and feelings involved in forming attachments.

Difficulty in differentiating self from other.
(17) David's boundaries have become most strongly blurred in his relationship with his mother, who died when he was 20. He seems to be carrying out her victimized stance, particularly reenacting her financial dependence on his stepfather. His mother clearly "martyred" herself by living with an unpredictable man with many borderline features, assuring herself, thereby, of some security for herself and her children. While David yearned to be separate, he does not seem able to internalize and integrate an identity of himself as a young man now living away from home.

(18) David fears strong attachments as indicated by his apprehension of losing anyone else, directed on a conscious level toward losing his grandmother. He has taken some steps to reduce the symbiotic nature of his interactions with her, which formerly involved three daily phone calls. Yet, he suffers guilt when he connects with her only on a weekly basis. He indicates that he did bond with his former therapists and he was frightened initially of repeating the sense of loss he felt when they terminated the therapeutic relationship with him, albeit due to their scheduling limitations.

Wish to conform at all costs (enormous fear of loss of love).
(19) David is anxious to assure me that he experiences my interpretations and comments as accurate and meaningful. He feels so depleted of resources for support that he does not wish to risk injuring the few he can draw upon. He tends to avoid interaction with peers, lacking the energy to stay focused on the needs of others. Exhausted from having been his family's primary alert caretaker, he views all other relationships as a potential demand upon him.

(20) He rarely acknowledged or affirmed himself as a separate individual with unique and important needs of his own, but adapted primarily by becoming whatever his mother and stepfather needed to insure for the ongoing survival of his family. His current academic difficulties as a business major reveal a flavor of his uncertainty about his own emotional needs.

(21) David has often fantasized about confrontations with family members, particularly his stepfather. He has continued to perceive himself in a dependent role in relation to his stepfather and has generally acted out his anger in indirect, avoidant behavior rather than in any observable assertive or individuating manner. He can acknowledge on an intellectual level my interpretation that his "carrying on the victimized role of his mother" in relation to his stepfather was a way of staying attached to his mother. Yet he was not able to separate

himself financially by finding alternative ways to fund his education. There was also an aspect of "he [stepfather] owes me this money" for all the suffering David endured throughout his childhood. He tends to avoid, with characteristics of avoidant personality disorder, rather than to confront the individuals who are significant in his life.

Marked anxiety when having to be alone (need for external sources for calming).
(22) David yearned for separateness from his family. Beginning at age 8 he dreamed of the day he could move far away to college. But rooming with other college students often was fraught with tension and disappointment. This past year he chose to live alone and is experiencing his aloneness as another assault on his sense of self. He interprets this as a sign of his being out of the mainstream of his friends' lives. He experiences his alone time as loneliness rather than as an achievement of autonomy.

Intensity of affect (lack of ability to modulate feelings).
(23) David tends to speak in a monotone voice, expressing a quality of heaviness and constant frustration. His underlying depressive quality leaves him with little energy to project the enthusiasm or the vitality of young men his age. His affective stance is often what one would associate with an elderly individual who is bemoaning the fate of a downtrodden life. Yet there is a childlike vulnerability to David that communicates a fragility and great fear of being wounded by the words or behaviors of others. He smiles when his therapist communicates a feeling of recognition and affirmation.

(24) David communicates a childlike sense of embarrassment when alluding to the sexual behavior of others, which he connects exclusively with his stepfather's dating behaviors. He averts his eyes and uses descriptors that a young adolescent would use to describe sexual intimacy. There is no sense in which he communicates his own sexuality; it is as if he has buried this symbol of adulthood, remaining connected to the childlike fantasies of a little boy who still seeks the protective mother. David also may unconsciously connect sexual behavior and feelings with the acting out behavior that caused great difficulties in his life and left him in a victim position. He was asked to be the referee for his stepfather's many relationships, predominantly with married women. He seems to connect sexuality with immaturity and has strongly defended against it in himself.

(25) David needed to repress his anger toward his mother's own dependency, rationalizing that she needed to stay with an emotionally abusive man in order that they survive financially. He is beginning to claim his right to his own anger, moving away from his disposition to feeling depressed and victimized.

Lack of inner sense of calm.
(26) David is growing increasingly intolerant of working ceaselessly (he would study six hours per night in high school) to attain his goals. The meaning of these external goals and his fantasy that they will provide him with safety and happiness are diminishing, leaving him less able to tolerate disappointment in his current classroom experiences. He is frustrated that nothing in life seems to provide him with a sense of peace or a experience of lasting pleasure. He is bored and feels unable to do anything to change his environmental experiences.

Need to idealize others as attempt to strengthen fragile sense of self by identification with idealized object.
(27) His tendency to idealize the lives of his friends leaves him feeling separated and detached from them; he experiences himself as left behind stuck in the same position. His tendency to romanticize the lifestyles of others serves to separate him from them, leaving him feeling jealous and immobilized to join them in any of their activities.

Need to be admired by everyone.
(28) David defends against anticipated rejection by avoidance at all costs, but responds with increasing tolerance to the positive affirmation he receives in therapy sessions. He struggles between his intense need to have others affirm him and his fear of the dependency that this triggers. His almost paralyzing fear of rejection by his peers results in his adapting to social experiences by exerting great effort to avoid them whenever possible.

Need to excel at everything.
(29) David initially worked six-hour days on his homework in high school, striving for successful grades. He no longer feels motivated to continue at this pace and is gravely disappointed that his academic performance is not relieving a core pain that he hoped would "go away" once college began. He feels betrayed by his fantasy and often wants to rebel against the demands that college places upon him.

High sensitivity to criticism.
(30) David agonizes before asking another person for a slight favor or expressing a wish to share a meal with another. He is immediately conscious of not wanting to

cause the other person a moment of discomfort, often avoiding taking a small risk to prevent a fantasized expectation of a rejection or moment of uneasiness for self and other. His fragile sense of self reveals a hypersensitivity to criticism. I feel I must be very careful not to communicate anything verbally that might be experienced as an injury. He ruminates over details to avoid risking the slightest verbal or nonverbal injury from another person.

A readiness to feel shame and guilt.
(31) David recognizes the limitations of his family of origin but remains very loyal to his idealized view of his mother. He was able to tolerate some brief moments in which he considered and experienced her emotional limitations. After five months of therapy, David was able to express some affect to the anger and disappointment he typically had communicated in without emotion. He often averts his eyes when sharing what he experiences as shameful family secrets. He did not learn until recent years, that his maternal grandmother, whom he calls "aunt," acted as his mother's sister in order that the grandmother raise his mother, nor did his own mother know until recent years that her real mother was her "sister" and that the woman who raised her as mother was her grandmother.

Need to identify with a victimized position (depression as the reverse of grandiosity).
(32) David holds on to painful statements for a long time:

David: *This bothered me and still stuck with me from three years ago. A friend of mine who I went to when I had problems said, "I don't understand. You were laughing a week ago. Why can't you today?" Her and everyone else assumes that if you smile you have no problems.*
T: *It shows how much it pains you. You can still feel it when you think of it now.*
David: *Yeah. We were really good friends. Haven't talked to her for a year. She backed away. I can understand it.*
T: *But it doesn't make it easier.*
David: *In my junior year, I wanted to commit suicide. She was there for a few weeks. Every time, every single time I came over she left. I got to feeling very self-conscious, like if I don't talk in a minute my time is over.*
T: *Her message was, "Make it quick."*
David: *She had everything going for her, good personality, everything going for her.*

(33) David goes through intense periods of depression. Prior to therapy he spent a great deal of energy creating a plan for suicide (carbon monoxide poisoning in the car). He reveals that if life ever again felt as heavy as it did shortly after his mother's death, it would comfort him to know that he had a way out of this life that was in his control. While he does not present now as imminently suicidal, he is unable to communicate a sense of looking forward to life. His early childhood lacked experiences that would communicate a hopeful outlook on life.

Parentified child behavior patterns (wish to rescue and save others, strong caretaker needs).
(34) David clearly functioned as the most adult figure in his family throughout childhood:

David: *[Stepfather] just got married this summer. He dated the "girl of the week." Ninety-nine percent of the time they were married—just having affairs with him [nervous laugh, self-conscious about sexual references].*
T: *He wasn't in his dad role?*
David: *He needs to prove he is still a man at age sixty.*
T: *You are real insightful.*
David: *I figured it out with a couple of counselors.*
T: *Sometimes it's hard, very hard to be the parent of your parents. Who wants to be the more mature person than your parent?*
David: *Yeah, yeah, exactly.*
T: *Then it feels like you are taking care of a kid when you need someone to turn to.*
David: *Exactly, then I have no one to turn to. My real dad lives twenty minutes away and sends no birthday card. When mom died, it totally fell on me. I had to ask [sister who is four years older] to call grandma, force [sister] to do it. Grandma lives for [sister] and I. I have to lie for everyone and know all the rules—you get in trouble if you don't know the rules. I'm tired of playing the game.*

Envy of the healthy.
(35) David frequently cites episodes with other students whom he "knows" deserve their good fortune. He does not understand why he is still stuck in the same spot while others move on with excitement, eager anticipation of the future, and a sense of accomplishment. He lacks these dynamic attributes, and communicates fear that he will remain frozen forever in this energyless state.

(36) During the second session, David reported feeling "struck" with envy and depression as he observed a

friend energetically engaging in a conversation with other college students. David often approaches life as one who is outside the candy store looking in the window with longing and sadness:

T: *Any thoughts or feelings since we talked last time?*
David: *A couple things. I went to see a friend, now an R.A.; I called him, waited in the lounge, happened to glance over, he was walking by and I had time to yell, but I didn't. He was walking with a couple of other people, laughing and having a good time. It was just like a three-second thing, but it stuck with me ever since. I just sat there stunned, not stunned. I don't know, I just sat there. Maybe I felt bad.*
T: *Yeah.*
David: *I'm kind of stuck. He's moved on and done well, and done well in everything he has done. I don't know.*

Use of symbiotic language (e.g., we, us, them).
(37) David often talked about his childhood by using the expression "we" to connote what has happened to himself, his mother, and his sister. The three of them had anxiously attached to one another in a needy and dependent merger. He spoke of his mother's friend as "our" friend on several occasions.

Reactiviation of Separation-Individuation Issues in Adolescence and Young Adulthood

(38) Adolescence affords a second significant opportunity to separate and further individuate from one's family of origin. Ideally, one can reenact unresolved issues left over from the first separation-individuation period, before three years of age (Mahler, et al. 1975). Often, the adolescent will embody additional corrective capability due to the maturation of ego development and to the extension of selfobject resources. David's behavioral and affective styles reflect struggles with adolescent and young adult developmental issues as well as with unresolved earlier developmental needs. The task of further separation and individuation requires new selfobjects with which to satisfy mirroring and idealizing needs. Friends often provide the role of "mirroring"—affirming one's own perceptions and experiences. Healthy adult role-models and mentors are often idealized and internalized, providing new experiences which serve to strengthen the inner sense of self. It is an indicator of health, according to Kohut (1987a), when adolescents and young adults seek and find satisfaction through outside relationships. The tasks of separating and individuating do not exclude the need for selfobjects:

> It is cardinal to Kohut's theories that separation and individuation leading to an end result in autonomy fail to define the essence of the human condition: we never outgrow the need for selfobjects though we do outgrow their exploitation by achieving mature empathy as a self-function. (Elson, 1986, p. 16)

(39) Kohut asserted that the "addictive person needs the object of his addiction with an absolute intensity that is not the same as the comparative relativity even of passionate love" (1987b, p. 124). The addictive personality is missing an aspect of psychological structure that hungers for needs to be met from external supplies, external selfobjects. This differentiates the addictive personality from more adaptive healthy-functioning individuals who can provide these supplies for themselves. Often, there is a lack of capacity for self-soothing. Such individuals are deprived of calming, protecting experiences with their primary caretaker. David suffered early deprivation, sudden loss, and phase-inappropriate responding that inhibited the development of his capacity to internalize the self-soothing function.

(40) Kohut suggested that such individuals initially turn to a psychotherapist to provide the impaired self-soothing function as well as other functions inadequately provided in early parent-child relationship:

> It was on the basis of feeling stumped that I began to entertain the thought that these people were not concerned with me as a separate person, but that they were concerned with themselves; that they did not love or hate me, but that they needed me as a part of themselves, needed me as a *set of functions* which they had not acquired in early life; that what appeared to be their love and hate was in reality their need that I fulfill certain psychological functions for them and anger at me when I did not do so. (Kohut, 1978, p. 888)

(41) Through the connection with the therapist's empathic responses, a client can experience the therapist as a new selfobject. The therapist initially gratifies unmet needs that the client can eventually transmute into his or her own psychic structure. Ultimately the client will be capable of meeting his or her own soothing, calming and mastery needs (Elson, 1986, p. 42).

(42) The client who suffers from early deprivation of appropriate mirroring needs is vulnerable to feeling addicted to the therapist, behavior manifesting in the transference. The individual who needs the object of addiction to perform the self-soothing, self-esteem maintaining function, is vulnerable to forming fanta-

sized attachments with others, particularly in the initial phase of relationships during which he or she turns to the object of addiction for gratification of missing emotional pieces:

> Many undergraduates experience acute anxiety as they try to find direction in their studies toward a goal which will confirm their worth. They cling to and yet seek escape from the familiar shelter of family and old associates. (Kohut, p. 171)

Adolescent Grief: The Loss of Childhood

(43) Hamilton (1988, p. 112) recalled these powerful lines of poetry by William Wordsworth, depicting a sense of resolve and strength following one's awareness of the loss of "innocent unity in infancy:"

> Though nothing can bring back the hour
> Of splendour in the grass, of glory in the flower
> We will grieve not, rather find
> Strength in what remains behind
> ("Ode on Intimations of Immortality from Recollections of Early Childhood")

(44) These lines touched Hamilton in their depiction of how successful differentiation and integration involve awareness of "gain in loss:" "The capacity to acknowledge and tolerate mutually contradictory emotions simultaneously is whole object relatedness" (Hamilton, 1988, p. 111). Wordsworth's words, "We will grieve not," disavow the grieving process that is essential if one is to internalize the "Strength in what remains behind." Ironically, the reading of Wordsworth's poignant poem stirs the very feelings of grief against which he defends.

(45) One of the critical tasks of adolescence, grieving the loss of childhood, requires that the adolescent have the capacity to tolerate and integrate good and bad self- and object-images:

> The grandiose self-images and omnipotent object-images do recede into the realm of fiction, mythology, and dreams. Salvation no longer beckons, but damnation no longer threatens. Knowledge of both good and evil together does result in a loss of paradise. (Hamilton, 1988, pp. 110-111)

"David's" Grief Process

(46) Grief and sadness have become "home" for David. His mother's death reactivated a grieving for a missing piece of his own self that began early in his development. The death of David's mother encapsulated a lifetime of emotional losses. It marked his loss of hope that she would protect him from an unpredictable stepfather and from an unpredictable life. She sacrificed David's childhood needs for consistency and calm by remaining in an abusive marriage for financial security. David was deprived of parental role models who could mirror and sustain the qualities of hope and optimism necessary to handle the vicissitudes of daily living. It is an ongoing battle for David to sustain any sense of hope for the future.

(47) David fears further loss. He is conscious of his wish to avoid "going through" again what he experienced when he lost his mother. For example, part of him now fears the death of his maternal grandmother and wants to begin separating from her now:

David: I'm tired of playing I'm close to grandma. I'm the only person she's got, but I don't want to go through her death. When she dies, I don't want to deal with it. I'm tired of being dependent. She [grandma] was spoiled when I grew up. I talked to her twice a day on the phone, so when I went to college it was even harder for her. It was hard for my mother. Now a few weeks will go by and I won't call grandma.
T: It's okay. It's appropriate.
David: Since I was a shy person and didn't have a social life, all I had was my family and grandma. Ever since my mom died, I've worked on not being dependent on anyone ever again.
T: That's hard.
David: It is hard. I'm feeling the effects now. I've pushed everyone away, and I'm feeling totally alone.

The Relationship Between Grief Work In Therapy and the Intensity of the Attachment to a Fantasy Bond

(48) David has experienced life at college as an ultimate blow; the fantasy that it would fill his inner emptiness has been slowly shattering. His strong attachment to the fantasy that college would bring him relief and happiness has been seriously challenged by the realities of his daily struggles and disappointments. He does not expect to be involved in a significant relationship in his life. He expresses a growing sense that he has never been truly happy.

(49) My work with David has affirmed that enabling the client to acknowledge and to grieve early childhood losses of necessary narcissistic supplies correlates with a growing capacity to engage in the realistic aspects of relationships with others without feeling devastated by their natural disappointments: "The reconstructive healing of psychotherapy could be accommodating. Thus, it

is evident that in the treatment of such patients, mourning and working through the fixation on the original traumatic situation is of paramount importance" (Shabad, 1987, pp. 197-198). While David had difficulty expressing his grief affectively, he is beginning to tolerate the limitations of reality in relationships and in work goals.

(50) My work with David supports Shabad's contribution to understanding the process of grieving in relation to feelings of remorse for "the lost childhood":

> a deep sense of regret over many lost years devoted to the pursuit of an illusory ideal may accompany the self-knowledge gained in psychotherapy . . . the defensive flight from remorse into unconscious action and how this defense is mobilized clinically as resistance to therapeutic progress . . . [the] therapeutic necessity of mourning the unrealisability of childhood wishes (Shabad, 1987, p. 116).

(51) The pain of remorse inhibits some individuals from engaging in the feelings that remind them of what they have indeed missed in their development. There were moments for David when it was easier for him to believe that he was "cursed" from the moment of birth than to give up the final shred of idealization of the limited parent. The death of David's mother strengthened his need to hold on to a somewhat idealized view of this primary caretaker. He was able, however, in significant moments in therapy to consider limitations in her ability to provide him with the enthusiastic, vital responses which he now finds difficult to provide for himself.

Termination as a Loss Issue

(52) David was able to verbalize that it would be a loss for him to end our therapeutic relationship. He nodded affirmingly when I initiated sharing with him what our work together has meant to me: I shared that I felt privileged to hear and to honor his life story, and that I believed what he went through. It was very important to him that I know about the significant people in his life, both past and present. David described the sadness of this ending more than he expressed it affectively, needing this cognitive framework to contain feelings of loss and sadness that continue to feel overwhelming.

Reflections

(53) We need to celebrate the human capacity to use fantasy to provide a creative, albeit sometimes dysfunctional, means of escaping from significant psychic pain. When a child appropriately seeks confirmation of self through the mother's approving and confirming responses and instead finds chaos, rejection, and uncertainty, this child is more vulnerable to forming attachments based merely on fantasy bonds—imagined connections with other persons, institutions, or groups. Alice Miller spoke of the despair one of her clients felt in recognition of her aging process, experiencing at a deeper level pre-oedipal anxiety about being abandoned. This woman was no longer able to receive the constant affirmation of her attractiveness from others from whom she sought a substitute confirmation and fantasized mirror for the missing piece her mother was unable to provide: "All her substitute mirrors were broken and she again stood helpless and confused like the small girl once did before her mother's face in which she had not found herself, but her mother's confusion" (1979, p. 66).

(54) These feelings of helplessness and confusion emerged to varying degrees in David's therapy. It is my greatest hope that there was some partial resolution for the missing mirroring piece through his internalization of the validating, mirroring self-object experience achieved through the therapeutic relationship. David achieved to various degrees an integrated, aware termination experience, with recognition of the loss of the relationship as well as recognition of many other significant losses, including the loss of the healthy parenting responses in his earliest developmental history. His capacity to mourn these losses directly impacts on his degree of recovery and ability to use more adaptive defenses: "The ability to mourn, i.e., give up the illusion of his 'happy' childhood, can restore vitality and creativity" (Miller, 1979). David may now be able to sustain our work in a way that permits experiencing his life with increased vitality and awareness and with a heightened capacity for self appreciation.

References

Elson, M. (1986). *Self psychology in clinical social work*. New York: W. W. Norton and Co.

Firestone, R. (1986). *Voice therapy* [Videotape]. Corona Del Mar, CA: Psychological and Educational Films.

Firestone, R. (1987). *The fantasy bond: Effects of psychological defenses on interpersonal relations*. New York: Human Sciences Press.

Firestone, R. (1988). *Voice therapy*. New York: Human Sciences Press.

Hamilton, N. (1988). *Self and others: Object relations theory in practice*. London: Jason Aronson.

Kohut, H. (1987a). Separation from family and the struggle to potentiate ideas and goals. In M. Elson, (Ed.), *The Kohut seminars on self psychology and psychotherapy with adolescents and young adults*. New York: W.W. Norton and Co.

Kohut, H. (1987b). Regulation of self-esteem. In M. Elson, (Ed.), *The Kohut seminars on self psychology and psychotherapy with adolescents and young adults*. New York: W.W. Norton and Co.

Kohut, H. (1978). *The search for the self: Selected writings of Heinz Kohut, 1950-1978*, P. Ornstein (Ed.), Vol. I & II. New York: International Universities Press.

Johnson, S. (1987). *Humanizing the narcissistic style*. New York: Norton.

Mahler, M., Pine, F., & Berman, A. (1975). *The psychological birth of the human infant: Symbiosis and individuation* (pp. 52-120). New York: Basic Books.

Miller, A. (1979). Depression and grandiosity as related forms of narcissistic disturbances. *International Review of Psycho-Analysis, 6*, 61-76.

Miller, A. (1981). *The drama of the gifted child*. New York: Basic Books.

Shabad, P. (1987). Fixation and the road not taken. *Psychoanalytic Psychology, 4*(3), 187-205.

Wolf, E. (1988). *Treating the self*. New York: Guilford Press.

Terms for Discussion

1. narcissistic (throughout article)

2. selfobject (paragraphs 1, 38, 39, 41, and 54)

3. intellectualize (paragraph 5)

4. symbiotic relationship (paragraphs 5, 10, 18, and 37)

5. rapprochement subphase of the separation-individuation process (paragraphs 12, 13, 14, and 38)

6. avoidant personality disorder (paragraphs 21, 28, and 30)

7. ego development (paragraph 38)

8. addictive personality (paragraph 39)

9. pre-oedipal anxiety (paragraph 53)

Questions

10. Do you agree with the author that using the grieving process is an appropriate intervention for repairing early injury? Explain.

11. What do the "markers for movement in therapy" in paragraphs 15 through 37 suggest to you about the seriousness of David's condition? In your opinion, could these just be temporary reactions to recent events (the death of his mother and starting college)? Explain.

12. David has seen several therapists, all of whom have terminated the therapeutic relationships for reasons beyond their control. Seeing several therapists might be beneficial for some clients. Do you think that it was in David's case?

13. What is your opinion on the therapist's hopes for David described in paragraph 54? Given the information in the article, would you recommend additional therapy for David?

14. There are more direct quotations of the client's and therapist's words in this article than there are in most of the others in this book. In general, do you believe that presenting quotations are useful in helping the reader understand the client and the course of therapy? In this article, were the quotations particularly useful? Explain.

15. Are there any other types of treatment that might have facilitated David's improvement? Explain.

16. Rate the article on the seven criteria described in the introduction to this book on a scale from 5 (highest quality) through 1 (lowest quality). Be prepared to explain your ratings.

Criterion 1: The demographics of the case are described: _____

Criterion 2: The condition(s) and behavior(s) that necessitated treatment are described in detail: _____

Criterion 3: The method of treatment is described in sufficient detail so that it can be replicated without additional information: _____

Criterion 4: A rationale is provided for the method of treatment selected: _____

Criterion 5: The client's improvement, if any, is clearly documented: _____

Criterion 6: Follow-up information on the client's improvement, if any, is presented: _____

Criterion 7: The study is appropriate for publication in a journal: _____

Notes:

Case 16

A Group Counseling Experience With the Very Old*

Brenda Garrett Hern
University of Akron

David M. Weis
University of Akron

ABSTRACT: The authors describe a group counseling experience using a modified remotivation and structured reminiscence format with six elderly female nursing home residents (ages 85-99). Much has happened in the area of group counseling for the elderly since Freud (1905) and Abraham (1949) espoused the futility of and lack of value inherent in psychotherapy of any kind for the aged. According to these analysts, the development of insight, the critical factor involved in psychoanalytic personality change, was not likely to occur in the elderly due to their presupposed rigidity and interpersonal withdrawal. This myth that the elderly are resistant to change, combined with many therapists' lack of experience with this age group and a consequent lack of familiarity with relevant treatment modalities, seems to have kept counseling of the elderly at a "developmental standstill" for years.

(1) Only since the 1950s have psychotherapeutic interventions been considered appropriate and beneficial for this particular age group. Group work has become increasingly popular and various forms have been developed for work with the aged. Creative therapies are being used more frequently with elderly groups. These include art therapy, dance therapy, and drama therapy and may range from being supportive in nature to insight-oriented in approach (Berland & Poggi, 1979). In addition, reality orientation, remotivation therapy, and reminiscence therapy have proven to be beneficial methods of group work with the elderly (Burnside, 1984).

(2) Although the literature is beginning to include more references to group work with the aged, journal articles pertaining to group counseling with the very old (those 85 and over) are still widely scattered. Due to the dramatic increase in life extension since 1900, the older age segment has increased over eightfold, while the general population has grown only threefold (Aizenberg & Treas, 1985). As the average age of the population of the United States increases and life expectancy also increases, a larger percentage of the population is in the "old-old" category. Data from the U.S. Bureau of the Census (1981) indicate that the population over 85 is the fastest growing percentage-wise of any cohort group in this country. In light of this emerging social trend, mental health professionals must begin to evaluate the importance of and explore the possibilities of group counseling with the very old.

(3) Corey and Corey (1987) encouraged counselors to consider doing group work with the elderly and recommended that the groups be oriented toward making the members' lives in the present more meaningful and enjoyable. Moss (1976) advised that the interpersonal-interactive nature of the group counseling experience may make it the most beneficial therapeutic modality

---

*Reprinted from *The Journal for Specialists in Group Work*, 16, 1991, pp. 143-151. Copyright 1991 by the American Counseling Association. No further reproduction authorized without written permission of the American Counseling Association.

for treating the elderly. The findings of Rattenbury and Stones (1989) suggest that both reminiscence and current topics group discussion are associated with significant gains in psychological well-being in a nursing home context. The current authors hope that the description and implications drawn from their experience with an "old-old" segment of the elderly population will motivate counselors to initiate group procedures in the treatment of this age group.

Description of the Group
The Clinical Setting

(4) The facility selected for the present group counseling experience with the "old-old" was a licensed intermediate-care nursing home with a capacity for 100 residents. Following a presentation of the design of the group to the Director of Social Services and subsequent administrative approval, six female residents were recommended by the staff for participation. The residents were referred on the basis of their tendency to isolate themselves in their rooms and to avoid social interaction with other residents. An intake interview was conducted with each of the residents referred by the staff in order to assess appropriateness for participation in the group. During the intake interviews, it became apparent that despite their varied backgrounds, unique personalities, and special needs, all of the potential group members were withdrawing and isolating themselves in their rooms much of the time. Therefore, the appropriateness of the staff's selection was validated and the six residents were accepted for participation in the group. Ages of the group members ranged from 85 to 99, with an average age of 91.5 years.

(5) The group was facilitated by the first author who is a doctoral student in counseling psychology. Consultation on the selection of group procedures and supervision was provided by the second author.

Group Members

(6) Jane, a 90-year-old widow, suffered from generalized osteoarthritis, a condition that left her confined to a wheelchair. She and her husband had no children and while their relationship was apparently stable, Jane was having trouble dealing with her feelings of anger toward him for not taking better care of himself and thereby leaving her alone. Withdrawn and depressed, she isolated herself in her room except for meals. Her serious hearing impairment proved to be yet another barrier that contributed to her increasing social withdrawal. Ruminating almost completely about the past, she seemed to dwell on the negative aspects of her life, referring to herself as "Hard Luck Jane."

(7) Helen, a 99-year-old in exceptionally good health, needed only occasional assistance to ambulate. She spent the majority of her time in her room reading, meditating, and memorizing poetry. She considered herself to be a happy and positive person who "takes one day at a time" and "looks forward and never back." Isolating herself in her room more and more of the time, she spoke of having only one friend who, according to Helen, was one of the few other residents besides herself who "made any sense." She expressed no interest in associating with the more debilitated residents of the home, perhaps knowing and fearing that she too might lose some of her abilities and independence at some point in the future.

(8) Alert, cooperative, and articulate, Nelda was a 94-year-old who was able to take care of the majority of her personal needs without assistance. In the intake interview, she readily discussed her background with regard to family life with her husband and son. Nelda was reluctant, however, to discuss her life as a child and her answers became guarded. After her parents divorced, she lived at times with her grandparents and at other times with a friend's family. Nelda maintained that she didn't have many friends at the home and spent most of her time reading in her room. With her roommmate severely mentally impaired, it seemed that Nelda had little opportunity for meaningful communication.

(9) Carrie, 85 and the youngest member of the group, suffered a cerebrovascular accident years ago, which left her with L. hemiparesis (a paralysis of the left side of the body) and confined to a wheelchair. Keeping up with news and current events, Carrie enjoyed reading, particularly a "good love story." Despite few family contacts and only "acquaintances" at the home, Carrie stated she was happy and, during the initial interview, showed neither symptoms of depression nor negative ideation about the past. With a charming sense of humor and positive attitude, it seemed that Carrie would be an excellent peer model for the group.

(10) Lucy, an 89-year-old confined to a wheelchair, was not always oriented to time and place. Never having married, she spoke primarily of her childhood, which she described as "not very happy." With her head bowed, she told of her father's drinking problem and the hardship it placed on her mother and the rest of her family. Feeling lonely, Lucy stated she didn't socialize much because "I'm not asked—I mean, I don't have the opportunity. You have to have made friends when you were young to have friends when you're old."

(11) Rachel, a 93-year-old who came to this country at the age of 10, was a deeply religious person with a fairly strong family support system. Though seeming neither anxious nor depressed, she spent most of the time in her room alone. Her visual acuity no longer permitted her to read and her hearing impairment made it difficult for her to carry on a meaningful conversation with others. It became easier for Rachel to remain alone in her room, recalling family memories and dwelling largely on the past.

Therapeutic Approach

(12) Because of the tendency of the group members to isolate themselves in their rooms and to avoid social interaction with other nursing home residents, it was decided, after a review of the literature, that a modified remotivation therapy approach in combination with a structured reminiscence format would be the intervention of choice for the group. Remotivation therapy, a technique devised by Dorothy H. Smith, has gained recognition and acceptance since its inception in the mid-1950s. In general, those involved in remotivation groups are helped toward resocialization. Each remotivation session includes five basic steps: (1) "Climate of acceptance," (2) "Bridge to reality," (3) "Sharing the world we live in," (4) "An appreciation of the work of the world," and (5) "Climate of appreciation" (Toepfer, Bicknell, & Shaw, 1974, p. 451-453). Each session is based on a different topic and these topics are geared to appeal to diverse interests and backgrounds.

(13) In remotivation therapy, issues dealing with personal problems and family relationships are avoided. This was one point of departure in this group experience from the standard remotivation format. Instead, members were encouraged to recall concerns and problems from the past if they wished to share these with the group. While some members chose not to do so, others seemed eager to share painful memories once group cohesiveness had formed. For example, Rachel spoke of the difficult times her family had when first in this country. She and her husband experienced similar financial hardship when raising their young family. This appears to be consistent with Lewis and Butler's (1974) concept of the life review, in that the very old cannot only tolerate, but may indeed benefit from focusing on painful life events in order to integrate all aspects of their past. At the same time, the encouragement and support Rachel received from other group members bolstered her sense of self-worth and enhanced her sense of purpose. The opportunity to interact in a supportive environment, sharing positive and negative aspects of one's life, may be essential to the strengthening of coping abilities in the elderly (Ingersoll & Silverman, 1978). Waters (1990) believed that when life review is used in a group, it provides an opportunity for members to share recollections with others in the group and helps them identify themes that run through their lives along with the strengths and coping techniques that they developed and the realization that these are still available to them.

(14) Reminiscence was also determined to be a viable technique in group therapy as early as the mid-1960s when Klein, LeShan, and Furman (cited in Poulton & Strassberg, 1986) suggested that reminiscence may be encouraged within groups of the elderly as a means to more rewarding extragroup social interaction. The process of reminiscence, which may either be spontaneous or purposive, consists of looking back over one's life, recalling people and events, thoughts, and feelings of personal significance (Havighurst & Glasser, 1972).

(15) Merriam (1989), after an analysis of reminiscence, concluded that there seem to be four basic components involved in the structure of reminiscence. These include "selection" of a topical stimulus; "immersion," in which the reminiscers fully immerse themselves in the remembered event or stimulus; "withdrawal" characterized by distancing oneself from the memory with more reflection upon the event; and finally, "closure" to the memory with some summing up of the experience. The authors' impressions from the current group experience lend support to Merriam's conceptualization of the structure of the reminiscence process. In addition, while reminiscence may be instrumental in the resolution of unresolved conflicts and the reintegration of the personality, it may also help establish common bonds and contribute to the development of trust and intimacy among group members. This was substantiated by this group experience with the very old. For example, the increase in both the number of verbalizations and the level of self-disclosure during group sessions indicate an increase in the trust and security experienced by the members. Additionally, the supportive feedback provided by group members for one another contributed not only to discussion, but also perhaps to resolution of prior conflict.

Therapeutic Process

(16) Originally, there were 12 weekly 75-minute group sessions planned. At times, depending upon the energy level of the members and with agreement of the members and facilitator, the sessions were shortened to 50 minutes. Expectations were set by the facilitator

during the intake sessions and again during the first group session. Group process and confidentiality were presented and discussed.

(17) At the beginning of each session, as the first step, the group facilitator attempted to model a "climate of acceptance," openness, and support through the use of warm greetings and positive comments to each group member. During the second step, "the bridge to reality," topics for discussion were chosen by group members in order that they might feel more involved in the planning of the session and share in the responsibility for the group's progress. Members were encouraged to bring an article, poem, or object from their rooms to share. The use of these concrete objects seemed to facilitate spontaneous verbalizations, social interaction, and reminiscence in the group.

(18) In the third step, "sharing the world we live in," the expression of past and present thoughts and feelings pertaining to the topic was encouraged and reinforced. During the fourth step, "appreciation of the work of the world," attempts were made to link the present topic to past occupations, hobbies, and interests through the use of reminiscence. In this way, the group members could relate current topics to their past in order to rediscover and reconfirm their own sense of identity in their present environment (Toepfer et al., 1974). In the final step, in which a "climate of appreciation" is fostered, a general enjoyment of the group effort was expressed by the group leader and group members as well. It was not uncommon for each of the members to comment at the end of the session about what a "good meeting" they thought we had and how much they enjoyed it and looked forward to the next session. As Moran and Gatz (1987) found, nursing home residents, regardless of the type of group modality involved in, like the group experience as evidenced in one way by a fairly low attrition rate.

Group Development
(19) The first group session included both an introduction of group members and structure of the group experience, including an explanation of the roles of group members and the function of the group leader. Also, the leader presented possible goals for the group. As was expected, there was little interaction among group members at this point. Because of the progressive social withdrawal that had been observed in these ladies and the novelty of the situation, group members were reluctant to speak and when they did, spoke only to the leader. It must also be noted that elderly people in this age range may not be accustomed to discussing their thoughts and feelings in a group situation.

(20) In the second session, there was more talking by the group members, although they continued to speak to one another through the group leader. At this time the decision was made to have each member bring in something tangible that was of significance to her as well as topic related. As previously stated, this resulted in more spontaneous verbalizations, an increase in group member interaction, and a decreased need to speak through the leader. As it was less threatening to speak about an object or article, members more readily could expand what they were saying to incorporate reflections on their past. Group members could then review and reaffirm past experiences that reinforced positive self-esteem and a sense of identity within the group.

(21) As the group sessions progressed over the next several weeks, the quality of the interaction continued to improve. Topics of discussion, chosen by the group members themselves, included Thanksgiving, Christmas, faith, patience, trees and other gifts from God. After the sharing of experiences and feelings by each group member, all members were encouraged to provide feedback about what was shared. This exercise facilitated group interaction, as similarities and differences were identified and explored. Each member became increasingly attentive to and supportive of other members. The sharing and cohesion experienced in the group became an effective method in terms of reducing feelings of alienation and isolation and increasing feelings of belonging among group members.

Group Member Development
(22) Jane initially focused on her arthritic condition and her severe hearing impairment allowed her to "tune out' what other group members were saying. This resulted in the need for much repetition and clarification on the part of the group members. After the first few session, however, Jane brought in an old photograph of her parents and was able to reminisce about her childhood in terms of both positive and negative life events. The supportive feedback she received from other group members proved to be a rewarding experience for her.

(23) During this period, Jane began to take more pride in her personal appearance as she wore her wig, make-up, and a clean dress instead of the hospital-style gown provided by the facility. Her sense of self-esteem increased as other group members took notice of this change and complimented her. As a result, Jane's depression began to lift and her negative ideation

decreased substantially as she increasingly made attempts to listen and interact with the group. She even began to speak of getting a hearing aid and went on to discuss this with her niece.

(24) Unfortunately, the gains Jane made were only temporary. Her dizziness became incapacitating and her arthritic condition worsened. Shortly thereafter, she fell and broke her ankle. At this point she refused to return to the group sessions despite attempts made by the group leader and other group members to persuade her to return. She again became depressed and withdrawn, lending support to Quinn's study (cited in Troll, 1986) and those of others, which found that health is a major contributor to psychological well-being in old age. Without therapeutic intervention, it is predicted that Jane will never be able to accept her late-life losses and her depression and withdrawal will only continue to worsen.

(25) Helen began the group experience feeling anxious and insecure. She initially resisted by stating she didn't feel this group experience was for her as she did not talk about or "live in the past" as she felt many other residents did. She interacted very little with other group members during the first few sessions. Then, at the group meeting before Thanksgiving, she recited a lovely original presentation about the origin of the Thanksgiving holiday to which all group members attentively listened. Through her story, Helen was able to discuss many of her feelings and values. The positive reinforcement she received from the group no doubt increased her self-esteem and sense of purpose.

(26) By selecting topic-related poetry or other written works that reflected her life philosophy, Helen was able to share her thoughts and feelings in a way that did not arouse uneasiness or anxiety for her. Group members were very supportive and Helen took pride in putting together her presentations for the weekly meetings. As a result, she came to interact more freely and spontaneously with other group members and eventually felt comfortable in joining hands at the close of the group session.

(27) Nelda, although quiet and somewhat anxious, appeared to enjoy the group experience from the beginning. Despite problems in childhood, she could always find something positive that came from her experiences. At the same time, she was positive and supportive of the experiences other group members chose to share.

(28) With little family contact, Nelda was quick to form friendships within the group. At the close of each session, she would help escort group members confined to wheelchairs back to their rooms. This seemed to make her feel needed and boosted her sense of self-worth and independence. Although she was sometimes reluctant to deal with her feelings, the group experience proved to be a positive one for Nelda, particularly in terms of resocialization.

(29) Although Carrie had not been eager to join in the social activities at the nursing home, she enjoyed the discussion and interaction of the group from the beginning. While activities and programs by facility volunteers provided entertainment, the group experience provided Carrie with the opportunity to share ideas and feelings and interact on a personal level with her peers.

(30) Through the course of group discussions, it became apparent that Carrie had a special love for children, although she had none of her own. She shared a photograph of the grandchildren of a lady with whom she had rented a room. She was also interested in the status and activities of other group members' children and grandchildren. Research has indicated that childless widows may often be more lonely and dissatisfied with their lives. In addition, it appears that to be physically incapacitated, as Carrie was, and at the same time widowed and childless contributes even more significantly to a poor quality of life (Beckman & Houser, 1982).

(31) Carrie, however, seems to have compensated for these factors rather well. Despite her paralysis and absence of children, she has been resourceful in finding other outlets and activities for her attention and affections. She expressed a genuine interest in all group members and was able to form friendships that endured outside the group experience. For example, she and another group member began to exchange and discuss different books. She was also supportive and helpful outside the group sessions to one member experiencing considerable illness and depression. Overall, the group sessions proved to be a positive and rewarding experience for Carrie.

(32) Initially, Lucy was very withdrawn and her verbalizations indicated depression, low self-esteem and often mental confusion as well. Never married and childless, she appeared to have very few family contacts or social network of any kind. Although her responses

were inappropriate and out of context at first, she increasingly became more attentive to what other group members were saying.

(33) As group cohesiveness developed, Lucy began to feel more and more a part of the group. For example, on one occasion upon entering the room where other group members had already assembled, she very forcefully shouted, "Hail! Hail! the gang's all here!" Lucy's self-image also seemed to improve as she attempted to identify with other members of the group. For example, her physical posture improved as others in the group encouraged her to "sit up straight" and stop bowing her head all the time. On one particular occasion, Rachel confronted her by saying, "Lucy, I like you, but it's not good for you to sit slumped over all the time. Sit up straight when you talk so we can see you!" Lucy replied, "Yes, I know, but a lot of times around here you forget yourself." Her reply was easy to understand when looking around the dining and social areas of each floor. With so many residents in wheelchairs lined up in front of the television, together yet all alone, it may be easy to lose one's sense of individuality with no interpersonal interaction to confirm it.

(34) Because of Lucy's visual disability and confinement to a wheelchair, it remained difficult for her to initiate contact with other residents outside the group. With the lapse of time between group sessions, the social gains Lucy was making in the group were partly diminished between meetings.

(35) A fairly new resident at the nursing home, Rachel seemed to prefer remaining in her room alone rather than participating in the social activities provided by the facility. With very frequent family contact, she at first didn't seem to feel the need for any other type of relationship. Nevertheless, as she began to share her values and religious beliefs as well as receive feedback from group members, she quickly came to view the group experience as a positive and fulfilling one. As group cohesiveness became stronger, she was able to discuss her thoughts and feelings easily. At the same time, she was attentive to and expressed genuine concern for the needs and feelings of other group members. Rachel came to look forward more and more to the group meetings where she could interact and identify with others in her age group. Even more importantly, her increased desire for meaningful social interaction transferred to outside the group situations as she began to participate in and enjoy many other activities at the home.

Implications

(36) Conclusions drawn by the authors from this group counseling experience with the very old seem to be consistent with the findings of Moss (1976), who suggested that because of its interpersonal-interactive nature, group counseling may indeed be the most beneficial therapeutic modality for the elderly. As Rattenbury and Stones (1989) revealed in their recent study, both reminiscence and current topics group discussion interventions were associated with significant gains in psychological well-being, with the amount of group participation affecting the benefit obtained. Anxiety, low self-esteem and somatic complaints are frequently responses to the losses and stresses of a lifetime. Myers (1990) suggested that, while people live most of their adult years with a highly internal locus of control, they come to experience an increasingly external locus of control when faced with the events and losses of later life over which they have no control. Physical disabilities and sensory impairments often contribute to the social isolation experienced by the very old.

(37) As elderly individuals increasingly focus on the negative aspects of their physical and emotional status, there may occur at the same time a decrease in their attention to external stimuli. This decrease in attention to external stimuli may be yet another source of withdrawal behaviors in the elderly. The findings of Bitzan and Kruzich (1990) suggest the need for caregivers to ensure nursing home residents an optimal level of functioning in terms of ambulation and hearing. Participation in counseling groups provide an opportunity for wheelchair-bound and hearing-impaired residents to interact with a variety of persons, thereby providing additional sources of external stimulation that may help in reducing their tendency to withdraw.

(38) Group progress was often slowed because of the sensory impairment on the part of some members and their tendency to isolate and avoid social interaction with other residents. The soft voices of some group members, their sometimes confused verbalizations, and the effects of hearing loss make attentive listening on the part of the facilitator and members essential. It is important that the leader function both as a teacher and a role model in setting the stage for member interaction. The expression of warmth, genuine caring, and concern are particularly important elements for success in group counseling with individuals in this age range. In addition, in light of the often severe sensory impairments of the members, patience on the part of the leader

and group members is a must.

(39) The use of touch was found to be one of the most effective forms of positive reinforcement in the current group situation. A pat on the hand or a quick hug seemed both to delight members and increase their feelings of belonging. In addition, it was observed that they increasingly took pleasure in the joining of hands as one of the group members offered a prayer at the closing of each session.

(40) Despite improvements made in the area of socialization and the apparent increase in individual morale, it is believed that the formation of other similar group activities within the nursing home is important in order to support and sustain the gains made in remotivation groups (Bowers, Anderson, Blomier, & Pely, 1967). While this particular nursing home had both a recreation therapist and social services director, as well as a number of committed volunteers, it was observed that many group activities planned allowed individuals to be only "passive participants." In other words, there were few activities in which direct interpersonal interaction was fostered. While residents were with a group when playing bingo or watching a musical show, there was little or no actual communication or interaction between group members.

(41) The authors found that group counseling with the elderly can often be frustrating in the face of multiple sensory impairments and tiring in terms of the effort involved to assemble the group. This is especially true when the majority are confined to wheelchairs and need assistance. Nevertheless, from the viewpoint of the authors, the reward of helping these very old social isolates to become more fully functioning individuals in their social environment more than makes up for any problems or inconveniences encountered in dealing with this age group. The members of this group of the very old seemed to have had a wealth of life experiences, wisdom, and insight to share. The group counseling experience provided an excellent medium through which the members rediscovered ways of relating and interacting that restored enjoyment and satisfaction to later life.

References

Abraham, K. (1949). The applicability of psychoanalytic treatment to patients at an advanced age. In K. Abraham, *Selected papers on psychoanalysis*. London: Hogarth Press.

Aizenberg, R., & Treas, J. (1985). The family in late life: Psychosocial and demographic considerations. In J. E. Birren & K. W. Schaire (Eds.), *Handbook of the psychology of aging* (pp. 169-183). New York: Van Nostrand Reinhold.

Beckman, L. J., & Houser, B. B. (1982). The consequences of childlessness on the social-psychological well-being of older women. *Journal of Gerontology, 37*(2), 243-250.

Berland, D. I., & Poggi, R. (1979). Expressive group psychotherapy with the aging. *International Journal of Group Psychotherapy, 29*, 87-107.

Bitzan, J. E., & Kruzich, J. M. (1990). Interpersonal relationships of nursing home residents. *The Gerontologist, 30*(3), 385-390.

Bowers, M. B., Anderson, G. K., Blomier, E. C., & Pely, K. (1967). Brain syndrome and behavior in geriatric remotivation groups. *Journal of Gerontology, 22*, 348-352.

Burnside, I. (1984). *Working with the elderly: Group process and techniques* (2nd ed.). Monterey, CA: Wadsworth Health Sciences.

Corey, M. S., & Corey, G. (1987). *Groups: Process and practice*. Monterey, CA: Brooks/Cole.

Freud, S. (1905). On psychotherapy. *The Complete Works of S. Freud* (Standard Edition, Vol. 7, 257-270).

Havighurst, R. J., & Glasser, R. (1972). An exploratory study of reminiscence. *Journal of Gerontology, 27*, 245-253.

Ingersoll, B., & Silverman, A. (1978). Comparative group psychotherapy for the aged. *The Gerontologist, 18*(2), 201-206.

Lewis, M. I., & Butler, R. N. (1974). Life-review therapy: Putting memories to work in individual and group psychotherapy. *Geriatrics, 29*, 165-173.

Merriam, S. B. (1989). The structure of simple reminiscence. *The Gerontologist 29*(6), 761-767.

Moran, J., & Gatz, M. (1987). Group therapies for nursing home adults: An evaluation of two treatment approaches. *The Gerontologist, 27*, 588-591.

Moss, E. P. (1976). A study of the relationship between group counseling, social activities, and aspects of life adjustment of older, sheltered workshop clients (Doctoral dissertation, New York University, 1975). *Dissertation Abstracts International, 36*, 2653.

Myers, J. E. (1990). Aging: An overview for mental health counselors. *Journal of Mental Health Counseling, 12*(3), 245-259.

Poulton, J. L., & Strassberg, D. S. (1986). The therapeutic use of reminiscence. *International Journal of Group Psychotherapy, 36*, 381-398.

Rattenbury, C., & Stones, M. J. (1989). A controlled evaluation of reminiscence and current topics discussion groups in a nursing home context. *The Gerontologist, 29*(6), 768-771.

Toepfer, C. T., Bicknell, A. T., & Shaw, D. O. (1974). Remotivation as behavior therapy. *The Gerontologist, 14*(5), 451-453.

Troll, L. E. (Ed.) (1986). *Family issues in current gerontology*. New York: Springer.

U.S. Bureau of the Census. (1981). *1980 census of population supplementary reports* (PC 80-S1-1). Washington, DC: Government Printing Office.

Waters, E. B. (1990). The life review: Strategies for working with individuals and groups. *Journal of Mental Health Counseling, 12*(3), 270-278.

Terms for Discussion

1. remotivation therapy (paragraphs 1, 12, and 13)

2. reminiscence therapy (paragraphs 1, 3, 12, 14, 15, 36, and 40)

3. current topics group discussion (paragraphs 3, 18, and 36)

4. self-esteem (paragraphs 20, 23, 32, and 36)

5. depression (paragraphs 23, 24, and 32)

6. anxiety (paragraphs 25, 26, 27, and 36)

7. internal locus of control (paragraph 36)

8. external locus of control (paragraph 36)

Questions

9. The clients were selected on the basis of their tendency to isolate themselves and avoid social interaction. (See paragraph 4.) Are there advantages to having a group in which all members have a common problem? Disadvantages?

10. Based on the information in paragraphs 6 through 11, which client seems least likely to benefit from the group therapy experience? Which one seems most likely? Explain.

11. What is your opinion on the authors' decision to deviate from the standard remotivation format? (See paragraph 13.)

12. In paragraphs 22 through 35, the authors describe the development of individual members of the group. Given that there were six members and that journal articles tend to be relatively short, have the authors provided adequate descriptions? Are there any clients on whom you would want more information?

13. Have the authors convinced you of the value of group therapy for the elderly who tend to isolate themselves? Explain.

14. In your opinion, is it, in general, probably easier to write a case report on group therapy or a case report on individual therapy? Explain.

15. Are there other types of treatment that might have facilitated the development of the group or the improvement of individal group members? Explain.

16. Rate the article on the seven criteria described in the introduction to this book on a scale from 5 (highest quality) through 1 (lowest quality). Be prepared to explain your ratings.

Criterion 1: The demographics of the case are described: _____

Criterion 2: The condition(s) and behavior(s) that necessitated treatment are described in detail: _____

Criterion 3: The method of treatment is described in sufficient detail so that it can be replicated without additional information: _____

Criterion 4: A rationale is provided for the method of treatment selected: _____

Criterion 5: The client's improvement, if any, is clearly documented: _____

Criterion 6: Follow-up information on the client's improvement, if any, is presented: _____

Criterion 7: The study is appropriate for publication in a journal: _____

Notes:

Case 17

Group and Individual Reactions to the Death of a Member of a University-Affiliated Women's Support Group*

Cynthia A. Griffin
Veterans Administration Medical Center, Martinez, California

Charles H. Gregg
The University of Utah, Salt Lake City

Jeanne M. Lee
Community Nursing Service Hospice, Salt Lake City

ABSTRACT: This article describes how a university-affiliated women's support group coped with the serious illness and subsequent death of one of its members. Both individual and group reactions are noted. The article also explores the normal grieving process, pathological grief reactions, and the relationship of death to group termination.

(1) In group therapy the process of termination often invokes a variety of feelings among group members, ranging from sadness and loss on the one hand to optimism and hope on the other (Corey & Corey, 1987). During the termination phase it is expected that group members will have the opportunity to review the group experience, resolve their feelings of separation, and be able to consolidate the therapeutic gains they have achieved. As a general rule, group therapists are expected to spend the last several meetings helping clients to sort out any unfinished business, identifying strategies to maintain new learning and behaviors, and resolve feelings about having the group experience come to an end. If handled effectively, the termination phase of group therapy should truly be a time when clients are able to transfer the personal gains they have made in therapy back into their everyday lives.

(2) Termination is, indeed, a normal and necessary part of virtually every group therapy process. When termination occurs as the result of the serious illness or death of one of the group's members, however, dynamics surrounding the whole group's termination change considerably. Few authors have written extensively on this topic, but Yalom (1980) has described "the wisdom and power of the dying" (p. 176) and noted that the interaction between patients facing death and other individuals in therapy can be a moving and powerful experience for all involved. Death is one of the great existential dilemmas and can set off robust emotions. Therapists and clients alike are compelled to examine their own feelings and reactions when one of their number is stricken with a terminal illness. The purpose of this article is to look at the relationship of the death of one member of a counseling group to the termination process of the entire group.

(3) Kubler-Ross (1975) has contributed extensively to the literature on death and dying with her stages of loss characterized by denial, anger, bargaining, depression, and acceptance. Other conceptualizations exist, however,

---

*Reprinted from *The Journal for Specialists in Group Work*, 16, 1991, pp. 230-235. Copyright by ACA. Reprinted with permission. No further reproduction authorized without written permission of the American Counseling Association.

that may prove just as useful for therapists who are faced with the dilemma of guiding a therapy group through the death of one of its members. Worden (1982), for example, identified specific tasks of mourning that need to be accomplished during the bereavement process. These tasks include: (a) accepting the reality of the loss, (b) experiencing the pain of grief, (c) adjusting to an environment that no longer includes the deceased, (d) developing new coping strategies, and (e) investing in new relationships.

(4) The process of bereavement that surrounds the death of a loved one can be an extremely difficult and taxing time for all concerned. The professional literature is increasingly making note of the potential benefits of counseling during this time of increased stress (Bowlby, 1980; Parkes, 1987). Several excellent resources have become available in recent years to assist the therapist who is actively involved in working with clients who are grieving (James, 1986; Rando, 1984). Moreover, it has been found that group therapy format, with the opportunity it affords for the sharing of mutual concerns and feelings, is an especially effective means of conducting grief counseling (Lehman, Ellard, & Wortman, 1986). Indeed, bereavement programs using a group therapy format have become increasingly more commonplace.

(5) The threat of severe personal loss is not, however, merely the province of those group therapists who choose to work with terminally ill patients and members of their immediate families. Serious illness and death, being part of the human condition, might occur at any time that one is working with groups and can have a profound impact on group members and therapists alike.

The Bereavement Process In Group Therapy

(6) As noted by Lewis (1983), the reactions that occur subsequent to the death of a loved one, such as anger, sorrow, and tears, have a homeostatic purpose in that they help to return the griever to a more normal state of functioning. In the case described in this section, the death of a member of a therapy group elicited many of these feelings; it also presented the group's other members and its two therapists with a profound challenge.

(7) The group was a university-affiliated women's support group consisting of seven members ranging in age from 31 to 63 years, and two therapists. The group had been meeting for approximately 1½ years. Originally introduced to each other via mutual membership in a life- and career-planning class, the group members elected to continue meeting after the class had ended for purposes of ongoing growth and support. Membership changed somewhat during the first 6 months of the group's existence, but then remained stable. The initial group therapist, a clinical social worker, had been one of the teachers in the original class. The senior author, Cynthia Griffin, joined the group as a cotherapist just after the onset of one member's illness. The process of bereavement experienced by the group and its members seemed to occur in stages that roughly approximated the views of Kubler-Ross (1975) and Worden (1982).

Initial Onset of Illness

(8) Approximately 6 months prior to the entry of the cotherapists, one of the group members, Annie (not her real name), was diagnosed as having cancer. Although Annie informed the other group members of her diagnosis, she chose to minimize the severity of the illness in subsequent group sessions, and she implied that her prognosis was favorable with proper treatment. For the next 6 months she continued to live a relatively active life, placing minimal emphasis on her declining health, both in group sessions and in her personal life.

(9) At about the same time that the cotherapist entered the group as part of her graduate school training experience, Annie's health began to rapidly deteriorate. She soon stopped attending the group sessions because of her illness, and she made a simultaneous decision to stop chemotherapy. Annie continued, however, to have regular telephone contact with the group's two therapists, who kept the group updated about her condition.

(10) Over the next 10-week period (the organizational unit around which the group had been meeting), events in the developmental life of the group were both noteworthy and diverse. When the group was first informed of Annie's rapid decline, several members attempted to find ways of continuing to include her in the meetings, denying her deterioration. Members discussed the possibility of setting up a schedule for each of them to bring Annie to and from future group meetings, assuming that she was physically able to attend. They also discussed the option of holding groups sessions at Annie's house. Annie's response was to decline the offer of transportation, and she requested that meetings not be held at her home, because she was too ill for this to occur.

Recognition of the Inevitability of Death

(11) With the direct intervention and confrontation of the therapists, who spent considerable time processing the overall reactions of the group, the group as a whole began to focus on issues pertaining to death, especially their apprehensions about seeing Annie deteriorate. Several members discussed their wishes for their own funerals. The latter topic was kept on a superficial and less threatening level, however, when one member remarked

that she would "want things to start off with the *William Tell* Overture and end up with 'Toot, Toot, Tootsie Goodbye'."

(12) In later meetings, group member reactions to the news of Annie's continuing physical decline remained divergent. Several members (and both of the therapists) maintained phone contact with Annie and kept the group informed of her condition. Personal visits by individual group members were also possible when Annie felt well enough. Annie's decision against both chemotherapy and radiation treatment was also discussed in the group, as was the fact that she was experiencing considerable pain.

Denial of Personal Loss
(13) One member suggested that "since the group means so much to Annie, perhaps we could tape the sessions and send them to her." The therapists viewed this suggestion as both a genuine effort to include Annie in the group as well as a denial of her separation from the group and a possible way of avoiding overt expression of serious concerns surrounding the illness. Group members, for example, might be tempted to censor their own remarks for fear of raising painful issues for Annie and the others to hear. Indeed, one woman explicitly stated that "maybe we should focus on the positive rather than negative," in terms of denying the pain surrounding Annie's illness.

(14) At this point, one of the therapists observed to the group that the members might be second-guessing Annie's frame of mind, that she might actually be more comfortable with the idea of her coming death than were the other members of the group. Although reluctant to discuss this topic directly, several group members responded by focusing on the need to "cherish the moment," and the need to value the quality, rather than the quantity of time that Annie had remaining.

(15) In the following weeks, group members were noticeably divided regarding their willingness to discuss the topic of Annie's coming death. In a phone conversation, Annie admitted to one of the therapists that she had become too weak to leave her bed, that she now required constant care, and that she probably had only a few more weeks to live. After some in-depth discussion between therapists surrounding their own levels of denial regarding the coming death, they made the joint decision (per Annie's wishes) to give the group explicit information regarding Annie's medical status and her impending death.

Responses to Grief
(16) This information was conveyed to the group at the following meeting. The members, in turn, reacted with expressions of considerable grief and loss. Themes that came up in subsequent meetings included a search for additional resources during a time of need. Several group members, for example, brought in inspirational readings for the group to share. In addition, the group was in conflict over individual members' willingness to discuss Annie's condition. Some of the women wished to focus considerable attention on Annie and her current situation, whereas others wanted to avoid the topic of death entirely and move on to other themes. This conflict became even more apparent when various group members reported their interest in having the group maintain close contact with Annie through visits, phone calls, cards, and letters. Others, in turn, began missing sessions and avoided all contact with Annie.

Increased Coping Strategies
(17) Coping strategies that group members adopted included elements such as anger ("Why didn't she tell us sooner about how sick she was!"), increased pursuit of inspirational readings, and further expressions of a desire to "live in the present," with a greater sense of purpose and meaning. Finally, the issue of "where do we go from here?" was addressed, suggesting the need for some members to acknowledge that life does, indeed, go on.

(18) Annie died 6 weeks after terminating her attendance in the group. The therapists informed the members of the group of her death and of the funeral plans. Both of the therapists and all but one of the members were in attendance at the funeral. Individual group members' feelings toward Annie were incorporated into the service via the reading of a poignant letter that one of the women had written to Annie 2 days before she died. In addition, the original group therapist was asked to speak at the service, and did so on behalf of all of the group members.

(19) Group sessions following the funeral vacillated between remembrances of Annie and affirmation that life would go on for the others in the group. An additional topic of discussion was the fact that Annie had donated a sum of money to the agency that sponsored the group. The agency, in turn, had designated that a portion of the money be turned over to the group. Thus, group members were faced with the task of deciding how the money should be spent.

Investment in New Activities
(20) After some discussion of their options, the members elected to hold a picnic at the end of the academic year in honor of Annie's memory. The timing of the picnic corresponded with the actual termination of the group

for the summer—a pattern that had also occurred during the previous year. This time, however, the group had no plans to resume its meetings in the fall. The picnic became symbolic of both a good-bye to Annie and a farewell to the formal structure of the group, because the original group therapist would be moving out of state and the cotherapist would be finishing her training experience. Group members talked openly about their sadness that the group was ending and their own individual plans for the future.

Normal Grieving Versus Pathological Grief Reactions
(21) The normal grieving process may last a few days, weeks, or months (Gregg, Robertus, & Stone, 1989). If the process is successfully completed, individuals should emerge ready to move on with their lives. Group therapists who find themselves faced with the terminal illness or death of a group member must prepared to assist the grieving process with the remaining members of their group. Rando (1984) offered a number of suggestions for therapists to employ when working with clients who are actively grieving. These suggestions include the following:

1. Be present emotionally as well as physically to provide security and support.
2. Do not allow grievers to become socially isolated.
3. Make certain that grievers have appropriate medical evaluation and treatment available if symptoms warrant.
4. Encourage the verbalization of feelings and recollections of the deceased.
5. Help grievers to identify any unfinished business with the deceased and look for appropriate ways to assist closure.
6. Help grievers to find a variety of new sources of personal satisfaction following the loss.
7. Encourage grievers to be patient and not set unrealistic expectations for themselves.
8. Help grievers to recognize that loss always brings about change and the need for new adjustments.
9. Assist grievers in getting and maintaining a proper perspective on what the resolution of grief will mean.
10. Encourage grievers, at the appropriate time, to find rewarding new things to do and people to invest in.

(22) In some cases, however, the process of mourning is not brought to a satisfactory conclusion, and the therapists are faced with a client or clients who are caught up in a pathological grief reaction. As noted by Bailey and Gregg (1986), pathological grief may be the result of any number of factors including an overdependence on the deceased, ambivalent feelings about the finality of death, a blocking of affect and a refusal to mourn, or an inability to depersonalize the loss.

(23) Group therapists need to be able to differentiate between normal and pathological grieving. Worden (1982) identified a number of signs to look for when therapists suspect the presence of an abnormal grief reaction These signs might often include the following: (a) the client is unable to talk about the deceased without experiencing intense renewed grief; (b) themes of sadness and loss continue to surface during subsequent group sessions; (c) behaviors and mannerisms manifested by the client imitate those of the deceased; (d) the client shows a history of depression; (e) self-destructive behaviors are present; (f) the client manifests physical symptoms like those experienced by the deceased; (g) the client manifests a phobia toward illness or death; and (h) the client avoids visiting the grave.

(24) Group therapists need to become aware of these manifestations of pathological grief, be able to recognize them, and make appropriate referral where necessary. In most cases, if circumstances warrant, a list of professionals who specialize in grief therapy can be obtained through local area hospice organizations.

Conclusion
(25) It might be said that the death of a member of a therapy group can be thought of as an exceptional form of termination. Group members need to be encouraged to express sadness over the loss of a cherished member and to bring closure to this valued relationship. Group members also need to be allowed to react to grief in their individual ways without criticism, ostracism, or attempts to change them from other members. In the situation described, one member did temporarily terminate her group participation. At the same time, however, group members must be helped to reaffirm the continuity of their own lives and be encouraged to express a willingness to move ahead and invest in new relationships. Therapists must be on the alert for pathological grief reactions among group members, and be ready to provide appropriate services as needed.

References
Bailey, B. J., & Gregg, C. H. (1986). Grief, pathological grief, and rehabilitation counseling. *Journal of Applied Rehabilitation Counseling, 17*(4), 19-23.

Bowlby, J. (1980). *Attachment and loss* (Vol. III). New York: Basic Books.

Corey, M. S., & Corey, G. (1987). *Groups: Process and practice.* Monterey, CA: Brooks/Cole.

Gregg, C. H., Robertus, J. L., & Stone, J. B. (1989). *The psychological aspects of chronic illness.* Springfield, IL: Thomas.

James, J. W. (1986). *The grief recovery handbook.* Beverly Hills, CA: Grief Recovery Institute.

Kubler-Ross, E. (1975). *Death: The final stage of growth.* Englewood Cliffs, NJ: Prentice-Hall.

Lehman, D. R., Ellard, J. H., & Wortman, C. B. (1986). Social support for the bereaved: Recipients and providers perspective on what is helpful. *Journal of Consulting and Clinical Psychology, 54,* 436-438.

Lewis, K. (1983). Grief in chronic illness and disability. *Journal of Rehabilitation, 49,* 8-11.

Parkes, C. M. (1987). Models of bereavement care. *Death Studies, 11,* 257-261.

Rando, T. A. (1984). *Grief, dying, and death: Clinical interventions for caregivers.* Champaign, IL: Research Press.

Worden, J. W. (1982). *Grief counseling and grief therapy.* New York: Springer.

Yalom, I. (1980). *Existential psychotherapy.* New York: Basic Books.

Terms for Discussion

1. group therapy (throughout article)

2. existential dilemma (paragraph 2)

3. denial (paragraphs 3, 13, and 15)

4. anger (paragraphs 3 and 17)

5. bargaining (paragraph 3)

6. depression (paragraphs 3 and 23)

7. acceptance (paragraph 3)

8. pathological grief reaction (paragraphs 22, 23, 24, and 25)

9. phobia (paragraph 23)

Questions

10. Lehman, Ellard, and Wortman suggest that group therapy is an especially effective format for conducting grief counseling. (See paragraph 4.) Do you agree? Why? Why not?

11. What is your opinion on the therapists' views described in paragraph 13?

12. If you were the therapist, how would you handle the situation in which some of the women wanted to focus on Annie while others wanted to avoid the topic? (See paragraph 16.)

13. Comment on the ten suggestions in paragraph 21. Are some more important than others? Are there additional things that might be done?

14. Have you ever observed other possible warning signs of pathological grief reactions other than those listed in paragraph 23. If yes, explain.

15. Are there other types of treatment that might have facilitated the clients' coping with the death of Annie? Explain.

16. Rate the article on the seven criteria described in the introduction to this book on a scale from 5 (highest quality) through 1 (lowest quality). Be prepared to explain your ratings.

Criterion 1: The demographics of the case are described: _____

Criterion 2: The condition(s) and behavior(s) that necessitated treatment are described in detail: _____

Criterion 3: The method of treatment is described in sufficient detail so that it can be replicated without additional information: _____

Criterion 4: A rationale is provided for the method of treatment selected: _____

Criterion 5: The client's improvement, if any, is clearly documented: _____

Criterion 6: Follow-up information on the client's improvement, if any, is presented: _____

Criterion 7: The study is appropriate for publication in a journal: _____

Case 18

Multiple Severe Sexual Dysfunctions Resolved in Brief Sex Therapy*

Philip Garippa
Clinical Social Worker and Sex Therapist in Private Practice

SUMMARY: The following case illustrates the use of integrative sex therapy techniques in treating a couple with numerous sexual dysfunctions. The integrative method enables the therapist to address sexual difficulties in both partners simultaneously and significantly reduce the time of treatment.

(1) This sex therapy approach, developed by Kaplan (1974, 1987), incorporates psychodynamic, cognitive, behavioral, and when necessary, psychopharmacological formulations in the treatment of sexual disorders. Psychodynamics are used to guide cognitive and behavioral interventions when encountering resistance and anxiety. The method encourages the therapist to bypass resistance whenever possible to promote effective treatment. When bypassing is unsuccessful, a psychodynamic mode is implemented to ameliorate the therapeutic impasse.

Evaluation
(2) Mr. and Mrs. B were 48 and 45 years old, respectively. They had been married 17 years and had two children. The couple was referred by their marital therapist, who had been effective in improving their relationship, but they remained sexually incapacitated.

(3) Each partner presented complaints of inhibited sexual desire (Kaplan, 1979). They had not engaged in any sexual experiences together for the past four years. Neither felt interested in sex, either experientially or psychically. Mrs. B never masturbated, and Mr. B stopped doing so during these years.

(4) Mrs. B had primary anorgasmia and also suffered from a sexual phobia to genital stimulation with an underlying panic disorder (Kaplan, 1987). Mr. B had an erectile dysfunction and primary premature ejaculation, especially during intercourse.

(5) These problems began about four years ago, when Mr. B experienced erectile difficulties during intercourse. (Previously, they would have intercourse about once or twice a week with minimal foreplay, and he would ejaculate quickly.) His initial erectile problem was precipitated by excessive alcohol intake. He then began to obsess about his erection, which served to worsen his condition, until he consistently lost the erection just prior to or upon vaginal penetration. Mrs. B could never tolerate genital stimulation (she would have a panic attack) and therefore only engaged in intercourse. Since Mr. B could no longer maintain his erection for intercourse, they began to avoid sex until it became nonexistent in their lives.

(6) Mrs. B was a warm, caring, and giving woman. She was also very sensitive to criticism and rejection and became upset quite easily. She displayed nonassertive and compliant behavior. Mr. B was quite dedicated to his family. He had an obsessive-compulsive personality style, was easily angered, and demanded perfection. They loved one another intensely, although there were significant power struggles in the marriage. Mr. and Mrs. B were eager to enter sex therapy, and I began seeing the couple on a weekly basis in conjoint sessions.

Treatment
(7) Given the information revealed in the evaluation, I began with the hypothesis that the couple's inhibited

---

*Reprinted with permission from *Journal of Sex & Marital Therapy, 17,* 1991, pp. 220-223. Copyright 1991 by Brunner/Mazel, Inc.

sexual desire was secondary to the panic disorder, phobia, anorgasmia, erectile dysfunction, and premature ejaculation.

(8) I gave an exploratory sensate focus (Masters, 1970) exercise without genital stimulation, which went quite well. However, Mrs. B experienced a full blown panic attack when mild genital stimulation was included. This event, coupled with her frequent spontaneous panic attacks (Klein, 1980) (Mrs. B had been in individual therapy on two previous occasions to address her panic attacks, but they remained with frequency), was the first issued addressed along with treatment for Mr. B's erectile dysfunction.

(9) Mrs. B was referred for antipanic medication (Kaplan, 1987, Klein, 1980). She was fearful of medication and her dosage was gradually titrated to Imipramine 25 mg., q.i.d. and Alprozolam .25 mg., t.i.d.

(10) During the time her medication was being regulated, I instructed Mr. B to masturbate (Zilbergeld, 1978) while watching an X-rated film. The film was used to enable him to focus on erotic thoughts that bypassed his obsessive spectatoring of his erection. Mr. B was able to have consistently firm erections (as well as morning erection) and ejaculated in one to two minutes. This information eradicated the need for an organic workup (Kaplan, 1983).

(11) About two months after beginning her medication, Mrs. B's panics subsided, and Mr. B was feeling confident about his erections. The couple was reintroduced to the sensate focus exercises with very gradual genital stimulation. Mrs. B was able to focus on herself (Barbach, 1975), and tolerate ever increasing clitoral stimulation. Within a month, she had her first orgasm. She continued to have orgasms throughout treatment. Mrs. B remained on her medication and was thrilled to have her panic attacks under control.

(12) While the above process was occurring, I was instructing Mr. B in the masturbatory stop-start (Kaplan, 1974, 1989) technique used for premature ejaculation. He did well and within the same time frame was able to last 10 minutes before ejaculation.

(13) Mrs. B then began stimulating Mr. B—first manually and then orally—using the stop-start technique. He would, in turn, stimulate her to orgasm, manually and orally. They were having sexual interactions two or three times a week, and their inhibited sexual desire disappeared. Mr. B responded well to the stop-start technique performed by his wife and was able to regulate his orgasm and maintain an erection for 10-15 minutes.

(14) As we entered the intercourse phase of therapy, Mr. B was quite apprehensive about his erections. When intercourse was contemplated, he worried about the experience for days. During sexual activity, he obsessed constantly about losing his erection. He either lost his erection upon entry or ejaculated quickly.

(15) I reintroduced the X-rated films and tried relaxation techniques, imagery, and cognitive (Beck & Emery, 1985) interventions in an attempt to bypass his anxiety and resistance (he had begun avoiding the exercises). A psychodynamic mode was then employed to address his obsessive-compulsive core. These interventions, which were carried out during individual sessions with Mr. B, were helpful in other areas of his life, but he still lost his erection or ejaculated quickly.

(16) I then offered the couple (in another attempt to bypass his severe performance anxiety) the option of using intrapenile injections (Lue & Tanagito, 1987) or the vacuum constrictor device (Marmar, 1990). Mr. and Mrs. B were both pleased with these suggestions and decided on a vacuum constrictor device. (These devices create a vacuum and mechanically draw blood into the penis and when sufficiently firm, a constrictor ring is placed at the base of the penis to maintain rigidity.)

(17) It took about two weeks for Mr. B to master using the vacuum pump effectively. He was able to have firm erections until he chose to release the constrictors.

(18) Mr. and Mrs. B began to have intercourse and they were able to use the stop-start technique during intromission since he was no longer concerned about losing his erection. Treatment lasted another eight weeks, wherein he was able to have intercourse for 10-15 minutes before reaching orgasm. Mrs. B, who could not have orgasms during intercourse, was instructed to stimulate herself manually during intromission and was then able to orgasm easily.

(19) They were both quite pleased with this outcome and had no resistance to using the vacuum pump. Also, about 40-percent of the time, Mr. B was able to have successful intercourse without the vacuum device, its mere presence reducing his performance anxiety. Mr. and Mrs. B continued in marital therapy (primarily addressing power and control issues), and their sexual successes were maintained, with satisfying intercourse occurring on an average of once or twice a week.

Concluding Thoughts

(20) Using an integrative approach to sex therapy, the inhibited sexual desire manifested by this couple was resolved. Mrs. B's panic disorder with concomitant sexual phobia and Mr. B's erectile dysfunction and premature ejaculation were also remedied within an 11-month period. The concept of creatively bypassing resistance and anxiety and using psychodynamics to guide interventions enabled the treatment to succeed in a rapid manner.

References

Barbach, L. G. (1975). *For yourself: The fulfillment of female sexuality*. New York: Doubleday.

Beck, A., & Emery, G. (1985). *Anxiety disorders and phobias: A cognitive perspective*. New York: Basic.

Kaplan, H. S. (1974). *The new sex therapy*. New York: Brunner/Mazel.

Kaplan, H. S. (1979). *Disorders of sexual desire*. New York: Brunner/Mazel.

Kaplan, H. S. (1983). *Evaluation of sexual disorders*. New York: Brunner/Mazel.

Kaplan, H. S. (1987). *Sexual aversions, sexual phobias and panic disorders*. New York: Brunner/Mazel.

Kaplan, H. S. (1989). *How to overcome premature ejaculation*. New York: Brunner/Mazel.

Klein, D. F. (1980). *Anxiety: New research and changing concepts*. New York: Raven.

Lue, T. & Tanagito, E. (1987). Physiology of erection and pharmacologic treatment of impotence. *J. Urology, 137*, 829-836.

Masters, W. H. & Johnson, V. (1970). *Human sexual inadequacy*. Boston: Little, Brown.

Marmar, J. (1990). Non-surgical treatment of impotence. *J. Med. Asp. Hum. Sex* (Special ed: Guide to the management of impotence), 44-48.

Zilbergeld, B. (1978). *Male sexuality*. Boston: Little, Brown.

Terms for Discussion

1. psychodynamic (paragraphs 1, 15, and 20)

2. phobia (paragraphs 4, 7, and 20)

3. panic disorder/attack (paragraphs 4, 5 7, 8, 11, and 20)

4. obsess/obsession/obsessive-compulsive (paragraphs 5, 6, 10, 14, and 15)

5. performance anxiety (paragraphs 16 and 19)

Questions

6. Based only on the information in paragraphs 1 through 6, what would your prognosis have been? Explain.

7. In your opinion, how important was the contribution of the antipanic medication to the overall course of improvement? Do you believe that the same degree of improvement could have been achieved without it? Why? Why not?

8. Does the use of X-rated films (see paragraphs 10 and 15) raise any moral/ethical issues for you? Explain.

9. If you had been the therapist, would you have also introduced manual and oral stimulation before entering the intercourse phase in this particular case? Explain.

10. Mr. B was able to have successful intercourse without the vacuum device about 40-percent of the time. (See paragraph 19). In your opinion, should a goal of therapy be to increase this to 100-percent? Why? Why not?

11. Given that the sex therapy was largely successful in this case, do you believe that the sex therapist and the marital therapist should have more closely coordinated their efforts than is indicated in this report? Explain.

12. Are there any other types of treatment that might have facilitated the improvement of Mr. and Mrs. B? Explain.

13. Rate the article on the seven criteria described in the introduction to this book on a scale from 5 (highest quality) through 1 (lowest quality). Be prepared to explain your ratings.

Criterion 1: The demographics of the case are described: _____

Criterion 2: The condition(s) and behavior(s) that necessitated treatment are described in detail: _____

Criterion 3: The method of treatment is described in sufficient detail so that it can be replicated without additional information: _____

Criterion 4: A rationale is provided for the method of treatment selected: _____

Criterion 5: The client's improvement, if any, is clearly documented: _____

Criterion 6: Follow-up information on the client's improvement, if any, is presented: _____

Criterion 7: The study is appropriate for publication in a journal: _____

Case 19

Childhood Neurotic Disorders with a Sexual Content Need Not Imply Child Sexual Abuse*

Nuala Healy
Mater Misericordiae Hospital, Dublin

Carol Fitzpatrick
The Children's Hospital, Dublin

Elaine Fitzgerald
The Children's Hospital, Dublin

ABSTRACT: Two cases are described of childhood obsessional states in which the content of the symptomatology led parents and professionals to suspect child sexual abuse. Following assessment it was felt, on the balance of probabilities, unlikely that child sexual abuse had occurred in either case. Both children had previously engaged in "sex play" with peers. Maternal attitudes to sexuality were felt to have influenced their daughters' views about sexual behaviour and to have contributed to the children's guilt feelings. Response to appropriate treatment was rapid and has been sustained in the short-term. The importance of avoiding lengthy and possibly damaging assessment procedures in such cases is discussed.

(1) Many children experience transient obsessional behaviour (Freud, 1966; Gesell, Ile, & Ames, 1974; Judd, 1965), but full blown obsessive-compulsive disorder involving significant handicap to child and family is a relatively rare cause of child psychiatric referral (Rutter, Tizard, & Whitmore, 1970; Rapoport, 1986). Outcome studies have tended to concentrate on children and adolescents whose disorder is severe enough to warrant in-patient psychiatric treatment (Warren, 1965; Bolton, Collins, & Steinberg, 1983). These studies have emphasized a mixed prognosis for the disorder, with many cases remaining symptomatic despite intensive treatment involving the child and his or her family.

(2) Child sexual abuse is a well recognized contributor to a wide range of behavioral and emotional disorders in childhood (Mrazek & Mrazek, 1981), although a specific association with obsessive-compulsive disorder has not been described. We describe two cases of obsessive-compulsive disorder where the sexual nature of their symptomatology led parents and professionals to suspect child sexual abuse. In both cases, following clinical assessment, sexual abuse was considered most unlikely.

Case Report 1

(3) Mary, aged 9 years, was referred to a Sexual Abuse Assessment Unit by a child psychiatrist, who was concerned that she may have been sexually abused. The referral to the child psychiatrist was instigated by her mother who had the same concern.

---

*Reprinted from *Journal of Child Psychology and Psychiatry*, 32, 1991, pp. 857-863. Copyright 1991 by Pergamon Press Ltd., Oxford, England. Reprinted with permission.

Family history
(4) Mary was the eldest of four children from an intact family. Her parents described their relationship as satisfactory. Mary's mother had suffered severe "scruples" in adolescence, when for several years she felt guilty and as if she was committing sins. She attributed this to the fact that she masturbated during adolescence. Mary's mother had suffered from gastro-intestinal symptoms over the past 10 years and had been referred to a psychiatrist, but had only attended once. There was no family history of sexual abuse in either parents' childhood. Mary's parents described her relationship with both of them as good. She quarreled with her younger brothers, this having increased since the onset of Mary's symptoms. Prior to the onset of her symptoms, Mary had friends and played out on the street with neighbouring children.

History of presenting complaint
(5) Mary was described by both parents as having become preoccupied with sexual matters over the previous three months. She had been told the facts of life by a school friend 1 year previously and had discussed this with her mother at the time and had not appeared upset. When she was 7 years old, her mother had found her playing with her 3 year old brother's penis for which her mother had reprimanded her.

(6) In the 3 months prior to assessment, Mary had started to masturbate frequently. She constantly wanted to sit on both her mother's and father's laps and told both parents that she could not stop thinking about their private parts and wanting to touch them. She was thinking of penises going into vaginas, bottoms, breasts, and of people she knew engaging in sexual activity. She kept thinking she wanted to touch her parents' and other peoples' private parts and was fearful she might do this. She also kept thinking she was going to call neighbours rude names. She had stopped going out to play, was crying a good deal, and had been unable to attend school for 3 weeks prior to attendance, because of her preoccupation and fears.

(7) Mary's parents had tried to reassure her. Her mother in particular was extremely sympathetic to her and "felt for her" because of her own adolescent scruples. At the time of assessment, Mary was spending all day with her mother seeking and receiving reassurance, which made the worries go away temporarily. Each evening was spent being reassured by both parents and she woke several times each night coming into the parents' bedroom for reassurance.

(8) A 10-day course of Diazepam had been prescribed for Mary by the referring child psychiatrist because of her marked anxiety. This had reduced her requests for reassurance somewhat, and had been discontinued prior to assessment.

Assessment
(9) Mary attended with both parents for assessment. Mary and her parents were interviewed together, this being followed by an interview with Mary alone. Her parents were also interviewed together without Mary. Mary's parents related warmly to each other and to Mary. Both parents were very concerned about Mary— her mother feeling that she could understand what Mary was experiencing because of her own experiences, her father more baffled but supportive.

(10) At interview alone, Mary was an articulate child who was clinically of average intelligence. She was mildly embarrassed when describing her "worries" but did not show the guarded hesitancy which is so common in children who have experienced sexual abuse. She talked with ease about her sexual preoccupations, the distress they caused and her attempts to get them out of her mind. Mary was asked indirectly and directly if anyone had touched her in the ways she was worrying about. She was not clear about this, answering "I think it might have happened" or "I think I might have thought it happened." She was equally uncertain when other topics were discussed, such as her return to school. Mary's mood was not depressed, nor was she anxious in the interview. A clinical diagnosis of obsessive-compulsive disorder (300.3, ICD-9 classification) was made. It was not possible at this stage to be sure whether or not she had been sexually abused.

Treatment and progress
(11) Following this initial interview Mary and her parents were told that what she was experiencing was an unusual but well described occurrence in children, that sometimes happened if children were upset about something. We said we were not quite sure what she was upset about, but that treatment should start and we would continue to try to find out what was upsetting Mary when treatment was under way. Parents were asked to give Mary a 15 minute "worry time" each evening when she would have their undivided attention and when she was to talk about her worries in as much detail as she wished. Other than this time, parents were asked to give a firm non-response when Mary sought reassurance, but rather to try to suggest some distracting activity to her. She was to be rewarded, using

social reinforcement, for normal behavior, such as going out to play. It was suggested that she might be able to return to school in the near future. Both Mary and her parents were very relieved to hear that she was not going mad.

(12) There was rapid and sustained improvement using this simple behavioural approach. Mary's parents had been becoming increasingly frustrated with her constant requests for reassurance and were thus able to stop reinforcing these requests. She returned to school the week after her initial interview and Mary was seen for three further interviews. She told us that about 6 months prior to assessment when she had been staying overnight with a 12 year old female cousin, that they had played the "mummies and daddies" game. This involved mutual kissing and fondling of the genital area. Mary had felt very guilty after it and refused to stay with that cousin again. Mary was now quite clear that no other older person had sexually abused her.

(13 Mary was discharged after 6 weeks, and at 6 months follow-up was asymptomatic.

Case Report 2

(13) Susan, aged 10 years, was referred to a Department of Child and Family Psychiatry by her family doctor. He had asked that she be seen as quickly as possible as she had been having "sexual hallucinations" for 3 months prior to referral and was very distressed. The family doctor wondered whether or not the child had been abused.

Family history
(15) Susan, the second eldest in a family of four and the only girl, was from an intact family. Her early history was normal. She had minor problems with mathematics but otherwise did well at school. She had been a good mixer prior to onset of symptomatology. She related well to her brothers. The parental relationship was good. Father had had a carcinoid tumour removed 2 years previously and had remained well since then. Mother had a phobic illness for some years prior to Susan's referral and at a later stage in therapy disclosed that she had been sexually abused by her brother who was 6 years her senior, when she was aged 10-13 years. She had not previously spoken of this to any professional. However, she had, 1 year before Susan's referral, confronted her brother whom she said tried to blame her for the abuse.

History of presenting complaint
(16) Susan was described by both parents as having become increasingly anxious about sexual matters during the 3 months prior to referral. She worried that other people might have touched her genital area or might have kissed her. She felt that she might have seen other people's genitalia, both male and female, and kept imagining what they looked like. The most casual encounter, e.g. brushing against a peer during playing or a stranger in a shop, became a source of great anxiety as she felt she might have touched their genital area. She also worried and experienced a considerable amount of guilt about sexual play in which she had engaged, on one occasion, with other small girls when 6-7 years.

(17) These thoughts made her very anxious, were difficult to control and made it impossible to concentrate at school or play with her friends. She sought constant reassurance from her parents and repeatedly questioned them about sexual matters. Her attitude to her father vacillated between extreme attachment and great antipathy. She tended to cling to her mother and wanted to sleep in her mother's bed at night. Mother, presumably because of her earlier experience, had become very upset and had feared that Susan had been sexually abused. She had been fearful of questioning Susan as she feared it might exacerbate the situation. Both parents had tried to reassure Susan. The father had at times adopted a firm approach which had appeared to help.

Assessment
(18) Susan attended with both parents for assessment. She was interviewed alone following parental interview. She was a pleasant child who related well and was of average intelligence. She discussed her "problem" in an open way and was quite at ease in discussing her sexual preoccupations. She appeared to realize that her "worries" were unrealistic, but still could not prevent them recurring. She did not appear depressed, but was somewhat anxious as the interview progressed. However, as in Case 1, she did not show the guarded hesitancy common in sexually abused children and when asked directly could not describe any incident of sexual abuse, although she again reiterated a worry that someone might have touched her.

(19) During the interview it emerged that 1 year prior to referral she had had a brief period of obsessional behaviours which had included prolonged and frequent hand washing. This had cleared up without any treatment.

(20) She also discussed her experience of "sex play" with two other girls of similar age when aged 7 years. This had only occurred on one occasion and involved

mutual genital fondling. She had not told anyone about this until now, but felt guilty at the time. As in Case 1, a diagnosis of obsessive-compulsive disorder (300.3, ICD-9 classification) was made.

Treatment and progress
(21) Susan and her parents were reassured as in Case 1. Parents were asked to give Susan a 15 minute "worry time" each evening when she could discuss her worries with them. She was not allowed to discuss them at any other time, but again parents were advised to distract her should she attempt to do so. She was encouraged to participate in normal social activities and was rewarded for doing so. She was encouraged to go to school and she managed to do this.

(22) Her improvement was dramatic following this approach and the symptomatology disappeared. She was seen for four further interviews and at no time did it appear that she had ever been sexually abused. This possibility was also discussed with the parents.

(23) Because of the mother's disclosure of sexual abuse, the parents were seen for two further sessions and the option of referral to another agency suggested. Mother, however, decided not to avail herself of this.

(24) Susan has remained symptom free and was seen for follow up 6 months later.

Discussion

(25) Child sexual abuse assessment is a complex process (Kolvin *et al.*, 1988; Jones & McQuiston, 1988; Butler-Sloss, 1988; Royal College of Psychiatrists, 1988) and it is never possible to be certain that sexual abuse has not occurred. In these children, it was felt, on the balance of probabilities, to be unlikely because:

(a) Neither child disclosed abuse despite this possibility being raised with them.
(b) Neither child showed any affective change when discussing the possibility of abuse.
(c) Neither child appeared to be burdened by a "secret."
(d) The family context of both children with good relationships with their fathers and particularly close mother/daughter relationships is unlike that usually seen in intra-familial sexual abuse.
(e) The rapid and sustained improvement in symptomatology which occurred without any disclosure of sexual abuse.

(26) Both girls did describe sex play with peers and Mary had, in addition, engaged in some sex play with her younger brother. The boundary between sexual curiosity amongst peers, leading to consensual sexual exploration, and sexual abuse is often unclear and contemporary norms are not available for sexual behaviour in young children (Cavanagh Johnson, 1989; Bentovim & Vizard, 1988). The work of Schofield (1965) suggests that sexual behaviour, often consisting of mutual masturbation, occurs in approximately twenty percent of male and ten percent of female preadolescent children. While the sexual behaviour described by Mary and Susan appears to have been of the "sexual curiosity" type, both girls expressed considerable guilt about it, and (using a psychoanalytic model) their symptoms could be seen as a major defense against sexual anxiety.

(27) The family dynamics appeared to be important in both the production of the girls' symptomatology and in their rapid response to treatment. Both girls had unusually close and protective relationships with their mothers, which preceded the symptomatology. This may have caused the girls to be fearful of and guilty about their sexual behaviour, as were their mothers based on their own painful memories of their emerging sexuality. For these girls and their mothers sexuality appeared dangerous. Both fathers were somewhat peripheral to and respectful of this shared mother/daughter attitude to sexuality.

(28) The straightforward behavioural approach aimed at target symptoms helped the parents to unite around the task of helping the child to maturity. Their success at this task confirmed them as competent parents. The mothers were enabled to distance themselves from their daughters and could stop projecting their fears onto them. The mothers were also given space for clarity about their own experiences. The fact that both fathers participated in treatment was felt to be important.

(29) The main aim of treatment was to affirm the parents in their parenting role. In cases of suspected child sexual abuse parents often feel threatened and undermined and it is easy for them to be rendered incompetent by their own feelings and by the professional system.

(30) Because of current preoccupations with child sexual abuse, these girls could have been engaged in exhaustive assessment procedures, with little help for their symptomatology. It is our opinion that such an approach would not have been helpful for these anxious and uncertain children. Instead the possibility of sexual abuse was explored while at the same time providing therapeutic help for the girls and their families. This appears to have been successful in these cases. It remains to be seen how these girls and their mothers

will cope with the physical and psychological changes of puberty.

References

Bentovim, A., & Vizard, E. (1988) Sexual abuse--sexuality in childhood. In A. Bentovin, A. Elton, J. Hildebran, M. Tranter, & E. Vizard (Eds.), *Child sexual abuse within the family.* London: Wright.

Bolton, D., Collins, S., & Steinberg, D. (1983). The treatment of obsessive-compulsive disorder in adolescence. *British Journal of Psychiatry, 142,* 456-464.

Butler-Sloss, E. (1988). *Report of the inquiry into child abuse in Cleveland in 1987.* London: HMSO.

Cavanagh Johnson, T. (1989). Female child perpetrators: Children who molest other children. *Child Abuse and Neglect, 13,* 571-585.

Freud, A. (1966). *Normality and pathology in childhood.* London: Hogarth Press.

Gesell, A., Ile, F. L., & Ames, L. B. (1974). *Infant and child in the culture of today* (revised ed.). New York: Harper & Row.

Jones, D., & McQuiston, M. (1988). *Interviewing the sexually abused child.* (3rd ed.). London: Gaskell.

Judd, L. (1965). Obsessive-compulsive neurosis in children. *Archives of General Psychiatry, 12,* 136-143.

Kolvin, I., Steiner, H., Bamford, F., Taylor, M., Wynne, J., Jones, D., & Zeitlin, H. (1988). Child sexual abuse: Some principles of good practice. *British Journal of Hospital Medicine, 39,* 54-62.

Mrazek, P. B., & Mrazek, D. A. (1981). The effects of child sexual abuse: Methodological considerations. In P. B. Mrazek & C. H. Kempe (Eds.), *Sexually abused children and their families.* Oxford: Pergamon.

Rapoport, J. L. (1966). Childhood obsessive-compulsive disorder. *Journal of Child Psychology and Psychiatry, 27,* 289-295.

Rutter, M., Tizard, J., & Whitmore, K. (Eds.) (1970). *Education, health and behaviour.* London: Longman.

Royal College of Psychiatrists (1988). Child psychiatric perspectives on the assessment and management of sexually mistreated children. *Psychiatric Bulletin, 12,* 534-540.

Schofield, M. (1965). *The sexual behaviour of young people.* London: Longman.

Warren, W. (1965). A study of adolescent psychiatric in-patients and the outcome 6 or more years later-II. The follow-up study. *Journal of Child Psychology and Psychiatry, 6,* 141-160.

Terms for Discussion

1. child sexual abuse (throughout article)

2. obsessional behavior (paragraphs 1 and 19)

3. obsessive-compulsive disorder (paragraphs 1, 2, 10, and 20)

4. preoccupation (paragraphs 6, 10, and 18)

5. anxiety/anxious (paragraphs 8, 16, 17, and 18)

6. social reinforcement (paragraph 11)

7. behavioural approach (paragraphs 12 and 28)

8. guilty/guilt (paragraphs 12, 16, and 26)

9. sexual "hallucinations" (paragraph 14)

10. phobic illness (paragraph 15)

11. defense against sexual anxiety from a psychoanalytic model (paragraph 26)

Questions

12. How important is the family history to your understanding of Mary's case? (See paragraph 4.)

13. Comment on the adequacy of Mary's assessment. (See paragraphs 9 and 10.)

14. In your opinion, how likely is it that Mary's experience with her female cousin (see paragraph 12) contributed to the onset of her disorder?

15. In Mary's case, were you surprised by her rapid improvement? Explain.

16. Compare Mary's "history of presenting complaint" (see paragraphs 5-8) with Susan's (see paragraphs 16-17). Are there important similarities? Differences?

17. Would you have suspected child sexual abuse in these cases based on the symptoms reported prior to assessment? Explain.

18. Do the reasons listed in paragraph 25 convince you that sexual abuse was unlikely in these cases? Explain.

19. Are there any other types of treatment that might have facilitated Mary's and Susan's improvement? Explain.

20. Do you believe that "exhaustive assessment procedures" (see paragraph 30) aimed at exploring the possibility of sexual abuse might, in some cases, be harmful? Explain.

21. Rate the article on the seven criteria described in the introduction to this book on a scale from 5 (highest quality) through 1 (lowest quality). Be prepared to explain your ratings.

Criterion 1: The demographics of the case are described: _____

Criterion 2: The condition(s) and behavior(s) that necessitated treatment are described in detail: _____

Criterion 3: The method of treatment is described in sufficient detail so that it can be replicated without additional information: _____

Criterion 4: A rationale is provided for the method of treatment selected: _____

Criterion 5: The client's improvement, if any, is clearly documented: _____

Criterion 6: Follow-up information on the client's improvement, if any, is presented: _____

Criterion 7: The study is appropriate for publication in a journal: _____

Notes:

Case 20

Pubescence: A Psychoanalytic Study of One Girl's Experience of Puberty*

Ruth M. S. Fischer
Philadelphia Psychoanalytic Institute
University of Pennsylvania School of Medicine
Institute of Pennsylvania Hospital

(1) Puberty is the coming of age, a time of sexual maturity, a coming to terms with one's body, a time of disengagement from parents and establishing relationships with peers. Burgeoning sexual maturity makes it necessary for the girl to confront her new body. Oedipal conflicts are revived, leading to regression and a reworking of infantile conflicts and relationships (Blos, 1979).

(2) We have traditionally understood this as a time when the girl experiences a revival of awareness of her castrated state, which leaves her feeling inferior, humiliated, deprived, and envious, a time of renouncing her masculine strivings and accepting her femininity, renouncing her wish for a penis and substituting it with a wish for a baby. She is left infantile and dependent with a faulty superego, never totally abandoning her wish for her father (Freud, 1931; Deutsch, 1944). This is indeed a time of reworking of old feelings, feelings related to sexual difference and sexual maturity. It is not, however, a time of giving up masculinity and becoming feminine. The girl is already and always has been feminine. Rather, it is a time of relinquishing masculine potential, of accepting limitations (Fast, 1979). One cannot be all things, both male and female. There is a loss of a sense of omnipotence in accepting these limitations.

(3) Major advances in our understanding of the girl's early psychological development have led to a new understanding of puberty. A review of some of the new ideas starts with Stoller's (1976) concept of primary femininity, the sense of self as female, beginning at birth and continuing and developing throughout life. This idea relates to Stoller's (1965) concept of core gender identity, the sense that one is masculine or feminine. Core gender identity results from three factors: the biological one of genes and hormones, the psychological one of sex assignment at birth and the meaning of that assignment to the parents and to the child in interaction with the parents, including early postnatal patterns of handling. The third factor is the developmental one of body ego (i.e., the body sensations around which the child organizes his or her world). It seems clear from clinical observation that little girls are feminine in nature prior to awareness of sexual difference. They walk, hold themselves, socialize in ways that are typically female, in ways that are different from the ways boys walk, hold themselves and socialize. Korner (1973) has noted intrinsic differences between male and female newborns in their reactions to diverse stimuli and differences in the way parents handle their newborn sons and daughters. From the beginning, there are inherent and environmental influences determined by the sex of the infant (Money & Ehrhardt, 1972). These are the elements that establish primary femininity, the girl's basic sense of herself as a girl.

(4) The presence of genital sensations throughout infancy and childhood is also basic to our new understanding (Barnett, 1966; Galenson & Roiphe, 1976). We can no longer maintain Freud's view (1931) that the girl experiences no inner genital sensations prior to puberty: that she is aware only of her clitoris, a view

---

*Reprinted from *Psychoanalytic Inquiry*, 11, 1991, pp.457-479. Copyright 1991 by the Analytic Press, Inc. Reprinted with permission.

on which our former understanding of femininity had been based. The ramifications of the presence of genital sensations in childhood are monumental. Awareness of sexual difference can no longer be credited with the devastating impact to which we have up to now attributed it. It can no longer be seen as the central factor in establishing femininity. Contrary to our former understanding, the girl has been aware of having an internal organ all along, and this gives her a very different perspective from which to deal with sexual difference. She no longer feels that she has nothing (i.e., no penis). She simply becomes aware of a difference.

(5) Our recognition that the girl has these sensations has required that we reevaluate our ideas of masturbation. It has allowed us to see and to acknowledge that girls do masturbate and that it is the absence of masturbation that is abnormal, not its presence (Clower, 1975).

(6) And we have changed our understanding of the girl's relationship to her father. She does indeed turn to him as a love object in response to her genital sensations. Her relationship with him, however, begins not with awareness of sexual difference, but much earlier, when she turns to him as an important person in her life with whom she desires a relationship (Yogman, 1982).

(7) And once we acknowledge the girl's inner genital awareness, we must also appreciate that her wish for a baby is not compensatory, but is a very basic feminine wish deriving from her anatomy, her sense of her body, and her object relationships (Parens et al., 1976).

(8) Our accepting the ideas of intrinsic sexual differences and of the girl's inner genital sensations leads us back to the concept of primary femininity and then to a new understanding of the impact of the awareness of sexual difference. Awareness of sexual difference does not establish femininity, for this has been established long before. Rather, it demands acknowledgement of difference, which has an impact of its own. It does not establish a relationship with the father, for this has been established long before. And it does not establish the basic feminine wish for a baby.

(9) Female and male development have similarities and differences. One is not the norm from which the other deviates. The girl is responsive to hormonal and genetic influences as well as to social pressures. She experiences genital sensations early in life. Her relationship to her mother and to her father, from day one, are important and different from those experienced by the boy. Her oedipal conflicts are her own, not entirely like those experienced by the boy. Her superego is not defective. It is different. Her wish for a baby is not compensatory, but, rather, it is an ingrained aspect of her inner self. Her separation and individuation experiences are her own. A girl is a girl from birth and develops along her own line of female development (Tyson, 1982). Primary femininity, the girl's sense of herself as female, has displaced penis envy as the central factor in femininity.

(10) With awareness of sexual difference, she arrives at another stage in her development. It is at this point that she deals with integrating her genital organ with its specific sensations as well as with penis envy, castration anxiety, triangulated object relationships, and the Oedipus complex. It is also at this point that she deals with a loss of omnipotence, as she accepts difference and limitations (Fast, 1979). This is a phase of development of great clinical relevance, but it is not the point at which the girl acquires her sense of herself as female.

(11) Penis envy is a normal developmental experience indicating awareness of sexual difference. It is superimposed on a primary sense of femininity. Normally, it is experienced transiently and resolved. When it persists and becomes overwhelmingly significant in a woman's life, we must wonder why this is so. It is a psychodynamic issue with multiple determinants. When it persists, it requires analysis of its component parts (Grossman & Stewart, 1976).

(12) What I have described is a very different concept of the girl as she enters puberty. She has a basic sense of herself as female. She thinks of herself as a girl. She is responded to as a girl. She has internal sensations which tell her that she is a girl. She has genitals, internal organs, of which she has some understanding.

(13) Our revised version of prepubital development calls for a revised understanding of puberty. There are aspects that are distinctive for the girl. Blos (1979) reminds us of the negative oedipal tie that is resolved in adolescence. For the girl, this is her tie to her mother. Revived longings for closeness with mother and the reactions against this are clinically highly evident. Body sensations are important, both those on the outside with the change in body contour (Benedek et al., 1979) as well as those on the inside. Menarche is an important developmental milestone (Kestenberg, 1961). As we

turn our attention to girls proceeding through adolescence, we note that intense, prolonged penis envy is not the norm. Contrary to traditional understanding, we often note a sense of joy that girls experience in their bodies. Menarche is not always experienced as a devastating, humiliating wound. Frequently, it is welcomed with a sense of pride (Hart & Sarnoff, 1971).

(14) An analysis of a girl as she progresses through puberty brings these issues into focus and allows us to observe, in depth and over time, reactions and progress through this phase. With this in mind, I present the following clinical material.

(15) Anne, at nine, suffered from multiple fears. She was unable to sleep at night for fear of the monsters hiding in the dark. She feared bodily injury and life-threatening illnesses. She had been sociable, but was now withdrawing from her friends. She was unable to attend sleep-over parties. She was excited by the idea of boys, but unable to tolerate even the hint of a relationship with a real boy. She was irritable and demanding of her parents and unable to concentrate in school.

(16) An apparently normal childhood other than occasional mild episodes of separation anxiety had been disrupted following a serious illness in the family which resulted in mother's preoccupation and transient withdrawal in depression when Anne was five. At first, it seemed Anne was coping, but as her symptoms persisted and intensified, therapy was sought.

(17) In the analysis, we played games of things lost and found: Guess What I See with My Little Eye, and Hide and Seek, hinted that she saw and knew more than she let on and that she was concerned with something she could not find. She drew mazes and spoke of reunions and lost objects. When feelings became too painful and she could neither talk, think, nor, more importantly, feel, she would list all the topics we had spoken of that day. It brought order to the chaos she was experiencing. Afterward, there were quiet periods when we would write letters to each other, a method she employed to give me an opportunity to write what she could not tolerate to be spoken. She explained that she was feeling that things were changing and that she no longer knew who or what she was. As the chaotic feelings were expressed in her sessions, her fears at home diminished and at school, she was better able to concentrate.

(18) Her inner confusion was reflected in her appearance, which was striking in its variety. I never knew who would enter the office. One day, she was a dirty, sloppy tomboy and the next, a made-up moll. Mostly, it was a combination: lipstick, eye shadow, nail polish, her hair in disarray with a baseball cap holding it down. She would hold a make-believe microphone pretending she was a rock star and then crawl on the floor, babbling baby talk.

(19) Gradually, her appearance grew neater, cleaner, and more predictable. She discarded the baseball cap, the baby talk, and the male characters she had portrayed: the baseball player, the race-car driver, the doctor. Now, she played at being women: teachers, nurses, rock stars, gymnasts, witches, interior decorators. I was to play the more subordinate role: the student, the patient, the audience.

(20) What had been an interest in mazes was converted into a fascination with floor plans. She drew them endlessly, floor plans of houses: her house, her grandmother's house, her friend's house, the analyst's house. She made comparisons. Whose was bigger, better, prettier, had more rooms, nicer rooms, the right combination of rooms, etc. But mostly she was concerned with how one moved from one room to the next: the connections between the rooms. She seemed to be desperately trying to make sense of her anatomy. Anxiety about connections in terms of relationships was in the background at this point. It surfaced later when relatedness to and connections between people, both emotional and physical, became more of a concern.

(21) Anxiety about her body was expressed in fears of heart attacks, cancer, pregnancy, of being with someone who is sick, of catching it and dying. Mostly, she tried to keep this in the background, out of her mind, to avoid being overwhelmed.

(22) Her favorite game was M.A.S.H.: listing mansion, apartment, shack, house; boys names, number of children, cities, and types of cars. To whom and under what circumstances would she marry? What kind of house would she have. Chance would decide. Meanwhile, she spoke of school dances and boy/girl parties, which fascinated her but in which she could not participate. I understood her to be thinking of marriage, penetration, and pregnancy: about her house, her floor plan, her inner space.

(23) She had to deal with the outer body as well. She gained weight in an effort to hide her changing body shape as her breasts developed. The clothes of the day

were just right to camouflage her emerging curves. She used these clothes both to hide and to emphasize her new body. She wore mother's clothes, noting how well they fit. There were constant comparisons with mother and with the analyst: constant measurement of limb size, hips, hair length, but never of bust, which she was making a desperate attempt to deny. Her hair became the focus of interest deflected from the rest of her body. She was preoccupied with its length, style, texture, color. She drew pictures of girls, differentiating them by weight, height, eye color, but mostly by hair style. Nothing other than physical attributes were pertinent, and breast development was pointedly absent. She was both preoccupied with and rigidly denying bodily changes. It seemed too much for her to deal with. Her "baby" brother had all the luck. No demands were placed on him. He was so inept, so helpless, and, somehow, she felt deprived of something that he was getting.

(24) As puberty progressed, the defensive aspect became more obvious. Anxiety about what was going on within her body was contained by "doing" her hair. She learned to make a French braid. This is a complex procedure requiring organization, concentration, and manual dexterity. It was a perfect defensive maneuver she utilized when she was experiencing a certain level of anxiety. She turned to it when things were beginning to feel chaotic, when body sensations were beginning to feel overwhelming, when she felt in need of organization. When anxiety increased beyond this limit, however, she could no longer manage the intricate process. At that point, she would hurriedly put her hair in a pony tail, talk nonstop, and start moving: changing positions in her chair, twisting, and turning, walking around the room. After working off some of the anxiety, she could return to braiding her hair. She wanted so much to organize, to get things under control, to produce her braid.

(25) The focus was on her hair, her body ornament, the braid, the phallic object. She spoke of feeling deprived and of the advantage her brother enjoys. She made frequent note of the yucky worms outside. She can't stand them. They make her sick. She walks out of her way to avoid them She "faints" at the sight of them. And then, she transiently developed a lump in her throat. She could not swallow. She felt she was suffocating. At one point, it became so intense that her parents considered laryngoscopy. She was preoccupied with ear piercing. She constantly thought of it, watched it done to friends. She was fascinated, frightened, unable to move on. Ideas about it kept coming back.

She recalled her first response to her mother when she had her period. Now, she could become pregnant—a very exciting, terrifying thought. Penetration and penetrating organs were never very far from her thoughts which were relieved by braiding her hair.

(26) Analytic sessions in her 11th year were particularly chaotic. Her life outside improved. She was more independent, was concentrating better in school, and was less frightened. In the analysis, she was unable to concentrate. She sang, moved about, changed the subject, talked fast and loud, forgot what she was saying, stammered, was unable to listen. Closeness with the analyst was frightening. But even more, she could not tolerate the closeness to herself: listening to herself, allowing herself to think, to feel, to pursue her own thoughts. It was too dangerous. All was chaos. The sessions were frequently demonstrations of how she felt: all mixed up; and of the way she handled it, "turning on MTV," as we grew to call it. She turned to singing and dancing to tune out her feeling. This, however, she only experienced as more stimulating and therefore resulted in increased excitement and chaotic feelings.

(27) After several months of this, she came in and reported that she had had her period. It was an event she had anticipated with some apprehension, mainly as to aspects of control and embarrassment. But the event itself elicited only pride. She was so pleased with herself. She felt so grown-up. She felt such contempt for her brother who was such a baby. She had discussed it all with her mother a long time ago and she knew everything she needed to know. (There was an element of denial here.)

(28) Most striking in the next several months was the diminution of the chaos. She was able to sit, to think, to fantasize, to listen, certainly not to everything but to some things. Her appearance changed. She became neater. She ate less. Earlier concerns returned but now in a more manageable form. She again expressed interest in piercing her ears. As earlier, she was interested, excited, frightened, thought of bodily injury and pain, but now she could tolerate thinking about it. There was a new dimension. The injury and pain seemed transient and therefore tolerable rather than devastatingly interminable and overwhelming.

(29) She returned to drawing pictures of different girls. This time, personalities emerged. She returned to drawing floor plans and exploring insides of houses, but with less urgency and anxiety, and with more interest and curiosity.

(30) And she noted the disappearance of her fears. She introduced this by suggesting that we put on a play. This was the first of many special shared activities in which she was to engage me. She wrote the script. She passed me a note inviting me to sleep overnight. School is dismissed. We go to her house, play, watch TV, eat dinner, and prepare for bed. She climbs into bed (the analytic couch) and then gets up again, swings her legs over the side and notes the absence of fear of anything hiding under the bed. She then turns off the light and we go to sleep. She remarks that there is no need to leave the light on or to carry a flashlight. We awake in the morning, unscathed. As I noted the lack of fear and the ease of falling asleep, she responded that she slept at night now. She no longer feared ghosts or witches hiding under her bed and in her closet.

(31) Concurrently, she was working harder at school. She explained that good grades are not attained without hard work and how good she would feel if she raised her grades. There was also a diminution of feeling slighted, unappreciated, and picked on by teachers. Massive ego and superego changes were evident as she turned from narcissistic omnipotence to acceptance of some vulnerability and of reality, from magical thinking to hard work to attain her goals, from immediate pleasure to longer-term goals, and from projection to more critical self-observation.

(32) Along with these changes, time assumed a new meaning. She was more aware and accepting of the passage of time in her own life and in the lives of those around her. She made note of grandparents' aging and of her own growing-up process. Things no longer seemed endless. They had a beginning, middle, and end. A striking psychic reorganization had taken place.

(33) Later, there was to be a return of anxiety and concerns about blood and bodily illness, but this was now in a more manageable form. She now had the ego capacities with which to deal with these conflicts. It seemed as if the experience of the menses was so powerful that it broke through some of the denial, demanding greater recognition of reality. She could no longer deny her pubertal experience, the aging process, her lack of omnipotence, her vulnerability to the forces of life, her genital sexuality, her femininity. Magical thinking had to be abandoned in the face of the pressure of this new reality. She now thought in terms of cause and effect. She was growing up. She could no longer continue to deny her maturation. Significant adjustments were made.

Discussion

(34) I have focused on Anne's physical maturation and its reverberations, noted in the psychological changes which manifested themselves in her analytic sessions. Of course her neurosis, her fears of bodily harm, are abnormal and influenced how she experienced her puberty. And of course the changes are not solely due to puberty, but very much indicate analytic progress which allowed these pubertal changes to occur. We are seeing the interdigitation of the two processes, the analytic and the pubertal. There is much here, however, that is typical of early adolescence.

(35) Anne presents us with events that are uniquely Anne's and are at the same time characteristic of the girl's pubertal experience. I would like to focus on three such experiences, clearly evident in Anne's analysis: the ambiguity of gender role in prepuberty, the role of the best friend, and the impact of menarche.

The Prepubertal Ambiguity of Gender Role

(36) When we first meet Anne, at nine, she presents as neither girl nor boy, adult nor child, or possibly as all of the above. Traditionally, we would say that with burgeoning adolescence, she is experiencing a revival of castration anxiety and penis envy. She is struggling with acceptance of her castrated state, abandoning her active masculinity, and turning to passivity and femininity (Freud, 1931). That she has not turned from her infantile masculinity to her genital femininity is indicated by her bisexual outfits and behavior. Her babyish behavior indicates regression in the face of this task. Here we see the girl's basic problem: giving up her masculinity and accepting her role as a woman.

(37) This playing at both female and male roles is not characteristic of boys at this age. Boys play at being boys. When they engage in girls' play, they are the object of derision, and we question their sexual identity. Then, we might wonder, is Anne experiencing a sexual identity problem? No doubt, her castration anxiety has been aggravated by her hostility and by the illness and loss she has experienced. It is certainly hinted at in the history of all of her fears. Playing at female and male roles may be an indication of castration anxiety and of penis envy. But in analyzing and observing girls of this age, one realizes that this ambiguity is not peculiar to Anne, but rather to the stage of development. Carson McCullers (1946), in *Member of the Wedding*, compellingly portrays this distinctive aspect of prepuberty in the development of the character of Frankie, the younger sister, caught between the world of

the child and that of the adult; not quite grown up and not quite child, not yet a woman, but no longer completely comfortable with her younger male friend. She moves back and forth between these worlds using the substitute nurturing mother figure to aid her in this passage. This is the fluidity that the girl experiences before puberty, a fluidity that boys either do not experience or do not allow themselves to play out.

(38) Girls of this age, as did Anne, speak of their freedom and of their confusion, of feeling neither infantile nor grown up, and yet a little of each: feeling not quite like their male peers and yet not like their mothers, playing baseball and doing gymnastics, not quite like the boys and yet not involved in the activities in which their mothers partake. They try each on for size. They play at each, maintaining some of their narcissistic omnipotence for just a little longer. At the same time, they feel quite small, without anything, not boy and not woman.

(39) In the beginning of her analysis, Anne demonstrated this both in characteristic fashion and defensively. It was noted in her appearance: the tomboy alternating with the rock star, the school teacher with the crawling baby. Each seemed equally possible and worth trying. Each seemed equally comfortable and uncomfortable as she turned from one to the other. She was not denying her basic femaleness, but, rather, playing out various roles--an expression of her omnipotentiality, an expression denied to the boy who must distance himself from girls and women, who must disidentify with mother in order to attain and maintain his masculinity (Greenson, 1968). For the girl, this is typical prepubertal ambiguity of gender role. Anne abandoned the bisexual role-play about six months prior to menarche. One can only speculate as to the biological impetus to the psychological change. It is tempting to understand this to be secondary to hormonal influence.

The Best Friend
(40) The second distinctively female characteristic noted in early adolescence is the best friend. This is something we all know about, that we all associate with girlhood, that is both the bane and saving grace of every girl's existence, to say nothing of her mother's and teacher's existence.

(41) Having a best friend is one way in which the girl attempts to resolve the preoedipal tie to the mother, a major task of adolescence. Puberty revives the longing for closeness with mother. The girl turns to her best friend to satisfy these longings, a task that can never be accomplished. So she turns in disappointment and anger and seeks solace with another best friend. At times, her need is played out with a boy in a pseudoheterosexual relationship. Frequently, she has multiple best friends as one is exchanged for another. These relationships are intense, exclusive, and interchangeable.

(42) As with the prepubertal ambiguous gender role, the best friend is a normal characteristic of female adolescence and is strikingly divergent from male adolescent behavior. The boy deals with his revived parental longings in a different way. Or possibly, that with which he is dealing is different, as has been suggested by Gilligan (1982), who points to a basic difference in male and female psychology: the primacy of connectedness in the life of the girl and of autonomy in the life of the boy, a basic difference that goes on to influence so many aspects of life including type of relatedness, games played, stories told, moral choices, life style, basic fears, and priorities. This idea is supported by Kestenberg's (1968) and Galenson and Roiphe's (1976) studies of body sensations, Bernstein's (1983) studies of superego differences as well as of the gender-specific vicissitudes of the separation-individuation experience (Olesker, 1990).

(43) Another mechanism the girl uses to deal with her need to break the tie with mother is to transfer it onto an idealized teacher or another woman in a position of some authority. This is most clearly presented in the well-known story by Muriel Spark (1961), *The Prime of Miss Jean Brody*. Jean Brody, a very opinionated, narcissistic woman who gathers her creme de la creme, "star girls" around her, is the idealized figure, and the girls are her admirers. Men are outside of this circle, and heterosexuality is relegated to fantasy.

(44) Anne's tie to her mother was intense. She was unable to turn to friends or teachers. She was retreating from her peers. In the analysis, she was desperately maintaining distance from the analyst. Her feelings were too intense, too exciting, too frightening. This brought a major problem into the therapeutic purview. At times, we were able to understand it and the analysis could proceed. At other times, we could not, as her feelings were too overwhelming. She feared loss of control. She feared becoming the analyst's baby. She feared taking over and being taken over. She feared that the analyst would object to her grown-up, independent ideas and feelings; she therefore could not allow herself to have them. She needed to fend me off both in the transference and as a new object.

(45) A major shift was noted several months prior to menarche. It was at this time that she wrote the script for the sleep-over story through which she announced her diminished fears and increased ability to sleep at night. With the psychic restructuring, there was a change in her ability to tolerate a relationship both in the transference and in reality. What was striking about the story was the use of the analyst as a girl might use a best friend. This story was followed by others, which she composed both during her analytic sessions and at home during breaks. In each, she and the analyst were engaged in activities that are usually shared with a best friend. The analyst was spoken of in terms more usually used describing a girlfriend, an important peer, not an adult. The importance of the story was in the activity and in the feeling of shared closeness. The stories were short and simple. Their importance to her was reflected by her careful typing and placing them in special protective folders. They were left in a safe place in the analyst's office. Occasionally, she kept a copy for herself. The first story she showed to her mother as if to be sure that it was acceptable to mother that we be friends in this way. The stories were of shopping and having lunch together, of going to the mall together, of playing in the snow together. The shared activities were in some way more indicative of a latency friendship than the shared secrets of adolescent relatedness, although features of both were present. There were times when this feeling became so pronounced that it was as if we were peers. The reality of the age difference was erased. One is reminded of Settlage's (1977) concept of the developmental use of the analyst.

(46) Over time, the intensity of the need to use the analyst in this way diminished. She was concurrently speaking of growing old and of growing up. She was dealing with acceptance of the passage of time. Slowly, she developed a friendship with a peer and then began to turn to the analyst as the idealized teacher. She brought in homework, asked questions, wanted to know "the" answer and tolerated no questioning of this transference manifestation. Further developmental progress was noted as parents reported they could say nothing that differed from her English teacher, who had suddenly become the source of all truth. And the analytic relationship took a new turn.

(47) From the beginning, it had been important to her not to allow herself to develop any strong feelings toward me. She feared loss of control. It was important to be in control, in charge. She played the teacher, the business woman, the employer. I was the student, the employee, the one who paid her endless amounts of money. The use of me as best friend was the beginning of a new developmental trend, indicating increasing comfort with her hostile dependent needs and increasing ability to move out of the parent/child relationship and into the world of peers. It was a developmental use of the analyst as an outlet for intense longings for closeness, which were so frightening to her. It demonstrated, in an exaggerated fashion, what the normal early adolescent girl experiences with her best friend.

The Impact of Menarche

(48) The need for activity in the session and in her life, the inability to sit and listen either to the analyst or to herself was not merely a function of her revived longings for union with mother. It was also an expression of the inner turmoil she was experiencing as she approached menarche.

(49) For her, the turmoil was multidetermined. She had no outlet in peer relationships. She was becoming increasingly anxious in her relationship with the analyst and with her parents, and, for want of another outlet, she turned ever more to her body which was already a source of excitement and discomfort. She was unable to sleep at night. There were all sorts of reasons why she could not get into bed. She came to her parents expressing fears of bodily illness and of death. To get into bed and give up the distractions of the day was to turn ever more to her body, to masturbation, which increased her excitement and her fears. She could not control it other than by staying vigilant. She would stay awake later and later, finally falling asleep exhausted, only to awaken in the middle of the night and repeat the process. She would not speak of these nightly vigils. The content of her fantasies was clear from her concerns with illness and death, with torture from ghosts who return from the dead seeking revenge, with eyes that bore into you, and with pregnancy resulting from contact.

(50) Breast development intensified her conflicts. She demonstrated both exhibitionistic impulses, pride in her developing body, and shame. She was a rock star entertaining thousands, exhibiting herself to her admirers. And in shame, she hid her body behind loose, baggy clothing. Ultimately this conflict was resolved by displacing all interest in her body to her hair which she endlessly arranged and rearranged.

(51) She was once more preoccupied with floor plans. She thought of marriage and family and endlessly played M.A.S.H. Who will be her husband, how many children will she have, what kind of car will she drive and in what sort of house will she live?

(52) Her inner sensations were inexorably drawing her attention to her body. Her interest in piercing her ears returned, this time in the service of integrating her vagina. She was fascinated by the piercing process, repulsed, disgusted, horrified. Thoughts of it brought to mind bodily illness, accidents and death. She wanted to get it over with. Do it and be done with it. She was dealing now with penetration. She went with a friend to have her ears pierced, watched while her friend's ears were pierced, and then was unable to tolerate the thought of piercing her own. She was still in great conflict over this "piercing" process. One sees here the importance and intertwining of various aspects of the developmental process. It is only with the ability to use peer relationships in this way that she will be able to proceed through adolescence. But development had to progress to allow this new object relationship to take place. Several important aspects of adolescence are now underway: the establishment of the best friend, peer relationships, and beginning integration of her genital sexuality.

(53) Menarche was a striking event in Anne's life, the psychological reverberations of which were noted in her analytic sessions. Mounting feelings of confusion and of inner chaos began to give way to a new sense of order. The organizing effect was notable. Her sessions had been chaotic. She felt chaotic and she expressed chaos. She was unable to concentrate, to feel, think, listen, or just be. She sang, moved about, spoke rapidly without order. She "turned on MTV," tuning in to dancing, singing, and action, which was only further stimulating, exciting, and chaos-producing.

(54) Then she got her period and there was a striking change in the nature of her sessions. She was calmer, more organized, and more comfortable relating. She felt more secure in her adult status and was less threatened by her regressive wishes to be cared for, babied, taken over by the analyst mother. She was more comfortable pursuing autonomous thoughts and feelings. The intensity of her hostile, aggressive feelings had diminished and, thereby, they became more manageable.

(55) The concept of menarche as an organizer derives from Spitz's (1965) observations of the first year of life. Development proceeds in spurts which are the result of a reorganization of the psyche, following which new capacities are noted. The smiling response, stranger anxiety, and the No, organizers of the psyche, indicate that there has been such a transition from one developmental level to the next. Once these milestones are attained, the personality is organized in a new way and new capacities are possible. The smiling response indicates that social interaction and connectedness are possible. Stranger anxiety indicates that the relationship to the mother has been established. This is followed by growth and development in a wide range of areas: cognition, perception, motoric skills, ideation, socialization, and a widening range of affect.

(56) For Anne, menarche seemed to organize her personality in a similar manner. She now was able to consider certain possibilities, to deal with certain realities that had previously eluded her. She thought in terms of passage of time and cause and effect. She and mother were not a unit. Separation was a reality with which she had come to terms. And she was a woman with the possibility of bearing a child. Menarche intensified internal genital sensations, which were now more organized and organizing rather than being experienced as confusing and producing chaos.

(57) Anne's concerns remained. What was different was that she was less overwhelmed by them. They felt less all-consuming, all encompassing. She developed a sense of continuity, of past, present, and future. Her problems no longer felt timeless, forever. Chaos need not be a permanent state. She dealt better with school work. She found that if she listened, she could learn. She did not feel defeated if she did not know it already or, at least, immediately. She began to be able to plan and to organize.

(58) And then she was faced with what she had been avoiding all along, the implications of her growing up. Acknowledgment of time meant dealing with growing up and with death: the possibility, the inevitability of her own death, of mother's and grandmother's death. And it was the idea of death that had brought her to therapy in the first place. Although an issue with which all adolescents must deal, it was particularly loaded and therefore difficult for Anne. Acknowledgment of the passage of time was the beginning of coming to terms with her place in her family. She must find her place in her own generation. She did not occupy the same space in time as did her parents or the analyst, much as she might try to deny this. Denial of this aspect of reality was of course part of the use of the analyst as best friend. She needed to move out of the entanglement with the analyst and with her parents and make her own life. And this meant dealing with her concerns of her destructive genital fears and wishes.

(59) She developed a transient school phobia. She was unable to go to school as she worried about leaving mother alone. Would she be all right? When she

returned to school, she needed to call home periodically to check in. Relieved once she heard her mother's voice, she could then return to class. Several hours later, she would need to make another call.

(60) Menarche meant dealing with herself as a woman. She defensively focused on the outside of her body as the menses forced her attention to the inside and evoked all her related fears. In denial, she turned things around. She protested, "It is not the inside I concern myself with. It is the outside." There was recrudescence of penis envy as she attempted to deal with the overwhelming fears surrounding the opening into her body. Her fears of penetration, displaced onto the ear-piercing and the preoccupation with floor plans, led to denial of the vagina and a focus on penis envy. Ultimately, this was resolved for Anne, at least temporarily, with the idea that girls do have special places inside of them in which babies grow. She would love to be a mother and to have a child. She will, however, adopt.

(61) Penetration and pregnancy, dealing with this opening into her body was particularly difficult as there was an overload of hostility with which she could not come to terms. It was as if all of the anger she was experiencing was being turned back on her either in the act of penetration or in the delivery of the baby. She feared some terrible retribution enacted on her body. She would be left horribly maimed, sick, or killed. We saw here the revival of feelings related to mother's pregnancy with her ambivalently loved brother: the jealousy of the baby and of the mother carrying the baby, as well as the wish to steal the baby from the mother. But, mostly, there was her anger at the withdrawn mother compounded by anger at the later withdrawal of mother in depression. The need for distance from the analyst was to avoid the terrible anger as well as the intolerable sense of loss and longing.

(62) Penis envy was evident in Anne's analysis from the very beginning as we played her favorite game of hide and seek. She was concerned with genital difference. Who has the object and who does not? Where is it hidden? Will she find it? But then she turned her attention to death and to what happens to the body after death. Where does it go and what does it feel like to be buried? The hidden object no longer represented simply the absent, hidden penis, but now also the dead, buried body which is in some mysterious location.

(63) The hiding place was really what fascinated her: the coffin, the box that holds the body. She thought about her body, her box, her vagina in which things can be placed. These thoughts were too exciting. She was unable to sit still and concentrate. She thought of illness and death and of the cruel controlling teacher who punished with after-school detention or even suspension if the child did not behave. Thoughts about her special box into which something could be placed, in which a baby could grow, which was life-giving, protecting, and also life-threatening, were very frightening.

(64) These thoughts intensified as she anticipated celebrating Halloween. For her, the holiday meant haunted houses, ghosts, and trick-or-treating: pretending to be something else, dressing up and going with a friend from house to house, filling her bag with candy. This was an enjoyable sublimation, but also a frightening one, for the haunted houses represented her inner space which she feared would be destructive in some way. The ghosts were dead children killed in the womb and bad children sent away from their homes, having to roam the earth.

(65) The game of hide and seek expressed concern with genital difference. Anne was looking for the penis. But there was so much more here. It was all interrelated with issues of destruction, separation, and loss. Penis envy had a very specific meaning to Anne, and she used it defensively. Behind it, she hid her concern about her hiding place, her box, her coffin, her inside space. To focus on envy of the penis, the hidden object, would be to support the defense and to miss an opportunity to understand what it was that she was defending against. What she was defending against were all of her feelings about the place in which the object is hidden.

(66) Penis envy, she could talk about. It was thoughts of her own body, of her hiding place, which led to sexual excitement, giggling, inability to sit still, and ultimately, turning on MTV. And it was to control such thoughts that the strict teacher with punishments of detention and suspension was called into play. She tried desperately to keep sexual thoughts and feelings under control, to keep her concerns about her femininity under wraps. Her feelings about her insides, her vagina, were too frightening. Anxiety about not having a penis was present, but anxiety about her own genital sensations and strivings was a more primary concern.

(67) The underlying, unspoken concern was of the place in which the missing penis, person, object might be hiding: the room in the house, the pathway to the inner chamber. She worried about the worms. She was intrigued by the ear-piercing, and she was frightened by

the lump in her throat. It all related to the inside of her body where she might someday be penetrated and impregnated, something she both wished for and feared so much.

(68) Here we see the role penis envy played in Anne's conflicts over her internal genital. She was concerned with the absence of the penis. She looked for it. She wondered about it. The focus on it, however, was to deflect a greater anxiety about her inside space into which the penis could penetrate and in which, someday, might grow a baby. This was her fear of bodily illness. If she gets too close, she might catch something from someone and die. This was too frightening to think about. So she focused on the absent penis. This was a distressing but far more bearable concern.

(69) Menarche intensified genital sexual sensations and thereby brought these concerns to the surface, making it possible, even mandatory, for Anne to consider them. She was now also better equipped to deal with them as she had developed a time sense, better reality testing, greater ego capacities. She was not so overwhelmed. It was safer as her adult status was more firmly established and regression was less threatening. Conflicts were raised and she became symptomatic as she reexamined these issues, indicating a new level of functioning.

(70) In discussing puberty, I have noted what appears to be distinctive characteristics: the prepubertal ambiguity in gender role, the role of the best friend in resolving the preoedipal tie to the mother, the role of menarche as an organizer, and penis envy as a defensive focus on the outside of the body while the primary concern is with the inside of the body, with the girl's own genital organ.

(71) Freud said that to understand women, we must turn to women for their help. He was referring to women analysts. We need to expand on this idea and turn to our women patients. We need to be open to what they have to teach us.

References

Barnett, M. (1966). Vaginal awareness in the infancy and childhood of girls. *J. Amer. Psychoanal. Assn.*, 14:129-141.

Benedek, E., Poznanski, E., and Mason, S. (1979). A note on the female adolescent's psychological reactions to breast development. *J. Amer. Acad. Child Psychiat.*, 18:537-545.

Bernstein, D. (1983). The female superego: A different perspective. *Int. J. Psychoanal.*, 64: 187-202.

Blos, P. (1979). Modification in the classical psychoanalytic model of adolescence. In *Adolescent Psychiatry* VII ed. S. Feinstein and P. Giovacchini. Chicago: Univ. of Chicago Press, pp. 6-25.

Clower, V. (1975). Significance of masturbation in female sexual development and function. In *Masturbation: From Infancy to Senescence*, ed. I. Marcus and J. J. Francis. NY: IUP, pp. 107-143.

Deutsch, H. (1944). *The Psychology of Women*. New York: Grune and Stratton.

Fast, I. (1979). Developments in gender identity: Gender differentiation in girls. *Int. J. Psychoanal.*, 60:443-453.

Freud, S. (1931). Female sexuality. *S.E.*, 21.

_____ (1933). Femininity. *S.E.*, 22.

Galenson, E. & Roiphe, H. (1976). Some suggested revisions concerning early female development. *J. Amer. Psychoanal. Assn.*, 24(Suppl.): 29-58.

Gilligan, C. (1982). *In a Different Voice*. Cambridge: Harvard Univ. Press.

Greenson, R. (1968). Disidentifying from mother: Its special importance for the boy. *Int. J. Psychoanal.*, 49:370-376.

Grossman, W. & Stewart, W. (1976). Penis envy: From childhood wish to developmental metaphor. *J. Amer. Psychoanal. Assn.* 24(Suppl.): 193-212.

Hart, M. & Sarnoff, C. (1971). The impact of the menarche. A study of two stages of organization. *J. Amer. Acad. Child Psychiatry*, 10:257-271.

Kestenberg, J. (1968). Outside and inside: Male and female. *J. Amer. Psychoanal. Assn.*, 16:457-510.

_____ (1961) Menarche. In *Adolescents: Psychoanalytic Approach to Problems and Therapy*, ed. S. Lorand & H. Schneer. New York: Hoeber, pp. 19-50.

Korner, A. (1973). Sex differences in newborn with special references to differences in organization of oral behavior. *J. Child Psychol. and Psychiat.*, 14:18-29.

McCullers, C. (1946). *The Member of the Wedding*. Boston: Mifflin.

Money, J. & Ehrhardt, A. (1972). *Man and Woman, Boy and Girl*. Baltimore/London: John Hopkins Univ. Press.

Olesker, W. (1990). Sex differences during the early separation-individuation process: Implication for gender identity formation. *J. Amer. Psychoanal. Assn.*, 38:325-346.

Parens, H., Pollock, L., Stern, J., & Kramer, S. (1976). On the girl's entry into the Oedipus complex. *J. Amer. Psychoanaly. Assn.*, 24(Suppl.): 79-108.

Settlage, C. (1977) The psychoanalytic understanding of narcissistic and borderline personality disorders: Advances in developmental theory. *J. Amer. Psychoanal. Assn.*, 25:805-833.

Spark, M. (1961). *The Prime of Miss Jean Brodie*. New York: New American Library.

Spitz, R. (1965). *The First Year of Life*. New York: Int. Univ. Press.

Stoller, R. (1965) The sense of maleness. *Psychoanal. Q.*, 34:207-218.

_____ (1976). Primary femininity. *J Amer. Psychoanal. Assn.*, 24(Suppl.):59-78.

Tyson, P. (1982). A developmental line of gender identity, gender role, and choice of love object. *J. Amer. Psychoanal. Assn.*, 30:61-86.

Viorst, J. (1990). *Earrings*. New York: Atheneum.

Yogman, M. (1982). Observations on the father-infant relationship. In *Fathers and Children. Developmental and Clinical Perspectives*, ed. S. Cath, A. Gurwitt, & J. M. Ross. Boston: Little Brown, pp. 101-122.

Terms for Discussion

1. Oedipal conflicts/Oedipus complex (paragraphs 1, 9, and 10)

2. superego (paragraphs 2, 9, 31, and 42)

3. penis envy (paragraphs 9, 10, 11, 36, 37, 60, 62, 65, and 68)

4. castration anxiety (paragraphs 10, 36, 37)

5. separation anxiety (paragraph 16)

6. defensive maneuver (paragraph 24)

7. narcissistic (paragraphs 38 and 43)

8. transference (paragraph 44)

9. denial (paragraph 60)

10. sublimation (paragraph 64)

Questions

11. What is your opinion of the concepts of "primary femininity" and "core gender identity"? (See paragraph 3.)

12. In your opinion, are any of the symptoms mentioned in paragraph 15 more serious than others? Explain.

13. What is your opinion on the use of letter writing as a therapeutic technique in this case? Might it be useful for other kinds of cases? Might it be effective with adults?

14. Comment on the interpretation of Anne's fascination with floor plans. (See paragraph 20.) Does the interpretation make sense in light of the other information about Anne? Are there alternative interpretations?

15. Anne's braid is viewed as a phallic object. (See paragraph 25.) Do you agree with this interpretation? Explain.

16. Shortly after having had her first period, Anne exhibited a number of changes. (See paragraphs 27 through 34.) Has the author convinced you that these changes were facilitated by psychoanalysis? Could the changes merely be the result of Anne's physiological changes? Explain.

17. In paragraphs 36 through 39, the author suggests that ambiguity of gender role is a normal characteristic of girls during puberty but not of boys. Do you agree? Explain.

18. The analyst allowed Anne to use her as a best friend. (see paragraphs 40 through 47). Was this appropriate in your opinion? Should the analyst have encouraged Anne to seek a best friend of her own age instead? Explain.

19. Do you agree that menarche has an important role as an organizer? Explain. (See paragraphs 48 through 70).

20. Do you find the concept of "penis envy" to be helpful in defining and understanding some of Anne's problems? Explain. (See "Terms for Discussion" for relevant paragraph numbers.)

21. Are there any other types of treatment that might have facilitated Anne's improvement? Explain.

22. Rate the article on the seven criteria described in the introduction to this book on a scale from 5 (highest quality) through 1 (lowest quality). Be prepared to explain your ratings.

Criterion 1: The demographics of the case are described: _____

Criterion 2: The condition(s) and behavior(s) that necessitated treatment are described in detail: _____

Criterion 3: The method of treatment is described in sufficient detail so that it can be replicated without additional information: _____

Criterion 4: A rationale is provided for the method of treatment selected: _____

Criterion 5: The client's improvement, if any is clearly documented: _____

Criterion 6: Follow-up information on the client's improvement, if any, is presented: _____

Criterion 7: The study is appropriate for publication in a journal: _____

Case 21

The Psychoanalytic Treatment of a Preschool Boy with a Gender Identity Disorder*

Calvin H. Haber
The Psychoanalytic Institute at New York University Medical Center
Schneider Children's Hospital of Long Island Jewish Medical Center

ABSTRACT: A three-year, nine-month-old boy began analysis by wishing he was a girl and pretending he was a superheroine. Over the course of almost five years, the cross-gender defense against fear of loss of the object, anal loss, and castration by the object reorganized in all libidinal phases through early latency. Developmental arrests seemed to occur during the anal rapprochement and oedipal phases that led to observable cross-gender strivings by two and a half years of age. The role of early childhood illness, narcissistic vulnerability, mother's childhood wish for a sister, the mother's adult wish for a daughter, a shared fantasy between mother and child, identification with the perceived power and beauty of mother and grandmother, pathological sibling rivalry that influenced identification with his sister, were demonstrated in his play during sessions. Interwoven in the background was the impact of an emotionally absent father, a dying grandfather, and an accident-prone uncle. This paternal matrix seemed to discourage budding masculinity and encourage feminine identifications.

The analyst's approach and the child's responses to interpretation of the transference manifestation, cross-gender behavior, fantasies, and play are presented. Finally, the gradual resolution of the conflicted wish to be a girl was supplanted by the emergence of appropriate gender identification. A two-year follow-up appeared to confirm his postanalytic gender stance and continuing consolidation of stable gender development.

(1) This paper deals with the five-year analysis of a three years, nine-months-old boy with a gender disorder. [See Friend et al. (1954) for an early description of gender disorder in boys.] It demonstrates that psycho- analysis during prelatency can be an effective method of treatment of this disorder. Clinical material is presented that contributes to the delineation of the origins and development of a subtype of a Gender Identity Disorder of Childhood, as defined by *DSM-III* and Coates and Zucker (1988). Clinical data are presented indicating that had he not been treated, the child would likely have developed into an adult homosexual.

(2) Two cases are cited in the literature which refer to this subgroup. Greenson (1966) described the psychotherapy of a transvestite boy whose mother was in simultaneous analysis (Stoller, 1966). His patient demonstrated the influence of tactile contact, identification with the object, failure to disidentify, and the role of father. The analysis of a five-year-old boy with tranvestite tendencies is described by Sperling (1964). The parity in masculine and feminine mental representations was also seen in her patient, who presented a dream in which he was half man and half woman. This child had a magic-potion dream which parallels a fantasy game my patient presented. Two cases of pretranssexual children that came to analysis are also known. An eight-month analysis of a five-year-old pretranssexual boy is described by Loeb and Shane (1982). This child exhibited disdain for his penis, and is part of another subgroup. In a completed analysis, the preoedipal determinants of a four-and-a-half-year-old is described by J. B. McDevitt (1985, unpublished). The child ex-

---

*Reprinted from *Journal of the American Psychoanalytic Association*, *39*, 1991, pp. 107-129. Copyright 1991 by International Universities Press, Inc. Reprinted with permission.

hibited separation anxiety. He showed disdain for his penis at the outset of the analysis. The continuum of childhood gender disorder linked to homosexual partner orientation, transvestism, or transsexualism is elucidated in a series of papers by Greenson (1964, 1966) and Stoller (1964, 1966). In adult analyses, interviews, psychotherapies, and anthropological studies (Stoller, 1975, 1985; Stoller and Herdt, 1982) have contributed a large body of information concerning the origins of adult gender disturbances. According to Stoller (1985), gender identity refers to the mix of masculinity and femininity in an individual, implying both masculinity and femininity are found in everyone, in differing forms and to differing degrees. Mahler and her coworkers (1975) noted that the rapprochement phase of boys is less stormy than that of girls. They thought the phase was less conflicted in boys when the mother respected and enjoyed the boy's masculinity all along, especially during the second half of the third year. They suggested that the presence of and identification with a father or brother facilitated the boy's early gender identity. If the mother was too intrusive and consistently interfered with the boy's phallic strivings, an ambitendent rapprochement struggle ensued which could give way to passive surrender. Kleeman (1965), and later Roiphe and Galenson (1981) have observed that boys discovered their penis by the age of eight to ten months. Although some briefly discovered their penis by four or five months, the majority developed a general interest by fifteen or sixteen months. Roiphe and Galenson describe an infant with "a disturbed sexual identity" who, during his first year of life, suffered severe traumas. The mother exhibited depression, anxiety, and intense hostile ambivalence toward her son that interfered with attempts at differentiation and separation (p. 222). Tyson (1982) examined the establishment of gender identity as a developmental line. Gender identity, she postulated, consists of three separate interrelated strands: (1) gender identity, i.e., all characteristics comprising the individual's sense of femininity and masculinity. This includes anatomy, biological sex, identifications, object relations, intrapsychic and bisexual conflicts, cultural and sociological influences. It begins with early core gender identity, the most primitive awareness of belonging to one sex and not the other, and is determined by genital anatomy and physiology, sex assignment, parenting and sibling relationships, object relations, cognitive capacities and ego functioning; (2) gender role—a person's overt behavior in relation to other people with regard to gender, originating in the earliest consciousness and unconscious interactions between the infant and its objects, interactions which may be influenced by parental attitudes to the child's biological sex; (3) sexual partner orientation, which refers to the sex of the chosen love object. In order to establish gender role the boy must disidentify with the mother and identify with father.

Presenting Problem

(3) A forty-five-month-old was brought for evaluation because of a persistent desire to wear his sister's clothes, shoes, and nail polish. Cross-gender behavior was first observed at thirty months when he wanted to wear nail polish. Beginning at thirty-three months, he made repeated requests for a doll, a doll carriage, and a kitchen set. Cinderella became his favorite her heroine, followed by Wonder Woman, Superwoman, and Princess Diana. In toy stores, Stanley continually showed stronger interest in the kitchen toys, dolls, and carriages. Cross-dressing and playing persisted during every free moment. Just before the consultation, his closest playmate observed that Stanley only wanted to play at being a girl and told him that that meant he wanted to be a girl. Stanley reported the event to his mother. His mother became upset because she was unable to stop his cross-gender activities. He told his mother he was a girl, and had a temper tantrum when she disagreed. He repeated the episode with his brother.

History

(4) Mother denied a sexual preference. Father was very proud that Stanley seemed able, at six months, to distinguish between his mother and father by voice recognition. He wanted another son. At six months Stanley developed chronic ear infection with elevated temperature, which persisted through part of his treatment. The chronic illnesses were the narcissistic fabric into which future injuries would be woven. Allergy immunization was begun during his first year, weekly at first, then bi-weekly during his second year, tri-weekly during his third, and once a month thereafter. These events ushered in a very close, stormy relationship with mother. The injections were traumatic. He was held down by his mother assisted by his grandmother, while the doctor held his arm and gave him an injection as he yelled, fought, and tried to escape. From early childhood, he took a favorite blanket to bed, and continues to use a fragment of it.

(5) Toilet training was attempted in close proximity to bottle weaning, at about twenty-one months, but it failed, as did a second attempt with a potty trainer a few months later. His mother tried to urine-train him by asking him to urinate into a paper cup. This occurred during a period of family chaos. A maternal uncle who lived in the house was seriously injured in a motorcycle accident. Both legs had to be bandaged and casted, and he underwent subsequent surgery. Stanley reacted to the

cast with fear and withdrawal. Three months later, he was frightened by his grandfather coming home with a bandage over an eye. Stanley developed a bandaid and bandage phobia after this. These very intense castration reactions during the latter half of his second year corresponded to the early genital phase (Roiphe and Galenson, 1981).

(6) When Stanley was thirty months old, his uncle required another operation. He again reacted to the cast with fear and withdrawal. Toilet training was attempted again, and this time was successful. His grandfather's health deteriorated, which ended their daily walks and conversations. Stanley was moved out of the parental bedroom, against his wishes, to a room of his own at three years, five months (four months before the consultation).

Family Background
(7) The family lived in a mother-daughter single family home. The grandparents, in their sixties, lived upstairs. Stanley lived downstairs with his parents, in their thirties, and his fourteen year-old brother and eleven-year-old sister.

(8) His mother was a matriarch who, together with his grandmother, exerted much more influence than his father and grandfather. His mother was prone to temper tantrums in which she screamed, cursed, and threw plates. As a child, she had felt isolated between her older brother and younger brother. She had found her younger brother troublesome and had wished he were a girl. A recommendation that mother seek therapy almost disrupted the analysis, allegedly related to financial hardship and time considerations.

(9) Stanley's mother initiated the consultation. His father opposed it, insisting that Stanley would outgrow the problem. He was very concerned with finances. He barely bothered with Stanley and immersed himself in home improvement projects during his free time. Four sessions a week with Stanley plus a fifth with either parent or both were met with opposition by the father. Mother feared Stanley might become a homosexual. Father's opposition diminished somewhat when it became financially possible to support the analysis. Thereafter, both parents supported the analysis throughout.

(10) Stanley's grandmother, a vital working woman, and his mother, were very close. Grandfather died at sixty-eight of vascular and cardiac problems. He had been retired, and did light house cleaning while his wife worked. Stanley had a close, pleasant relationship with him. His grandfather began to fail when Stanley was thirty months old. During the next eight months, attention was drastically focused away from Stanley and toward his ill grandfather, who finally was hospitalized. A hospital bed was delivered to the house in anticipation of his discharge, and Stanley eagerly awaited his return; but his grandfather died the next day. The boy reacted with unusual silence and diminished interest in play. A period of turmoil followed, and Stanley was left in the care of a neighbor. He reacted to his beloved grandfather's death by asking to visit him in heaven. When he was told it was impossible, Stanley demanded a rope to climb to heaven. He was furious when he was told that God had taken his grandfather; he refused to attend church "because God would not allow him to visit his grandfather." When the family dog died two months later, Stanley commented that it was good because now his grandfather would not be alone.

The Analysis
(11) The analysis began when Stanley was three years, nine months old and ended when he was eight years, seven months old. He was a tall, muscular, well-dressed, unsmiling child. He was alert and very serious, and tended to be aloof, surly, and preoccupied with his things and ideas. He had been told that I was a doctor who helped children who worried about going to nursery school and had sleepless nights. He reacted positively to the idea that I would help him. In nursery school he cross-dressed and played in the kitchen and was anxious about separating from his mother. During his analytic sessions, he insisted that his mother stay in the consultation room. He exhibited intense cross-gender activities from the moment of entrance until he left. He refused to acknowledge my existence for a month. He ordered me not to look at him and to "shut up." From his dollhouse play, it was evident that he viewed his grandparents as part of one continuous extended family. He disagreed with or ignored any comments of mine that connected avoidance of me with his grandfather's visits to physicians. On several occasions, upon saying "grandfather," Stanley reacted either by leaving the room or emitting a loud, anguished scream. He could not separate from mother for the first few weeks, so she sat in the consultation room. For another year, he was in and out of the waiting room. His first play was as the bride, Princess Diana, marrying Prince Charles. I was assigned the role of the priest who married them. After a month he seemed to become aware that I did not interfere, and his play shifted to playing (1) a powerful superheroine, such as Wonder Woman, who had a lasso with which she caught male wrongdoers; (2) a woman being chased by a monster with my role being that of

saving the woman by stopping the monster; and (3) moving and relocating. He moved furniture from one room to another, and in his play he adopted unmistakably feminine mannerisms in his way of walking and talking. He either ignored me or issued commands to me in a contemptuous way. Cross-gender activities continued in the waiting and consultation rooms.

(12) He was a vulnerable child in that he had frequent sore throats, earaches, fevers, and allergies. He saw his pediatrician several times a month and took a lot of medication. He missed many sessions because of illness.

(13) After a while, when he played with dolls in the dollhouse, a repetitive, clear "upside down 69" theme emerged accompanied with sexual excitement that may have been connected with primal scene experiences in the parental bedroom. Dolls hung from the ceilings. Hair was washed upside down. I had to close my eyes while the boy and girl dolls faced down and kissed each other in a 69 position. He frequently played mother. At one point I said I thought he liked to play mother because he loved her a lot. He disagreed, called me ugly, and chased me outside to stay in the cold. I complained and said he was sending me away because I was a man.

(14) At home he was a finicky eater and threw a temper tantrum if solid food came in contact with a semi-solid food on his plate. He would cry and refuse to finish his meal. He played a girl during the entire day. He tended to be quarrelsome, obstinate, bossy, and defiant at home and with me. During sessions he intentionally and repetitively spilled water, became upset, and then would leave abruptly. He would not assist in cleaning up after sessions, and tested me frequently. He would turn over all the furniture in the room that he could and then say he wanted to leave and that I could straighten everything up. I linked these episodes into a genetic reconstruction. He listened carefully when I said he turned over the furniture and wet my couch because he was angry about having been moved out of his parents' bedroom and felt alone.

(15) Stanley's first separation from his parents, for a period of one week, occurred during the first year of analysis. He stayed with his grandmother and siblings. In play, he made me sit alone and silent in another make-believe apartment with the door closed. When I connected the loneliness I felt with what he must have felt with his parents away on vacation, he did not disagree. This was a major concession for him to make at that time. He put on a skit of "Mirror, mirror on the wall, who is the fairest of them all?" He was annoyed with me when I said he ignored me because I was a boy. I indicated that Stanley had to be the fairest to insure against being left alone. He referred to a doll as "he-she." During a subsequent session, Stanley was brought by his grandmother and sister. He combed a Barbie doll's hair while directing the analyst to assist in changing the doll's clothes. He went into the waiting room and showed the doll to his sister. She replied with a disapproving facial expression. I asked if his sister approved. He replied, "She says boys play with boys and girls play with girls!" He disagreed with his sister who indicated that she would not play "Dolls" with him. I answered, "You like to play with both." He replied with enthusiasm in his voice, "Yeah." Several minutes later he was back in the waiting room again. This time he returned with a distinct exaggerated wiggle of the hips that mimicked a girl or woman. He told me to shut up and called me ugly when I said he walked like a girl when he was with the girls. He then sat in the analyst's chair, and I wondered aloud if he was playing a boy doctor now. He shouted that this was a girl doctor's office now and that I could get out. I could wait in the waiting room, and his sister could come in. He pushed me into a closet with the door open and repeated several times that he was a girl. I said, "Oh, you like girls, so it must be hard to like yourself as a boy." He returned to the waiting room, once again rebuffed by his sister. He repeated his sister and mumbled, "Boys play with boys." As we cleaned up, I said, "Because you like girls so much, you like playing a girl." He did not respond. However, during subsequent sessions I was called "Ugly." The name lasted for more than a year.

(16) After the parental vacation, I said to him that when he was a baby he had felt love for his mother and had thought that he would have to be like her or he might lose her. As if to say he agreed, he went into the waiting room, said hello to his mother, returned, and told me the boy doll had died. When I said, "Boy dolls die," he became fearful and said, "The boy doll came back to life." Fear of loss, abandonment, and death returned when he developed a loose tooth. I interpreted this as his being reminded of his fear of losing his mother when he thought of losing his tooth. He responded by grooming a girl doll. In an apparent shift from passivity to activity, and assuming a cross-gender role, he took loving care of the doll mother to defend against his fear of his aggression and of hers.

(17) During Stanley's earliest years, he was afraid of going to the doctor. Mother had reacted to her brother's motorcycle injuries and her father's illness by acting with Stanley the way he now was acting with me on an

almost daily basis. He screamed, threw things, and walked out on me. His mother, in her tantrums, had screamed, thrown dishes, and abruptly abandoned Stanley and left the house for hours. He apparently was utilizing identification with the aggressor and denial of gender differences to allay his fear of separation and loss. When I said he could show his anger without temper tantrum he asked, "What other ways are there?" I said I thought he screamed because he thought I would not listen to him. With further working through, his temper tantrums stopped in school and became less frequent in the sessions.

(18) Stanley's rapprochement phase, weaning and toilet training had been complicated by his uncle's motorcycle accident and recuperation and his mother's reaction to it. In his sessions, he spilled water and had temper tantrums as he fed the dolls. He became cantankerous and furious with me whenever he spilled water on his clothes or on the furniture, and left the room abruptly. To spill produced a fear that necessitated being angry with me and going into the waiting room. Reversal of his mother's anger at him when he had soiled and wet himself, associated with his anxiety at seeing his uncle's and his grandfather's bandages and the need to reassure himself against maternal abandonment, seemed to be involved. His grandfather's death seemed to have represented the castration threat, when you "cross" mother and incur her wrath. After some months, urethral phase derivatives surfaced in a different way. While playing "House," and serving tea, he ritualized spilling water. At one point, his naughty smile betrayed his pleasurable excitement. During a session with mother, she complained about boys who don't aim right. She added, "Girls are just easier." In public bathrooms, he refused to accompany his father and expected to join his mother in the ladies' room.

(19) A solution to his dilemma appears to have been suggested to him by the very special relationship his mother had with his sister and with his grandmother. His mother always had wished for a younger sister and had found her younger brother, the one who had the motorcycle accident, troublesome. She also would have preferred her daughter, Stanley's eleven-year-old sister, to have had a sister rather than a younger brother. In his sessions, Stanley expressed admiration for his sister in his play. He twirled a baton as she did, adopted her favorite color, purple, and preferred her television programs. I interpreted his idealization of his sister as the wish to be his mother's favorite. I added once he may have wanted to be like his grandfather but was upset with him because he was weak and died.

(20) Stanley disliked his older brother, whose hobby was World War II memorabilia. His brother was the most active in interfering with his cross-dressing, which made him angry. A fake necklace or ring was enough to enhance his fantasy that he was a girl. He did not express negative feelings toward his penis. On the contrary, he proudly told his mother how large it was.

(21) A castration reaction surfaced when he sustained a superficial paper cut. He became anxious and irritable. The thought of a bandaid made him even more anxious, and he wanted to leave. In subsequent sessions, he spoke about memories of his uncle's bandages and his own fear of being injured. The bandaid phobia ended, which seemed to infer that his castration anxiety eased slightly. By the end of the first year, Stanley seemed to be fond of me. However, he never sought physical contact.

(22) During the second year of analysis, when Stanley was five and a half years old, chronic throat infections and ear complications caused a reduction in his auditory acuity. A tonsillectomy and adenoidectomy was recommended by several consultants. Attempts to engage him about the upcoming hospitalization and procedure were ignored. However, he responded with interest and enthusiasm to a suggestion that we write about the operation. At his suggestion, the "book" was named after the surgeon. He would sketch the story, and I would write a line or two to explain the drawing. The "book" consisted of eleven pages. In addition to his fantasies concerning the surgical instruments, as might be expected, tall, important nurses played a prominent role. The patient was a pretend girl who "didn't like being sick or taking medicine." The surgery transpired with little or no fear, and his wish was fulfilled. His health improved and medications were discontinued. He was able to attend school and sessions regularly. Stanley's shyness did not allow him to speak about sexual fantasies. He found it easier to communicate as "an author" and artist. During the course of the analysis and successive levels of development, he wrote "books" titled: *A Little Lost Lamb* and *The Anatomy Book* that correctly depicted the anatomical differences between the sexes. In *The Love Book* he sketched the way he appeared to himself when he pretended he was a girl. At the age of seven, he wrote *A Nude Book* which more accurately illustrated the male and female body.

(23) During the first half of the analysis, we analyzed derivatives of cross-gender defense against damage, loss of his mother, loneliness, and castration. The use of denial of gender in fantasy, identification with the aggres-

sor, and a shift from passivity to activity to defend against his fear of his mother when she brought him to the doctor and held him for injections were focused upon. We reflected upon his observation of his sister's and grandmother's special relationship with his mother. He accepted my suggestion that he, too, wanted a special relationship with his mother, so he played at being a girl. Stanley's father was submissive and had little to do with him. He had loved his grandfather, but he had died, and his uncle had sustained injuries requiring repeated surgery. When I commented on his apparent idea that injuries and death occurred to men, so that he felt it was safer to be a girl, he listened quietly and did not disagree.

(24) Oral-phase derivatives surfaced in the form of a threat that I drink and eat immediately or he would take a meal away from me. In his identification with his mother, he told me, "Eat, drink or be left hungry." He understood when I said that it seemed to him that whoever is in charge of the food is powerful. Anal-phase derivatives defended against his intense fear of spilling and messing and loss, followed by his bursting into an angry tirade and leaving the consultation room, threatening never to return. This seemed to recapitulate his weaning and early toilet training failures. He utilized gender denial, reversal, and identification with the aggressor to punish the analyst, instead of being punished himself for losing control of his bowels and urine. The ultimate defense against castration anxiety was to be a powerful female, a superheroine.

(25) By the end of the third year, we had an alliance that was very workable. He called me "Doc" and referred to me outside the consultation room as "the Doc." He listened to my interpretations, and although he did not usually comment on them, he frequently revealed his thoughts via his play. By this time, cross-gender play no longer took place at home or in school, but only during his sessions. He revealed during "69" doll play that he had seen his aunt and uncle kissing. I suggested that he had seen them in the position in which he had placed the dolls, while they were staying at his home to babysit for him. I added that it apparently had confused him about who was on top and who was on the bottom, and about who was the man and who was the woman. He told me rather apologetically that he had just peeked under the door, so that he had seen feet only. This led to play in which he was a millionaire woman who married a series of men who then died. As a result, she had many husbands. I suggested he had felt that men died all over the place, like his grandfather and later his grandfather's brother and he never had known of a woman who had died. He replied, "I don't want to have a fifth husband. This is my fourth." He then made love to the husband with loud passion. I observed his obvious fun in this activity.

(26) After I reassured him that I would not tell his mother, he cunningly told how he was able to secretly satisfy his mother's request that he not play girl and at the same time satisfy his own desires. At bedtime, when no one was close by, he could pretend he was a favorite female character he had seen on one of the "soaps" he saw on television. He refused to reveal the content of his bedtime fantasies for some time. Finally he revealed that the women were beautiful, and inferred that they were desired by men. I proposed that we pretend I was a reporter and he was a television star. He agreed, but insisted that I ask him questions in writing, although I might have to read the question to him since he was only in the middle of first grade (almost six-and-a-half-years old) and could barely write, and then only phonetically. He wrote that he had strange switch fantasies at bedtime. He "punched a guy's lights [breasts or chest) out," but if he liked him he kissed him. He added that he especially liked tall, dark, and handsome men.

(27) In his daydreams, Stanley stated, he was a pretty girl. An appointment with a guy consisted of dinner, movie, and dancing. He appeared physically as three feet, three inches tall, as well as "gentle and reasonable." Sexual excitement seemed to be associated with his fantasies. I asked him what caused his penis to get hard. After initially denying that his penis gets hard, with a smile on his face, he exclaimed, "Men do!" He thought his penis became hard when he was in the company of men in nice clothes who did not wear shirts. His penis became soft when he did not think of men. In response to a written question about a nicely dressed girl, he wrote, "I don't care if I was the girl, but if the girl made a pass at my boyfriend I would punch her lights out." It seemed that sexual excitement in the form of cross-gender fantasies, masturbation, and erections was present at this age and existed earlier, before he was able to be open with me.

(28) During the fourth year of analysis, a new theme surfaced in his play with dolls. Men died, but women who were in danger were saved by a fearless man. A man who lived and who saved women appeared. This led, after further analysis of fears about dying, to oedipal themes of males who were in combat with each other and were being injured. He ended by playing at being a woman in love with a strong, handsome boy. I suggested that he hid being a boy because he wanted to steal strength from a strong, handsome boy. He smiled and "made love" to his imagined boy lover. His wish to

hide his masculine strivings out of fear of dying or of injury (especially to his penis) was interpreted many times in connection with his play.

(29) When Stanley started school, he attempted to play with the girls and to stay separate from the more athletic boys. He refused to talk about this. We played teacher and flash cards. He accepted a flash card interpretation: "Stanley stays home for lunch longer because he's afraid his 'pishy' will be hurt if he plays sports in the school yard with the boys." This was a forbidden, embarrassing topic, and he forbade me to talk about it. He did allow me to write a flash card so he could read and comment on it.

(30) First grade was marked by periods of curiosity and learning interspersed with problems with teachers. He reacted with fear and humiliation to the teacher's corrections or criticisms. He aspired to be perfect to defend against further narcissistic injury. The classroom scene was reversed in his play with me. I was made the student who wanted to be perfect for fear the teacher would insult, scream, and break things like his mother had done in the past. I was the helpless boy with fragile self-esteem. He always took the role of the teacher and always told me what kind of student I was to be. In the play, under questioning by him, I admitted I was afraid of being a boy lest my feelings be hurt and I die. I added that I might think of hiding myself in girls' clothes. He offered me solace and told me he would help me stop my worrying.

(31) The periods of playing as a boy, which had always existed, became longer and longer. During the analytic sessions, there were brief periods when he played with the Ken doll, playing as a boy. His self-esteem seemed to stabilize, and a feeble sense of masculinity was surfacing. We came to know the moment of changing gender as the "switch" or "switching." He came to expect some "figuring out" after he switched to discover what thoughts had led him to assume a cross-gender position. At one point, his cross-gender play persisted. Interpretations that followed his play had no impact. I offered a series of interventions that meant he was playing girl because he was mixed up. He thought, because I said it, it was okay to play girl here in my office, that it meant I wanted him to be a girl like he thought his mother did when he was a baby. Stanley did not take issue with my interpretation, and his cross-gender play subsided but did not stop. He appreciated genetic interpretations as long as the word "baby" was included. He appreciated the time relationship because his narcissism was not injured. In his scheme of things, he recognized he was now older, smarter, and had no need for his former ways. In part, he accepted the interpretation as recognition or gratification of his wish to be considered older and grown-up.

(32) During the latter part of the fourth year of analysis, his switching was less frequent and a male fantasy emerged in his play that had three forms. The first involved a doctor and a nurse. It had started a year earlier with the book he wrote, with pictures about an anticipated hospitalization for a tonsillectomy. When danger was perceived, he switched from being the doctor to being a nurse. When he felt secure, I was the patient and he was the doctor. He identified with his allergist, giving me shots to make me well. Another frequent theme involved a detective who figured out clues and always won in the end. Occasionally, in a variation of this theme, he rescued a beautiful rich woman to whom he had made love. The last theme, which persisted until the end of the analysis, involved an architect/real estate tycoon who was the richest man in the world and had contact with presidents and kings. Occasionally, he turned out to be president, and eventually he designed, planned, and led the first civilization on the moon.

End of the Analysis

(33) During the last seven months of analysis, Stanley stopped switching altogether. He told me he thought he did not have to come so often. At this point, he was in latency and advancing smoothly. The day we agreed on a termination date, a negative oedipal theme unfolded that was to be played out and interpreted over several sessions. I was assigned to play the President, and he played "the killer robber." After killing me and Nancy Reagan, he robbed "my place." He then took my attaché case to smuggle out of the country. The wish to steal my powerful penis in order to be a fearless boy had emerged, as well as his fantasy that termination equaled death, that if he left me I would die. During termination, the symptoms related to each prelatency phase reemerged. Each phase reorganized the gender symptom. Oral incorporation of his mother surfaced again in a game he created. He concocted a powerful magic potion while playing a witch. Then, playing a boy, he ingested the potion. He fell to the floor, seemed to faint or die, and was revived or reborn a boy. These were interpreted and worked through once again.

(34) In school, Stanley had started first grade with a separation crisis that lasted several weeks. He was considered immature and his mother was prepared by the school psychologist for him to be left back. He made friends with difficulty and avoided sports. By the

middle of third grade, in contrast, he had become a popular youngster who played obligatory sports but did not involve himself in elective athletics. He had the highest grades of any of the boys in his class and was placed in a gifted track. In one class, he sat with fifth graders. During his fifth year of analysis, his parents described him as a delight to have, in contrast to their initial comment that he was "busting up" their home.

(35) During the analysis, Stanley's father brought him one day a week. He informed me that occasionally they spent the rest of the day together. In his play, Stanley eventually brought a carpenter and a construction man onto the scene. These reflected his father's favorite avocations. After his father had taken him to his office, he imagined himself a tycoon in a "high rise."

(36) Stanley visited me three times after termination, at his request. He was pleasant and friendly. He related to me as one might to a close friend he had not seen in a long time. He took inventory of the office to note changes. He checked out his old drawer, which still was unused and empty. He asked me if I still had his "book," and appeared pleased that I had it. He reviewed it carefully, and blushed at one point. He informed me about his current activities and suggested we meet again. His parents later reported by telephone that all was well and that "he was a pleasure." With some ambivalence, his mother commented on how complicated it was to rear such a bright child. She thought at times that it might be better to have a child of only average intelligence. She thanked me again and gave permission for me to present an account of Stanley's analysis. A visit two years later, when Stanley was ten, revealed a likable, talkative youngster who thought he might like to be a writer. It appeared we both understood when and where that notion began. The parents asked me if they could consult with me as time went on. They felt that Stanley might appreciate visiting me from time to time. They were clearly concerned that the changes that had taken place in Stanley's personality might not hold through adolescence. I agreed to be available for follow-up.

Discussion

(37) Stanley appeared to have a sense of being or wishing he was a girl by the age of two and a half years. After six months of analysis, it became evident that by telling his mother how proud he was of his penis, he wished to hide his masculinity. The opening phase began with successive images of playing powerful women. Princess Diana appeared to be the only woman who was famous and admired. All the others in a series (Wonder Woman, Superwoman, Fire Girl, She-Ra) exhibited the superego elements of a woman or girl apprehending male wrongdoers. Intrapsychic conflict persisted through successive phases of development. Simply put, to be a girl was to be a victor and defended against being a weak boy who is taken to task by a pretty superheroine for his wrongdoings. Each libidinal phase reorganized the gender symptom and was recapitulated in the transference.

(38) In this case, the mother played a pivotal role, as in other cases (Greenson, 1966; Stoller, 1966; Loeb and Shane, 1982; McDevitt, 1985, unpublished). Stanley's family background, consisting of the distant father, dying grandfather, and accident-prone uncle, also contributed to the arrest in gender development. The type of father or father surrogate available seemed to be the issue in Stanley's case. The role of the father in separation-individuation and identification has been documented by Abelin (1971) and Ross (1975). Mother wished for another daughter who would have been, in her mind, more manageable. Her preference was projected by her experience of having an older and younger brother. Stanley was influenced in sharing mother's wish by multiple factors. She wished her younger brother had been a girl. Stanley's older sister was healthy and did not suffer with repeated problems of allergies, immunizations, otitis and tonsillitis. His sister was appealing in that she was not only healthy but also compliant and pretty. It seemed that she fulfilled the mother's fantasies. It may have been that during his first two years Stanley recognized and came to share his mother's fantasy that sister, mother, and grandmother represented strength, health, and goodness when compared to his dying grandfather, injured uncle, and father.

(39) The father was an emotionally insignificant figure prior to the analysis. He seemed healthy at the time I first met him. However, shortly thereafter he developed Grave's disease with severe exophthalmos. The mother's temperament during the stress of the grandfather's and uncle's illnesses cannot be minimized since it peaked during the patient's separation-individuation phase. The elements of overt hostility as expressed by a temper tantrum, consisting of flinging dishes followed by an exit from the home for hours, was repeated in the transference. This shaping environment existed from Stanley's birth. The scene was repeated many times during the first year of analysis when he played the powerful, cruel girl, and the analyst was the boy in the corner, facing the wall, who was warned not to speak lest he be deprived of his meal. The cross-gender symptom was reorganized with oral-phase derivatives and defended against the threat of food deprivation. Later in the

analysis, oral-phase derivatives emerged in the form of a magic potion concocted by a witch that changed boys into girls. The fantasy, a food-gender link, involved oral incorporation of the cruel mother, death of the masculine self-representation, and rebirth as a powerful female. The symptom was expressed as urethral- and anal-phase derivatives when Stanley spilled water and messed, became infuriated with me, and left abruptly for the waiting room. These repetitive transference reactions suggest a reconstruction of the preoedipal determinants that led to recognizable cross-gender behavior.

(40) "During the rapprochement and phallic phases, the boy ordinarily copes with the separation and castration anxiety by moving emotionally and physically away from his mother and toward the father" (McDevitt, 1985, unpublished). This process has been referred to as "disidentification" (Greenson, 1968). When a male figure is emotionally available, the boy's primary identification is replaced and becomes gender-appropriate. In order for individuation to proceed, other elements in addition to father's availability should be present. The mother might encourage the boy's budding masculinity and his interest in boyish activities. The young boy shifts away from his mother. The sight of her reminds him of the threat of object loss and the threat of castration (McDevitt, 1987, unpublished). He moves toward his father who, like himself, has a penis. Father, at this phase of development, can be idealized and can assuage his anxieties. During the oedipal phase, Stanley's masculinity was discouraged as he attempted to shift toward his beloved grandfather. His grandfather's health failed rapidly, causing the boy's anxiety to mount rather than to ease.

(41) Instead of masculinity, his mother encouraged femininity. At this point, Stanley seemed to have shared his mother's fantasy that he be a girl. His emotionally absent father allowed Stanley's budding masculinity to wane. The phallic aggressive qualities of Wonder Woman and the superheroines must have seemed appealing compared to the injured, dying, distant men who were available. His sister was favored and was someone to be admired and idealized. The omniscient mother was to be respected, feared—a person not to be crossed. Identification with mother and difficulty in disidentifying with her seemed to be profoundly influenced by a fantasy he shared with her (Blum, 1988)—mother's wish for a daughter. Father's effort to placate his wife and Stanley's fear of his mother's wrath added to his desire to fulfill mother's wish. Disidentifying with mother was partial, and gender individuation progressed in a deviant form best described by Stanley when he referred to his dolls or pictures as "he-she." This mental representation suggests a parity between his masculine and feminine self-representation that is conflict-ridden. The use of the pronouns "he-she" as a noun I also heard from an adult analytic patient who tended to restore conflicted gender identity and depleted sense of masculinity by visiting and referring to transvestite homosexual prostitutes as "he-she." Core gender, the "he" in "he-she," is conflict-free and would not seem to be involved in Stanley's case. Rather, the issue of gender role, the "she" in the "he-she," and the aim of the sexual drive or sexual orientation is in question.

(42) Prognosis and adult outcome is still uncertain. Without analysis, it seems that gender development would have moved toward a homosexual orientation (Friedman, 1988; Green, 1987). Follow-up during adolescence and early adulthood is required to validate the tentative conclusion that psychoanalysis during prelatency can be effective in gender identity disorders, and offers an alternative in some cases to a brittle sense of masculinity and/or homosexual orientation in the future adult.

References

ABELIN, E. L. (1971). The role of the father in the separation-individuation process. In *Separation-Individuation: Essays in Honor of Margaret S. Mahler*, ed. J. B. McDevitt & C. Settlage. New York: Int. Univ. Press, pp. 229-252.

BLUM, H. P. (1988). Shared fantasy and reciprocal identification, and their role in gender disorders. In *Fantasies, Myths and Reality: Essays in Honor of Jacob A. Arlow*, ed. H. P. Blum, Y. Kramer & A. D. Richards. Madison, Conn.: Int. Univ. Press, pp. 323-338.

COATES, S. & ZUCKER, K. J. (1988). Gender identity disorders in children. In *Handbook of Clinical Assessment of Children and Adolescents*, Vol. 12, ed. C. J. Kestenbaum & D. T. Williams. New York: N.Y. Univ. Press, pp. 893-914.

FRIEDMAN, R. C. (1988). *Male Homosexuality: A Contemporary Psychoanalytic Perspective*. New Haven: Yale Univ. Press, pp. 33-48.

FRIEND, M. R., SCHIDDEL, L., KEIN, B. & DUNAEFF, D. (1954). Observations on the development of transvestism in boys. *Amer. J. Orthopsychiat.* 24:563-574.

GREEN, R. (1987). *The Sissy Boy Syndrome and the Development of Homosexuality*. New Haven: Yale Univ. Press, pp. 99-113.

GREENSON, R. R. (1964). On homosexuality and gender identity. *Int. J. Psychoanal.*, 45:217-219.

_____(1966). A transvestite boy and a hypothesis. *Int. J. Psychoanal.*, 47:399-403.

_____(1968). Disidentifying from mother: its special importance for the boy. *Int. J. Psychoanal.*, 49:370-374.

KLEEMAN, J. (1965). A boy discovers his penis. *Psychoanal. Study Child*, 20:239-265.

LOEB, L. & SHANE, M. (1982). The resolution of a trans-sexual wish in a five-year-old boy. *J. Amer. Psychoanal. Assn.*, 30:419-434.

MAHLER, M. S., PINE, F. & BERGMAN, A. (1975). *The Psychological Birth of the Human Infant.* New York: Basic Books.

ROIPHE, H. & GALENSON, E. (1981). *Infantile Origins of Sexual Identity.* New York: Int. Univ. Press.

ROSS, J. M. (1975). The development of paternal identity: a critical review of the literature on nurturance and generativity in boys and men. *J. Amer. Psychoanal. Assn.*, 23:783-818.

SPERLING, M. (1964). The analysis of a boy with transvestite tendencies. *Psychoanal. Study Child*, 19:470-493.

STOLLER, R. J. (1964). A contribution to the study of gender identity. *Int. J. Psychoanal,* 45:220-226.

_____(1966). The mother's contribution to infantile transvestite behavior. *Int. J. Psychoanal.* 47:396-403.

_____(1975). *Sex and Gender. Volume II: The Transsexual Experiment.* New York: Aronson.

_____(1985). *Presentations of Gender.* New Haven: Yale Univ. Press.

_____ & HERDT, G. H. (1982). The development of masculinity: a cross-cultural contribution. *J. Amer. Psychoanal. Assn.*, 30:29-61.

TYSON, P. (1982). A developmental line of gender identity, gender role, and choice of love object. *J. Amer. Psychoanal. Assn.*, 30:61-87.

Terms for Discussion

1. gender identity disorder (paragraphs 1 and 42)

2. rapprochement phase (paragraphs 2, 18, and 40)

3. narcissistic (paragraphs 4, 30, and 32)

4. phobia (paragraphs 5 and 21)

5. castration reactions/anxiety (paragraphs 5, 21, 23, 24, and 40)

6. oral-phase derivatives (paragraphs 24, 33, and 39)

7. anal-phase derivatives (paragraphs 24 and 39)

8. oedipal theme/phase (paragraphs 28, 33, and 40)

9. libidinal phase (paragraph 37)

10. transference (paragraphs 37 and 39)

11. separation-individuation phase (paragraphs 38, 39, 40, and 41)

12. preoedipal determinants (paragraph 39)

13. phallic phase (paragraph 40)

14. disidentification (paragraphs 40 and 41)

Questions

15. Are the three strands of gender identity that Tyson identified in paragraph 2 helpful in conceptualizing Stanley's case? Explain.

16. What is your opinion on the issue of whether homosexuality can or should be cured and whether its development can or should be prevented? In your opinion, is homosexuality the central issue in Stanley's case? If yes, explain why. If no, what is the central issue?

17. Initially, Stanley's father insisted that Stanley would outgrow his cross-gender behavior. (See paragraph 9.) In your opinion, is it possible that that is what happened in this case (i.e., that the psychoanalysis was merely coincidental to a natural maturational process)? Explain.

18. If you were the analyst, how would you have responded to Stanley's question in paragraph 17?

19. Speculate on why Stanley refused to discuss his upcoming hospitalization but was eager to write about it. (See paragraph 22.)

20. What elements of the analysis in paragraphs 11 through 32 distinguish Stanley's treatment as "psychoanalytic" as opposed to other forms of mental health treatment?

21. The author states that prognosis and adult outcome are uncertain. (See paragraph 42.) Based on the information in the article, what is your prognosis for Stanley?

22. Are there other types of treatment that might have been used with Stanley? Explain.

23. Rate the article on the seven criteria described in the introduction to this book on a scale from 5 (highest quality) through 1 (lowest quality). Be prepared to explain your ratings.

Criterion 1: The demographics of the case are described: _____

Criterion 2: The condition(s) and behavior(s) that necessitated treatment are described in detail: _____

Criterion 3: The method of treatment is described in sufficient detail so that it can be replicated without additional information: _____

Criterion 4: A rationale is provided for the method of treatment selected: _____

Criterion 5: The client's improvement, if any, is clearly documented: _____

Criterion 6: Follow-up information on the client's improvement, if any, is presented: _____

Criterion 7: The study is appropriate for publication in a journal: _____

Case 22

Identity Formation in an Adolescent Girl: Boundaries between Psychotherapy and Counselling*

Catherine Schmidt-Löw-Beer
Institut für Tiefenpsychologie (Vienna, Austria)

(1) Adolescence has been characterized as a period in life, when many typical changes both in body growth and emotional development take place. It is often accompanied by various degrees of turmoil (Freud, 1958; Rutter et al., 1976).

(2) Physical, cognitive and emotional growth spurt ahead, creating pressure for new adaptation, as well as opportunities to reconcile and resolve older conflicts. All adolescents struggle with a heightened awareness of body changes and body concerns (Cooper & Wanerman, 1984).

(3) One of the main tasks of adolescence is to develop one's own unique identity (Erikson, 1965), thereby weakening ties to strong internalized parental objects, allowing the recognition of the self, with its special strengths and weaknesses, likes and dislikes (Loewald, 1979).

(4) However, sometimes the ability to form a stable and integrated sense of who one is can be impaired and instead an adolescent can feel overwhelmed by confusion, fragmentation, anxiety and frequently somatic symptoms.

(5) Possibilities of helping such young people, other than by suggesting they go into long term psychoanalysis or intensive psychotherapy will be considered. Depending on the child's or adolescent's psychopathology a balance between time spent with learning, curiosity and peers, and in a therapist's office should be found.

(6) It will be suggested that seeing even very disturbed adolescents only once a week over a certain period of time can be highly successful; the aim of the treatment being to join forces with and allow the normal strife for growth and development, characteristic in adolescence to take over.

(7) A case of an eleven and a half year old girl will be presented to show how such development was achieved and the question will be raised as to which interventions led to growth and change. Are they strictly psychotherapy or do they also belong to the realm of counselling? Where are the boundaries?

(8) Throughout the therapy the parents received counselling by the client's therapist. They were seen irregularly, about twice a month, because they often changed their appointments.

(9) What did the counselling imply?
   a. The parents' own wish to be good parents was supported.
   b. The reality of the here and now remained the central focus of the meetings.
   c. The child was shown to have both lovable and dislikeable aspects.
   d. Questions were raised, regarding the parental need to create "a crisis" about everything and their inability to set limits or to take responsibility on themselves.

(10) Before going into the details of the history, typical

International Journal for the Advancement of Counselling, 14, pp. 181-191. Copyright 1991 by Kluwer Academic Publishers. Reprinted with permission of Kluwer Academic Publishers.

interventions that were applied in the process of the treatment and which have been described by Kernberg et al. (1989) will be considered:

    a. Problems were discussed by the therapist and the client in an attempt to sort and figure things out. (Clarification)

    b. The client was confronted with unconscious aspects of her behaviour. (Confrontation)

    c. A stable relationship between therapist and patient slowly developed.

    d. The therapist made interpretations, interpreting the transference, especially the relationship in the here and now. Often it was related to infantile material, thereby addressing unconscious conflicts.

    e. Proplan interventions were made according to the "control" hypothesis of Weiss and Sampson (1986).

(11) This is a psychoanalytical cognitive theory, claiming that every human being develops a specific pathogenic belief concerning his life at a very early age. For instance, the notion that his or her mother does not want him or her to succeed in life. A patient with such a belief will go through life unconsciously hoping that this belief will prove to be wrong. He will devise an unconscious plan of success testing his environment with the hope, that it will allow him to develop, thereby disconfirming his pathogenic belief. Patients have many pathogenic beliefs.

(12) Such a test could manifest itself in the following exchange (please forgive me for the oversimplification; it is not just a way of strengthening self-confidence):

Patient: I was offered a very good job yesterday (pause), but I really am no good, I can't type, I haven't learnt languages....

Therapist: (after having assessed that the patient's arguments are unrealistic) How come you cannot allow yourself a good job? I think you are worried that your mother does not want you to be independent. (That would be a proplan intervention, which would lead to immediate progress in the treatment.)

Whereas:

Therapist: Tell me more about not being qualified?... (Would confirm the patient's pathogenic belief that he is not supposed to be successful—he would go on complaining, becoming depressed and angry.)

(13) I am assuming that both in psychotherapy and in counselling such proplan interventions are made, leading to progress and growth of personality. My claim would be that unknowingly therapists and counsellors are achieving much more in terms of real changes, than they are aware of. *It is suggested that both in psychotherapy and in counselling such proplan interventions occur frequently* leading to progress and growth of personality.

(14) However, what it was that really helped and led to the growth and change that was achieved in the course of the therapy can merely be speculated on.

(15) Six years after the treatment had ended, the client was contacted in an attempt to find out how she had experienced the therapeutic work: had it helped her and if so, could she share her impressions and her experience with her therapist?

(16) Forgive me for oversimplifying the rich and complex material, in spite of which I hope to give you a first hand impression of what really went on in the sessions and how these were experienced by the client. The material will be limited to the last two years of the treatment concentrating mainly on the identity problems.

(17) I should like to introduce my patient Lisa. She was eleven and a half years old when I first met her. Lisa would also like to introduce herself, at least in writing. Today she is twenty-four years old and has moved to another country. She sent me a tape, reflecting on her therapy and reading from her diary, which she had begun to write during the last two years of the treatment. I shall attempt to describe a psychotherapy which lasted five and a half years comparing the client's point of view with the therapist's point of view. We met once a week. The sessions lasted fifty minutes; only during the last eight months we would meet for one and a half hours.

(18) Lisa was small for her age and plump. Her brown hair was greasy, neither short nor long and somehow hung around her head sadly and limply. She wore baggy, shabby pants and a washed-out colourless sweater. When she moved she seemed to feel awkward; it was as if she were crippled under a heavy weight. The liveliness of a teenager was completely missing; instead she was clearly deeply unhappy and depressed. Now and again she would quickly glance at me expressing anxiety, insecurity, with an air of impatience and boredom. It was as if she were saying: when can I go, there's no more to say, you know everything, I have no problems. Can't you leave me in peace? At the same time she was nervously sliding around on her chair. I found myself struggling with feelings of helplessness and anger, wondering if I wanted to work with Lisa, who so

Identity Formation

obviously had had enough of psychotherapy.

(19) I should mention that Lisa had been in all kinds of treatments since age three including drug treatment which had led to a psychotic episode and the doctor's view that Lisa should be removed from her harmful environment. Also at the age of four she had an operation on the urethra in an attempt to cure the symptom of enuresis (bed wetting), the reason for which she was now supposed to see me. No wonder she was sick of therapists.

(20) Lisa's parents, when I first met them, seemed to fill the office like two giants continuously expanding, causing me to feel smaller and smaller, and nearly to disappear into the corner of the room.

(21) They talked about Lisa describing her as a very difficult burden in contrast to her beautiful, intelligent sister who was one and a half years older. She wets both during the day and at night. The children at school often call her "smelly." She was never dry although the parents tried everything to get rid of the wetting, both with patience and threats. But Lisa was stubborn and aggressive, unwilling to cooperate. Her grades at school are bad and she has no friends. They had provided therapies for her since she was three years old.

(22) It is hard to describe Lisa's parents briefly, due to the complexity of their personalities, and the aspects in which they differ and, on the other hand, are similar. Mother works in the social field and father is an artist. Basically they love their children and are themselves lovable people. However, these qualities are buried under severe narcissism and their infantile personalities. Partly they are still children, easily hurt and perpetually in competition with one another. They are unable to provide security, themselves searching for security from their children. They cannot postpone their wishes, and therefore are incapable of helping each other. Each parent wishing to be the child, looked after and cared for by the other, the good mother, who fulfills all wishes.

(23) Initially, when I began to see Lisa she lived in a chaotic world, confused about who she was, male or female, whether her parents were men or women. The absence of boundaries between the generations and between the sexes flooded the family with confusion.

(24) And last but not least meet Blacki, the youngest family member, a small dog who moved into the flat several months after the therapy with Lisa had begun. He caused numerous conflicts, mostly having to do with issues around toilet training. I met him personally.

(25) As it turned out Lisa had many complaints: she was depressive and full of anxieties: she was afraid of doctors, had carcinophobia. She frequently somatized, suffering from headache and stomach-ache. She hated school and had no friends. She had several symptoms: Bulimia (like her mother) followed by attempts to lose weight. Periods of terrible boredom. Enuresis during the day and at night.

(26) Frequently, before wetting, Lisa would have a recurring dream: she dreamt she has to go to the bathroom so she calls her mother. Mother does not come. Lisa gets up, goes to the bathroom and to the toilet. There she suddenly becomes aware of mother's leg hanging into the room from the window. She is terrified, and at the same time she hears a voice telling her to save her mother. Only one of them can live, the other must die. She wakes up in a wet bed, confused, because she did the right thing namely to go to the bathroom.

(27) In the dream her struggle for independence and autonomy and her fear of annihilation in her symbiotic relationship to mother are apparent. Therefore, I decided to avoid the role of a controlling mother by initially not addressing the enuresis.

(28) Lisa does not know why the wetting stopped. She only remembers being glad that I did not mention it. It was connected to so much pressure. How did the symptom disappear in my view?

    a. Although I did not address the symptom I used Blacki metaphorically, asking Lisa how she could help him to become clean? Does she imagine he feels hurt when everybody yells at him? When they hit him? Lisa soon stopped wetting, but Blacki developed into an enuretic dog.
    b. We spent a lot of time thinking about issues of control.
    c. I helped her to see the connection between the feeling of wet and other emotions. Wet can make her glad, cause her to be sad, make her mad, or make her feel bad. She thereby learns to differentiate and to separate. Lisa stops wetting; however, the urge to stuff herself with food is coupled with a panicky wish to lose weight.

(29) *In April 1988 six years after the therapy ended Lisa says:* I know that I was a very unhappy child, that I was always unhappy. There was always something gnawing inside me and it usually had to do with my body image. Talking to you was so important, because I

was just unhappy and I had to talk.

(30) *Let us compare this memory with a session in October 1980:* Lisa shows me photographs of the first beautiful holiday she spent with friends in Italy. Beautiful, although Steven did once call her a hippopotamus which was very upsetting. She is making such an effort to lose weight. She mentions mother's eating problems and her doubts that psychotherapy could help mother.

Mother wonders whether acupuncture would help. Lisa also wonders and talks about her fear of being unable to lose weight. I point out how doubtful she is as to whether I can help her and her wish for magic. Magic would help her to avoid considering her fantasies and fears about losing weight. Could it be that, on the one hand she does have the wish to lose weight, yet, on the other hand, she is afraid of losing weight?

Lisa becomes extremely anxious, she is nearly in tears and for the first time she remembers her experiences in hospital, when she was four years old and her fantasies about operations. (She was operated on the urethra at age four and had her tonsils out when she was five.)

Lisa: Something happens inside me. I keep thinking of having my appendix out. (She has never had her appendix removed). People are attacking me. They are tearing something out of me. Dieting seems to lead to an increase in weight.

Therapist: That sounds very confusing.

Lisa: Yes, because that means something must be growing inside me, some sort of tumour. (Lisa is getting very tense).

Lisa: In my tummy there are many horrible little doctors. Their noses and their chins are very pointed. Every time when I try to lose weight they appear and tease me and they do something. I don't know what. They cut and they pull and I don't lose weight. I can never understand why I can't lose weight when I diet.

Lisa and I wonder when and how these doctors got into her? She thinks it was when she had the bladder operation, although she has never had these "imaginations" so clearly before.

This session was not only characterized by strong emotions, it was decisive for Lisa's development. It is interesting, that shortly thereafter Lisa began to write a diary.

In the following weeks she keeps talking about being unable to lose weight.

(31) *In January 1981 she writes:* I'm keeping a very strict diet. Only 400 calories per day. How much have I lost? Nothing! Nothing at all! I can't eat less. I want to be slim, I want to be beautiful.

(32) *In January 1981 she writes into her diary:* I just told Dr. Schmidt that love and sex don't go together. If you don't want to have sex with somebody you really love him. (Her fear of sex and of her strong feelings of confusion become very clear. A diffuse relationship between sexuality, her fantasies of what is going on inside her body, and her weight begins to emerge. In the following sessions we remember her disgust with respect to her menstruation, that was connected to fantasies of bleeding to death, and of body injury. During this period she is still unsuccessfully trying to lose weight.)

(33) *In January 1981 Lisa writes into her diary:* I am so ugly. I look into the mirror and what do I see? I start from the bottom: Slippers that are falling apart. Jeans that are cut badly at the bottom. Fat, fat, fat legs, fat stomach, tiny torso lengthwise, sideways I have enough. No neck because I am wearing a surgical something because I twisted a muscle doing a somersault. Thick lips with a mustache over them. If I smile teeth with those stupid brown marks. Face that looks dirty. Small pimples everywhere and a big one on my cheek. Messy eyebrows and greasy hair. What a sight! I hate myself so much I am sick of myself I am so disgusting. No wonder I don't have a boyfriend. I feel so "yucky" so fat. I am sick of this sadness all the time.

(34) *A session in March 1981:* Lisa looks quite chubby. Less attractive. "Grows" on me as the hour progresses.

Lisa: I read a book . . . I found myself in it; it was about a man turning into a rock; giving up his life because it brings no pleasure. It reminds me of the time in hospital when I wanted to have everything. She would like to be able to sing in a musical, although her sister says she sings wrong . . . .

Lisa: Oh yes, I really do . . . (want to have everything). That reminds me of a story: A fairy says to a good twin (one twin is good the other bad). I will marry you when you become a man. Only when the twins good and bad join does she accept him. I suppose it's the same with me. I can't accept the bad parts of myself.

Therapist: (I nod) That you are good at some things and bad at others. Good ideas and thoughts, bad ideas and thoughts.

At the end of the hour Lisa wonders what the doctors removed from her at the operation. She imagines that maybe they removed a penis. She always thought she was a boy.

(35) *In May 1981 Lisa writes into her diary:* I think I am disgusting and that is what I don't want people to know. I hate life, I hate mummy, I hate my friends . . . I wish I could become beautiful and wonderful. Only then

Identity Formation

could I become happy. I don't want to go through life hiding myself out of shame.

(36) At this point I would like to remind you of Lisa's recurring dream.

On September 16, 1982 she writes the following passage into her diary: This was written after the therapy had ended, when for a while Lisa continued to write into her diary.

A psychology book mentions something interesting. It dealt with the study of children who were placed in a residential nursery-home for some weeks: I quote: "During the first few days they cried frequently and desperately clung to some favourite toy they had brought along. After a while their crying abated, ... They become apathetic and hostile and lose previously acquired bowel control." Doesn't that sound familiar? I had a brain storm the other day when I saw a little child cling to her mother's leg. I remember that I used to do that all the time. It protected me from the world. I suddenly thought of the persistent dream I used to have of my mother's leg on top of the closet. I imagine that that could have been what was chopped off in the hospital. That was mine and my mother's. It makes sense because I felt cut away from her in the hospital and that could also account for my feelings of guilt with her leg up there, since it was because of me and in me that it happened. (Probably Lisa was furious with mother wanting her to die in her fantasy). That's what I wrote to Dr. Schmidt. I think it makes a lot of sense though it's hard to express.

(37) *Lisa's thoughts about the dream today:* I can remember having talked with you about my dreams a lot and that it helped me. But I can't remember any details. I remember thinking about the dream where my leg, no it was my mother's leg, hung into the bathroom from the window. We discussed the dream in depth and it was very disturbing and upsetting. I think we came up with many explanations and finally I stopped dreaming this dream. However I still don't know what it means and I don't know if I was convinced by your interpretations. The main thing is I don't have the dream any more.

In Lisa's fantasy the doctors are connected with the sadomasochistic parents, who always exposed their child to doctors.

In order to understand the dynamics of the case it does not suffice to take only Lisa's symptoms and problems into account. Her interactions with her parents must be considered. As I have mentioned before, they are infantile, narcissistic personalities, transferring their own anxieties on to their daughter, the daughter therefore becomes the object on to which the parents attempt to undo their own castration anxiety. For this reason Lisa repeatedly has to face medical procedures.

It is not surprising that Lisa feels castrated. The material shows that Lisa has the fantasy of being a castrated boy. In the everyday language that was used with Lisa her fear that something was missing and that she had been injured, was pointed out. Therefore she feels ugly, incompetent, and stupid. Others have something she has not got (Freud, 1923).

The recurring dream can serve to understand the underlying psychodynamic processes. It can also be seen as an attempt to deal with the trauma of castration, which was triggered by the urethral operation. The traumatic separation from the mother at the same time involved a separation from mother's leg (a symbol for integrity and holding). Lisa lost two things at once: Her nurturing and vitally important mother, her imagined penis and thereby her integrity. In the child's fantasy the two elements, Lisa's penis and mother's leg became unified. In the dream mother and her protective qualities are symbolized through her leg, whereby we even know that in real life Lisa would feel protected when clinging to mother's leg, the leg being her transitional object (Winnicott, 1971). From now on every separation from mother is connected with fear of castration and very threatening. She also loses her integrity and feeling of safety and security, remaining damaged, helpless and furious. That is why Lisa has to fail in her attempts to lose weight, because unconsciously she is resisting the attempts of the doctors, and/or the mother to tear out her integrity.

(38) *Lisa remembers the sessions in May 1981 in the following way:* She had the feeling of being two people. A pleasant person who her friends knew and a person she had to hide.

"I know Dr. Schmidt that you liked me and that was very important to me and you liked me because of my soul and because of the things I had to say."

(39) *Let us take a look at a session from that period:* May 1981: Lisa looks very pretty. She hands me a poem: I am I.

"I wrote a poem for you and me (she is obviously very proud). You know (reluctantly at first. She is obviously struggling with something) everybody wants to change me to improve me. My friends, my mother, my father. Help that also sounds like the doctors. They also wanted to help me." She talks about being two people.

Lisa: One of them is happy, and alive, I think. The other is bad and naughty—that's me. Sometimes—actually that's the problem I often don't know who is me or the other person. I frequently feel as if I were lying when I say: this is how I feel—because suddenly I don't really know who it is who is feeling—me or the other me. (Lisa is struggling, worried, nervous, excited; there is an atmosphere of something very important happening. Tension combined with the awareness of discovering a new dimension within herself.)

Therapist: How confusing for you.

Lisa: We must name them: (thinks) One of them is the judge, that's the super-ego. The other is the actor. When I am alone the two of them are present and they talk together. Yesterday I stood in front of the mirror and I wanted to shake hands with myself. But I couldn't. I hate my body. You know what: I just remembered when I was in hospital I had to walk through this long corridor and I wanted to turn into a rock. I wonder if that's where the split actually started. I had to save one part of my body.

The fantasy of turning into a rock can also be understood in terms of an attempt to save herself from the pain and anxiety of separation. A rock symbolizing something that is without feelings, lifeless and without sex, but, on the other hand provides safety and protection through its stability.

In the final year Lisa developed into a lively active adolescent. To a large extent she had succeeded in separating from her parents and was involved with her peer group. There were numerous fights with father, but also respect and even some love for one another. Mother started to turn to her daughter for her own needs and her dependence on her daughter was striking. However Lisa was often able to ignore her parent's needs and was able to go ahead with her own life. She won prizes, played the piano in a cabaret, and was elected into the school council. She had several friends and her first sexual experiences.

(40) I shall now briefly reconsider the boundaries between psychotherapy and counselling.

(41) The treatment lasted several years and we met regularly. I developed a psychoanalytically oriented hypothesis with respect to the underlying dynamics and I also aimed at achieving structural changes of the personality. These are features characteristic for psychotherapy. However, looking through my process notes (covering the entire therapy) I actually became aware of the fact that I rarely offered deep interpretations, which would be considered to be the heart of psychoanalysis. Through listening, I created a facilitating environment (Winnicott, 1960) thereby allowing Lisa to discover her own ideas and develop her own creativity. My interventions most frequently consisted in helping Lisa to become aware of connections between the increasingly rich material that was presented.

(42) Both in counselling and psychotherapy one is confronted with having to establish a certain type of relationship, whereby I worked hard on creating an atmosphere of trust, reliability, and stability. Maybe one could say that as a psychoanalyst I actually did a good job in counselling?

(43) Lisa, anyway was able to express her thoughts, feelings and understanding of what had gone on much more clearly than I was, both in poems and in her diary.

(44) As the end approaches I ask myself if Lisa will manage to hold on to her newly acquired abilities and skills. Has she developed into an autonomous human being?

(45) Saying good-bye was sad. She writes about it in her diary and decides to replace me through her diary. The diary becomes the transitional object. She took her ability to analyze with her; her own version of her therapist which had now become mother's leg, that she had finally internalized. She had achieved object constancy and found her own identity.

(46) A few months after the therapy ended, Lisa ends her diary. Her final words are as follows:

This diary has meant a lot to me. It has been my on and off companion for about two years. Only two years! It seems like more, because so much has happened within those two years. In essence I consider my childhood to be unhappy. This diary has witnessed the termination of my perpetual unhappiness. And it has witnessed the termination of my childhood. Actually at the time when I started this diary I had already made a significant part of the journey. I had learnt to listen to my thoughts and tried to interpret them. This was a major change from when I was used to being unhappy and remained feeling terrible without being aware of "that I am unhappy." Just knowing I am unhappy makes it so much more concrete and acceptable. It's like the difference of hearing a song in a foreign language and then in both cases you hear the music, but only in the English one, can you truly grasp it. This does not mean you understand the meaning of all the words, but you do have some idea. This was the point I was at, at the beginning of my diary. The song was finally in a comprehensible language. Anything I would have written before that would have been very, very, jumbled up, because I hadn't been with Dr. Schmidt enough to incorporate her way of figuring things out. I am sorry I did not write before I did, but I still think this diary contains the most important years of my psychological rebirth. I am definitely a happier person, than I used to be. What happened when I spilled out my heart enough to let go of a lot, interpreted a lot and began to feel better about myself. This is drastically oversimplified, because I really don't know what happened to change the way I feel. I am sure it was partly due to the magic of psychotherapy, which I am sure that nobody fully understands.

References

Cooper, S., & Wanerman, L. (1984). *A casebook of child psychotherapy*. New York: Brunner/Mazel.

Erikson, E.H. (1965). The problem of ego identity. *J. Amer. Psychoanal. Assoc. 4*: 56-121.

Freud, A. (1958). Adolescence. *Psychoanal. Study Child. 13*: 255-78.

Freud, S. (1923). *Die infantile Genitalorganisation*, Gesammelte Werke, Band 13. Frankfurt: Fischer, 1969, 6. Aufl.

Kemberg, O., Selzer, M., Koenigsberg, H., Carr, A., & Appelbaum, A. (1989). *Psychodynamic psychotherapy of borderline patients*. New York: Basic Books.

Loewald. H. (1979). The waning of the Oedipus complex. *J. Amer. Psychoanal. Assn. 27*: 751-776.

Rutter, M., Graham, P., Chadwick, O., & Jule, W. (1976). Adolescent turmoil: fact or fiction. *J. Child Psychol. Psychist. 17*: 35-56.

Weiss, J., & Sampson, H. (1986). *The psychoanalytic process: Theory, clinical observations and empirical research*. New York: Guilford Press.

Winnicott, D.W. (1960). The theory of the parent-infant relationship. In: *Maturational processes and facilitating environment*. New York: International objects and transitional phenomena. International Universities Press.

Winnicott, D.W. (1971). Transitional objects and transitional phenomena. In: *Playing and reality*. Great Britain: Hazel Watson & Viney Limited.

Terms for Discussion

1. transference (paragraph 10)

2. proplan intervention (paragraphs 10, 12, and 13)

3. psychoanalytic cognitive theory (paragraph 11)

4. pathogenic belief (paragraph 11)

5. psychotic episode (paragraph 19)

6. narcissism (paragraphs 22 and 37)

7. infantile personality (paragraphs 22 and 37)

8. carcinophobia (paragraph 25)

9. bulimia (paragraph 25)

10. castration anxiety (paragraph 37)

11. transitional object (paragraphs 37 and 45)

12. super-ego (paragraph 39)

13. Object constancy (paragraph 45)

Questions

14. What is your opinion on the assertion that "every human being develops a specific pathological belief concerning his life at a very early age"? (See paragraph 11.)

15. Does it surprise you that the therapist struggled with feelings of helplessness and anger? (See paragraph 18.) Explain.

16. Do you believe that clear boundaries between generations and sexes is desirable for healthy family functioning? (See paragraph 23.) Explain.

17. If you had been the therapist (assuming that you do not have the hindsight provided by this article) would you have asked Lisa directly about her bed wetting? (See paragraph 28.) Explain.

18. Are there measures that could have been taken when Lisa was in the hospital to reduce her psychological trauma? (See paragraph 30.) Explain.

19. How would you answer the question posed in paragraph 42?

20. Are there other types of treatment that might have facilitated Lisa's improvement? Explain.

21. Rate the article on the seven criteria described in the introduction to this book on a scale from 5 (highest quality) through 1 (lowest quality). Be prepared to explain your ratings.

Criterion 1: The demographics of the case are described: _____

Criterion 2: The condition(s) and behavior(s) that necessitated treatment are described in detail: _____

Criterion 3: The method of treatment is described in sufficient detail so that it can be replicated without additional information: _____

Criterion 4: A rationale is provided for the method of treatment selected: _____

Criterion 5: The client's improvement, if any, is clearly documented: _____

Criterion 6: Follow-up information on the client's improvement, if any, is presented: _____

Criterion 7: The study is appropriate for publication in a journal: _____

Case 23

Occupational Therapy Intervention for an Adult with Depression and Suicidal Tendencies*

Valerie L. Custer
The University of Texas Medical Branch Hospitals

Kathryn E. Wassink
Texas City Independent School District

(1) Depression and suicidal tendencies are common problems among patients in both inpatient and outpatient mental health settings. To help patients work through depression and overcome self-destructive tendencies, the psychiatrist, occupational therapist, and patient must work cooperatively to set goals. The following report describes the steps taken to help a suicidal patient improve his self-image through occupation and selected work activities.

Background Information

(2) Ralph, a 40-year-old married man, was admitted to the psychiatric unit of The University of Texas Medical Branch Hospitals, Galveston, in April 1988 with major depression and diabetes controlled by diet. At the time of admission, he had symptoms of depression with suicide ideations. He reported that he kept a loaded gun at home and on several occasions had held it to his head. The patient lived with his wife of 11 years and his teenage stepdaughter.

(3) The patient's mental health problems were first diagnosed when he was 14 years old; at that time, he was hospitalized for 4 months for "antisocial" problems. Several subsequent hospitalizations followed for substance abuse and panic attacks. Because of his work history since that time, we assumed that he had been treated with some success.

Clinical Program

(4) Early in this hospitalization, Ralph was referred to occupational therapy, where he was evaluated with the occupational therapy department's initial interview, Peloquin's interview (Peloquin, 1983), the coin purse evaluation (Allen, 1985), and clinical observation. During the interviews, Ralph reported multiple life stressors, with the major problem being his difficulty in finding work and in maintaining work in his interest area. He reported being a writer and having had difficulty publishing or obtaining rewarding employment. Other problems he identified were difficulty with his father-in-law, chronic fatigue, decreased enjoyment of pleasurable activities, frequent awakening at night, and feelings of despair.

(5) The psychiatric occupational therapist noted several functional problems. The patient's lack of social skills was exhibited in his tending toward isolation. Ralph's self-perception seemed to fluctuate between grandiosity and feelings of worthlessness and of being a failure. Ralph was resistant to authority and had difficulty accepting constructive criticism. His stress management

*Reprinted from *The American Journal of Occupational Therapy, 9,* 1991, pp. 845-848. Copyright 1991 by the American Occupational Therapy Association. Reprinted with permission.

and time management skills were poor, and he showed traits of compulsive perfectionism. He even admitted that he placed unnecessary stress on himself while trying to do things perfectly, and this began to impair his function in daily activities.

(6) Because many of Ralph's problems were related to his inability to find or maintain satisfying employment, the therapist referred Ralph to the occupational therapy department's work program. This program administers many types of work evaluation, offers work hardening, and has a program to develop job-search skills.

(7) The patient's performance on the various work evaluations indicated that he had good potential for competitive employment. Academic and cognitive testing was performed with the Microcomputer Evaluation and Systems Screening Analysis (Valpar International, 1984) and the Wide Range Achievement Test (Jastak & Jastak, 1978), which showed that he had good skills in such areas as concentration in following complex instructions and problem-solving. On two interest inventories—the Self Directed Search (Holland, 1985) and the Gordon Occupational Checklist (Gordon, 1967)—the patient scored high in the areas of artistic and people-related occupations. These results are comparable with the patient's previous work interests. A physical capabilities assessment with the WEST 2 system (Work Evaluation System Technology, 1985) and the Round Blocks subtest of the Physical Capacities Evaluation (Smith, 1983) revealed scores within normal limits and showed that the patient had no significant problems in lifting strength, hand speed, or endurance. [The Round Blocks subtest of the Physical Capacities Evaluation score was 80% with the right (dominant) hand and 85% with the left hand. The physical capabilities assessment showed a medium work level, in which the maximum lifting weight is 50 lb, with frequent lifts of 25 lb.]

(8) Observation of Ralph's social and worker behaviors during the testing of the work program, however, revealed several problem areas that had been noted previously in the occupational therapy clinic. During the initial interview in work programs, Ralph verbalized severe feelings of failure; although as a writer he sometimes had articles published, he was unable to maintain a steady income by writing. He stated that he often had writer's block and would sit at his typewriter and play Russian roulette with a loaded gun. He believed that he had the intellectual potential to be successful in the job market, yet he had continually failed. Ralph's job titles, as reported in the work program evaluations, included writer, copier, machine operator, office technician, bindery worker, and warehouse operations manager. He expressed deep disappointment in himself because he had nothing to show for the 2 years he had spent in college. He had not completed an associate's degree. He had started a program in architecture, which had been financed by the Texas Rehabilitation Commission, but had dropped out because he thought that he knew more than the instructor. At 40 years of age, Ralph believed that he had wasted his life and was not "man enough" to earn a steady income with which to support his family.

(9) During the testing sessions in the work program, the patient showed poor social skills, such as interrupting and arguing with the staff, and refused to listen to others' opinions if they conflicted with his own. He would intellectualize by telling others how to do things better. He often made grandiose statements about his abilities, perhaps to compensate for his insecurities and fear of failure.

(10) While in the work program, Ralph continued to question authority and had difficulty accepting criticism. He exhibited compulsive traits that increased his anxiety unnecessarily and often slowed his rate of production. He exhibited limited insight regarding his strengths and weaknesses, as revealed in the testing, and had no vocational plans or goals to improve his situation. His pessimism impeded his potential and caused him to look first at the negative aspects of situations. An additional vocational barrier was his limited knowledge of marketable fields in his interest areas (arts and people) and available educational programs that could enhance his skills.

Treatment Plan

(11) After reviewing the results of the work program evaluations, we began a work preparation treatment plan that focused on the following goals:

1. Improvement of time management skills to promote effective use of time in preparation for balancing work, rest, and play once employment was secured.

2. Training in stress management skills, with a focus on techniques that could be used either at work or at home.

3. Improvement in self-image to facilitate a more confident impression during the employment interview process and once employment was achieved.

4. Improvement of social skills in preparation for positive interactions with co-workers and authority figures.

5. Improvement of knowledge of vocational sources and markets in the areas of artistic and people-related occupations so as to plan and implement a realistic vocational goal.
   6. Improvement of job-hunting skills to facilitate and improve marketability as a potential employee.

(12) The vocational treatment plan was implemented for 3 weeks, until Ralph was discharged. Discharge plans included follow-up with a psychologist at a mental health-mental retardation facility near Ralph's home and continuation with antidepressant medications. Because Ralph still had suicidal thoughts, the occupational therapist recommended referral to outpatient occupational therapy for continued structure and time management so as to keep Ralph's depression from causing a rehospitalization.

(13) During his outpatient care, the patient often contacted the occupational therapist outside of his daily treatment sessions, at which time the therapist provided him with continual nurturing and encouragement. The therapist continued to remind him of his accomplishments and improvements. When Ralph verbalized negative thoughts, he was redirected to more positive thoughts and solutions.

(14) Initially, the occupational therapist assisted the patient in determining his first realistic vocational goal, which was to return to school to pursue a degree. Because the patient was threatened by the possibility of another failure, the therapist insisted on positive thinking and practical step-by-step planning. The therapist aided the patient in a search through college catalogues for a program compatible with his decision to pursue a communications degree with a major in radio broadcasting. The therapist contacted the Texas Rehabilitation Commission, and Ralph's case was reopened and financial support was allocated. Because this was accomplished in June and school did not begin until September, constructive activities in addition to occupational therapy were needed in the interim. The patient began work, through the volunteer division of the hospital, in the occupational therapy department, which kept him productive and challenged as he waited for school to begin. His tasks were to care for the plants in the occupational therapy greenhouse and to help geriatric patients work with the plants. He also performed light clerical work, such as copying and collating for the occupational therapy department, and helped volunteer services with their hospitality cart. He sometimes talked with new patients who had been referred to the job readiness program and told them how he was being assisted.

(15) Initially, Ralph's treatment progressed slowly. He created unnecessary crises by perceiving problems as obstacles in his recovery and giving up on his goals. For example, the therapist worked to plan a school program, which Ralph was quick to abandon when a transportation problem (i.e., who would use the family car) arose. The therapist taught the patient problem-solving techniques, which involved the following steps:

   1. Break problems down into small steps to decrease the tendency to become overwhelmed.
   2. Use a goal work sheet (Hughes & Mullins, 1981) to visually assess the problem and solve only one part of the problem at a time until the problem is alleviated.
   3. Understand that there may be more than one way to solve a problem; do not give up if one plan does not work.

Concerning Ralph's problem with use of the family car, the therapist's guidance in using this problem-solving process helped Ralph find an alternate mode of transportation.

(16) The therapist also taught the patient basic stress management techniques, as described by Courtney and Escobedo (1990), to promote calmer, clearer thinking. Later, more complex stress management techniques involving biofeedback; visual imagery; slow, repetitive, deep breathing; and progressive muscle relaxation (Charlesworth & Nathan, 1984), were taught as ways to reduce overall anxiety. The patient found that visual imagery and breathing techniques worked best for him, and he successfully incorporated them into his daily routine.

(17) The therapist taught Ralph to keep a log of his daily activities to improve his time management skills (Larrington, 1970). Every hour of every day was documented. Once the patient did this consistently, the therapist discussed ways in which to achieve a greater balance between work, rest, and leisure activities and provided practical suggestions to improve his productive use of time. The therapist helped Ralph develop a structured schedule; he was required to spend a certain amount of time each day doing things that were important to him, such as volunteer work, planning for school, and making extra time for family activities, as well as doing something especially meaningful to him.

(18) To improve the patient's self-esteem and feelings of self-worth, the therapist used role-playing. In addition, the patient was required to report on one positive thing he had done for himself every day. To improve

the patient's social skills and acceptance of authority, the occupational therapist confronted the patient whenever he questioned the therapist's authority or verbalized grandiose, unrealistic statements about himself or a situation.

(19) Ralph used his good academic and writing skills by instructing another patient on résumé writing. The situation provided an opportunity for Ralph to experience immediate feedback from the therapist on his social interactions while simultaneously showing him that he was making a contribution. Role-playing techniques were used to solve difficult social situations. Ralph was shown ways to respond tactfully to authority, even when there was disagreement; provided with suggestions for appropriate conversation; and taught positive interview techniques and ways to make a good first impression in preparation for job hunting (Wassink, 1988).

(20) When the patient started school, he began to experience more success in his life. During this time, the task in treatment was to reduce the patient's dependency on the therapist and to help him develop more confidence in his own strengths and abilities. The patient's motivation for positive changes in his life became stronger. He was thus able to plan and present a program on mental health as a class project. During mental health week, he was asked to present the program on a local radio station. Ralph received much positive feedback from his instructors and classmates, which helped to reinforce his feelings of self-worth. Ralph wanted to help others by sharing his experience of battling depression. He allowed the second author to interview him on videotape as he gave testimony of his problems and rehabilitation.

(21) During the second half of his class work, Ralph was selected by his instructors to receive training from one of the more competitive radio stations in the area as a disc jockey and to help with the day-to-day running of the station. As he became more involved with his education and in his progress in the rehabilitation program, his hours of volunteer service were gradually reduced. Because he had accomplished all of the occupational therapy goals outlined in his original treatment plan, he was discharged from occupational therapy. His testimony on videotape indicated that he was no longer suicidal.

(22) Ralph's inpatient care had been covered by his spouse's insurance. As an outpatient, Ralph's position with the hospital volunteer services and placement in occupational therapy permitted the therapist to monitor his behavior until school started. His school expenses were paid for by the Texas Rehabilitation Commission.

Follow-Up
(23) Ralph finished the 1-year program required for certification in broadcasting and communications and continues to work at the local radio station. During the week he operated equipment for the radio station, and on weekends he serves as the disc jockey. While monitoring equipment, he has blocks of time when he is allowed to work on other projects and is currently writing a novel. Since his discharge from the occupational therapy program, he has survived the crisis of a separation from his wife. Ralph used the coping skills learned in occupational therapy to handle the crisis and to continue to pursue his occupational goals.

(24) This patient received considerable individual time with the therapist, in contrast to the usual occupational therapy programming. Specific patients, because of their insight and motivation, will benefit more from one-on-one intervention for goal attainment. Ralph was such a patient.

Summary
(25) A hospitalized patient with depression and suicidal tendencies was referred for occupational therapy. The patient's evaluations while hospitalized indicated a lack of social skills and unrealistic expectations concerning abilities and aspirations. A work evaluation showed high scores in artistic and people-related occupations.

(26) Treatment focused on improvement of self-image, social interaction abilities, and stress management skills that would assist the patient in obtaining and keeping a job. Increased knowledge of vocational options and selection of an appropriate training program led to a job placement that the patient has enjoyed and maintained for the past 2 years.

References

Allen, C. K. (1985). *Occupational therapy for psychiatric diseases: Measurement and management of cognitive disabilities.* Boston: Little, Brown.

Charlesworth, E. A., & Nathan, R. G. (1984). *Stress management: A comprehensive guide to wellness.* New York; Atheneum.

Courtney, C., & Escobedo, B. (1990). A stress management program: Inpatient-to-outpatient continuity. *The American Journal of Occupational Therapy, 44,* 306-310.

Gordon. L. V. (1967). *Gordon Occupational Checklist.* New York: Harcourt, Brace & World.

Holland, J. L. (1985). *Self Directed Search*. Odessa, FL: Psychological Assessment Resources.

Hughes, P. L., & Mullins, L. (1981). *Acute psychiatric care: An occupational therapy guide to exercises in daily living skills*. Thorofare, NJ: Slack.

Jastak, J. F., & Jastak, S. (1978). *Wide Range Achievement Test*. Wilmington, DE: Jastak Associates.

Larrington, G. G. (1970). *An exploratory study of the temporal aspects of adaptive functioning*. Unpublished master's thesis, University of Southern California, Los Angeles.

Peloquin, S. M. (1983). The development of an occupational therapy interview/therapy set procedure. *The American Journal of Occupational Therapy, 37*, 457-461.

Smith, S. L. (1983). Physical Capacities Evaluation. In H. L. Hopkins & H. D. Smith (Eds.), *Willard and Spackman's occupational therapy* (6th ed., pp. 168-173). Philadelphia: Lippincott.

Valpar International, Inc. (1984). *Microcomputer Evaluation and Systems Screening Assessment, MESA*. Tucson: Author.

Wassink, K. E. (1988). Job search skills for unemployed psychiatric patients. *Occupational Therapy in Health Care, 5*, 149-158.

Work Evaluation System Technology. (1985). *WEST 2. Work capacity evaluation device*. Long Beach, CA: Author.

Terms for Discussion

1. depression (paragraphs 1 and 12)

2. antisocial (paragraph 3)

3. panic attack (paragraph 3)

4. stress management (paragraphs 5, 11, 16, and 26)

5. time management (paragraphs 5 and 17)

6. compulsive perfectionism/compulsive traits (paragraphs 5 and 10)

7. role-playing (paragraphs 18 and 19)

8. intellectualize (paragraph 9)

Questions

9. In paragraph 1, the authors mention cooperation between a psychiatrist and an occupational therapist. What other types of professionals, if any, might have provided effective assistance in this case if called upon?

10. What journal would you refer to if you wanted to know more about Peloquin's interview, which is mentioned in paragraph 4?

11. In your opinion, are all of the problems mentioned in paragraph 5 functional problems?

12. Are the results of testing (see paragraph 7) described in sufficient detail?

13. Comment on the goals listed in paragraph 11. (Are any important goals missing? Are some of them more important than others? Should some of the goals have been pursued earlier in the course of treatment than others?)

14. Is Ralph's quick abandonment of his school program (see paragraph 15) consistent with his other symptoms? Explain.

15. What is your opinion on the use of confrontation for the purposes mentioned in paragraph 18?

16. Is the evidence that Ralph is no longer suicidal adequate? Explain.

17. Have the authors convinced you of the value of occupational therapy in Ralph's case? Explain.

18. Are there any other types of treatment that might have facilitated Ralph's improvement? Explain.

19. Rate the article on the seven criteria described in the introduction to this book on a scale from 5 (highest quality) through 1 (lowest quality). Be prepared to explain your ratings.

Criterion 1: The demographics of the case are described: _____

Criterion 2: The condition(s) and behavior(s) that necessitated treatment are described in detail: _____

Criterion 3: The method of treatment is described in sufficient detail so that it can be replicated without additional information: _____

Criterion 4: A rationale is provided for the method of treatment selected: _____

Criterion 5: The client's improvement, if any, is clearly documented: _____

Criterion 6: Follow-up information on the client's improvement, if any, is presented: _____

Criterion 7: The study is appropriate for publication in a journal: _____

Case 24

Extended Inpatient Treatment of a Refractory Heroin Addict: A Multidisciplinary Approach to Patients with a Dual Diagnosis*

Lindsay A. Levine
The Menninger Clinic

Patricia N. Harper
The Menninger Clinic

ABSTRACT: Chemically dependent patients may also have a psychiatric problem (e.g., thought disorder, affective disturbance, character pathology). They may suffer as well from concomitant neurological deficits. Consequently, such patients are difficult to treat, and they tend to relapse after achieving sobriety in a short-term treatment program. Traditional chemical dependency programs thus may run the risk of oversimplifying the needs of these refractory patients. The authors present a clinical case to illustrate how an in-depth assessment and extended inpatient care by a multidisciplinary treatment team can achieve more lasting success with refractory dual-diagnosis patients.

(1) When treating patients with a serious history of drug abuse, clinicians should consider the possibility of additional psychiatric diagnoses, including severe character pathology (Blume, 1989; Hellman, 1981; Roszell, Calsyn, & Chaney, 1986; Vaccani, 1989). Failure to recognize the breadth of psychiatric difficulties in some patients who are substance abusers may frustrate treatment efforts to maintain sobriety (Mirin, Weiss, Michael, & Griffin, 1988). It is also important to consider the possibility of concomitant organic impairment (Meek, Clark, & Solana, 1989). In short, substance abusers deserve a "careful evaluation, followed by individualized flexible treatment planning" (Weiss & Mirin, 1985, p. 364).

(2) This paper describes the assessment and treatment of a patient with a dual diagnosis who had failed nearly two dozen prior inpatient attempts to achieve sobriety. The assessment and treatment took place in the chemical dependency unit of a tertiary psychiatric care facility that specializes in the treatment of patients with "difficult-to-treat" problems, particularly affective disorders, thought disorders, and severe character pathology. The majority of beds in the hospital are for patients requiring extended treatment. The chemical dependency unit, however, has an average length of stay of only 4-6 weeks. Nevertheless, on occasion this unit treats patients with a dual diagnosis for a longer time. This case illustrates the difficult diagnostic and treatment issues related to dual-diagnosis patients.

(3) Numerous articles have been written on the treatment of the dual diagnosis alcoholic and drug-addicted patient (e.g., Dodes, 1988; Kaufman, 1989; Kaufman &

---

*Reprinted with permission from *Bulletin of the Menninger Clinic*, 55, 1990, pp. 384-393. Copyright 1990 by The Menninger Foundation.

Reoux, 1988; Khantzian, 1986; Kleber, 1985; Rosen, 1981; Roszell et al., 1986; Vaccani, 1989; Wallen & Weiner, 1989). There is a paucity of literature, however, on the assessment and treatment of the refractory dual-diagnosis patient.

(4) Treatment approaches described in the literature on substance-abusing patients have included the use of a multidisciplinary treatment team (Angres & Benson, 1985). Such an integrative effort may be essential for the comprehensive assessment and treatment of patients with multiple diagnoses (Wallen & Weiner, 1989). Although psychiatric inpatient programs are generally considered most helpful for "the older, more middle-class or health professional patient, and the adolescent user who has not been using drugs long enough to develop many of the secondary characteristics of drug addiction" (Kleber, 1985, P. 409), structured inpatient programs of longer stay may also benefit refractory addicted patients with concomitant psychopathology.

(5) Wallen and Weiner (1989) have suggested that most substance-abusing patients with a dual diagnosis require ongoing help with their social, familial, and occupational functioning. With regard to the latter, the inability to succeed in work situations has been linked to excessive early narcotic abuse (Kleber, 1985). This extended care should include participation by patients both in traditional chemical dependency treatment programs (Alcoholics Anonymous, Narcotics Anonymous, Cocaine Anonymous) and in other psychiatric therapies (Dodes, 1988; Kaufman & Reoux, 1988; Rosen, 1981). The value of family intervention has also been noted (Kleber, 1985; Menicucci, Wermuth, & Sorenson, 1988), because collusion is prevalent between family members and the patient (Angres & Benson, 1985).

(6) Although there are inherent limitations in presenting a single case study, the case report that follows illustrates the application and benefits of such an integrated treatment plan. This patient's 15-month hospitalization on a 12-bed inpatient chemical dependency unit followed a highly individualized treatment approach based on the guiding principles of Alcoholics Anonymous. This treatment program strongly emphasizes relapse prevention, which is a plan developed by the recovering person; in relapse prevention, friends and family members watch for warning signs of impending drug or alcohol use (Miller, Gorski, & Miller, 1982). On admission, patients are evaluated both medically and psychologically. Rehabilitation also involves a multidisciplinary treatment team. With this patient, a psychiatrist coordinated the treatment, which involved a nursing team, a psychologist who served as a consultant and also conducted neuropsychological and psychological testing, a social worker who addressed family issues, a chemical dependency counselor, an activities therapist, a vocational counselor, a psychotherapist, and, when medical problems arose, medical consultants.

Case Report

Patient History

(7) At admission, Robert was 40 years old and in the midst of his second divorce. For more than 25 years, he had been a polysubstance abuser, with intravenous heroin as his drug of choice. Prior to coming to the hospital, he had been maintained on methadone (65 mg/day). Six months before admission, he had begun injecting an additional gram of heroin each day. Just preceding admission, he had experimented with "speed balls" (a cocaine-heroin mixture). He reported that he had spent as much as $12,000 on illicit drugs in only a few weeks.

(8) Following a pattern common to young poly-drug abusers, Robert had abused alcohol heavily in the past, beginning at age 10, with his first black-out in junior high. By age 15 he was using street drugs, and by his early 20s he began consistently abusing marijuana and cocaine. He said that he had never sold drugs or had legal difficulties connected with his drug use.

(9) Robert said that he had made nearly two dozen prior attempts to resolve his addiction in various treatment settings. He explained that he usually relapsed either while in treatment or soon after discharge. He had never maintained more than 3 or 4 months of sobriety. His attempts to stay sober by living in chemical-free halfway houses or by taking drugs such as naltrexone (Trexan) and disulfiram (Antabuse) had also been unsuccessful. Over the years, he had overdosed on drugs several times.

Family History

(10) Robert was the second of three siblings from an upper middle-class family who lived on the East Coast. His family history was significant for two grandfathers with alcohol dependence, and he had both a niece and a nephew who had undergone chemical dependency treatment.

(11) Robert's home life was characterized by compromised and inconsistent parental emotional availability and attunement. During his early childhood, for example, he had a poor relationship with his parents, who provided minimal structure and few consequences for

unacceptable behavior. Thus, from his earliest years, he had little tolerance for dysphoria and frustration, and even now he had difficulty modulating aggression. Robert's early emotional disturbance was signaled by poor school performance, destruction of property, and increasing substance abuse from a young age. He described his wealthy parents as "great enablers" who provided much of the money to support his drug habit.

(12) By adolescence, Robert was heavily dependent on illicit substances and had become sexually active. At age 16, he fathered an illegitimate child. His pattern of unstable relationships, poor job stability, and chemical dependency appeared to have become ingrained. Robert explained his perennially poor school performance as being due to his lack of motivation. He had attended only one year of college at a state university. He had been married briefly in the early 1970s, then several years later had married his second wife, who was a recovering alcoholic. They had no children, and now they were going through a divorce.

(13) The patient had worked at various jobs, primarily as a salesman. He had sold cars, vacuum cleaners, carpets, and shoes. Robert's wife said that it was easy for him to acquire jobs because of his good interpersonal skills, yet he had great difficulty holding onto them. She believed that their marital relationship was destructive because it thwarted his sobriety as well as her own. Despite their impending divorce, their relationship was notably amicable.

Assessment
(14) Following an extensive assessment, the patient was diagnosed as having polysubstance dependence, borderline personality disorder, and cognitive and attentional problems. His medical assessment, including a physical examination on admission, was negative for active problems. Initial laboratory work included an electrocardiogram (EKG) that revealed slight QRS prolongation, a chest X ray that showed mild to moderate parenchymal fibrosis, and electroencephalogram (EEG) and head computerized tomographic (CT) studies that were normal. Blood work, including testing for human immunodeficiency virus (HIV), revealed no abnormalities. Drug screens were initially positive for methadone.

(15) Despite Robert's history of heavy narcotic addiction, when he arrived on the chemical dependency unit, he was easily detoxified on methadone (65 mg/day, reduced slowly over a 21-day period). In addition, clonidine (which suppresses autonomic symptoms of withdrawal, enhancing the patient's physical comfort) was available to him, but he seldom requested it. Robert's withdrawal symptoms were relatively mild until the last few days, when he complained of sleeplessness, muscle stiffness, headache, and gastrointestinal distress. During detoxification, his vital signs remained stable. He attributed the relatively mild withdrawal symptoms to "psychological factors," that is, his strong motivation for treatment.

(16) Medical problems that arose during the course of Robert's hospitalization included degenerative disc disease of his thoracic spine and a hernia that necessitated surgical repair. Robert was also undergoing extensive dental work. During and after the surgical procedure to repair his hernia, he required narcotics for pain control. Both he and the chemical dependency unit staff were concerned that he might relapse after being given prescribed narcotics. The patient talked at length about his fear of relapse. He talked to his NA sponsor, who had also undergone major surgery that required narcotics. Perhaps as a result of the working through that Robert carried out with staff and peers, he was able to avoid abusing the prescribed narcotics given for the procedure.

(17) Psychological testing indicated that Robert's core conflict revolved around aggression and dependency needs. He struggled to reconcile two contradictory sides of his ego ideal. On the one hand, he viewed himself as a compliant, cooperative, well-liked individual who pleased others, but on the other hand, he presented himself as a hedonistic, aggressive person who had difficulty controlling rebellious impulses. His intense dependency needs were manifested sometimes in more adaptive, compliant behavior that elicited nurturance from others and, at other times, in more self-destructive behavior, such as brief sexual liaisons. As a result of his underlying affective turbulence, Robert had difficulty modulating affect and sometimes acted impulsively. At times of intense affect, for example, Robert craved opiates, in a pressured attempt to find a peaceful haven. His psychological test profile suggested a borderline level of ego organization. Testing was not consistent with a pattern of antisocial development, but instead suggested a more treatable condition in a highly motivated patient.

(18) Neuropsychological testing documented cognitive limitations, both generic and acquired in the course of several near-fatal drug overdoses. The patient evidenced residual effects of premorbid verbal learning disability and reported early attentional problems in school. He tended to misperceive or misunderstand communication, and to have difficulty with verbal and visual memory, perhaps because of his mild-to-moderate

deficits in registering and assimilating complex verbal and visual material. He also demonstrated difficulty with abstract reasoning, problem solving, and verbal expression as manifested in occasional mispronunciations.

(19) Vocational testing confirmed the existence of cognitive limitations. Robert was reading at the 8th grade level, spelling at the 10th grade level, and doing arithmetic at the 11th grade level. He scored quite low on achievement (6%) and practical-mindedness (2%). Despite good interpersonal skills and an ability to follow simple-to-semicomplex verbal instructions, Robert was unable to function well vocationally.

(20) A family evaluation revealed that Robert's family had colluded with, enabled, and rescued him for more than 20 years. His parents kept his addiction a secret, even from other family members, which indicated that "looking good" was their priority. When Robert had been treated in other chemical dependency settings, his parents told friends that he was traveling in Europe. During his extended inpatient stay at our clinic, they supported his treatment financially, but maintained considerable distance emotionally. They did visit the hospital a few times to meet with their son and the unit social worker, and they also attended a family educational workshop conducted by staff members of the treatment unit. The parents were well versed in the language of addiction. Robert and his ex-wife continued to maintain a close "friendship" and talked weekly by phone, although she rarely visited because she lived some distance away. Robert talked openly about his ambivalent feelings toward her and about not wanting to be mothered by her as in the past.

Treatment

(21) This patient's multiple problems and character pathology required every member of the multidisciplinary treatment team to maintain communication and to integrate individual treatment efforts. Robert was the subject of weekly team meetings and regular review conferences held each quarter with outside consultants. His significant personality disturbance, problems of impulse control, superego deficits, and affective instability manifested in moodiness at times. His fragmented and empty sense of self led him to compare himself during psychological testing to a chameleon. In general, the treatment team believed that Robert's personality disorder, history of end-stage addiction, significant cognitive difficulties, and multiple treatment failures could be most comprehensively addressed in an extended inpatient treatment process.

(22) The members of the treatment staff regarded this patient's treatment with reservations. Their concerns included the question of whether a primarily addiction-focused unit could work effectively to address Robert's characterological difficulties. But they were also concerned that a general extended-stay psychiatric unit might be unable to maintain a focus on the patient's potentially fatal chemical dependency. Ultimately, they decided (given the gravity of Robert's addictive illness) that the preferred site of treatment was the chemical dependency unit itself. However, once this decision was made, they also deliberated about the difficulty of treating a patient requiring extended treatment on a primarily short-term unit. To help Robert develop stable and consistent peer relationships, they encouraged him to cultivate friendships with members of AA, NA, and CA in the community.

(23) The treatment team was particularly concerned with how to help Robert maintain a strong alliance in the current treatment when so many prior treatments had failed. The team also focused on what it meant to him to be a "special" patient. Fellow patients on the chemical dependency unit often mistook him for a staff member, and he sometimes had difficulty refraining from acting as though he were indeed on the staff. Robert's treaters were quick to point out that he needed to concentrate on his own emotional and sobriety concerns. Countertransference difficulties included a tendency to excuse or minimize the patient's behavior because of the treatment team's close attachment to him.

(24) Treatment goals were oriented toward helping Robert establish and maintain sobriety while he also slowly developed a capacity to modulate affect, tolerate dysphoria, contain impulses, and delay gratification. The ultimate goal was to help him internalize the external controls supporting sobriety.

(25) Robert spent the first months of treatment in detoxification and participated in the didactic and group meetings that make up a traditional addiction treatment. He gradually achieved increasing levels of responsibility and began to participate in community-wide AA, NA, and CA meetings. Throughout his stay, he voluntarily attended at least six meetings every week. He obtained community sponsors, including a drug and alcohol counselor who played a major supportive role in his treatment. During his stay, he worked on at least seven relapse prevention and sobriety plans. He worked through the AA steps slowly. Once he was detoxified, his random weekly drug screens were negative.

(26) The treatment team challenged Robert to talk openly about his cognitive limitations, which he found difficult to accept. Nevertheless, he expressed relief at having his cognitive disability defined. This problem had not been addressed in his previous treatments, and its omission had perhaps made relapses inevitable because of his frustration at being unable to sustain work. Team members also encouraged Robert to keep lists and to make notes about information he wanted to remember. These memory aids proved helpful to him. He soon began to demonstrate increased comfort in acknowledging and asking for clarification when he did not understand verbal communications.

(27) Because of Robert's long history of feeling frustrated with activities that required manual dexterity and cognitive comprehension, he was assigned to work in our clinic's wood shop with activity therapists who were sensitive to his limitations. When he completed a wooden cutting board, Robert reported that it was the first project he had ever done well from start to finish. He later progressed to the greenhouse and to computer activities, with similar success. Nevertheless, Robert continued to struggle when given a complex task or a series of tasks with verbal instructions. At times he still hesitated to ask questions that might reveal his limitations. He eventually began volunteer work as an orderly at a local medical center with geriatric patients. For the first time in his life, he received positive evaluations on his work performance.

(28) The patient was assigned a psychotherapist, with whom he met twice a week in expressive-supportive psychotherapy. During this process, he became increasingly self-reflective and invested in his psychotherapy. His therapy sessions centered on themes of abandonment and neglect from early childhood. He said that his parents were emotionally undemonstrative, showing their love instead through material gifts; they also were averse to any display of anger. They often traveled, leaving their children behind in the care of others.

(29) Much of Robert's early life had been spent in an attempt to gain attention. As a child, he would tear up his room, leave drug paraphernalia in sight, and even return home intoxicated—all with little effect. In part, his flight from painful depressive feelings through drug use was motivated by his perception that his parents wanted nothing to do with him when he was angry or sad. The patient did not believe, however, that the sessions with his therapist caused drug cravings, despite discussions that aroused painful affect. The containing environment of the hospital was a source of support for the patient while in psychotherapy. Throughout Robert's treatment, sobriety was the main priority.

(30) Several times during the treatment, Robert "relapsed" without actually using illicit drugs. On one occasion, he signed an insurance check he had received and sent it to a drug dealer. Fortunately for Robert, the dealer did not send drugs (although he kept the insurance money). The patient did not tell his treaters about this incident until a year later. Prior to discharge, he also revealed that three or four times during his stay he had approached various people on the street to buy drugs. Somehow, he had never managed to complete a transaction. Such secrets were obviously detrimental for Robert's ongoing sobriety.

(31) Brief sexual involvements also detracted from treatment. In addition, Robert had difficulty controlling his anger on a number of occasions. At least three times, he nearly came to physical blows, but was able to regain control before actually hitting someone. On each occasion, staff members intervened to help prevent a fight. The patient acknowledged that his rage frightened him and that he often felt helpless to control his overwhelming sense of anger.

(32) Long before Robert's transition from inpatient to outpatient status, the treatment staff began a thoughtful, graduated relaxation of external control while assessing the patient's internalization of his treatment process. To prepare the patient for discharge, they outlined specific tasks, including mastering of some independent living skills, such as opening a checking account and getting a drivers license. Robert was encouraged to work out a financial agreement with his parents so that he could buy a car with their assistance but not receive one as an outright gift as he had in the past. He was also encouraged to negotiate with his parents regarding payment for his day hospital treatment. These tasks allowed Robert to deal with hitherto unresolved issues of adolescence (i.e., establishing an identity not based on opposition to others, separating from parental figures, increasing his level of autonomy, accepting responsibility for his own actions, developing initiative, and channeling energy into personal interests, career development, and more mature interpersonal relationships).

(33) Prior to discharge from the inpatient unit, Robert met with the day hospital staff to discuss his transition process. They talked about his feelings of sadness and loss at leaving the hospital and its security. In addition, Robert continued his volunteer work at the local medical center, while participating in some day hospital activities. During this time, he also continued to work on his seventh relapse prevention and sobriety plan for use

by the day hospital staff members during the transition process. To support his ongoing sobriety, he was placed in an alcohol and drug-free halfway house. He also became involved in a weekly outpatient chemical dependency group. He continued his active participation in AA, NA, and CA. In the last few months prior to discharge, Robert was begun on naltrexone (50 mg/day). After discharge, he returned each day for 6 months to the chemical dependency unit to obtain the medication. He currently has maintained 3 years of sobriety, more than 1½ years outside the inpatient setting.

Conclusion

(34) This case illustrates how biological and environmental forces can create entrenched patterns of addictive behavior. Only by paying adequate attention to the complicated interacting variables shaping such a patient course of addiction can a chemical dependency unit staff address the full range of treatment needs (Frances, 1988). Although the chemical dependency problems of many addicted patients can be addressed in traditional programs, standard approaches carry the risk of oversimplifying the treatment necessary for the refractory patient (Wallen & Weiner, 1989). Basic elements of chemical dependency programs (e.g., AA and NA) are not competitive with more individualized treatment approaches to refractory patients with a dual diagnosis (Dodes, 1988; Rosen, 1981).

(35) Critics of long-term hospitalization might contend that, after more than two dozen previous attempts to resolve his problems, this patient was simply "ready" for the success he experienced in our hospital. We believe, however, that the extended, multidisciplinary treatment was a crucial factor in his success, particularly in light of his previous refractoriness. Because of his many prior treatment failures, the patient entered the hospital for what he himself called a "long-term" rehabilitation process. He acknowledged that he was at the "end stage" of his addiction, and he knew that he would "die like many of my friends" if he was unable to change the course of his life. Indeed, he was ready for the extended inpatient treatment that he believed was essential to recovery.

(36) This patient's characterological difficulties endured throughout his treatment, and they may continue throughout his life. But the work begun in the hospital enabled him to achieve more adaptive functioning, which he has maintained on an outpatient basis. This patient will always be at risk for using drugs in response to dysphoric feelings, but he has been able to maintain sobriety in a safe enviromnent that allowed him to experience alternative ways of addressing emotional conflict and interpersonal difficulties. Although brief traditional addiction treatment programs provide this experience, they cannot adequately address underlying personality disorders and long-standing cognitive impairments, which can only be modified in intensive extended treatment.

Acknowledgment

The authors would like to thank Shirley Wilds for her help in manuscript preparation and Lee I. Ascherman for his helpful insights.

References

Angres, D. H., & Benson, W. H. (1985). Cocainism—A workable model for recovery. *Psychiatric Medicine 3*, 369-388.

Blume, S. B. (1989). Dual diagnosis: Psychoactive substance dependence and the personality disorders. *Journal of Psychoactive Drugs, 21*, 139-144.

Dodes, L. M. (1988). The psychology of combining dynamic psychotherapy and Alcoholics Anonymous. *Bulletin of the Menninger Clinic, 52*, 283-293.

Frances, R. J. (1988). Update on alcohol and drug disorder treatment. *Journal of Clinical Psychiatry, 49*(9, Suppl.), 13-17.

Hellman, J. M. (1981). Alcohol abuse and the borderline patient. *Psychiatry, 44*, 307-317.

Kaufman, E. (1989). The psychotherapy of dually diagnosed patients. *Journal of Substance Abuse Treatment, 6*, 9-18.

Kaufman, E., & Reoux, J. (1988). Guidelines for the successful psychotherapy of substance abusers. *American Journal of Drug and Alcohol Abuse, 14*, 199-209.

Khantzian, E. J. (1986). A contemporary psychodynamic approach to drug abuse treatment. *American Journal of Drug and Alcohol Abuse, 12*, 213-222.

Kleber, H. D. (1985). Treatment of narcotic addicts. *Psychiatric Medicine, 3*, 389-418.

Meek, P. S., Clark, H. W., & Solana, V. L. (1989). Neurocognitive impairment: The unrecognized component of dual diagnosis in substance abuse treatment. *Journal of Psychactive Drugs, 21*, 153-160.

Menicucci, L. D., Wermuth, L., & Sorensen, J. (1988). Treatment providers' assessment of dual-prognosis patients: Diagnosis, treatment, referral, and family involvement. *International Journal of the Addictions, 23*, 617-622.

Miller, M., Gorski, T. T., & Miller, D. K. (1982). *Learning to live again: A guide for recovery from alcoholism* (3rd ed.). Independence, MO: Independence Press.

Mirin, S. M., Weiss, R. D., Michael, J., & Griffin, M. L. (1988). Psychopathology in substance abusers: Diagnosis and treatment. *American Journal of Drug and Alcohol Abuse, 14*, 139-157.

Rosen, A. (1981). Psychotherapy and Alcoholics Anonymous: Can they be coordinated? *Bulletin of the Menninger Clinic, 45*, 229-246.

Roszell, D. K., Calsyn, D. A., & Chaney, E. F. (1986). Alcohol use and psychopathology in opioid addicts on methadone maintenance. *American*

Journal of Drug and Alcohol Abuse, 12, 269-278.

Vaccani, J. M. (1989). Borderline personality and alcohol abuse. *Archives of Psychiatric Nursing, 3*, 113-119.

Wallen, M. C., & Weiner, H. D. (1989). Impediments to effective treatment of the dually diagnosed patient. *Journal of Psychoactive Drugs, 21*, 161-168.

Weiss, R. D., & Mirin, S. M. (1985). Substance abuse as an attempt at self-medication. *Psychiatric Medicine, 3*, 357-367.

Terms for Discussion

1. severe character pathology (paragraph 1)

2. affective disorders (paragraphs 2, 17, and 21)

3. refractory patients (paragraphs 3, 4, and 34)

4. Alcoholics (Narcotics and Cocaine) Anonymous (paragraphs 4, 5, 22, 25, 33, and 34)

5. methadone (paragraphs 7 and 15)

6. Antabuse (paragraph 9)

7. dysphoria (paragraphs 11, 24, and 36)

8. borderline personality disorder (paragraphs 14 and 17)

9. cognitive and attentional problems (paragraphs 14, 18, 19, 21, and 26)

10. clonidine (paragraph 15)

11. ego ideal (paragraph 17)

12. superego deficits (paragraph 21)

13. countertransference (paragraph 23)

14. expressive-supportive therapy (paragraph 28)

Questions

15. The authors state that there are inherent limitations in presenting a single case study. (See paragraph 6.) Speculate on what they mean by this statement.

16. Given the information on patient history, family history, and assessment in paragraphs 7 through 20 (without considering the rest of the article), what would your prognosis for Robert have been?

17. In paragraph 17, the authors refer to brief sexual liaisons as an example of self-destructive behavior. Do you agree? Brief sexual involvements are also mentioned in paragraph 31. In your opinion should these be discouraged for a patient such as Robert?

18. Do you agree with the "critics" mentioned in paragraph 35 or with the authors? Explain.

19. Are there other types of treatment that might have facilitated Robert's improvement? Explain.

20. Rate the article on the seven criteria described in the introduction to this book on a scale from 5 (highest quality) through 1 (lowest quality). Be prepared to explain your ratings.

Criterion 1: The demographics of the case are described: _____

Criterion 2: The condition(s) and behavior(s) that necessitated treatment are described in detail: _____

Criterion 3: The method of treatment is described in sufficient detail so that it can be replicated without additional information: _____

Criterion 4: A rationale is provided for the method of treatment selected: _____

Criterion 5: The client's improvement, if any, is clearly documented: _____

Criterion 6: Follow-up information on the client's improvement, if any, is presented: _____

Criterion 7: The study is appropriate for publication in a journal: _____

Case 25

Alcoholic Women's Feminine Self-Concept and Mothering: The Importance of Reinforcing Self-Esteem in Treatment*

Carolyn Bersak

State University of New York, New Paltz and Albany

(1) A case study, "Enhancing Self-Esteem As a Strategy for Treating Female Alcoholics" (Alcoholism Treatment Quarterly, 7(3), 1990) applied specific psychotherapeutic interventions developed by Cleveland (1987) for self-esteem enhancement as a treatment method with a female alcoholic population. The approach was distinguished from Cleveland's by its focus on the unique needs of female alcoholics in contrast with those of Cleveland's co-dependent women. The model outlined also differed from Cleveland's in being "inter-," rather than "intra-" personal, providing the added therapeutic dimension of an ideal human relationship with the therapist. Optimally, this ideal relationship is modeled and extrapolated to other relationships outside the therapeutic interaction.

(2) One of the subjects discussed in the previous case study was Ms. M. At the time of treatment Ms. M had been an active alcoholic and marijuana abuser who was also sexually promiscuous and prone to food bingeing. In the course of treatment she had been referred to Alcoholics Anonymous, and I learned she had successfully maintained sobriety for 10 years. Her treatment with me had begun to focus on other self-esteem issues like those of feminine self-image, self-hatred, and internalized rage. At the time of the therapy's successful termination, Ms. M was happily married, was expecting her first child, was drug-free (several years), and was actively pursuing a satisfying career.

(3) Also at the time that treatment was terminated, it was observed that Ms. M could have benefited from further intervention following the same strategy of encouraging her to develop greater autonomy. It was projected that she might accomplish this by continuing to cultivate her self-esteem apart from the residual anger that she had internalized from her mother. The two techniques of self-disclosure and redirection of affect had proven to be the most beneficial for enhancing Ms. M's self-esteem and thereby for treating her substance abuse.

(4) The present discussion expands on the previous focus on the treatment techniques of self-disclosure and redirection of affect to examine new issues that arose when Ms. M returned to treatment for additional work on what she described at reevaluation as "boundary problems."

Case Re-Evaluation

(5) Ms. M had left treatment just after marrying, and part of her rationale for returning to treatment was her difficulty with the complexity of the new roles that she had taken on as wife and mother. She was experiencing anxiety about her ability to be a good mother which I associated with her role change from respected career woman to full time housewife. But paramount among her concerns was her feeling threatened and trapped by the burden and responsibility of having to take care of her baby, whom she "loved to death."

(6) Ms. M reported to her first session with her baby in a portable car seat which she set down across the room, so that the sleeping newborn's face was turned away

---

*Alcoholism Treatment Quarterly, 8, 1991, pp. 113-118. Copyright 1991 by the Haworth Press, Inc. Reprinted by permission.

from her, out of sight, and toward the corner. She sat facing me and told me how needy she was and how much she resented the baby's intrusion into her life. She complained that this intrusion had come just when she had begun to achieve a balance between her career and her marriage.

(7) In contrast with the therapist's (my) model, which afforded continuing work after childbirth, Ms. M had selected a more traditional approach to child rearing which required staying at home with her newborn. When we last met she had given me the impression of being ready to return to work full time; so that her readiness to abandon this career option was surprising to me. She stated that for the first time in her life, she had enjoyed having developed a close relationship with her mother which previously had been characterized by distance and anger. Yet behind her self-reported contentment with that relationship, she still harbored sufficient displeasure with staying at home to prompt her visit to discuss her feelings with me.

(8) She expressed that she was depressed and attributed her depression to an inability to fit into the community's mainstream whose values positioned full time motherhood as the major priority for her. She obviously had internalized these values at her own expense. She could not see that she was having difficulty because she was unable to identify and acknowledge in herself a right to have needs other than those of the traditional, mainstream model. I perceived an additional reinforcer of this perspective in her newly established closeness with her mother who reinforced the traditional mainstream emphasis on the importance of her staying at home with the baby.

(9) It was interesting to me how her physical behavior at our first session expressed a desire to retaliate against her baby when she walked into my office: she literally put *the baby* in a corner the way its arrival had put *her* in a corner, i.e., trapping her at home without the social supports that she needed both as an active career woman, and as a recovering substance abuser. In this regard her success with AA, which stimulated her to reach out to a support network of newly found friends, was being undermined by the lifestyle she had fallen into. Her immediate community of full time stay-at-home mother/housewives offered no support or comfort for former career women and active AA members. So in keeping to herself and remaining isolated and lonely she was regressing into behavioral patterns that were dysfunctional. She was slipping into her previous pattern of attacking herself, exaggerating minor events into a cycle of tortuous and destructive self-criticism.

Discussion

(10) As her therapist, I used the rapport that I had previously built in our earlier sessions to suggest to her that she had internalized a value that could never be true for her: that staying at home could be fulfilling and satisfying. I had to validate for her that it was all right for her to be angry with having just to stay at home and sort laundry. A therapist with a more traditional orientation might have attempted to focus on some inadequacy in the patient's mothering that had left her unable to feel satisfied in her stay-at-home role. Work would be carried out to help such a patient adjust to feeling more loving toward the baby despite her difficulty with the associated lifestyle. The important, distinguishing factor in the two therapeutic approaches was that changing the lifestyle would not be an option in the traditional model whereas it would be in the nontraditional model; where for the traditional approach changing the patient would be the only area of focus, for the nontraditional approach changing the lifestyle would be an added option.

(11) It should be qualified that this approach emerged from the uniqueness of Ms. M's needs (the AA model of recovery) rather than from any idealized, universally applicable notion of career salience. Ms. M fit into the model suggested by Silvia, Sorell, and Busch-Rossnagel (1988) who observed that alcoholic women had lower self-esteem, were more depressed, and were more committed to fulfilling stereotypical expectations of the "feminine" sex-role and saw themselves as less successful in satisfying the expectations of important people in their lives. According to the findings suggested by this research it would be critical for Ms. M to be allowed to fulfill the therapeutic requirements suggested by AA of reaching out to others in her situation to provide and receive the support and reinforcement so vital to recovery. Internalizing a lifestyle that precluded this option should be seen as destructive for such a client.

(12) Thus, Silvia et al.'s (1988) research corroborates my intuition that attempting to mold Ms. M into a traditionally "feminine" life style pattern would not resolve the internal conflicts that were at the root of her self-destructive behavior. As noted above, however, another group of researchers disagree. Williams (1984), for example, suggested that masculine sex role patterns were predictive of increased drinking in a sample of female alcoholic patients. The picture Williams drew was one of rebellion, low self-esteem, impulsive acting out, rejection of traditional feminine patterns, and more

psychological conflict than was evident in the profiles of women who did not abuse alcohol.

(13) Had I applied Williams' (1984) model to the treatment of Ms. M I would have attempted to mold her into the traditionally feminine role of staying at home as a curative measure. I would not have encouraged her to move into a therapeutic model appropriate for her needs regardless of traditional male/female stereotypes. Like Sylvia et al. (1988), however, Vannicelli (1984) cautions against following restrictive approaches like that of Williams: Vannicelli expressed concern that therapists' having sex-role expectancies can limit and disrupt the patient's potential for growth.

(14) Concerning the feminine self-concept of alcoholic women Bersak (1988) also observed that great therapeutic power lies in creating environments and reinforcement of alcoholic clients' self-concepts apart from traditionally drawn images of female roles. Bersak stressed the value of creating an environment to enhance alcoholic clients' feelings of self-worth in the treatment effort to enable them to accept and affirm themselves as people. Bersak contended that such an approach can work hand-in-hand with abstention to help alcoholics grow both physically and emotionally healthier.

(15) The case of Ms. M illustrates the importance of including support *for* an alcoholic client while placing her in a demanding role requiring that she constantly provide support for others. In this light, it can hardly be predicted that Ms. M will successfully achieve fulfillment and satisfaction for herself or continue to build a healthy environment for her children and husband when she is cut off from the support that she really needs. Validation in career function and in AA support groups can help Ms. M and other women in need of self-concept reinforcement. Attempting to impose stereotypically "masculine" or "feminine" roles on alcoholic women like Ms. M would seem to be working against this effort.

(16) In recent sessions, Ms. M has begun actively to pursue her career, to obtain quality child care, and to improve her sexual relationship with her husband. All of these changes were encouraged by her therapist's telling her symbolically that it is not only OK, but necessary to take care of herself in addition to her baby.

References

Bersak, C. (1988). Feminine self-concept of alcoholic women. *Affilia, 3,* 17-25.

Bersak, C. (in press). Enhancing self-esteem as a strategy for treating female alcoholics. *Alcoholism Treatment Quarterly.*

Cleveland, M. (1987). Treatment of co-dependent women through the use of mental imagery. *Alcoholism Treatment Quarterly, 4*(1), 27-41.

Silvia, L., Sorell, G., & Busch-Rossnagel, N. (1988). Biosocial discriminators of alcoholic and nonalcoholic women. *Journal of Substance Abuse, 1,* 55-65.

Williams, C. (1984). Personality variables in the female problem drinker. *Dissertation Abstracts International, 45*(3), 1034-B.

Vannicelli, M. (1984). Barriers to treatment of alcoholic women. *Substance and Alcohol Actions/Misuse, 5*(1), 29-37.

Terms for Discussion

1. self-esteem (paragraphs 2, 11, and 12)

2. internalized rage (paragraph 2)

3. self-disclosure (paragraphs 3 and 4)

4. redirection of affect (paragraphs 3 and 4)

5. depression (paragraphs 8 and 11)

6. internalized values (paragraphs 8, 10, and 11)

Questions

7. Does the apparent contradiction between what Ms. M said about her baby (see paragraph 5) and what she did with her baby in the session (see paragraph 6) surprise you? Explain.

8. Has the author convinced you that staying at home could never be fulfilling for Ms. M? Explain. (See paragraph 10.)

9. What is your opinion on the distinction between "changing the lifestyle" and "changing the patient"? Do you agree that this is an important distinction in the case of Ms. M? (See paragraph 10.)

10. Do you agree that a therapist's sex-role expectancies can limit and disrupt a patient's potential for growth?

11. Are there any other types of treatment that might have facilitated Ms. M's improvement? Explain.

12. Rate the article on the seven criteria described in the introduction to this book on a scale from 5 (highest quality) through 1 (lowest quality). Be prepared to explain your ratings.

Criterion 1: The demographics of the case are described: _____

Criterion 2: The condition(s) and behavior(s) that necessitated treatment are described in detail: _____

Criterion 3: The method of treatment is described in sufficient detail so that it can be replicated without additional information: _____

Criterion 4: A rationale is provided for the method of treatment selected: _____

Criterion 5: The client's improvement, if any, is clearly documented: _____

Criterion 6: Follow-up information on the client's improvement, if any, is presented: _____

Criterion 7: The study is appropriate for publication in a journal: _____

Case 26

Hypnotherapy for Agoraphobia: A Case Study*

Gina M. Harris
Private Practice of Psychology

(1) Fierce anxiety without warning. Multiple symptoms of light-headedness, dizziness, difficulty in breathing, racing heart and pulse, hit the patient with stupefying force, unpredictable in time or focus. These symptoms, as a burgeoning literature attests, are the essence of panic disorders.[1]

(2) Current demographic studies have documented that millions of individuals are victimized by the unpredictable tyrant of panic each year. In the case of panic disorder, the fear of fear exercises a profoundly disabling effect on the individual and his/her functioning. Agoraphobia is one of the most common panic disorders that afflicts individuals in our society. Agoraphobia has been defined as an exaggerated or abnormal dread of traversing or being in open spaces. As has been previously described by many investigators, among them Goldstein,[2] Tyler,[3] Weeks,[4] most victims of agoraphobia begin to restrict or avoid these situations in which panic attacks have occurred. Soon, the individual's sense of control is so compromised, that he/she retreats to the home, confused and overwhelmed by the experience of agoraphobic symptoms and the associated panic.

(3) Effective treatment for agoraphobic patients is complicated by the fact that before seeking psychological consultation, they have frequently sought assistance from a wide variety of medical specialists. The services of healers as diverse as allergists and neurologists have been sought by those seeking surcease from the malady within.

(4) A wide variety of approaches have been used in the treatment of agoraphobia. Unfortunately, those techniques, such as desensitization, that offer such quick effective assistance for simple phobias, have mixed results in the case of agoraphobia.

(5) The key feature to overcoming entrenched patterns of avoidance is exposure to those very same target situations that elicit the symptoms. Burns[5] has provided an excellent summary of components of this pervasive syndrome. As he describes it, there are strong responses affecting:

A. The cognitive senses: the sufferer experiences feelings of apprehension and fear. Patterns of thought frequently are unproductive, irrational, and anxiety generating; they appear to be often related to an inability to cope with the feared situation and the psychophysiological arousal evoked by it. Thoughts about the need to escape from the situation may become prominent; if such escape occurs, the sufferer may engage in ruminative self-defeating thinking, involving poor self-esteem, a sense of failure and of being demoralized.

B. The psychophysiological symptoms: a higher level of arousal of the system may involve increased muscular tension, rapid heart rate, hyperventilation, feelings of faintness, heightened blood pressure, etc.

C. The behavioral system: the intense distress may result in withdrawal from the provoking situation; if contact is maintained with a situation, impaired performance may be expressed. Alternatively, if the fear produced by the anticipation of entering the phobic situation becomes overwhelming, avoidance behavior may

---

*International Journal of Psychosomatics, 38, 1991, pp. 92-94. Copyright 1991 by the International Psychosomatics Institute. Reprinted with permission.

take place, followed by a rapid decrease in the fear and the psychophysiological symptoms.

(6) According to Burns,[1] there are strong responses which are beyond involuntary control. Attempts on the part of the sufferer to manage the fears of psychophysiological symptoms usually end in failure. In such situations, strong responses may develop which are excessive and quite out of proportion, bearing in mind the demands of the situation. These strong responses have a tendency to persist, albeit with fluctuations in intensity, over a lengthy period of time; are often not allied to the development of the individual nor age specific, or may be thought of as adaptive. The sufferer may possess good insight and recognize that such responses are not reasonable and that most people do not manifest such reactions in similar situations. In addition, there are frequently strong responses which involve social components; thus, the sufferer may try to conceal the problems because of embarrassment.

(7) A study of agoraphobia is particularly intriguing because while clearly an avoidance disorder, it shares many characteristics with a mood disorder such as anxiety state and is sometimes associated with minor depression. Surprisingly agoraphobic sufferers are most attuned to autonomic and somatic accompaniments of the symptoms and are less concerned with cognitive psychological components. The key feature in overcoming entrenched patterns of avoidance is exposure to those very same target situations that elicit the symptoms.

(8) In the following case study, a young woman was successfully treated for a variety of agoraphobic symptoms through the combination of hypnosis and in vivo desensitization.

Case Report

(9) Mrs. L, a college graduate, was employed in the past as an English teacher. She now works solely in her home as a housewife and serves a number of charitable organizations in her community. Her medical history was unremarkable, and she enjoyed good health and a stable family life in spite of her agoraphobic symptoms. One of the motivating forces for Mrs. L's seeking treatment at this time was the fact that her husband had to forgo three business trips to exotic and interesting foreign lands because of the limitations his wife's agoraphobic fears imposed on family activities. Not surprisingly, he was growing increasingly more impatient with Mrs. L's behavior.

(10) Mrs. L had, as a consequence of her relative inactivity and malaise, gained weight, which further increased her frustration and level of self-criticism.

(11) She had previously sought assistance from a variety of psychologists and psychotherapists of different orientations, including neurolinguistic programming, and insight oriented psychotherapy. She was referred by a psychologist who found he was making little headway in relieving her constellation of symptoms and bouts of panic.

(12) Having experienced so little success with these various treatments at the outset, Mrs. L was leery of any new treatment, particularly on embracing hypnosis. Her knowledge of hypnosis was limited to the hypnosis of entertainment and she was not familiar with the psychological applications. Therefore, significant gradual efforts at therapeutic re-education had to be employed.

Progressive Relaxation

(13) The first stage of treatment involved teaching this patient progressive relaxation. The type of relaxation training employed was the one developed by Susskind.[6] It involves the tensing and relaxing of various muscle groups. Mrs. L enjoyed relaxation treatment and she found her "air hunger" and anxious thoughts significantly diminished after such a relaxation session. The use of progressive relaxation was considered first because of Mrs. L's trepidation about utilizing hypnosis. Unfortunately, myths about hypnosis perpetuated by some popular articles on stage hypnotists have served to frighten many individuals and set up powerful misconceptions about the nature and efficacy of hypnotherapy. Mrs. L, particularly fearing loss of control, was loathe to venture into this new area until she had more confidence in the practitioner.

Hierarchy Development

(14) The second stage of psychological treatment consisted of the development of hierarchies of particular events, activities and settings that elicited Mrs. L's agoraphobic symptoms and their associated symptoms of panic.

(15) These hierarchies were of the standard temporal spatial form and revolved around five main areas: going to restaurants (site of her first panic attack), movie and sound stage shows, elevators, driving, and travel. Mrs. L was able to effectively utilize the imaginal behavioral rehearsal inherent in the desensitization combined with graded practice assignments, e.g., attend a play in the evening, go to a particular restaurant. While Mrs. L was making steady progress, she was informed by her husband that he needed to travel to Paris in April, two

months later. Determined not to be sidelined by her fears this time, desperate to go to Paris in the spring, buoyed up by the diminution of anxiety and significant decrease of feelings of panic, she consented to try hypnosis.

(16) Extensive descriptions of her travel destinations and hotels were obtained by Mrs. L. At this time, she acknowledged a deep fear of airplane travel as well as going through United States Customs.

Hypnosis Techniques Employed

(17) In phase II, hypnosis techniques employing the use of positive imagery, heaviness and self-efficacy training were introduced. Mrs. L, within the context of deep progressive relaxation instructions, was given suggestions which emphasized her body's ability to cope with stressers and tensions. In her conversation with me post-trance, Mrs. L most clearly recalled the statement, "Your body knows what to do." She found the recollection of that statement helpful in reducing her anxiety. That she found such a statement helpful is very important since in an agoraphobic disorder, one sees a patient who feels helpless and out of control in dealing with the symptom.[7] The most essential step is to buttress the patient's belief in him/herself and of his/her retaining confidence and control. The utilization of positive imagery, emphasizing pleasant imaginal scenes juxtaposed with behavioral imaginal rehearsal of the proposed itinerary through Paris also had a beneficial effect for Mrs. L. One of the images that was of particular value to Mrs. L was the image of a "safe place". A brief example of the narrative induction utilized follows:

(18) "Think of the words peace . . . safety . . . comfort . . . and happiness . . . now let your mind spontaneously take you to a place . . . it may be a place that you go to frequently or one that you have visited only in the distant past . . . or maybe one that is totally imaginary . . . but stay with the first place that comes to your mind . . . if you find yourself just going from place to place, those are tricks being played on you by the conscious part of your mind, the part of your mind that says you can not do something and puts judgments on things, that leads you to an external rather than to an internal experience . . . appreciate the aroma, touch and feel the environment . . . and objects therein, appreciate the taste . . . perceive about you, you and all around you . . . explore in full detail all the ingredients of the scene, whether it be outside or inside."[8]

(19) After the hypnotic relaxation was established, imaginal rehearsal of portions of the trip were carried out step-by-step, conducted entirely in hypnotic trance. After 10 weeks of combined hypnosis combined with in vivo desensitization, Mrs. L made her trip to Paris successfully which included a number of shopping trips that she made by herself. This confidence translated itself into the determination to lose thirty pounds which Mrs. L proceeded to do. As of this writing, she has been symptom free for over two years.

(20) An interesting post script has presented itself in that Mrs. L recently referred her sister who is suffering from much the same constellation of agoraphobic symptoms.

References

1. Burns, L.E., and Thorpe, G.L. *The agoraphobic syndrome*, 1983.

2. Goldstein, A.J. Case conference: The treatment of a case agoraphobia by multifaceted treatment program. *Journal of Behavior Therapy and Experimental Psychiatry.* 9, 45-51, 1978.

3. Tyler, P., Horn, S., and Lee, I. Treatment of agoraphobia by subliminal and supraliminal exposure to phobic cinema film. *Lancet. 1*, 358-360, 1978.

4. Weeks, C. Simple, effective treatment of agoraphobia. *American Journal of Psychotherapy. 32*, 357-369, 1978.

5. Burns, L.E. Fears and phobias-epidemiological and phenomenological aspects. *Psychiatry in Practice.* 1, 8, 25-28, 1982.

6. Susskind, D. The idealized self-image (ISI): A new technique in confidence training. *Behavior Therapy.* 1, 538-540, 1970.

7. Alman, B.M. *Psychology and counseling.* 306, 1983.

8. Pratt, J., and Wood, D.P. *A clinical hypnosis primer*, 1984.

Terms for Discussion

1. anxiety (paragraphs 1, 7, 13, 15, and 17)

2. panic disorder (paragraphs 1, 2, 11, and 15)

3. agoraphobia (paragraphs 2, 3, 4, 7, 9, 14, 17, and 20)

4. desensitization (paragraphs 4, 8, 15, and 19)

5. syndrome (paragraph 5)

6. mood disorder (paragraph 7)

7. hypnosis (paragraphs 8, 13, 15, 17, and 19)

8. progressive relaxation (paragraph 13)

9. positive imagery (paragraph 17)

Questions

10. The author does not discuss the underlying cause(s) of agoraphobia. Is this a flaw in a case report of this type? Speculate on possible causes in this case.

11. The author mentions that Mrs. L had to be re-educated regarding hypnotherapy. (See paragraph 12.) Suggest some methods that might be used to re-educate a client such as Mrs. L.

12. The author used both desensitization and hypnosis in treating the client. In your opinion, was one more important than the other? Could one have been used effectively without the other?

13. What was your opinion on hypnotherapy before reading this report? What is your opinion now? Explain.

14. Are there other types of treatment that might have facilitated Mrs. L's improvement? Explain.

15. Rate the article on the seven criteria described in the introduction to this book on a scale from 5 (highest quality) through 1 (lowest quality). Be prepared to explain your ratings.

Criterion 1: The demographics of the case are described: _____

Criterion 2: The condition(s) and behavior(s) that necessitated treatment are described in detail: _____

Criterion 3: The method of treatment is described in sufficient detail so that it can be replicated without additional information: _____

Criterion 4: A rationale is provided for the method of treatment selected: _____

Criterion 5: The client's improvement, if any, is clearly documented: _____

Criterion 6: Follow-up information on the client's improvement, if any, is presented: _____

Criterion 7: The study is appropriate for publication in a journal: _____

Notes:

Case 27

A Case Analysis in Human Sexuality: Counseling to a Man with Severe Cerebral Palsy*

Robert Joseph
United Cerebral Palsy of New York

ABSTRACT: This article is a case analysis of a 25-year-old man, named Michael, who has cerebral palsy, generalized athetosis. His physical disability is severe and he has a profound speech disorder. Michael is functioning cognitively within the range of borderline intelligence. Michael requested human sexuality counseling. At the onset of counseling Michael stated that due to his physical disability he was neither able to masturbate nor could he find a sexual partner. Four key areas in sexuality and disability are discussed: (1) recognition of the individual with a severe disability as a sexual being, (2) masturbation as a valid sexual activity, (3) seeking an appropriate romantic involvement, and (4) the process involved in making a referral to a sex surrogate. The entire course of treatment is outlined along with the impressions of the counselor.

(1) Individuals with physical and/or developmental disabilities are often the recipients of a wide range of therapeutic services. If this individual attends a Day Treatment, Day Training, or Sheltered Vocational Workshop Program he or she most likely receives any combination of, or all of the following services: occupational therapy, physical therapy, speech therapy, and psychological services. The process of being examined, probed, manipulated, and assisted by therapists, doctors, and other staff members is always present throughout the individual's life span. Often the client is a passive recipient of the prescribed treatment. Rarely does the client (patient) have the opportunity to request a certain intervention or to control the course of treatment. On the other hand, it is my contention that a good therapeutic process always includes dialogue. A relatively new area of therapy for the disabled has been growing over the past decade. This area is human sexuality services. Proponents of providing this service recognize the legal, moral, and ethical right of all individuals to have access to sex education, information, and counseling. Everyone must be guaranteed the freedom of opportunity and sexual expression.

(2) This burgeoning area is setting the tone for a most interactive therapeutic process that considers dialogue paramount while addressing the sexual lives of the disabled. The introduction of human sexuality has allowed, and welcomed, individuals with disabilities to express their desires to love and be loved, to touch and be touched, and to enjoy the pleasures of erotic and autoerotic stimulation. The unfortunate history of people with disabilities is that they have been treated as asexual beings. The present, and promising future, is giving the disabled the opportunity to explore their own sexuality without the fear of reprisal or punishment, or the pain of being ignored. United Cerebral Palsy of New York City, Inc. has employed a Human Sexuality Specialist virtually uninterrupted since 1977. The specialist has historically offered education, information, and counseling, as well as a healthy dose of encouragement and support.

(3) Many of the individuals who attended programs in United Cerebral Palsy of New York City, Inc. are faced with the dual problem of cognitive/intellectual deficits and a physical disability. This physical disability compromises, to varying degrees, their ability to physically perform what they want to do. The cognitive deficits

---
*Reprinted from *Sexuality and Disability*, 9, 1991, 149-159. Copyright 1991 by Human Sciences Press, Inc. Reprinted with permission

can cause untold problems in the areas of comprehension, retention, and expression. The human sexuality specialist must attend to both concerns simultaneously to be effective. This is a case study of an individual who represents many of the challenges of working with the disabled in the area of human sexuality. This article will follow the course of his treatment. I will present the case as it unfolded for me in terms of actual session content, and my analysis of the issues at the time they arose and in retrospect.

(4) The individual's name is Michael. He was twenty-five years old in 1988 when I first met him. Michael has a diagnosis of cerebral palsy, generalized athetosis. His speech is severely dysarthric and extremely difficult to understand. Although Michael's arms and legs are in almost constant motion, he is able to move his own wheelchair by pushing with his feet. On the Wechsler Adult Intelligence Scale, Michael attained a Verbal IQ score of 78. The examiner was unable to administer the performance subtests due to Michael's uncontrollable movement. Michael's functioning is within the range of borderline intelligence.

(5) Michael attended the United Cerebral Palsy Day Treatment Program. He would spend his days engaged in general academic activities and pre-vocational activities. Michael was friendly and was often seen in the company of peers. They were also severely physically disabled and ranged in IQ from moderately retarded to borderline intelligence. Michael lived at home with his mother and father. He is their only child.

(6) In my position as the human sexuality specialist I would travel from classroom to classroom offering the people in the program a basic lecture on sex education. Michael was in attendance at one of these sessions. At the end of each session I would suggest that, if anyone had any questions or had something they wanted to talk about in private, they could come to my office or ask their group leader to call me to set up an appointment. Two days after the group session Michael made his way to my office and asked if we could talk. An appointment was scheduled.

(7) At the beginning of our first session Michael told me that he had never had sex, nor had he ever masturbated. I was somewhat surprised (but did not express this) to hear that he had never masturbated, as I knew that he was very much a part of a peer group that talked a lot about sex and had a fair amount of sexual experience. I didn't feel that his physical disability would make it impossible for him to masturbate. I wanted to make sure that he knew what masturbation was. His response was that "masturbation was playing with yourself." I asked what he meant by "yourself." He responded, "Jerking your penis until you see the white stuff shooting." I asked him why he had never attempted to masturbate. He claimed that it was because of his disability. It had been my experience that even the most profoundly disabled people with cerebral palsy (as opposed to a paralyzed person who may have no movement) claim to be able to manipulate their genitalia in some way to get sufficient erotic stimulation. There seems to be a strong drive towards finding an effective position or method. While I was taking a sexual history Michael stated that he does wake up in the morning with an erection, and often gets erections when he observes attractive woman and when he watches X-rated videos on his VCR at home.

(8) Michael and I discussed how he could possibly maneuver his body into a position which would allow for direct stimulation. We talked about his ability to grasp his penis, or to rub his crotch against his pillow, blanket, or even headboard. I offered various suggestions. The session ended with Michael saying that he would "fool around" with my suggestions. An appointment was set for the following week. The reader should keep in mind that Michael's severe speech disorder makes it difficult for the conversation to flow easily, and the content of an individual session is comparatively reduced as a function of my need, and his benefit, to understand every word that he says.

(9) I did not believe that Michael had never attempted to masturbate. However, I felt that I must deal with his statements as if they were the absolute truth. As noted earlier my impression was that he was highly sexually motivated as he talked often about sexual matters with his peers and staff members. I also found out shortly after our sessions started that Michael had a healthy appetite for sexually explicit magazines and videos. Regardless, my aim was to avoid the fundamental error of expressing surprise, which could be dangerously perceived by him as my lack of trust in his honesty. I was very curious over why he would lie to me, if he was, at this very early point.

(10) At our next session, and for the few thereafter, Michael would describe exactly how he had tried to masturbate during the past week. One approach was to rub his penis along his arm when he was able to twist his body into an appropriate position. There was little success in this approach and certainly no orgasm. He did find some success in "humping" his pillow. Michael felt that he was getting closer to orgasm as he was maintaining an erection but would tire after not

climaxing for upwards of one hour. Our sessions had become a training course on how to masturbate when you are unable to use your hands.

(11) After two months Michael revealed to me that he had lied. He was fully capable of masturbating to orgasm and does it regularly. His main method is to rub his legs together which causes direct stimulation to his penis. Although this was difficult he would orgasm after thirty to forty-five minutes. I was angered by him for engaging us in such a long deception but I kept that to myself. I did ask why he had lied. He claimed that he did not trust me. He had seen many therapists come and go after offering all kinds of help. He had grown disappointed, rejected, and distrustful. If he was going to talk about his sexual feelings and behavior he needed to know that I would listen, understand, and help him. Michael controlled my commitment without risking any of his own commitment.

(12) I had never faced such a manipulative beginning to a therapeutic relationship. My experience with the physically and developmentally disabled had taught me that a key theme is often their passivity and dependence which often drives a willingness to tell anyone who asks, anything about themselves. In a very active way Michael had effectively tested my ability to deal with his sexuality.

(13) On the other hand, I also felt very satisfied. I had correctly diagnosed the possibility that he was lying, and resisted any line of inquiry that would reveal my suspicions. I provided total trust to an individual who didn't believe that was possible. Interestingly paradoxical, Michael stated, "I liked you because you believed me even when I was lying." I chose this point to discuss the importance of honesty and mutual trust.

(14) Now that Michael and I were able to move out of this protracted trust-building stage we began the work. I took a full (true!) sexual history. Michael spoke easily about his desires and frustrations. He was tremendously frustrated over never having a sexual partner. I probed regularly into his fantasy life. I often asked, "What would you want if you could have anything?" I asked that he describe these fantasies in vivid detail. It has been my contention that people often develop a restrictiveness, or reluctance, to explore the full possibilities of their sexual pleasure. In addition, people with disabilities are often unaware of what possibilities even exist. Michael was frustrated and angry over not having a partner, and this was adversely and unnecessarily ruining his enjoyment of masturbation. There are many avenues to explore for enhancing one's sexual pleasure that have nothing to do with a partner. My plan of treatment was to first resurrect his masturbatory activities, and increase his enjoyment of them. This treatment plan asks the multi-leveled question, "Can one create a better fantasy, masturbate more effectively, and have a more intense and satisfying orgasm?" A wide range of activities that are valid sexual involvements for autoerotic pleasure are available that will provide a resounding yes to the above question.

(15) The second major therapeutic milestone occurred at this point. The first milestone was the development of trust. This milestone was the beginning of the process of validating Michael as a fully sexual individual. He would be a person who possesses an active sex life of his own choosing, one that he works on and feels good about. Michael was learning that there wasn't anything inherent in his disability that limited his ability to attain sexual pleasure. We often spoke of how he could incorporate his involuntary movement into possible sexual movements, and how he could create fantasies that played on his disability.

(16) At the six-month point of counseling Michael began talking about having a friend. I believed that he would reach this point a short time after we successfully worked on masturbation and fantasy. An interesting aspect of sexuality counseling with the disabled is that, in using a step-by-step approach, success on one level is almost invariably followed by a renewed frustration over the next level. In cases of a delayed onset of "validated" sexual activity the individual exhibits an "I want more, I need more, and give me more" attitude. Michael's need to become more sexually involved manifested itself in his preliminary discussions about having sexual intercourse. He clearly wanted to find a partner to become involved with interpersonally.

(17) At this point I introduced various techniques that Michael could use to widen his social involvements in his search for a girlfriend. We also took a look at the women that may be available to him in the program. This aspect of counseling was severely hampered by Michael's compromised ability to travel independently. Basically he could not get himself to a social gathering. He would need accompaniment for long-distance travel. However, Michael had a few friendships with nondisabled people who were willing to take him places. Because of these people we were able to explore various activities that would expose him to potential partners.

(18) While we were working on becoming more socially involved, we also spoke a lot about sexual activity between two people. Although he had seen oral sex and

intercourse on videos Michael asked numerous questions about what was actually happening. He questioned how he could make love when he had so much involuntary movement. He was concerned that his deformed body would be a turn-off. And ultimately he asked if anyone could actually love him.

(19) For many months Michael received a series of rejections in his attempt to meet someone. He was hurt, angry, and his self-esteem was very low. He regressed in the area of masturbation to the point where he felt that it was a poor substitute for the "real thing." My impression was that Michael was particularly dismayed because he was closely following our plan, but without any success. He had widened his social involvements, and had become quite extroverted in his attempts to meet people, but he still did not have a girlfriend.

(20) A major turning point occurred in June 1986. Michael told me that he had been speaking with his friend Jimmy. Jimmy also has cerebral palsy and severely dysarthric speech. Although Jimmy is ambulatory he has a very awkward gait and he uses a Rollator (walker). More importantly Jimmy was sexually experienced. Jimmy had befriended some neighborhood "tough guys" who helped him obtain the services of prostitutes. Jimmy had offered to help Michael get a prostitute. They were making arrangements to meet in lower Manhattan and together they would hire a prostitute.

(21) The problem in this arrangement was that Jimmy had an inflated sense of his own capabilities. His "friends" had clearly done all of the work to get the prostitutes. It would be a dangerous situation if Jimmy and Michael met on a street corner and tried to hire a woman. In addition, Michael was going to travel further than he ever had alone because he didn't want to tell anyone what he was doing.

(22) I was extremely anxious over this plan and expressed my reasons to Michael. Somewhat surprisingly, Michael agreed with me and dropped the idea. He was clearly scared himself. We discussed the possibility of him asking someone more responsible to help him get a prostitute. Michael named his father, a friend, and his home attendant as possible candidates. The next few sessions were spent scripting what Michael would say to these people. Unfortunately (or fortunately?) Michael was rejected by all three people as they each felt that it would be too dangerous. They did suggest that he find a girlfriend. This well-intentioned advice was "old news" as Michael put it. Michael was depressed and growing resentful of his disability as the reason for his inability to experience intimate physical contact.

(23) For the first time I considered the possibility of a sex surrogate. I had been aware of a woman who identified herself as a sex surrogate with a specialty in working with physically disabled people. I felt that for me to make this kind of referral two conditions had to be met: (1) Michael had to have tried every available means to gain sexual experience through traditional methods, and (2) the surrogate was acceptable to me in terms of what service she was truly providing. I am making the assumption that my readers are at least somewhat familiar with the controversy that surrounds sex surrogacy.

(24) I telephoned the surrogate whose name was Amy. After identifying myself and my relationship to Michael we began talking about his case. I described him to her and how the treatment had been progressing. Amy told me that she had worked with similarly disabled people. I asked about her professional credentials. She spoke about her Masters Degree in Rehabilitation Counseling and her one-year intensive surrogacy training in California. She also outlined the differences in attitudes towards surrogacy in California and New York, and the attempts by surrogates to obtain official recognition through certification or licensing. Although Amy sounded intelligent I needed to meet her. We agreed to meet in my office the following week. At this point I chose not to tell Michael what I was considering.

(25) On the morning of the meeting I found myself to be anxious. The receptionist called at precisely 10 A.M. to say that my visitor had arrived. I left to meet her in the lobby. As I extended my hand to say hello my first impression was that she was a little older-looking than I had expected (mid-forties). Amy was also a little "messy" looking as her hair was long past her shoulders and heading in various directions. Her blouse was also a little low-cut. Simply put, and for a sense of comparison, she was dressed more provocatively than my coworkers in the center. As we walked to my office I thought to myself that she was probably selling a little of her appearance along with her skills. Amy talked about her family and their opinions of her profession (her teenage daughters thought she was "cool"). I shared my thoughts about working as a human sexuality specialist. We shared our common concerns for, and specific interests in, people with disabilities.

(26) As we spoke I found myself attracted to Amy. Attracted in the way that one becomes when they are with a bright, articulate, and sensitive human being. She possessed warmth and sincerity, and exuded a soft sensuality. My instincts told me that she was for real and was not consciously "marketing" herself. Amy

spoke about sex freely and easily, combining anecdotal stories and clinical impressions in a way that was professionally empathetic and insightful. The referral would be made if Michael wanted it. I told Amy about Michael's history. Amy mentioned that it was possible that an entire session could be spent just talking. I was confused as I thought I had communicated clearly that Michael was seeking sexual experience. He was not experiencing any sexual dysfunction. He wanted to engage in foreplay and intercourse for the first time. Michael and I had worked on his thoughts, feelings, and needs. He had met my first requirement for making the referral and now he needed to have sex with a partner. Amy responded that she understood. They would only talk long enough, prior to foreplay, to make sure that he was calm and relaxed. As I escorted Amy out of the building I told her that I would call to schedule the appointment.

(27) At my next session with Michael I told him everything. He was excited and anxious, and he wanted to know more. Primarily Michael wanted to know what this woman would do for him. He asked how much it would cost and when would he have to pay her. I told him that it would cost seventy dollars for a 1½-hour session. Michael earned ten dollars per week helping his father sell blank videotapes at a flea market. He told me that he had saved forty dollars and asked if I could hold it for him while he earned the additional thirty dollars he needed. In terms of the session I explained that the sex surrogate would talk to him for a short time to get to know him and to make sure that he was comfortable. When he was ready she would help him undress in the bedroom and they would have sex together. I was then taken aback when Michael asked how this was different from prostitution. It seems that everyone asks the same question. When I outlined the differences Michael's reaction was that this was "much better than prostitution because she would take the full time to work with me." He asked about birth control and sexual disease. At least in this instance my fear that no one ever listens to my basic lectures was assuaged. I explained that she would help him use a condom and that she could not get pregnant. Michael was satisfied that this was an excellent way for him to have a sexual experience with a partner. He was thrilled as his frustration was nearing an end. Everything was set except a third condition emerged before I would schedule the appointment. Michael would have to arrange for his own transportation to New Jersey. He would once again have to find someone he trusted and could count on to get him there. He would try again with his friend Eric.

(28) Michael and I discussed exactly what he would tell Eric. This included who Amy was, and what Eric would be asked to do. In this case it was only to provide transportation.

(29) Michael told me that Eric had responded very favorably. I wanted to meet with both of them to make sure that everyone knew what was going to happen. The next day we met and everything was set.

(30) Although I was confident that I had made the correct decision, something was troubling me the rest of the day. That something was that I was not solely functioning as Michael's therapist, but also as a representative of United Cerebral Palsy of New York City, Inc., an agency that may have a fundamental disagreement with my use of a sex surrogate in the treatment plan. I sensed that the agency could be particularly concerned about the legal issues surrounding surrogacy. I felt that I should inform my superior, Ms. Giovanna Nigro, of my plans. Ms. Nigro was the Manhattan Borough Director and she is a certified sex educator. I told her that I was not seeking her approval, but that I wanted her to be fully aware of this case. I have to admit that I was concerned that Ms. Nigro would disapprove and tell me that I could not complete the process. More important than this approval-disapproval issue I knew that I had worked hard and diligently with Michael and developed this course of treatment in a sound and professional manner. I was counting on Ms. Nigro to recognize that I had laid down the necessary therapeutic groundwork to render this referral the next logical step in an effective treatment plan. I explained the entire course of treatment and tried to anticipate her questions. When I finished, Ms. Nigro leaned back and stated that it appears that I have considered all relevant issues and that she wished Michael good luck. Although, as I stated earlier, I was not looking for approval, her response gave me more than I could have wished for as a therapist and an employee of the agency. It also confirmed my sense of communion with others who care deeply about the quality of life for people with disabilities.

(31) Two days before Michael was to see Amy, Eric canceled. He claimed that he had pressing family matters to attend to. Michael was devastated. I now faced an extremely difficult decision. Should I take Michael? I was conflicted because I had always been of the school that says the counselor counsels, the counselor does not do. I had always been absolutely against doing more for the individual than he or she could do for themselves. But, on the other hand, I often heard the criticism of our field that we can talk "all day long" about socializing for the physically disabled but if they can't get out of their house are we really providing a useful service. Could it be true that we are really contributing to the

individual's frustration? In my resolution I had to be convinced that Michael had done everything humanly possible to get himself to this point. He had, and I knew what I would do. I would take him to his first sexual experience with another person.

(32) On August 8, 1986 I picked Michael up at 7 P.M. He was freshly bathed and dressed in a pair of shorts and polo shirt. He was excited and he stated that he was looking forward to today more than anything he had ever looked forward to before. Michael asked what I would do during his session? I was surprised by his seemingly calm disposition. I searched my memory for how I felt before my first sexual experience. I was extremely nervous, but then again I had not faced the obstacles that he had to overcome. His sense of calm may have been the result of his frustration nearly being over. There was a self-satisfaction in his accomplishment, a success after a long-sought-after endeavor. His accomplishment was measured neither by a sexual conquest, nor a satisfying sexual experience. But rather by his personal attainment of normalcy. His severe disability, the source of relentless frustration, was being rendered irrelevant. Michael would make love like anyone could make love.

(33) My only fear at this point was that I was totally wrong. Could it be that his calmness was a figment of my imagination, and the sexual encounter would be a disaster? Michael and I chatted about sports as I drove over the George Washington Bridge.

(34) We arrived at Amy's apartment. I told Michael to wait in the car as I would make sure that she was home. Amy greeted me at the door. She was dressed casually. I commented briefly again about the extent of Michael's disability and how he could be transferred out of his wheelchair. I mentioned that his movement would become more spastic if he was to get nervous or fear for his physical safety. Amy suggested that it would be a good time to bring Michael in. They exchanged hellos and Amy told me to come back at 9:30 P.M.

(35) When I returned Michael and Amy were talking quietly. They greeted me briefly, whispered something to each other, hugged, and said good-bye. I pushed Michael into the street and helped him into the car. He was laughing and talking simultaneously which made it impossible to understand him. He was so excited and wanted to talk so much that I pulled the car into a supermarket parking lot.

(36) Michael wanted to tell me exactly what happened moment-by-moment. They started by talking about each other's day. After a few minutes of friendly conversation Amy asked about his sexual experience. Michael told her that he masturbates often but had never been with another person. Amy asked if he was comfortable enough to get undressed. She then wheeled him into the bedroom and helped him onto the bed. She slowly undressed him and then herself. Amy caressed his chest and told him how sexy and attractive his body was. They fondled each other and licked each other's skin. Amy showed Michael how to touch her skin and helped guide his hands. They engaged in foreplay for over thirty minutes. When Michael was thoroughly aroused, Amy from the top position inserted his penis into her vagina. They rocked slowly back and forth together. Michael had an orgasm. He told me that his movement had never been so calm.

(37) Michael was proud and expressed how he felt like an adult for the first time in his life. His sense of elation was so great that he wanted to tell me the whole story again. I was happy to hear it again as I drove him home. I couldn't understand a word he said as I concentrated on the road, but it didn't matter. Michael savored each memory as it solidified in his mind.

(38) Our next session was on Monday. We talked about the evening but not in detail. I inquired if he was troubled by anything that had occurred. He said that he wasn't. Michael spoke about feeling good, feeling normal, and feeling like he wanted to do it again.

(39) Over the course of the next few months Michael would find a few moments here and there to talk about that evening. More importantly he had become intent on developing an intimate relationship with a woman that he could care about.

(40) As I think back now I entered into this aspect of counseling with fear and trepidation. In this case the referral was the next logical step in the treatment. In many cases a referral would not be advised as the individual either cannot, or refuses to, meet the requirements I outlined as prerequisites. Is sex surrogacy therapy or prostitution? Whatever it was, or is, Michael's life was forever changed. Everything I had hoped for was far surpassed. Michael gained a high level of confidence and self-esteem, and a positive self-image far beyond what he would have if we only talked. Occasionally I am troubled by that conclusion. But I am never troubled by how we proceeded, and what he did. Michael had gone through every step that I felt was necessary for the experience to be truly an outgrowth of

Human Sexuality

his own trials, tribulations, and abilities. For Michael, in his heart, becoming a "truly sexual being" was much more than just words.

Terms for Discussion

1. human sexuality services (paragraph 1)

2. borderline intelligence (paragraph 4)

3. manipulative [client] (paragraph 12)

4. trust/trust building (paragraphs 13, 14, and 15)

5. validated sexual activity (paragraph 16)

6. sex surrogate (paragraph 23, 24, 27, 30, and 40)

Questions

7. In paragraph 1, the author states that "Everyone must be guaranteed the freedom of opportunity and sexual expression." Do you agree? Why?

8. In paragraphs 7 and 9, the author says that he was surprised that Michael reported having never masturbated; the author did not express his surprise. If you were the counselor and were surprised, would you have expressed it? Why?

9. Michael lied about masturbation for the first two months of the therapeutic relationship. Do you agree with the author's decision not to voice his suspicions for a two-month period? Explain.

10. In paragraph 12, the author refers to the passivity and dependence of the physically and developmentally disabled. In your opinion, is such a view of the disabled stereotypical or is it a factual observation? Explain.

11. In paragraph 16, the author refers to a "step-by-step" approach. Speculate on what the author means by this term in this particular case. Do you agree with this approach in this case? Explain.

12. Michael ultimately asked if anyone could love him. (See paragraph 18.) If you were the counselor, what kind of answer would you have given? Be specific.

13. The author discussed with Michael the possibility of getting a responsible person to help Michael get a prostitute. (See paragraph 22.) In your opinion, did this pose any moral or legal problems? Explain.

14. What is your understanding of the difference between a prostitute and a sex surrogate?

15. Do you agree with what the author told Amy about just talking with Michael in their initial session? Explain. (See paragraph 26.)

16. Comment on the author's decision to inform his superior about arranging the surrogate and the timing of his decision. (See paragraph 30.)

17. What is your opinion on the author's decision to drive Michael to be with Amy? (See paragraph 31.)

18. In your opinion would it be possible for a person such as Michael to become dependent on prostitutes and surrogates, precluding the development of an intimate relationship with a woman? Explain.

19. Do you agree that Michael had become a "truly sexual being"? Explain. (See paragraph 40.)

20. Both the client and the counselor were men. Do you believe that in this case it was important for the client to have a male counselor? Explain.

21. Are there other forms of treatment that might have facilitated Michael's improvement? Explain.

22. Rate the article on the seven criteria described in the introduction to this book on a scale from 5 (highest quality) through 1 (lowest quality). Be prepared to explain your ratings.

Criterion 1: The demographics of the case are described: _____

Criterion 2: The condition(s) and behavior(s) that necessitated treatment are described in detail: _____

Criterion 3: The method of treatment is described in sufficient detail so that it can be replicated without additional information: _____

Criterion 4: A rationale is provided for the method of treatment selected: _____

Criterion 5: The client's improvement, if any, is clearly documented? _____

Criterion 6: Follow-up information on the client's improvement, if any, is presented: _____

Criterion 7: The study is appropriate for publication in a journal: _____

Notes:

Case 28

Treating Adolescent Satanism in Art Therapy*

Amy M. Speltz

(1) Increasingly, adolescent psychiatric patients have interests in satanic symbols and rituals, or have had previous membership in satanic cults (Bourget, 1988). Although some adolescents merely dabble in satanism as they might with new forms of music, for others satanism can become so integrated into their identity that they cannot reject it. This paper is to call attention to the role of the art therapist in "containing" satanic expression while allowing the angry feelings associated with it to be worked through.

(2) Most of the professional work done to counteract the influence of satanism has concentrated on sessions to build awareness of the phenomenon. This has been done even with very young children (Gould, 1986). In the current psychiatric literature, satanic cult victims are often lumped together with members of fundamentalist religious cults and are not differentiated for special attention (Olsson, 1980). However, currently there is a draft for legislation in some states to require those in the health and law enforcement fields to learn about satanic rituals and practices in order to recognize possible victims. Because of the threat of ritualistic murders associated with satanic cults, local police departments have become well informed.

(3) Primary sources for learning about satanism are not easily available. There was a burgeoning of literature on the occult and witchcraft in the 1970s, but the current dearth of published mainstream literature has left mental health professionals to deal with the problem in isolation and with few guidelines. Occult bookstores will now yield more information on this topic than will libraries.

(4) Satanism appeals to both near-normal rebellious adolescents as well as to the emotionally disturbed. Because it thrives on secrecy, not much information about it has become available. This secrecy, which has great appeal for adolescents, is also present because those who join satanic cults may be terrorized into keeping the secrets; they are threatened that they or their loved ones will be punished if they do not.

(5) Satanism provides an ultimate form of rebellion because it is the opposite of parental beliefs. Good equals bad. Bad equals good. It is against social norms and is usually not acceptable, even in the most permissive society. Because other forms of rebellion, such as sexual acting out and experimentation with drugs, are tolerated, satanism may be one of the few remaining forms of rebellion with a capacity to shock. It appeals to adolescents with deep insecurities and low self-esteem. It provides a sense of belonging and a deviant identity against the conventional society that may have rejected them. The recruitment of children is usually targeted toward those having problems at home, and it is believed that children with stable home lives are not recruited (Gould, 1986).

(6) For many adolescents, satanism provides a sense of power and control in that it allows the believer to put spells on others. This is often paradoxical in that true participants in a satanic cult place themselves under the control of the cult's high priest. For emotionally-disturbed adolescents, satanism provides an outlet for anger and violence. In satanic groups it may be acceptable to act very angry and be respected for it. Aggressive acts, such as the killing of animals or animal sacrifices, are condoned.

---

*The Arts in Psychotherapy, 17, 1990, pp. 147-155. Copyright 1990 by Pergamon Press Ltd., Oxford, England. Reprinted with permission.

(7) Satanism is reinforced by elements in the existing teenage culture. Many believe that heavy metal music has a definite link with the satanic. Although there are reasons to question this, the popularity of such music may have introduced satanic themes in a way to make them acceptable to adolescents.

(8) Wass and colleagues (1988-89) discussed the lyrics of such music in a recent article. One-fifth of all adolescents in their study were attracted to rock music with destructive themes. Their findings seriously questioned the notion of the recording industry that teenagers do not know the lyrics, are only interested in the sound of music, and listen only for fun. Interest in this music may often be the first step toward the acceptance of satanism. Patients have informed me that there are many underground music groups that are satanic and that the musicians themselves practice satanism. Some patients have referred to LaVey (1969, 1972). Some music reinforces satanism by suggestion, with slow and hypnotic rhythms that make the adolescent relax. The longer the adolescent concentrates on the music the more hypnotic it becomes.

(9) Leisure activities such as Dungeons and Dragons may have special meaning for those involved in occult or satanic activities. Some recent films have allusions to satanic practices, which can only be understood by those who are involved. For example, in a recent film, "The Golden Child" (Paramount Pictures, in association with Eddie Murphy Productions, 1986), Eddie Murphy is recruited by people from a foreign country to find the golden child who has the "Midas touch"—everything he touches turns to gold. He can bring things back to life. The child is kidnapped by an evil person with evil powers who wants the child's powers, but, in order to achieve them, must possess him and substitute evil for the good. The child is given oatmeal with blood, which will make him more vulnerable, is also put in the center of an area with four points around him, four beings who concentrate on weakening his goodness and substituting evil. This is a very minor part of the film, and unless one is familiar with the ritual it would probably have no meaning. "The Golden Child" may be one of the only mainstream films with allusions to satanism, but other films, such as the video "Faces of Death" (MTI Home Video, produced by Rosilin F. Scott, 1978), deal with satanic themes. Patients report that this film is about real-life experiences people have had with supernatural powers. Some of the deaths are connected with satanic rituals, which have connections to the drug culture—patients have reported the use of drugs in rituals.

(10) There are various levels of involvement in satanism. At one level are the "dabblers," the largest groups of patients. Beyond this, according to Gould (1986), are self-styled satanists, organized groups, and an international network.

(11) Satanic symbols proliferate quickly among an adolescent group. They begin to appear, inked or carved on the body, on jeans and jean jackets, in graffiti, and everywhere else. Some patients will draw the symbols simply to attract attention, others because someone they consider to be "cool" is doing it. Symbols usually include the pentagram, the goat's head, 666, the upside-down cross, horns, and the devil.

(12) Although some patients will draw satanic symbols in the art therapy session, patients more involved in satanism usually draw pictures that are very violent and bloody. Anger radiates from their pictures and sometimes specific satanic symbols are incorporated. Some patients do not have the imagination or ability to draw the violence and will rely only on the symbols.

The Response to Satanism

(13) Satanism should be closely monitored in mental health settings. It is especially dangerous with psychiatric populations, who are needy and extremely subject to peer influence. Because the therapeutic effort is to diminish destructive ways of living and to replace them with healthier alternatives, many patients are left without forms of rebellion or control. Satanic rituals can then become even more inviting. At the same time, one must be prepared for that rare patient who professes satanism to be his or her legitimate religion and establish guidelines for such cases. The destructive impulses behind these expressions require therapeutic attention —satanism is merely an outlet. To deny the expression of satanism in art therapy would be to constrict the release of anger and aggressive feelings and undermine the therapeutic potential of working the feelings through. The use of satanic symbols are very graphic representations of angry feelings and it is necessary to provide a safe, structured environment where the patients can work through these issues.

Varying Levels of Involvement in Satanism: Three Patients

(14) As an art therapist working with such patients, I have observed varying levels of involvement in satanism. Three adolescent patients I will call David, Christina, and Doug illustrate three levels of participation in satanic practices. In each case the patients were

treated by an individual verbal psychotherapist and by me as their art therapist.

(15) David was willing to teach me a great deal about satanism. He was a 16-year-old adolescent diagnosed as having a major recurrent depression, with psychoactive substance abuse, and an Axis II diagnosis of borderline personality disorder. He had become involved with satanism at the age of 11 after attending a satanic mass with friends, but seemed to maintain objectivity as to the part it played in his life. He reported that many others were too frightened to become involved at that time, but he did because of the feelings of power and control that it gave him, although it did not seem to fulfill any other emotional needs.

(16) He spoke of a ritual called "Proposals." When one does a proposal, he or she concentrates on raising a spirit or a demon. A proposal is based on concentration and includes no music, blood, or sacrifices, but is still an expression of a religious belief. It is believed that if one concentrates, or sends a proposal to the Devil or Satan, someone can be harmed through this telepathy. The more engaged one is and the more time one spends on proposals, the more powerful one may become within the network of the satanic religion. This motivates one to become more deeply involved. In addition, combining proposals with others greatly increases the power to raise demons and spirits.

(17) David had no fear of speaking about satanism and sharing his experiences. He spoke of doing the proposals, and described the ritual as the formation of a "compass" with four others (North, East, South, and West) and someone in the middle. The outside people are to concentrate on evil, negative things. Eventually the spirits that are raised will be possessed by the person in the middle. David described out-of-body experiences. He reported that if one is possessed by a spirit or demon as a result of a proposal, if one is hit, only the spirit or demon will feel the pain. Even when the spirit leaves, one will no longer feel pain, unless it is a flesh wound.

(18) David told me of an experience of having "pissed off" one of the demons, and believed that this demon followed him around for a week. It was like a sixth sense, and he could feel it as if it were another person. The only way to get rid of the demon was not to act as if one were scared. He also reported that one should never wear a cross because demons will then "go for you." However, if one is powerful, one can control spirits. Spirits become even more powerful by taking control of other spirits.

(19) He spoke of conventional satanism and contrasted it with non-conventional satanism. In the latter, aggressive and angry feelings are displayed through satanic art and rituals. The satanic religion becomes a sanction for aggression and is seen in the negative and hostile tendencies that are part of the rituals. David talked about concentrating on hurt and pain. He believed that his developing ability to control his impulses may have had something to do with what he described as "letting go" of satanism. Although he dabbled in it after he had gained more self-control, it did not have the same effect.

(20) David believed that satanism had not really affected his daily life, and said, "I just have more knowledge now. You're never really out of it. Like Vietnam, it's always with you." He continued to believe that people should respect satanism and be afraid of it. He reported that vulnerable people tend to become easily engulfed by the music and the satanic symbols, and that they weaved the rituals into their daily life to the point of lost objectivity and reality.

(21) David's illness was perhaps less severe than Christina's or Doug's. He was of higher than average intelligence, and a strong individual. His personality tended to be more antisocial than the other two patients and consequently he was attracted more by the promise of power and control than the others and less attracted by its potential for releasing his anger. He really did not have the hatred and anger of patients who became more deeply involved. He was obviously intrigued by supernatural powers and rituals, but somehow kept satanism in perspective.

(22) Christina, a 17-year-old female, represented a different level of involvement. She had an Axis I diagnosis of major depression and an Axis II diagnosis of borderline personality disorder. Her predominant affect was anger. She was able to trace this anger back to her early childhood and focused much of it on her mother. She had some degree of self-awareness and realized that she often turned her sad feelings into angry feelings because they were easier to deal with.

(23) For Christina, satanism became a way to live out a fantasy. When her anger arose she was not really able to express it verbally and directly, but retreated into the use of satanic symbols. She seemed to be displacing the anger she felt toward her parents; satanism became a way for anger to be expressed and to be acceptable to others. Because she was so angry she used satanic beliefs as a way to inflict pain. By inflicting pain through

satanic fantasy she could do so within the confines of her religious beliefs.

(24) Christina was also using satanism to rebel against her parents' religion. She did not keep her satanism a secret from her family. When her mother asked her directly about her satanic beliefs, Christina told her that there was nothing good in the world and that was why she liked satanism. She read her mother a poem about drinking blood that had been written by one of her friends.

(25) On certain days, Christina would present her "Alice Cooper look." She would draw black make-up heavily around her eyes, draw a black tear on her face, and dress all in black. Her paranoid ideation became so severe that she began carrying a knife. A revised diagnosis of a psychotic disorder was considered, as well as that of schizoid personality disorder. She was finally able to talk about her satanic thoughts in her psychotherapy sessions. She began to see these beliefs as deeply influenced by her own life history. She defended her view that evil predominates by saying, "I've never seen God do his stuff."

(26) She later began to spend a great deal of time writing letters and stories. During the course of art therapy, she went from satanic fantasy to utilizing the fantasy of fictional characters as a way of expressing feelings. The fictional characters she drew still seemed to represent other aspects of herself (much as satanic symbols had expressed the angry side of her identity)—the powerful and controlling aspects of the self, as they came to be developed through the course of her treatment.

(27) Doug, a 15-year-old white male, revealed little about his satanic practices. I was not able to learn from him whether he actually belonged to a satanic group or whether he had selected these expressions in an almost private and solitary way. His diagnosis was major depression, recurrent and borderline personality disorder. His MMPI described his personality configuration as associated with both paranoid schizophrenia and personality disorder. Individuals with this profile are, by adult norms, usually seen as defensive or evasive, sensitive, easily hurt by criticism. They are distrustful, fear emotional connection, keep people at a distance, and misperceive the motives and actions of others.

(28) There were early indications during his treatment that Doug might be vulnerable to satanism. His fascination and response to newspaper articles about vampire murders spoke to his inner turmoil. He was upset by the movie "Nightmare on Elm Street" (New Cinema Corporation, 1986), and often talked about *Helter Skelter,* the book about Charles Manson (Bugliosi & Gentry, 1975) and about Charles Manson the man. Doug appeared quite depressed and paranoid in his stance toward others. He liked to see his blood drawn and had mentioned a wish to become a mortician. He was interested in heavy metal music.

(29) In his first interview, Doug expressed an interest in art. When he began working in art therapy, he verbalized much knowledge about satanic cults and symbols. He knew a great deal about the history of the pentagram, its sources, and some of the other items related to satanism. When he was questioned for information about certain symbols, he talked about them freely, but if questions were of a personal nature about how his artwork affected him or how satanism affected him, he did not answer or denied any personal attachment to it.

(30) Doug's artwork was always done in lead and colored pencil, a very controlled medium. In the beginning it was confined to demons, configurations of the goat head and pentagram symbols. They seemed to be safe images because they were familiar symbols, recognized by others, and not configurations of his own fantasies. It appeared that as he progressed in treatment and was being confronted, his connection to satanism and the role it was playing in his emotional state became clearer to him. His drawings then became more three-dimensional and vivid. His art increased in violence and seemed to take over, not only in art therapy but also outside of the sessions. When his violent and bloody drawings were discussed, he said that this was reality and that drawing mountains and trees was not.

(31) It finally became clear that Doug was engaging in satanic activities with peers. He admitted that his interest in satanism was a source for self-esteem. He was viewed by some peers as a leader and the priest in the ceremonies he conducted. Other peers came to him for information about satanic rituals. He described his involvement in these activities as a means of attaining both physical and mental power over adversaries. He reported that during the rituals he became possessed by a black demon who had given him the power to make small objects and awake evil powers to cause misfortune to peers.

(32) It appeared that Doug took his beliefs seriously. He participated in a seance with several peers. He asked to be possessed by a demon and then asked the demon to possess another peer. Sometimes these beliefs seemed to conflict with Doug's emotional self, as when he expressed needing to keep his love for his girlfriend secret

from Satan. Satanism can be a vehicle for denying feelings of love and expressing intense feelings of anger toward others.

(33) When he was asked to think seriously about the torture and dismemberment of small animals in satanic practices, he saw nothing wrong with it and said, "Why should I care about anyone when no one cares about me?" This seemed to emphasize the intense anger Doug felt, perhaps as unresolved rage at his mother. At times like this Doug was not able to rationalize or acknowledge his love for his girlfriend.

(34) During Doug's fourth month of treatment, the verbal therapist and I decided that his morbid drawings of mutilated bodies and other satanic pictures should be limited to the art therapy sessions to provide opportunity and encouragement to process the therapeutic interpretation of the artwork. Doug's response was that he simply did not understand why these drawings were offensive to others. He seemed quite puzzled that others might be repulsed by this violent art. This strange innocence recalls Haeseler's (1987) statement that patients can learn to understand their artwork and its meaning to them but also must learn to see it in its likely reception by others.

(35) Doug was allowed to draw anything that he desired in art therapy. It was not known that if he were prevented from drawing violent art the aggression would be expressed in other, more dangerous ways. Does art provide an adequate substitute for more dangerous acting out by such patients? Could such primitive rage, violence, and aggression be worked through in art therapy combined with individual psychotherapy? Haeseler (1987) has distinguished between art as reenactment and art as metaphor. That is, rather than patients using their art to "commit" the destructive act, it would be "far more beneficial if patients were to use their art to identify and express the strong feelings that the reenactment helps them to avoid—in other words to find a metaphor for the internal feelings they are experiencing" (Haeseler, p. 12).

(36) Doug found it extremely difficult to accept the rule limiting his drawings to art therapy. Because art was a source of both self-esteem and catharsis, the patient truly suffered. The prohibition against drawing seemed to remove a layer of his identity and he was lost. This period also coincided with increasing violence on his part. His identification with Charles Manson continued, and he painted "Die Pigs" in red paint on a wall. A chart note by the supervising psychiatrist stated the dilemma:

> He was struggling to draw as he often does, but was unable to decide what he might produce. It is as if he is afraid that what he would convey would be too horrible for our world to accept. We are in a dilemma as to whether or not we can contain his present inclination toward a plunge into the world of blood or gore, or if he should be allowed to express himself.

(37) Without his former reliance on art, Doug often verbalized very violent thoughts. He spoke about committing murder. He was vague about it, but spoke about omnipotent powers. Instead of speaking directly about his relationship with his verbal therapist, he spoke at great length about his hostile, aggressive, and morbid fantasies about both therapists and other authority figures.

(38) During this intense period, art therapy also lost its attraction. In the earlier phase of his treatment, art therapy was so valuable to him that even when he was unable to go to the sessions, he called the art therapist to come to see him. He became quite argumentative about the value of art therapy and quite angry when pressed to discuss it. A note described his dilemma:

> He is obviously trying to keep the lid on. He may fear that if he lets emotional issues out by discussing his artwork, it will get out of control for him, which would be a desperate situation.

Working with the Satanic Patient: The Art Therapist's Experience

(39) There were rumors that Doug was talking about human sacrifices, and he was getting older peers "stirred up" and involved. His verbal therapist worked very diligently with him about the satanism; he was told that he could not draw satanic pictures except in art therapy sessions and that he could not have certain satanic posters in his room. Some of his music was temporarily taken away from him.

(40) Following these restrictions, Doug retreated from his drawings and seemed to be placing his energies into verbal therapy. It was evident from his lack of investment in art therapy that he could not make an equal investment in both. He seemed really in conflict about what he could draw. He was hesitant and very guarded in what he displayed in his artwork. In the months that followed, the art seemed to be contingent on his verbal therapy sessions. When therapy became too much for him or issues that were too difficult arose, he backed off

from verbal therapy and reinvested energy into his drawings and in the art therapy sessions.

(41) During the next few months, he was faced with the prospect of the departure of significant people who had been associated with his treatment. He was struggling with how to express his feelings toward people. Both his verbal therapist and his case supervisor were leaving; he felt that a great deal of support had been withdrawn from him. The drawings during this two-month period were more illuminating. They seemed to be configurations of his own imagination and not taken from other artwork. The drawings were more direct, depressive acts, such as having an ax in the forehead or having a head chopped off. There were two pictures of particular interest. One was of three demons disemboweling a person. This gory picture was a gift for his mother. The second picture, equally gory, was a gift for the birthday of a person who had contact with Doug through his treatment program. The drawings, despite their gory content, still expressed a wide realm of emotions, including affection and caring, as well as anger. When he made these drawings for people he actually liked, it was a clue to the fact that he was unaware of how such pictures would be received. He seemed to be very focused on the grotesqueness, the gore, and the blood of his drawings.

(42) A power struggle ensued because the birthday gift picture was turned over to me. I tried to process his drawing with Doug. When I learned that it was a gift and how important it was to him, I emphasized that his gesture was genuine and important and how it was good that he wanted to share his talent with someone he liked. This was an attempt to separate the gesture from the content of the picture. It was difficult for him to do this. He had a hard time making the distinction between the two. Because the art therapist had possession of the picture, he felt that his privacy had been violated and that I had invaded his personal space. He later came to art therapy and tore and threw away this picture. If its intended recipient couldn't have it, no one was going to have it. He had been told that he could draw his pictures but keep them completely private.

(43) Doug's feelings during this time demonstrated the importance of his artwork for him and how painful it was when others tried to put some controls on it. His artwork seemed to serve several purposes: (a) as a means of expression, (b) as a coping mechanism, and (c) as a source of pride. The art was one way in which Doug could maintain his fragile self-esteem. He struggled with whether or not to give up his drawings. To give them up would be to sacrifice a strong outlet for expressing emotions. He had stated that he would "cut up heads and sit them on a platter or mutilate the therapists" if he had to give up his drawings. This is an example of the amount of aggression, anger, and hostility that he had internalized and that seemed to be expressed when his artwork was threatened.

(44) Art therapy was one means by which Doug could be aggressive and hostile and carry out his threats without having to pay the consequences. The anger, which he had internalized for many years, had reached a point where he could no longer control its expression; it was projected through his drawings.

(45) In processing the artwork during this time, Doug became very angry with my questions. He said, "If you would ask me straight out, I would tell you instead of playing games." I then asked him straight out. Because of his great resistance, I had previously taken an indirect way to let him know that artwork is sometimes purely artwork and sometimes a self expression. I had told him that when it was self expression, it was important for him to give feedback as to what the art meant to him or what message he was trying to give to the drawings. But responding to his wishes, I then asked him directly what meaning he was trying to convey when he gave the drawing as a birthday gift, once again trying to separate the gesture from the content. He responded that the drawing meant nothing. He had difficulty acknowledging personal ownership of his drawings despite his pride in them. They were just pictures he liked to draw; they were things he knew how to draw. He was able only once to say that when he was angry he put everything into his drawings. When this was repeated back to him, he said, "No, I was talking about another person. " He was always very guarded and used a great deal of denial. When discussing the benefits of art therapy for this patient, we have to say that such benefits became clear only in their absence. Art therapy became a catharsis for him; it provided little insight or cure. It temporarily contained his aggressive and violent impulses.

Some Guidelines for Working with the Patient Interested in Satanism

(46) I have related the work with Doug in greater depth to illustrate some of the dilemmas present in working with such patients. Although I cannot advocate special techniques for working with them, my work has suggested some general guidelines, some of which are basic art therapy principles and others are specific to the work with such patients.

Allowing the Expression of Anger

(47) Patients such as Doug, Christina, and David, like all patients in art therapy, are encouraged to use their art to express feelings. They need to be told that they are free to express their anger in their artwork. They need to be told that it is okay to be angry in sessions, but if they feel that their anger is going to be destructive they can leave the session with no apologies. Art therapy provides an unrestricted environment where these patients can express themselves and release the feelings that have somehow become associated with satanism. Because art therapy is a means by which unconscious material becomes conscious, a graphic record of unconscious feelings becomes possible. This free expression releases these feelings before the patient can censor them.

(48) In contrast to some restrictions that may apply toward satanic expression in various settings, art therapy provides patients with a less restrictive environment to express themselves and release feelings that had previously been satisfied by participation in satanic practices. An ultimate goal of therapy is to release these feelings and disassociate them from satanic practices. Later, patients should be able to re-associate their anger with real objects or persons so that this can be worked through in psychotherapy. Margaret Naumburg (1975) wrote that neutralization of aggressive energy characteristic of sublimation occurs in the area of artistic execution. The role that free expressive art served for Doug became obvious when his freedom to use it was restricted. The art served to release these angry feelings, and without it there was a greater danger of harm to others—or at least a mounting expression of desires and threats.

Controlling the Therapist's Response to Sensationalism

(49) In working with patients involved with satanism, the first rule is to not acknowledge the sensationalism of satanic work. How it affects the patient not the therapist should be addressed. Some of these patients do the sensational kind of artwork because it produces an immediate reaction, particularly from adults. It can force adults away from the patient. Attention can become focused on the sensationalism of the drawing rather than on its meaning. The patient may also use the artwork as a way to avoid closeness to others, and as a way to test the therapist on how he or she will react or will deal with it. In not providing the conventional reaction of shock or horror a beneficial uncertainty is aroused in patients. Asking them what the art means in a nonthreatening way provides a new challenge.

Dissociating the Work and the Person from Satanism

(50) If the artwork is accepted as signifying something other than satanism, the therapist gives support for the patient to explore it or see it in another way. With Doug and others, the art therapist's methodology is to talk first about the artistic ability shown in the drawings. This is in contrast to the usual practice in art therapy—technique is not discussed because the therapist fears that it may inhibit freedom and defeat the real purpose of art therapy. But for patients who use satanic themes, addressing technique neutralizes the discussion. It moves the art one step away from satanism. The artistic avenues used should be explored, particularly if the patient is not verbal about the meaning of his or her artwork. Doug was first able to say that he made his drawings simply because he liked to draw. By complimenting him and increasing his self-esteem about his work, I gave him some ego strength, which allowed him to move to a verbal level in which he could begin to acknowledge and deal with his artwork. The therapist can then begin to explore art's meanings and expression indirectly. One way is to talk about famous artists and artists in general. Showing the patient similar works by other artists provides support and gives the message, "You are not the only one who draws these things or for whom the artwork is so intense." This gives the therapist an opening to say that famous artists release much energy and personal expression into their art to display a meaning or give a message to people.

Discussion of Meaning

(51) When their unconscious feelings are expressed in graphic images by some patients, the art therapist can begin to discuss the meanings of satanism for them. The therapist informs patients that the meaning of the artwork is different for each person and that it is important to verbalize what their art means to them. This helps to separate occult or satanic meaning and to substitute an individual interpretation. It helps patients to examine the role of satanism, how it affects them personally, and what emotions are being used or expressed through satanism. Satanism can become a "container" into which the patient projects these feelings of aggression and violence. Some patients will be able to finally identify their use of satanism and develop the strength to be released from it.

(52) There is great variation in patient response to the discussion of meaning, and some of this variation depends on verbal ability. One female patient influenced by satanism always allowed her drawings to tag along behind her verbal skills. She could make a very simple

drawing and talk at length about its meaning. Her drawings were not always satanic. Satanic drawings seem to have been produced when she was angry or displaying some near-psychotic characteristics. Another patient always drew very intense drawings. His pictures always had some violence and anger in them. He never verbalized about them. Very few of these patients combined intense drawings with developed verbal skills. When they expressed their emotions graphically, it seemed to take up all of their energies. Once their emotions were at a more conscious level, they could process the meaning, and verbal skills seemed to correlate with the level of emotions expressed graphically.

(53) As a patient develops in the art therapy process, he or she may have less intense angry works of art and more intense verbal processing of unconscious material. When graphics predominate, they are more uncontrolled and there is a greater need for art therapy. When meanings reach conscious level, there is more control and greater censorship is involved. Once patients reach this level of awareness, they can be very direct about what they want to express in art therapy. If they want their art to express anger, they can do so with an awareness of what they are doing either before or after the drawing.

An Alternative Approach to Meaning: Objectification
(54) If a patient is unable to express the meaning of his or her work the art therapist can approach it by saying, for example, that every work of art has different meanings for different people. The therapist might ask, "If someone were to walk in here and see your picture, what message do you think they might get?" This is a gentle challenge to the patient to step back and view the art objectively. Patients are not always able to do this. Another question asked might be, "If this picture were looked at by someone who didn't know you, what do you think it would say about you, or how does it represent you?" Some patients may be frightened by the question, but the experience may still be positive. If patients are frightened about what the pictures say, it is an indication that they have some conscious awareness of how intense their feelings are—how angry and frightened they are. If they are not ready to acknowledge these feelings they are not really ready to be affected by them.

Conclusion

(55) There are no specific techniques with guaranteed effectiveness for patients with satanic interests. Each patient should be assessed concerning his or her ability to process abstract material. The patient's ego strength, self-esteem, and how he or she uses the art should be considered. This paper has attempted to call attention to what seems to be an expanding population of adolescents interested in satanism. The primary goal of the therapist is to weaken the link with satanism between the patients' emotions and their art productions. For some patients, artwork can release emotions that were somehow satisfied by satanism. Some helpful techniques for therapists have been: (a) avoiding acknowledgment of the sensationalism in the artwork, (b) discussing artistic techniques in the early stages when there is great resistance to the exploration of meaning, (c) exploring meaning when the patient is ready, and (d) developing objectification when the patient is not.

References

Bourget, D. (1988). Satanism in a psychiatric adolescent population. *Canadian Journal of Psychiatry, 33,* 197-202.

Bugliosi, V., & Gentry, C. (1975). *Helter skelter.* New York: Bantam.

Gould, C. (1986). *Information on satanism.* Unpublished manuscript.

Haeseler, M. P. (1987). Censorship or intervention: "But you said we would draw whatever we wanted." *American Journal of Art Therapy, 26,* 11-20.

La Vey, A. S. (1969). *Satanic bible.* New York: Avon.

La Vey, A. S. (1972). *Satanic rituals.* New York: Avon.

Naumburg, M. (1975). Art therapy: its scope and function. In E. F. Hammer (Ed.), *Clinical application of projective drawings.* Springfield, IL: Charles C. Thomas.

Olsson, P. A. (1980). Adolescent involvement with the supernatural and cults. *Annual of Psychoanalysis, 8,* 171-196.

Wass, H., Rapu, J. L., Cerullo, K., Martel, L.G., Mingione, L. A., & Sparring, A.M. (1988-1989). Adolescent's interest in views of destructive themes in rock music. *Omega, 19* (3), 177-186.

Terms for Discussion

1. major depression (paragraphs 15, 22, and 27)

2. psychoactive substance abuse (paragraph 15)

3. Axis II borderline personality disorder (paragraphs 15 and 22)

4. antisocial personality (paragraph 21)

5. paranoid ideation (paragraph 25)

6. psychotic disorder (paragraph 25)

7. personality disorder (paragraphs 25 and 27)

8. MMPI (paragraph 27)

9. paranoid schizophrenia (paragraph 27)

10. self-esteem (paragraphs 31, 36, and 55)

11. catharsis (paragraph 36)

12. coping mechanism (paragraph 43)

13. internalized anger (paragraphs 43 and 44)

14. denial (paragraph 45)

15. near-psychotic characteristics (paragraph 52)

16. ego strength (paragraph 55)

Questions

17. Do paragraphs 1 through 15 convince you that satanism is an important problem among adolescents? Explain.

18. What is your opinion on the issue of satanism being a legitimate religion for rare patients. (See paragraph 13.) If you believe that it can be a legitimate religion for some, is it appropriate for a therapist to try to redirect it or discourage its expression? Explain.

19. Does David's interpretation that learning to control his impulses helped him to let go of satanism make sense clinically? Explain. (See paragraph 19.)

20. Are there other types of treatment that might have helped Christina in addition to encouraging her to write about fictional characters? Explain. (See paragraph 26.)

21. What is your opinion on the decision to limit Doug's drawing activities to the art therapy sessions? (See paragraphs 34 through 40.)

22. For Doug, art therapy "provided little insight or cure." (See paragraph 45.) Does this surprise you? Would you, nevertheless, recommend art therapy for a patient like Doug? Explain.

23. In paragraphs 46 through 54, the author presents guidelines. Briefly comment on each. Consider whether the rationale for each is clear, whether each one seems important, and whether there may be circumstances in which it might be inappropriate to apply them.

24. Rate the article on the seven criteria described in the introduction to this book on a scale from 5 (highest quality) through 1 (lowest quality). Be prepared to explain your ratings. *Note: Because Doug's case is described in more detail than the others, apply the criteria only to his case.*

Criterion 1: The demographics of the case are described: _____

Criterion 2: The condition(s) and behavior(s) that necessitated treatment are described in detail: _____

Criterion 3: The method of treatment is described in sufficient detail so that it can be replicated without additional information: _____

Criterion 4: A rationale is provided for the method of treatment selected: _____

Criterion 5: The client's improvement, if any, is clearly documented: _____

Criterion 6: Follow-up information on the client's improvement, if any, is presented: _____

Criterion 7: The study is appropriate for publication in a journal: _____

Case 29

Summoning a Punishing Angel: Treatment of a Depressed Patient With Dissociative Features*

Eliezer Witztum
Jerusalem Mental Health Center–Ezrath Nashim

Jacob T. Buchbinder
Jerusalem Mental Health Center–Ezrath Nashim

Onno van der Hart
Institute for Psychotrauma, Utrecht

ABSTRACT: The authors describe their treatment of a 24-year-old repentant, extremely observant Jewish man with major depressive disorder who complained of persecution by a personal angel. The therapists initiated a culturally sensitive psychotherapy of the patient, enacting a ritual summoning of the angel that resulted in the angel's transformation into an ally. The authors discuss the relationship of the patient's symptomatology to pathological mourning, trance, and dissociation. They advocate the use of a strategic combination of culture-specific concepts with modern psychiatric approaches in similar cases.

(1) Both traditional healing practices and modern psychotherapeutic approaches are based on a rationale or a healing myth that includes an explanation of illness and health, deviancy and normality (Frank, 1973). In traditional societies, the myth is compatible with the world view (usually religious) shared by the patient and the therapist. The traditional healer—a shaman, for example—makes a diagnosis by performing certain acts, and then offers a remedy that may involve drugs or the performance of specific symbolic acts and incantations. According to Frank (1973), the healing efficacy of these procedures lies in the patient's expectation of help and the perception that the healer possesses a special healing power. Not only in traditional healing practices, but in all health care systems, including modern psychotherapy, explanatory models accepted by patients and practitioners alike guide the choice among therapies and therapists and cast personal and social meaning on the experience of sickness (Kleinman, 1980).

(2) A potential conflict exists when the patient belongs to a subculture or religious group with beliefs and explanatory models that differ substantially from those employed by practitioners in the mental health establishment. Psychotherapists can solve this conflict strategically by adjusting to the world view of the patient (cf. van der Hart, 1978/1983, 1988; van der Hart, Witztum, & de Voogt, 1988). Within the context of cross-cultural therapy, these therapists endeavor to help patients articulate their symptoms and solve their problems in the mold of the prevailing idiom and with metaphors from their unique cultural background (cf. Crapanzano, 1975; Good & Good, 1986; Obeyesekere,

---

*Reprinted with permission from the *Bulletin of the Menninger Clinic, 54,* 1990, pp. 524-537. Copyright 1990 by the The Menninger Foundation.

1970). Elsewhere, we (Bilu, Witztum, & van der Hart, 1990) have described the successful treatment, based on this approach, of an ultraorthodox Jewish patient by two secular therapists in a mental health clinic in Jerusalem. After being exposed to a terrorist attack, this patient developed posttraumatic symptomatology, including hallucinations of a demon who threatened to kill him. These hallucinations appeared related to the patient's traumatic grief about his father's death in a traffic accident when the patient was 8 years old. Treatment included instructing the patient to use traditional incantations intended to keep the demon at a distance and metaphoric imagery work in which the patient moved from the desert (where the demon and his aides were threatening him) to an oasis called the "Lower Paradise" where he reunited himself with his father, a mystical experience that successfully concluded therapy for him.

(3) Here we report a comparable cross-cultural therapy from the same clinic. This patient also expressed unresolved mourning regarding his father's death in the idiom of his subculture: A personal angel appeared and ordered him to perform self-afflictive behavior. The two therapists (one an observant Jew) were equally able to join the patient's cosmology. Treatment combined a standard psychiatric approach, consisting of the prescription of psychotropic medication and supportive therapy, with a culturally sensitive approach in which the therapists carefully entered the patient's mystical world and confronted the maladaptive aspects found there.

Case Report

The patient
(4) The patient, whom we shall call Ezra, was a 24-year-old married man who had been a Jewish penitent for 2 years; he was brought by his brother to the clinic because of "bizarre behavior." During the previous 6 months, while Ezra had been immersed in studying the *Zohar* (the key mystical Jewish text), he had heard voices, had dreams in which his late father appeared as a threatening black apparition, engaged in ascetic practices such as frequent fasting, often visited the graves of Zaddikim (Jewish saints), and had ritually lit candles on these graves and in his house. All these symptoms and practices became more intense 4 months prior to his admittance to the clinic after the birth of his first child, a girl.

(5) Ezra appeared unkempt and was only partially oriented to place and time. His cooperation was minimal. His affect was depressed, but his formal thought processes were intact. The content of his thinking indicated auditory and visual hallucinations of a personal angel. Ezra also experienced nightmares in which he saw his father dressed in black with a sad, suffering facial expression. These experiences began after the birth of Ezra's daughter.

History
(6) Born in Israel and of North African descent, Ezra was the younger of two boys. His father had been a quiet, sad man who began to drink in mid-life and became a chronic alcoholic; at home he drank himself to oblivion and often slept covered with his own vomit. One night 9 years earlier, his father had asked Ezra to bring him a glass of water and to stay by his side because he felt ill. Ezra, then 15 years old, brought him the water but refused to stay with him. The next morning the father was found dead. The boy felt guilt ridden and developed a depressive reaction. He subsequently started using hard drugs. When Ezra was 18, his older brother persuaded him to quit taking drugs and join the military service. After successfully finishing his duty 2 years prior to admission, Ezra became religiously observant, married, and started praying for a son to name after his late father. During the pregnancy, he excitedly awaited the birth of this son.

(7) Ezra was shocked when the child was a girl instead of a boy. He began to hear a voice that he identified as belonging to a personal angel who, instead of protecting him, had come to punish him for the neglect that had led to the death of his father. The angel told him to afflict himself by fasting frequently and otherwise eating minimally, by abstaining from sexual relations, and by wearing old and tattered clothes. This self-affliction, the angel said, would eventually bring him forgiveness. Ezra also began to visit grave sites of Jewish saints, praying there for several hours at a time. At night he ritually lit candles in his house.

Treatment
(8) In the second session, one of the therapists prescribed a small dose of the antipsychotic medication thioridazine (Ridazin, U.S. trade name, Mellaril), and started psychotherapy with the assistance of Ezra's older brother, a rabbi and a penitent of many years. Recognizing that Ezra's symptomatology was related to guilt-ridden pathological mourning, both the therapists and the brother explained that Jewish law forbids mourning a dead relative for longer than a year. The therapists asked Ezra to take an important step toward completion of his unresolved mourning by writing a letter to his father in which he asked for forgiveness and for permission to continue to

live (cf. van der Hart, 1978/1983, 1988). One week later, Ezra brought his letter to the third session and read it out loud while crying and trembling:

Father, I just want to ask for your forgiveness and pardon. I know that I am to blame for your death, but I ask forgiveness. I did not know that this is how it would turn out. I want to see you alive. But only say, "I forgive you." Until I see you alive, I will not believe that you have forgiven me. I have an angel that helps me to afflict myself. Please appear to me. I do not want to be reincarnated as a stone, and therefore I cry the whole night. I wait for the angel to teach me mystical secrets of the upper spiritual worlds. Then I will know that you have forgiven me.

(9) After writing the letter, Ezra reported that he felt slightly improved and slept better. However, he also reported the continuation of his self-affliction, his frequent visits to the grave sites, and his ritual lighting of candles. The therapists told him that he was functioning as a person suspended between life and death. They stated that a personal angel should be protective rather than punitive. The therapists and the rabbi sought to improve Ezra's outer appearance, an action they believed could positively influence his inner world. Ezra complied with their request to remove his tattered, dirty jacket because they convinced him that such dress was inappropriate for a religious student. Finally, the therapists asked him to bring a picture of his late father to the next session. The therapists realized that Ezra was pursuing an ecstatic religious experience, which would signify to him that God had forgiven him. Only then would he permit himself to resume enjoyment and involvement in everyday life.

(10) At the fourth meeting, his brother reported that Ezra had taken off his dirty jacket for one day, but when his angel warned him that he would be reincarnated as a stone, he had resumed wearing it. Nevertheless, the patient showed some overall improvement. The therapists and the brother negotiated with Ezra and reached an agreement that he would have his coat dry-cleaned. Ezra then took his father's picture, stared at it with great intensity, and began to cry. The therapists asked him to investigate the angel's nature, in particular its name and intentions: Was the angel concerned with Ezra's benefit or was it just an evil spirit in disguise?

(11) At the fifth session, the therapists noted some deterioration in Ezra's condition. He was more afraid of the angel, and he refused to change or clean his clothing. After some negotiation, he agreed to remove his dirty coat following the upcoming "Ninth of Av," a Jewish day of fasting that commemorates several national tragedies. Ezra had been unable to ascertain the name of the angel, but said that it belonged to the inner circle of the angel Raziel. (This important angel, according to its name, is connected with the "mysteries of God.") Ezra added that he summoned his angel by lighting eight candles aligned in a specific geometric form and by reading a text from the mystical tract *The Book of the Angel Raziel*. This book is a collection of Jewish mystical, cosmological, and magical material, first printed in 1701 and reprinted many times because of the popular belief that the book protects its owner's house from fire and other danger (Dan, 1972a).

(12) The therapists noted modest improvement in the patient during the sixth and seventh sessions. Ezra began to smile and made eye contact on a few occasions. However, he still rarely spoke. The angel had responded to this symptomatic improvement by ordering Ezra to initiate harsher ascetic practices, including reducing his food intake even more. In the eighth session, Ezra reported no change in his condition but added that he planned a pilgrimage to the grave site of the Holy Ari in Safed (Rabbi Isaac Luria, the 16th-century founder of a cabalistic mystical school) and to the graves of other saints in Tiberias.

(13) During the ninth session, he recounted his experiences from the pilgrimage; he had recited special penitential cabalistic prayers. Although the angel was still "deep inside," after the pilgrimage Ezra felt less frightened by its threats. Because the angel still insisted that Ezra's father had not forgiven him, Ezra felt compelled to continue the afflictions and to stop taking medication. However, the therapists and the brother were able to persuade him to resume taking his medication, to which small doses of clomipramine (Anafranil) were added to combat depression.

(14) Ezra appeared for the 10th session wearing a fancy new hat. He reported that the angel now wanted him to mourn the destruction of the Jewish temple in Jerusalem [70 Common Era (CE)] rather than the death of his father. The therapists advised him that such mourning is practiced in Av, the preceding month. Ezra began to cry. The therapists then gave a positive interpretation of his behavior by saying that indeed the month Elul (the current month) was the proper time for self-reflection about deficiencies in one's spiritual condition. Now they had a sign that he was moving toward a normal life: Ezra realized that because he had been so busy mourning his father, he had neglected the appropriate mourning of the destruction of the temple during Av and the required soul-searching during Elul in preparation for the Jewish

New Year and Day of judgment. His brother reported that Ezra could concentrate better and that he had resumed his study of the *Talmud,* a compendium of generally legalistic and nonmystical material compiled during the 6th century CE. Ezra studied alone, however.

(15) During the 11th and 12th sessions, Ezra's functioning had improved but, as ordered by his angel, he also practiced more self-affliction by eating less; and he still refused to take any medication. The therapists realized that they must confront the angel directly. Perhaps they could summon the angel and order it to cease afflicting Ezra. The brother, excited about this possibility, accepted the suggestion that he and the two therapists could serve as a lay Jewish religious court of three for this purpose. They planned to enact the ritual procedure during Ezra's next therapy session. The therapists' intention was to reframe the modus operandi of the angel and to reach a modus vivendi, making the angel an ally and friend instead of a punishing agent. This intervention would accord with the patient's and his brother's subcultural beliefs. What actually happened during the ritual deviated from the therapists' design and expectations because the brother, who as a religious authority was head of the court, tried to exorcise the angel and rushed the ritual in that direction. He presumably felt that maintaining any connection with the angel might be deleterious to Ezra.

Summoning the angel
(16) Although Ezra was late for the next session, the therapists and the brother decided to proceed with the ritual as soon as Ezra arrived. The brother hastened to lock the door, turn off the lights, and close the windows and shades. The therapists understood that these actions served to transform the room into a setting conducive to the induction of a trance. Ezra set up his candles in the form of an 8-stemmed candelabrum. After he lit them, the therapists and the brother ceremonially stated that a Jewish court of three was formally constituted. Leading the ritual, the brother requested that one of the therapists read a formula from *The Book of the Angel Raziel,* which the patient used to summon the angel (a formula originally used to swear or adjure the king of demons not to cause harm or damage). During the reading, Ezra spontaneously began swaying, moving his body and head in an increasingly rhythmic, vigorous manner. While adding his own ecstatic singsong of a two-syllable phrase with increasing loudness and force, he seemed to enter a trance-like state. Suddenly he became quiet and informed the others that the angel was present. The atmosphere in the room was charged and thick. The brother was tense, and the therapists noticed that the patient had become vague and distant. The brother, obviously impressed, hurriedly stated that, on behalf of the court, he was ordering the angel to cease afflicting Ezra and to return no more for "good or bad"—not even to reveal mystical secrets. Ezra seemed stunned and confused because he was still ambivalent toward the angel. One of the therapists then explained to him that, from then on, the angel had no right to disturb him because the angel belonged to another realm. The brother, tense and emotional, told Ezra to blow out the candles in one breath, thereby ending the ritual. Ezra did so, and the court declared that Ezra was now a free man, under his own control. The brother hurriedly opened the shades and windows, and turned on the lights. He handed *The Book of the Angel Raziel* to the therapists, saying that Ezra no longer needed it. Ezra nodded in agreement.

(17) The therapists had planned to convert the angel from a punitive antagonist to an ego-supportive ally. However, the brother was determined to drive the angel completely away once and for all. Nevertheless, the angel behaved according to the therapist's expectations by returning infrequently in the role of an ally

Follow-up
(18) At the next session—the 14th—Ezra appeared smiling, and his brother reported several significant changes: Ezra now ate normally, he had resumed sexual relations with his wife, and for the first time, he had played with his infant daughter. However, the angel had still appeared a number of times without being summoned and had instructed Ezra to study the *Talmud,* a nonmystical work, and to read from the cabalistic book *Tikkunei Zohar.* Because Ezra still showed depressive affect, the antidepressive medication was increased 25 mg. During the 15th session, Ezra reported that the angel had not reappeared. His brother said that Ezra was functioning better at home, was more sociable, and took much better care of himself and of his appearance. At the 16th session, Ezra reported that the angel had appeared twice, both times only to praise his *Torah* study. Moreover, although Ezra's father had previously appeared in Ezra's dreams as a mournful old man in a black cloak, he now appeared dressed in white and bathed in light. The brother remarked that Ezra had chosen life, but was still saddened by the loss of his father. To elevate the soul of their father, the brothers were studying the *Mishnah* (a compendium of laws edited at the end of the 2nd century CE) and chapters from the mystical *Zohar.* Such studies are culturally normative for Sephardic Jews. The brother related that a memorial meeting would be held soon in honor of their late father, when the brothers would ritually celebrate the completion of their studies. The thera-

pists now had objective indications that Ezra was working through his guilt and grief using normative rituals, and that he had forsaken his idiosyncratic, pathological behavior. In addition, the therapists regarded the memorial meeting as an apt leave-taking ritual that would further aid the working through of the unresolved mourning.

(19) The brother was planning to move from Jerusalem to become head of a religious seminary elsewhere, and Ezra and his family planned to join him. However, 4 months later Ezra arrived at the clinic with his wife (the brother was abroad). Although Ezra's medication had been mistakenly stopped, he was not psychotic. He was neatly dressed and was oriented to time and place. His cooperation was good. His affect was sad, and his formal thought processes were intact. The angel had ceased to visit him. One therapist advised Ezra to take the antidepressant medication again, and he complied. After taking the medication for 2 weeks (75 mg/day), Ezra showed improvement over his former depressed state.

(20) A year after treatment ended, the patient remains stable. He dresses well and attends the religious seminary full time with his brother. The personal angel appears rarely and then only as an encouraging ally.

Discussion

Diagnosis and cultural aspects

(21) A formal psychiatric examination indicated that the patient's symptom complex fits the *DSM-III-R* (American Psychiatric Association, 1987) description of a major depressive episode with psychotic features: His mood was depressed; he showed markedly diminished interest in almost all usual activities; he had stopped eating and therefore had lost a good deal of weight; he exhibited psychomotor retardation, a strong feeling of worthlessness, and excessive, inappropriate guilt feelings to a delusional degree; and he had mood-congruent delusions and hallucinations associated with unresolved grief, accompanied by a sense of guilt and a feeling of deserved punishment. This manifestation was, in fact, the patient's second depressive episode; the first episode had occurred at age 15 when his father died. Ezra blamed himself for his father's death. At that time, he did not seek therapy, but instead tried to overcome his intense emotional pain by using hard drugs. The second episode occurred after the birth of a daughter instead of a son reactivated the patient's traumatic grief. At that point, his brother brought him to the clinic.

(22) The diagnosis of major depressive episode with psychotic features ignores some important aspects of the patient's symptomatology. The psychotic features involved not only his involuntary, spontaneous hallucinations of an angel; they also concerned his deliberately summoning and communicating with this angel. The patient appeared to be a highly hypnotizable subject, whose trance induction and summoning procedures were inspired by traditional mystical sources. Both spontaneous and deliberately evoked hallucinations involved trance states similar to hypnosis. Thus the patient's psychotic-like experiences are reminiscent of the rare diagnosis of hysterical psychosis, of which high hypnotizability is an essential feature (Janet, 1898/1908; Spiegel & Fink, 1979; Steingard & Frankel, 1985; van der Hart, Witztum, & Friedman, 1989). Although we do not advocate a reintroduction of this diagnostic category, we stress the incidence of this feature in psychotic patients because it makes psychotherapy—especially hypnotherapy—the treatment of choice.

Possession and nonpossession trance

(23) The patient's self-induction of a trance state similar to hypnosis can be analyzed using Bourguignon's (1979) study of altered states of consciousness (ASC), the different ways of inducing them, and their use in various societies. She proposed dividing the supernatural explanatory model of ASC into two basic categories: *possession trance and nonpossession trance*. Possession trance involves the impersonation of another personality, while nonpossession trance characteristically involves imaginary interactions with one or more personalities, beings, or forces through the hallucinatory experience.

(24) The "trancer" (i.e., the one who experiences the trance) in a nonpossession trance (usually a man) sees, hears, feels, or interacts with one or more beings, or forces, through the hallucinatory experience. In contrast, the subject of a possession trance (usually a woman) performs and impersonates another personality. The trancer, who prepares for the experience by learning what to expect and how to interpret what is perceived or felt, initiates the nonpossession trance through a hypoglycemic condition induced by fasting, sensory deprivation, mortification, or drugs. Possession trance, however, is induced by drumming, dancing, crowd contagion, or, more rarely, drugs.

(25) During the relatively passive nonpossession trance experience, the subject receives instructions from the spirit, which he or she will be expected to remember and subsequently enact. In contrast, the actively performed possession trance will be followed by amnesia for the performance.

(26) From these descriptions, it is clear that this patient

was experiencing a nonpossession trance: He was passive and receptive to the angel's admonitions, and he remembered them. In preparation for the trance, he fasted and isolated himself. He used rhythmic body movement and a repeated melody to induce the trance, and he used an incantation formula to summon the angel.

Pathological mourning
(27) The patient's symptoms stemmed from unresolved mourning complicated by remorse. The patient continuously blamed himself for his father's death. This self-blame was probably based not only on his guilt feelings about letting his father die alone, but also on previously cherished wishes to rid himself of his drunken father. Ezra initially suffered from depression, which he subsequently tried to resolve by using hashish and hard drugs, then with religious fervor, and finally through marriage and the expectation that he would have a son who could be named for his father. His mystical studies during this time seemed to be an attempt to purify himself, to spiritually obtain forgiveness, or to escape pain by instigating mystical experiences. The birth of a daughter shattered his hopes for achieving forgiveness for his supposed complicity in his father's death. Deep depression followed, this time accompanied by auditory and visual hallucinations of a personal angel who provided spiritual guidance and prescribed ascetic practices; Ezra also experienced painful dreams of his father dressed in black and appearing to suffer.

The personal angel as a cultural phenomenon
(28) The patient's personal angel was similar in many ways to the traditional Jewish mystical phenomenon of the *maggid*, and may have been inspired by it. The maggid (literally meaning "one who relates" cf. 2 Sam. 15: 13) is an angel or supernatural spirit that, in mysterious ways, conveys teachings to scholars worthy of such communication. A maggid is thought to pass secrets to the cabalist, the student of Jewish mysticism, when he is asleep or awake. The maggid speaks through the student's mouth or induces automatic writing (Dan, 1972b).

(29) Probably the most important appearance of a maggid occurred to Rabbi Joseph Caro (1488-1575). There are some interesting similarities between his maggid and the angel that appeared to our patient. In his biography of Caro, Werblowsky (1977) emphasized the ethical and ascetic orientation of Caro's maggid. Werblowsky regarded the maggid's presence as evidence of the rabbi's strict, guilt-ridden conscience. The maggid verbally lashed out at various sins Caro had committed. "Take no pleasure from this world," the maggid told Caro, and it prescribed ascetic avoidance of eating and drinking, and the adherence to fasting and self-flagellation.

(30) From a psychodynamic point of view, the appearance of the maggid might be explained as a culturally sanctioned projection of a harsh superego. Culturally, the maggid embodies key fundamentalistic religious values and ideals. Through his mystical studies, our patient found in the figure of the angel a recognizable and culturally sanctioned expression of his deep remorse.

The personal angel as a dissociate phenomenon
(31) According to Werblowsky (1977), the phenomenon of the maggid is comparable to a dissociative state, although the former is more complex. Lewis (1978) concurred with Werblowsky to some extent; he regarded Caro's maggid as a mild dissociation resembling a hypnotic state, and added that he hesitated to consider the experience pathological because Caro's consciousness remained clear and his content and outlook were consistent with a non-dissociated state and with a clear memory of the experience. "Taking his times, cultural setting and personal qualities into account, his conduct can be held . . . to be within the normal range " (Lewis, 1978, p. 15).

(32) Janet's (1889/1973, 1907/1965) definition of dissociation as the splitting off, separation, and isolation of certain parts of the personality *(dedoublement de la personnalite)*, offered a century ago, is as relevant today as it was then (cf. van der Hart & Horst, 1989). The dissociation often results from traumatic experiences, and the dissociated parts (or states) escape control—and sometimes the awareness as well—of the habitual personality. They begin to lead lives of their own and either take over the patient's behavior or coexist with it. In line with Werblowsky's theory, the former could be conceived of as occurring when the maggid is evoked and speaks through the person's mouth. A switch into the maggid state has then taken place. Janet (1898/1908) reported that the "devil" appeared in this way in his patient Achille. Interestingly, his patient's dissociative disorder was also based on extreme feelings of remorse. The existence of two personality states side by side occurs when the person hears or sees an angel—that is, hallucinates the angel's presence—as was the case in our patient.

(33) Both Janet and modern authors have linked dissociative symptoms and disorders to the experience of psychological trauma (cf. Putnam, 1985, 1989a, 1989b; Spiegel, 1988). Dissociative reactions occur in the context of acute trauma as an adaptive process that provides protection and allows the individual to continue functioning, although often in an automatonlike manner (Putnam, 1989a). Dissociative states may be little more than traumatic imagery, that is, the unassimilated

memories of traumatic events, but these states can also develop a sense of self. The latter condition is most clearly seen in patients suffering from multiple personality disorder (MPD) (Putnam, 1989a). Both phenomena seemed to exist in Ezra. His discovery of his father's death constituted a psychological trauma that evoked violent emotions, especially feelings of guilt and remorse. Ezra's personal angel may be seen as a kind of alternate personality, comparable to those of MPD patients. However, unlike the alternate personality in MPD, the personal angel (like the demon in demonic possession) is grounded in normative subcultural beliefs in the existence of such supernatural beings.

The experience of the personal angel as hypnotic state
(34) The patient's trance state seemed similar to the hypnotic state. Breuer (1895/1955) and, more recently, Bliss (1986) stated that dissociations are basically self-hypnotic phenomena. According to Janet's (1889/1973) dissociation theory, however, high hypnotizability is based on the existence of dissociative states. Whatever the relationship between the two, recent research findings indicate that traumatized individuals tend to be highly hypnotizable (Bliss, 1986; Spiegel, Hunt, & Dondershine, 1988; Stutman & Bliss, 1985).

Treatment
(35) The strategic therapy for our patient was essentially an experiment in combining two different approaches. The first approach was a traditional social psychiatric approach of diagnosis, medication, and support, and the second was a culturally sensitive approach that comprised a mixture of modern strategic treatment techniques with the use of the patient's own belief system. From the beginning, the therapists did not question the reality of the patient's hallucinations and his belief in the existence of a supernatural personal angel. Supported by the religious authority of his brother, the rabbi, they could focus on the basic problem of guilt-ridden pathological mourning and explain that Jewish law forbids mourning a dead relative for longer than one year. By emphasizing this injunction, the therapists and the rabbi motivated the patient to accept their guidance to complete his mourning. The patient reported that writing a leave-taking letter to his father and asking him for forgiveness and permission to live helped him to feel slightly better. As the continuation of the self-afflictions and related practices indicated, however, this writing assignment was insufficient to resolve all or most of his guilt feelings. In hindsight, it would have been better if the patient had been instructed to write—at a fixed time and place—a *continuous* leave-taking letter to his father, to be finished only when the patient felt he was ready to say good-bye to his deceased father and start living again. Such an assignment is especially effective for resolving ambivalent grief when the relationship with the deceased is conflicted and guilt feelings may dominate (cf. van der Hart, 1988; van der Hart & Goossens, 1987).

(36) Instructions to the patient to change his subjective sense of self by improving his outer appearance were based directly on Jewish tradition. The therapists originally believed that the patient's compliance in giving up his old, tattered jacket indicated substantial progress; that is, separating from this *linking object* signified a step toward leave-taking from his deceased father. But as the angel's continuing admonitions and the patient's ascetic practices showed, Ezra still harbored unresolved guilt feelings.

(37) The therapists then again joined the patient's idiosyncratic experiences and mystical beliefs—which many ultraorthodox Jews follow—by planning to directly confront the punishing angel in a ritual summoning the angel to the lay court. Although this ritual took a course different from the one the therapists had planned, it nevertheless proved to be an effective way of treating the patient's dissociative experience. The patient and his brother were easily persuaded to participate in the summoning ritual because of its cultural congruence. However, the rabbi/brother took an unexpected course of action. Following such modern therapeutic approaches as ego state therapy and the treatment of malevolent alternate personalities in MPD patients, the therapists had intended to discuss with the summoned angel its reasons for punishing the patient and then to negotiate a more benign influence. Attempts at exorcism are considered to be therapeutically contraindicated (Putnam, 1989a). However, this approach contradicts traditional Jewish law, which does not regard such entities as dissociated ego states but rather as malevolent supernatural beings that must be completely removed. For this reason, and perhaps because he was frightened by the presence of the angel, the brother/rabbi, as head of the lay court, hurriedly ordered the angel to immediately disappear and never return. Interestingly, the angel did return a couple of times in the benign way the therapists had hoped for. Treatment was eventually successful in resolving the angel's psychological foundation, as well as the patient's remorse and mourning regarding his father's death.

(38) This case history illustrates that cross-cultural therapy conducted in a culturally sensitive way offers unique treatment opportunities. It supports the policy of strategically combining a culture-specific approach with modern psychiatric approaches in similar cases. As the course of the summoning ritual indicates, this report also shows that the potential conflicts between traditional

religious approaches and modern treatment techniques, based on secular therapeutic myths, are not always easily bridged.

Acknowledgment

The authors gratefully acknowledge a grant from the Israeli Ministry of Immigrant Absorption to the second author which partially supported this study. They thank Yoram Bilu, PhD, for his helpful comments on an earlier draft of this article.

References

American Psychiatric Association. (1987). *Diagnostic and statistical manual of mental disorders* (3rd ed., rev.). Washington, DC: Author.

Bilu, Y., Witztum, E., & van der Hart, O. (1990). Paradise regained: "Miraculous healing" in an Israeli psychiatric clinic. *Culture, Medicine and Psychiatry, 14*, 105-127.

Bliss, E. L. (1986). *Multiple personality, allied disorders, and hypnosis.* New York: Oxford University Press.

Bourguignon, E. (1979). *Psychological anthropology.* New York: Holt, Rinehart & Winston.

Breuer, J. (1955). Studies on hysteria: Theoretical. Part III. In J. Strachey (Ed. and Trans.), *The standard edition of the complete psychological works of Sigmund Freud* (Vol. 2, pp. 183-251). London: Hogarth Press. (Original work published 1895)

Crapanzano, V. (1975). Saints, Jnun, and dreams: An essay in Moroccan ethnopsychology. *Psychiatry, 38,* 145-159.

Dan, J. (1972a). Book of Raziel. In *Encyclopedia Judaica* (Vol. 13, cols. 1592-1593). Jerusalem: Encyclopedia Judaica.

Dan, J. (1972b). Maggid. In *Encyclopedia Judaica* (Vol. 11, cols. 698-701). Jerusalem: Encyclopedia Judaica.

Frank, J. D. (1973). *Persuasion and healing. A comparative study of psychotherapy.* Baltimore, MD: Johns Hopkins University Press.

Good, B., & Good, M. D. (1986). The cultural context of diagnosis and therapy: A view from medical anthropology. In M. R. Miranda & H. H. L. Kitano (Eds.), *Mental health research and practice in minority communities: Development of culturally sensitive training programs.* Rockville, MD: National Institute of Mental Health.

Janet, P. (1908). *Néuroses et idées fixes* [Neuroses and fixed ideas] (Vol. 1). Paris: F. Alcan. (Original work published 1898)

Janet, P. (1965). *The major symptoms of hysteria* (2nd rev. ed.). New York: Hafner. (Original work published 1907)

Janet, P. (1973). *L'automatisme psychologique* [Psychological automatism]. Paris: Societe Pierre Janet. (Original work published 1889)

Kleinman, A. (1980). *Patients and healers in the context of culture: An exploration of the border between anthropology, medicine, and psychiatry.* Berkeley: University of California Press.

Lewis, A. (1978). Psychiatry and the Jewish tradition. *Psychological Medicine, 8,* 9-19.

Obeyesekere, G. (1970). The idiom of demonic possession: A case study. *Social Science and Medicine. 4,* 97-111.

Putnam, F. W. (1985). Dissociation as a response to extreme trauma. In R. P. Kluft (Ed.), *Childhood antecedents of multiple personality* (pp. 65-97). Washington, DC: American Psychiatric Press.

Putnam, F. W. (1989a). *Diagnosis and treatment of multiple personality disorder.* New York: Guilford Press

Putnam, F. W. (1989b). Pierre Janet and modern views of dissociation. *Journal of Traumatic Stress, 2,* 413-429.

Spiegel, D. (1988). Dissociation and hypnosis in post-traumatic stress disorders. *Journal of Traumatic Stress, 1,* 17-33.

Spiegel, D., & Fink, R. (1979). Hysterical psychosis and hypnotizability. *American Journal of Psychiatry, 136,* 777-781.

Spiegel, D., Hunt, T., & Dondershine, H. E. (1988). Dissociation and hypnotizability in posttraumatic stress disorder. *American Journal of Psychiatry, 145,* 301-305.

Steingard, S., & Frankel, F. H. (1985). Dissociation and psychotic symptoms. *American Journal of Psychiatry, 142,* 953-955.

Stutman, R. K., & Bliss, E. L. (1985). Posttraumatic stress disorder, hypnotizability, and imagery. *American Journal of Psychiatry, 142,* 741-743.

van der Hart, O. (1983). *Rituals in psychotherapy: Transition and continuity* (A. Pleit-Kuiper, Trans.). New York: Irvington Publishers. (Original work published 1978)

van der Hart, O. (Ed.). (1988). *Coping with loss: The therapeutic use of leave-taking rituals.* (C. L. Stennes, Trans.). New York: Irvington Publishers.

van der Hart, O., & Goossens, F. A. (1987). Leave-taking rituals in mourning therapy. *Israel Journal of Psychiatry and Related Sciences, 24,* 87-98.

van der Hart, O., & Horst, R. (1989). The dissociation theory of Pierre Janet. *Journal of Traumatic Stress, 2,* 397-412.

van der Hart, O., Witztum, E., & de Voogt, A. (1988). Myths and rituals: Anthropological views and their application in strategic family therapy. *Journal of Psychotherapy and the Family, 4*(3/4), 57-79.

van der Hart, O., Witztum, E., & Friedman, B. (1989). *Hysterical psychosis, dissociation, and hypnosis.* Manuscript submitted for publication.

Werblowsky, R. J. (1977). *Joseph Caro: Lawyer and mystic.* Philadelphia: Jewish Publication Society of America.

Terms for Discussion

1. psychotropic medication (paragraph 3)

2. *DSM-III-R* (paragraph 21)

3. depressive episode with psychotic features (paragraphs 21, 22, and 27)

4. hypnosis (paragraphs 22 and 31)

5. hysterical psychosis (paragraph 22)

6. possession trance (paragraphs 23, 24, and 25)

7. nonpossession trance (paragraphs 23, 24, 25, and 26)

8. dissociative state (paragraphs 31, 32, and 33)

9. multiple personality disorder (paragraphs 33 and 37)

Questions

10. How certain are you that Ezra's hallucinations were pathological and not merely an expression of a legitimate religious experience? Explain.

11. Do you believe that the brother's behavior described in paragraphs 16 and 17 was more beneficial than the course of action planned by the therapists? Explain.

12. Is the fact that Ezra experienced nonpossession trances rather than possession trances important to his diagnosis and course of improvement? (See paragraphs 23 through 26.)

13. Do you believe that Ezra's wish to rid himself of his drunken father might have contributed to Ezra's guilt when his father died? (See paragraph 27.) Explain.

14. Do you agree that Ezra did not suffer from multiple personality disorder? (See paragraph 33.) Explain.

15. Do you believe that Ezra would have eventually showed significant improvement if only a traditional psychiatric approach had been used? (See paragraph 35.) Explain.

16. Are there other types of treatment that might have facilitated Ezra's improvement? Explain.

17. Rate the article on the seven criteria described in the introduction to this book on a scale from 5 (highest quality) through 1 (lowest quality). Be prepared to explain your ratings.

Criterion 1: The demographics of the case are described: _____

Criterion 2: The condition(s) and behavior(s) that necessitated treatment are described in detail: _____

Criterion 3: The method of treatment is described in sufficient detail so that it can be replicated without additional information: _____

Criterion 4: A rationale is provided for the method of treatment selected: _____

Criterion 5: The client's improvement, if any, is clearly documented: _____

Criterion 6: Follow-up information on the client's improvement, if any, is presented: _____

Criterion 7: The study is appropriate for publication in a journal: _____

Case 30

Therapy for an Anxious Patient Who Believes His Symptoms Are Caused by a Medical Problem*

Baruch Fishman
New School for Social Research
Cornell University Medical College

The Patient

(1) Mr. A, a 41-year-old music teacher, was referred for a psychological consultation after an extensive workup disclosed no medical basis for symptoms of chronic fatigue, faintness, palpitations, and pain in his head and chest. These symptoms had begun in September, at the start of a new academic year, and had progressively worsened. By the middle of November he was convinced that his life was forever ruined by an undiscovered physical illness, even though his internist assured him that he was healthy. In mid-December the internist suggested that his symptoms might be due to "stress" and convinced Mr. A to accept a psychological evaluation.

(2) Mr. A began the first appointment by acknowledging that he was upset about his physical symptoms but expressed skepticism that they were caused by emotional distress. No traumatic event preceded their onset—"and besides, everything's been going so well in my life." To support this view, he explained that he had a tenured position in a suburban school district that already paid very well and that, assuming he carried off a new assignment teaching younger children, a substantial pay raise would follow the next year. Furthermore, the job was undemanding and allowed him lots of leisure time to spend with his wife and two daughters and to teach a class in a prestigious music academy. Now this physical affliction might destroy everything.

(3) With little prompting, Mr. A went on to describe the toll his symptoms were already taking. Teaching untalented grade-school kids how to finger the saxophone or the trumpet required concentration and patience, but because of his symptoms Mr. A worried that he would become impatient, would overreact and embarrass himself, or would do his work so poorly that he would lose the expected promotion and even get fired. This constant worry was already affecting his home life. Typically, he retreated to the TV when he got home and after dinner escaped to bed and sleep. Interaction with his family had gone from being irritable to nonexistent.

(4) Mr. A said that he never before experienced symptoms like these and never had any psychiatric illness. He reported some difficulties during his childhood, but generally it was quite positive. Although his parents were caring and devoted to him and his brother, they were divorced when he was four years old, and his father remarried shortly thereafter. His father continued to be involved with raising Mr. A until he died three years later. His mother also remarried, and Mr. A formed a loving relationship with his stepfather. In fact, over the years Mr. A remained close to his mother and his stepfather and was currently living in the same apartment building where they did.

(5) For as long as Mr. A could remember, he always felt inferior to his older brother. He described him as being outgoing, attractive, sharp, quick, witty, and ultimately successful, obtaining a Ph.D. and then becoming an international consultant. In contrast, Mr. A saw himself as shy, unattractive, nonverbal, slow, and awkward. His musical talent was not valued much by his parents, but

---

Hospital and Community Psychiatry, 43, 1992, p. 583-585. Copyright 1992 by the American Psychiatric Association. Reprinted by permission.

he felt proud of it. He never completed his doctoral dissertation, and rather than take the risks of a performing career, he chose the security, and boredom, of being a teacher. Choosing safety over ambition was a general characteristic of Mr. A, and until recently it had at least provided peace of mind.

(6) Based on Mr. A's months of excessive worry, the absence of primary depressive or panic symptoms, and the presence of motor tension, autonomic hyperactivity, and irritability, the initial *DSM-III-R* diagnosis was:

Axis I:	Generalized anxiety disorder
Axis II:	None
Axis III:	None
Axis IV:	Psychosocial stressor: new teaching assignment. Severity: 2, mild (predominantly acute event)
Axis V:	Current global assessment of functioning (GAF): 65. Highest GAF past year: 85

The Expert's Opinion

(7) To engage a patient like Mr. A, who has trouble believing his physical symptoms are due to anxiety, I take a five-step approach. First, I sidestep the issue of what is causing what. I do so by clarifying right up front that I am a psychologist, not a physician, and that I am in no position to offer an opinion on medical matters. I rely on the medical expertise of the patient's physicians, and I avoid a struggle over what the physical examination and laboratory tests did or didn't prove. The very last thing I want to do is try to convince the patient that his problem is primarily emotional and "all in his head."

(8) The second step is to define a specific, limited, and feasible therapeutic goal. Having stated that I do not deal directly with medical illness, I explain what I can do: I have an expertise in training individuals how to improve their ability to cope with all sorts of problems—situational, interpersonal, and vocational as well as medical. To bring this point home, I identify specific areas of maladaptive coping by the patient; in Mr. A's case, he is responding to his physical symptoms with unremitting worry, irritability, difficulty concentrating, and social withdrawal. The goal of treatment is for Mr. A to acquire skills to cope with the physical symptoms regardless of what the cause of these symptoms may be.

(9) The third step is to describe the theoretical rationale behind the planned approach, in this case cognitive-behavioral therapy.[1] While I try to avoid excessively intellectual discussions, I want the patient to understand that the therapy makes good sense. I explain that all of us become anxious when we perceive a potentially dangerous situation, be it social (a cocktail party), economic (job loss), symbolic (a fight with the boss), or physical (a pain in the chest). Such anxiety is part of life, and everyone has some, but the difference between normal and abnormal anxiety is the degree to which the person expects to be able to cope with the perceived danger.

(10) If the person feels unable to cope, then anxiety itself becomes the problem. It takes on a life of its own, generating excessive worry and producing muscle tension throughout the body. The worry and tension then escalate if the threat seems chronic (like the fear of losing a potential promotion) and the ability to control seems minimal (like the fear of losing one's temper with untalented kids). Now a vicious cycle is at work: the person is worried and tense about being worried and tense. Feeling out of control, he or she becomes even more anxious. Thus the task for the patient is to break this cycle by acquiring skills to cope with the anxiety-provoking situation.

(11) Most patients don't grasp all of this information initially, but I emphasize that the aim is not to eliminate anxiety; that's impossible. The aim is to learn skills to cope with inevitable anxiety and thereby restore a sense that one is in control. In explaining this intention, I achieve two additional therapeutic goals. I frame the problem explicitly as one of deficient coping rather than of unexplained physical symptoms, and by taking a respectful didactic approach, I begin to set up a collaborative relationship of teacher and student or, even better, of trainer and trainee.

(12) Patients like Mr. A can often be motivated by this approach. After countless doctors' appointments and extensive tests, they have become fixed into a passive medical model. They expect to be told what disease they've got and expect others to cure it. Instead, I frame the targeted problem as deficient coping skills that we are going to improve together. At this point the patient conveys his belief that he is not up to the task, as Mr. A did by saying, "I'm not sure I can handle this."

(13) Accordingly, the fourth step is to accept the patient's resistance as expected and understandable. For example, with a patient like Mr. A, I might say, "Of course you feel you can't do it. It's that very expectation of failure we will focus on. And from what you've told me, that expectation has been around a long time. Compared to your older brother, you always believed you were weak, dumb, and inept, and once people think of

themselves as inferior, they spend their lives hiding out, avoiding challenges, anticipating failure, and interpreting situations as evidence of their defects.

(14) "So it's no surprise that you're expecting failure now. But it'd make no sense if I told you that you had to get better in order to get treatment. What does make sense is to learn skills to increase your confidence and, along the way, also take a look at this belief you have about being inferior."

(15) With Mr. A, I might continue, "The irony is that you're convinced that you can't do it, but actually your musical background makes you an ideal candidate. You've already learned the importance of releasing tension before you play an instrument, attacking a new piece of music a phrase at a time, practicing what you've learned until it comes naturally, examining what you're doing, and correcting a technique that isn't working. Cognitive therapy follows very similar principles and techniques."

(16) This quotation illustrates that, like all psychotherapies, cognitive-behavioral therapy requires as much art as science. Although the focus is on the here and now, placing the intervention in the context of the patient's cognitive style and life course makes the patient feel understood and thereby enhances the therapeutic alliance. Similarly, although transference is not interpreted and regression is actively discouraged, the therapist uses the power inherent in the doctor-patient relationship to direct, motivate, encourage, and reinforce. The more the therapist as a teacher can be empathic and tailor language, examples, and recommendations to the specific patient, the more the "trainee" will feel motivated and hopeful about achieving the expected goals.

(17) As the fifth step, I indicate that the "training course" will be time limited, usually about 12 to 16 sessions over three or four months. For patients like Mr. A who are inclined to feel hopeless and helpless, setting a finish line in advance conveys concretely that I expect the task to be accomplished within a defined period. This expectation implies that although the patient's character style may be chronic, the process of acquiring better coping strategies can be relatively brief.

(18) Further, setting a limit helps keep the focus on the present assignments without giving the patient time to ruminate about this pain or that ache. Even if additional sessions are added at the end, the time limit helps diminish regressive tendencies that often accompany physical symptoms, as when the sick child was mothered in bed and excused from school. A set time limit also encourages an anxious patient to move ahead.

(19) After taking these five steps to engage the patient in therapy, I use the techniques of cognitive-behavioral therapy as with other patients with anxiety disorders—that is, training the patient in skills to control symptoms, such as deep breathing, distraction, and relaxation; helping the patient identify and correct catastrophic thoughts and other misinterpretations of situations; and helping the patient examine and restructure basic beliefs of inferiority and vulnerability.[1-3]

Mr. A's Outcome

(20) After the above five-step induction into treatment, Mr. A agreed to start a course of 12 sessions of cognitive-behavioral therapy to learn how to cope better with his physical symptoms. The therapy actually consisted of 15 sessions: six twice a week, six once a week, and three booster sessions over the following two months.

(21) I began by asking Mr. A to note the situations in which his physical symptoms were most pronounced. This is a relatively easy task and generally meets with little resistance; most patients like Mr. A are more than willing to focus on their somatic problems. The assignment also sets the stage for doing homework and examining internal and external situations between sessions.

(22) Mr. A reported that his physical symptoms tended to be most frequent and intense while he was interacting with fellow teachers at school. I asked him to write down in detail the thoughts and feelings he had in these situations, with the stated aim of examining them to make sure they were not getting in the way of his coping when the physical symptoms were at their worst.

(23) Mr. A arrived at the third session somewhat surprised that in every case he was having worries about public humiliation and failure: being a lousy teacher, not getting promoted, and failing as a performing musician. We spent the rest of the session learning how to examine such thoughts to determine how realistic or distorted they were. We identified several common distortions, such as catastrophizing and all-or-nothing thinking, and the homework assignment was then to practice the skills of thought monitoring and examination.

(24) Like many such patients, Mr. A had learned by the sixth session that the more unrealistic his thoughts, the

more intense his physical symptoms. I had only implied this connection; when Mr. A recognized it, it was a profound turning point for him. With the awareness that his catastrophic thoughts were contributing to his physical distress, he was now more willing to consider his problem as emotional rather than physical. He became highly motivated to learn ways to relax the tension in his body and to correct exaggerated and distorted images.

(25) My attempt to train Mr. A in relaxation was not very successful. He felt some relief with deep abdominal breathing, but when I attempted modified hypnosis with suggested imagery, he actually became more anxious. This experience is not uncommon with individuals who have maintained rigid control over their thoughts and feelings to defend against a disruptive childhood and chronic insecurity. I chose not to push the issue, instead indicating that some people just don't like the experience of altered consciousness and that many other coping strategies are available.

(26) Mr. A did respond to learning skills that focused on changing his fears that he would be humiliated, an expectation based on his underlying sense of inferiority. He began each session with self-deprecating remarks about how he hadn't done a good job with his homework. ("I could only come up with four images of failure.") I countered with praise and encouragement. ("Four! That's great, and plenty to work on. Some patients go weeks before they come up with any.") We then systematically reviewed these images, such as colleagues at the musical academy ridiculing his menial position in a grade school.

(27) By examining these images rationally and connecting them with latent beliefs about his worth, we gradually reinterpreted his current situation and past life. The result of this "reframing" was that he no longer saw his teaching position as an inevitable consequence of his weakness and fears, but rather as an opportunity to instill a sense of pride and personal accomplishment in children, giving them what he had missed during his youth. By the tenth session he was practically symptom free. He realized that he could make rational choices when faced with challenges, and that his feelings need not be dictated by imbedded and distorted notions about himself.

(28) The last few sessions were devoted to consolidating these changes and to correcting distorted beliefs and images evoked by termination, such as the notion that he was a weak child whom nobody ever really wanted. Follow-up phone calls six and 12 months later indicated that Mr. A had continued to apply his acquired skills and had maintained his gains without relapse.

References

1. Beck AT, Emery G: *Anxiety Disorders and Phobias: A Cognitive Perspective.* New York, Basic Books, 1985.

2. Deffenbacher JL, Suinn R: Generalized anxiety disorder, in *Anxiety and Stress Disorders.* Edited by Michelson L, Ascher LL. New York, Guilford, 1987.

3. Meichenbaum D: *Stress Inoculation Training.* New York, Pergamon, 1985.

Terms for Discussion

1. motor tension (paragraph 6)

2. autonomic hyperactivity (paragraph 6)

3. irritability (paragraphs 6 and 8)

4. *DSM-III-R* (paragraph 6)

5. generalized anxiety disorder (paragraphs 6, 7, 9, 10, 11, and 19)

6. psychosocial stressor (paragraph 6)

7. global assessment of functioning (paragraph 6)

8. cognitive-behavioral therapy (paragraphs 9, 15, 16, 19, and 20)

9. passive medical model (paragraph 12)

10. transference (paragraph 16)

11. regression (paragraphs 16 and 18)

12. catastrophic thoughts (paragraphs 19 and 24)

Questions

13. Is choosing "safety over ambition" (see paragraph 5) necessarily a symptom of a psychological problem? Is it a symptom in this particular case? Explain.

14. Is there an advantage to describing a diagnosis in terms of the *DSM-III-R* rather than a more general description?

15. Do you believe that it was appropriate to describe the rationale behind the treatment approach to this client? Why? Are there other cases with which it might clearly be inappropriate? (See paragraphs 9 through 12.)

16. What is your opinion on the statement that "like all psychotherapies, cognitive-behavioral therapy requires as much art as science"? (See paragraph 16.) Does this case study illustrate the statement? Explain.

17. Do you agree that it was a good idea to indicate that the course of treatment would be of limited duration in this particular case? (See paragraphs 17 and 18.) Are there other types of cases where this would be clearly inappropriate? Explain.

18. Mr. A had a "turning point." (See paragraph 24.) Given what you know about this client, does this surprise you? Explain.

19. In this case, do you believe that a follow-up by phone rather than in person was appropriate? Explain.

20. Are there any other types of treatment that might have facilitated Mr. A's improvement? Explain.

21. Rate the article on the seven criteria described in the introduction to this book on a scale from 5 (highest quality) through 1 (lowest quality). Be prepared to explain your ratings.

Criterion 1: The demographics of the case are described: _____

Criterion 2: The condition(s) and behavior(s) that necessitated treatment are described in detail: _____

Criterion 3: The method of treatment is described in sufficient detail so that it can be replicated without additional information: _____

Criterion 4: A rationale is provided for the method of treatment selected: _____

Criterion 5: The client's improvement, if any, is clearly documented: _____

Criterion 6: Follow-up information on the client's improvement, if any, is presented: _____

Criterion 7: The study is appropriate for publication in a journal: _____

Case 31

Psychotherapy by Telephone: A Therapeutic Tool for Cancer Patients*

Hindi T. Mermelstein
Memorial Sloan-Kettering Cancer Center

Jimmie C. Holland
Memorial Sloan-Kettering Cancer Center

ABSTRACT: Medically ill patients who cannot come to the psychotherapist's office on a regular basis frequently are encountered in consultation-liaison settings. For these individuals the telephone becomes the only link to psychological counseling. Two cases presented in this article of successful telephone therapy with cancer patients exemplify and highlight the effect of this mode of interaction on the therapeutic process and relationship. Telephone communication also differs from face-to-face interaction in areas of therapist-patient accessibility, control, formality, and anonymity, which make it an especially effective psychotherapeutic tool for the medically ill patient.

(1) Just 3 years after Alexander Graham Bell's invention of the telephone, a report of a physician's use of the instrument to diagnose a child's cough and to reassure the child's grandmother appeared in 1879 in the *Lancet*. Since then, the telephone has become the major means of rapid communication between patients and physicians. In primary medical care practice today, 15% of patient contact time is via the telephone.[1] In the mental health field, telephone and telecommunications systems have been central to the development of suicide hot lines, 24-hour counseling services, consultation, and teaching programs to remote areas.[2-4]

(2) Despite the wide use of the telephone in health care, there are few reports of its use in psychotherapy. Saul[5] described several cases in which the distance and separation provided by the telephone decreased the patients' fear of intimacy. These individuals who found it too anxiety provoking in the therapist's office to express themselves were able to interact with the psychotherapist via the telephone. Other reports of psychotherapy by telephone describe cases in which either the therapist or patient was absent for prolonged periods of time or, in some cases, made a permanent move to another city.[6-8] A survey of 40 psychiatrists in 1977 determined that 86% followed at least some patients by long-distance telephone.[9] Yet, the events that prompted the departure from standard face-to-face therapy were exceptions to the rule, often unexpected, and initially perceived by both patient and therapist as an experimental trial in therapy.

(3) Patients with significant medical illness require frequent contact with their medical doctors and often with mental health professionals as well. This is particularly true of cancer patients. The psychiatry service at the Memorial Sloan-Kettering Cancer Center (MSK) often evaluates and treats patients who are unable to come to the outpatient office on a regular basis. Generally, these individuals cannot come because of their physical condition, because of distance, or because of the presence of a concurrent psychiatric disorder that makes travel or the intimacy of face-to-face contact intolerable. For these patients, the telephone is the sole avenue for psychological counseling; likewise, it is a major and integral therapeutic tool in our work with such patients. In this paper, we present and discuss two cases of telephone therapy with cancer patients at MSK, high-

---

**Psychosomatics*, 32, 1991, pp. 407-412. Copyright 1991 by The Academy of Psychosomatic Medicine. Reprinted with permission.

lighting some of the issues that arise while using this means of conducting psychotherapy.

Case Reports

Case 1

(4) A 50-year-old woman with advanced ovarian cancer was referred to psychiatry for the evaluation and treatment of depression. In the hospital, she complained of anxiety and of feeling a loss of control over her disease and her body. Though she reported no feelings of depression and no change in her usual interests, appetite, or sleep pattern, her husband described frequent crying over the past month, accompanied by weight loss and feelings of hopelessness. Psychiatric examination indicated that she met criteria for an adjustment disorder with depressed mood. A trial of medication and supportive therapy was undertaken to help her deal with the likely progression of her disease and its poor prognosis.

(5) This housewife lived in Georgia and came to MSK monthly for chemotherapy. Several referrals to doctors in the Savannah region were suggested, but the patient was reluctant to follow up on them. She and her husband called frequently to ask advice about her increasing feelings of depression and anxiety. During almost every call, they reminded me (H.M.) of how soon they would be back in New York City and of how eager she was to be seen. It became clear that she was not going to transfer her psychiatric care to a local doctor. She saw me as a significant part of the MSK team that was caring for her. This added to her sense of security and trust in our relationship. By insisting that she switch therapists, I realized that I was actually doing her a disservice. She needed psychotherapeutic intervention and support more frequently than the once a month she was seen during her brief stays in New York City. I had had some limited experience with telephone therapy in the past and agreed to try telephone sessions during the weeks she remained at home. These appointments were planned with the same structure as face-to-face sessions and with a regular fee schedule. Other telephone contacts, such as urgent situations, rescheduling, and medication questions were on an "ad-lib" basis and were done without extra fee, just as in standard therapy. The patient was initially started on amitriptyline and was switched to methylphenidate when the tricyclic antidepressants exacerbated her constipation and dry mouth.

(6) We continued treatment with this arrangement of telephone sessions once or twice a week for over 3 months. When possible, the patient initiated the appointment by calling, just as though she were coming to the office. The average length of the calls was approximately 30 minutes. In our early sessions, the themes revolved around her feelings of guilt for being sick and her terror of the loss of control that the disease represented. She mourned the loss of her future and her unfulfilled dreams. For example, construction of a house that she had designed had just begun. She knew that it was unlikely she would live to see it completed, which she did not. The patient had to face leaving her teenage children "unsettled." She was concerned that they would not complete her plan for their lives without her to guide them.

(7) As she neared the terminal phase of her illness, the thrust of the telephone sessions focused even more on her progressive disease and her entitlement to and need for care. Through the positive transference that was established early in our relationship, she accepted my permission to be sick and slowly gave up her responsibilities. She needed frequent reassurance that it was all right to become more dependent upon her husband and others. Finally, she agreed to allow a nurse in the house instead of insisting that her husband, who had begun to feel overwhelmed, continue to be her sole caretaker. The above issues could be dealt with over the telephone.

(8) Less easy was the assessment of her depression as her terminal state developed. Without visual cues, it was hard to assess her general physical state and thus its contribution to her psychological state. When her voice sounded weak or when she wanted to end sessions early, I found it hard to assess whether this was due to depression, pain, physical weakness, or fatigue. Was she still attending to her dress, or was she too regressed to do so? On several occasions I spoke to her husband briefly to fill in the gaps in information I could not get from the telephone appointments with the patient.

(9) At our last face-to-face visit, I was shocked by her appearance. She had aged greatly, become cachectic, and looked almost moribund. As a counterphobic reaction to her increasing physical debilitation, she needed to maintain a visual facade of wellness. At that visit, she wore an excessive amount of rouge and other makeup, which gave her face a clown-like appearance. It was a surprise to see these changes because the patient had not mentioned them during the previous 3 weeks of telephone contact. One month before her death, she entered a hospice program in Savannah. The patient chose to transfer all her care to the hospice team, as she had done previously when she wanted all care, including psychiatric, at MSK. She agreed to contact me if she needed or wanted additional help and support. Though I

did not speak to the patient after that, her husband called from time to time for support over the 4 weeks until her death.

(10) Even with its limitations, once I became more comfortable with my decision to conduct most of the therapy by telephone, it worked out well. Through our sessions I was able to offer this patient some of the psychosocial support she needed through the last phases of her illness.

Case 2

(11) A 34-year-old woman with lymphoma was referred for psychiatric evaluation at the time of her third relapse. At the initial interview she was extremely distressed about her medical situation, which was very serious. However, upon further questioning, it became clear that she had never made an adjustment to her illness over its 10-year duration. In addition, she had signs and symptoms of a chronic depressed state, which I felt probably predated her illness.

(12) I agreed to see her for ongoing evaluation and supportive treatment during her chemotherapy. Over the 6 weeks that followed, her anxiety continued unabated, and she developed conditioned nausea and vomiting prior to her treatment; these also were provoked by any reminders of the chemotherapy. She could not sit at a table with anyone wearing Opium perfume because the smell reminded her of one of her chemotherapy drugs and nauseated her. As she began to lose her hair, she became more socially isolated and depressed. Using crisis intervention and cognitive techniques, progressive relaxation, and medication, I began to work to lessen her symptoms and to help her function at her maximum level.

(13) As part of the treatment of her disease, however, she was sent to Seattle for a bone marrow transplant. Though I referred her to a psychiatrist in the area who specialized in the psychological care of medically ill patients, she asked if we could continue our sessions by telephone instead of having to see a new psychiatrist in her distant city. In this case, it was more difficult to schedule regular sessions because of her hospitalization. We tried to speak once a week over the 4 months she was there. The length of the sessions varied because of her poor physical state. She often could not tolerate more than 15 minutes of contact. The major theme of our sessions was the change in her body image and her fear of being engulfed by the tubes and medication bottles that surrounded her. The goals of treatment were to support her throughout her difficult "here and now" situation of the transplant procedure and to help her remain connected to the medical personnel at Memorial Hospital and to her former pretransplant world. Finally, I hoped that by continuing the telephone contact, I was maintaining the therapeutic relationship so that when she returned to New York City, our work together could continue, particularly since there were many issues that remained unresolved when she left for Seattle.

(14) Once she recovered and returned to New York City, she was eager to resume face-to-face contact. She told me that the telephone calls helped her feel that I cared for her no matter how sick she was and no matter how her appearance had changed. However, because I was unable to see her and her environment, she felt a sense of alienation during our telephone sessions. At one point, she had trouble remembering what I looked like and began visualizing me as older and similar in appearance to a dear friend of hers. The long-distance treatment was more difficult than with the first patient, in part because of issues that arose. I did not know what she looked like, and I did not know the appearance of the laminar flow rooms in which she was isolated for over 2 months. This added to concerns about how helpful I could be to this young woman who was undergoing a life-threatening treatment. Concerns about how much to charge for the telephone sessions reflected doubts about therapeutic efficacy. Countertransference issues dealt with fears of personal death and inadequacy. Still, the patient and I agreed that maintaining telephone contact during the period that she was away was beneficial. In fact, since her return, she continues in psychotherapy, which has enabled her to return to work and to begin to reconnect with her friends. Her physical health remains good, and she is looking forward to remaining disease-free and to being a cancer survivor.

Discussion

(15) These two cases of psychotherapy with cancer patients demonstrate the use of telephone sessions as an important part of psychotherapeutic treatment. Some aspects of telephone work should be highlighted since they are relevant to this mode of psychotherapy with medically ill patients.

(16) Psychotherapists spend a considerable amount of time on the telephone in a range of contacts with patients. Although all contact with the patient (or even with others about the patient) is part of the therapeutic relationship,[10] the telephone therapy in these cases was structured as regular psychotherapy sessions that were conducted over the telephone. In this mode of psychotherapeutic communication, the same therapeutic processes occur as in standard treatment.[5,6,8] Rosenbaum[7] described 19 years of continued treatment of a woman

by very brief phone calls (often 5 minutes or less in duration) and letters. He emphasized the patient-therapist bond that grew. In the cases presented, the content of the material discussed in telephone sessions of usual length was as important as the bond between patient and therapist. For example, the first patient's view of her therapist as an authority figure empowered the therapist to help the patient feel that she had permission to be sick. It also allowed the therapist to bolster the patient's failing ego and self-esteem while increasing physical debility narrowed her activities.

(17) Because there are no visual cues in telephone contact, the transferential representation of the therapist may be vividly apparent in the patient's visual image of who the person on the other end of the telephone wire is. This is exemplified by the patient with lymphoma who visualized her therapist's face to be that of her dear longtime friend. In a case reported by Shepeard,[11] all contact during the first 6 months was by phone. When patient and therapist finally met, the patient was upset to see that the therapist was the same age as the patient's daughter, whom she described as self-centered and uncaring, and not an older person like herself, as she had imagined. The patient's intense disturbance at the reality she saw probably contributed to her inability to meet face-to-face again for the remainder of the treatment. As Williams and Douds[12] noted, if patients can make of the counselor what they will, they may also be able to make of the counselor what they need.

(18) For the individual who is unable to come into the therapist's office because of physical or even psychological reasons, we feel that treatment by phone is an important therapeutic tool. This may be especially true for people who are homebound because of physical disability, such as cancer patients. These individuals often feel isolated; the telephone contact helps to maintain their sense of connectedness to others, and it decreases their fears of abandonment. These effects, as well as the accessibility and immediacy of telephone communication,[13,14] may be particularly helpful in the period immediately following discharge from the hospital. Patients are excited about going home but are often also anxious about leaving the protection of the hospital. They are anxious about the return of disease, the loss of the readily available monitoring of the staff, and the responsibilities to be met at home. Follow-up telephone sessions reassure patients and diminish their distress,[15] just as they do with adolescents away at school or at other trial separation periods.[16] There have been preliminary reports that suggest that such follow-up contact by phone improves compliance with treatment regimes[17] and lessens the utilization of medical services.[18]

(19) Another feature of the telephone is that it equalizes the power between patient and therapist.[14,19] Usually the patient comes into a "stranger's" office. In theory, the patient is free to leave, but in reality this is hard to do before the formal end of the session. With the telephone, patients are on their own "turf" and know that they can hang up. This increased sense of control on the part of patients may allow them to feel less guarded. For oncology patients, whose illness has already thrust them into a dependent role and who often feel helpless, this relative empowerment of the individual during the telephone sessions may be particularly therapeutic.

(20) There may be less formality in patient-therapist interactions via the telephone. According to Grumet,[19] this facilitates the development of a parental or older sibling relationship. These roles may be particularly beneficial in crisis intervention and supportive therapy, in which the power of therapeutic suggestion, advice, and manipulation can be pivotal. A related difficulty noted by others who have reported on telephone therapy is the risk of switching to a social or conversational mode of interaction.[20] Our clinical observation is that though this can be a problem, it seems to depend more on the individual therapist and patient, rather than on the use of the telephone as a therapeutic tool.

(21) Another feature is the anonymity and decreased scrutiny that may allow patients with paranoid ideation to feel more at ease in this mode of therapeutic contact.[21,13] A 45-year-old man with a chronic delusion that he has a brain tumor is a patient of our service. When his psychotic symptoms worsen, his paranoia and fearfulness of people increase until the closest contact he can allow with his therapist is keeping his office appointment by telephoning the psychiatrist from another location in MSK.

(22) The main negative features of telephone therapy are the loss of visual and nonverbal cues, which normally tell us a great deal about patients and our own responses to what is going on in therapy.[22] In the case of the woman from Georgia, it was hard to assess the timbre of her voice. The significance of the parameters of a patient's voice—its tone, volume, rate, rhythm, and progression—are harder to evaluate in the medically ill. My inability to see the transplant patient and her environment was an obstacle to my feeling connected to her and her to me as the therapist. We are currently conducting a trial of the use of videophones in homebound cancer patients. The videophone projects a still Polaroid-like picture of the caller and receiver that can be

changed every few minutes. Our preliminary results strongly suggest that the presence of this picture exchange between therapist and patient markedly reduces the impact of this major disadvantage of standard telephone contact. Improvements in technology, which include color pictures and the capability to project the images on a regular TV screen, hopefully will be available in the near future.

References

1. Knopke HJ, McDonald E, Siverton JE: A study of family practice in Wisconsin. *J Fam Pract* 8:151-156, 1979

2. Wittson C, Benschoter R: Two way television: helping the medical center reach out. *Am J Psychiatry* 129:136-139, 1972

3. Straker N, Mostyn P, Marshall C: The use of two-way T.V. bringing mental health services to the inner city. *Am J Psychiatry* 133:1202-1205, 1976

4. Maximen J: Telecommunications in psychiatry. *Am J Psychother* 32:450-456, 1978

5. Saul L: A note in the telephone as a technical aid. *Psychoanal Q* 20:287-290, 1951

6. Robertello R: Telephone sessions. *Psychoanal Rev* 59:633-634, 1972

7. Rosenbaum M: Continuation of psychotherapy by "long-distance" telephone. *International Journal of Psychoanalytic Psychotherapy* 3:483-495, 1974

8. Lindon J: Psychoanalysis by telephone. *Bull Menninger Clin* 52:521-528, 1988

9. Rosenbaum M: Premature interruption of psychotherapy: continuation of contact by telephone and correspondence. *Am J Psychiatry* 134:200-202, 1977

10. MacKinnon R, Micheis R: The role of the telephone in the psychiatric interview. *Psychiatry* 33:82-93, 1970

11. Shepeard P: Telephone therapy: an alternative to isolation. *Clinical Social Work Journal* 15:56-65, 1987

12. Williams T, Douds J: The unique contribution of telephone therapy, in *Crisis Intervention and Counseling by Telephone*. Edited by Lester D, Brockopp G. Springfield, IL, Charles C Thomas, 1974, pp 80-82

13. Miller W: The telephone in outpatient psychotherapy. *Am J Pschother* 27:15-26, 1973

14. Lester D: The unique qualities of telephone therapy. *Psychotherapy: Theory, Research, and Practice* 11:219-221, 1974

15. Holland J, Rowland J: Reactions to cancer treatment: assessment of emotional response to adjuvant radiotherapy as a guide to planned intervention. *Psychiatr Clin North Am* 2:347-358, 1979

16. Toichin J: Telephone psychotherapy with adolescents. *Adolesc Psychiatry* 21:332-341, 1987

17. Catanzaro R: Telephone therapy. *Current Psychiatric Therapy* 11:56-60, 1971

18. Infante-Rivard I, et al: A telephone support service to reduce medical care use among the elderly. *J Am Geriatr Soc* 36:306-311, 1988

19. Grumet G: Telephone therapy: a review and case report. *Am J Orthopsychiatry* 49:574-584, 1979

20. Lester, D, Brockopp G (eds): *Crisis Intervention and Counseling by Telephone*. Springfield, IL, Charles C Thomas, 1973

21. Rosenblum I: Telephone therapy. *Psychotherapy: Theory, Research, and Practice* 6:241-242, 1969

22. Jacobs T: Posture, gesture, and movement in the analyst: Clues to interpretation and countertransference. *J Am Psychoanal Assoc* 21:77-92, 1973

Terms for Discussion

1. depression (paragraphs 4, 5, 8, and 11)

2. anxiety (paragraphs 4, 5, and 12)

3. adjustment disorder (paragraph 4)

4. supportive therapy (paragraphs 4, 12, and 20)

5. positive transference (paragraph 7)

6. counterphobic reaction (paragraph 9)

7. conditioned nausea (paragraph 12)

8. crisis intervention (paragraph 12)

9. cognitive techniques (paragraph 12)

10. progressive relaxation (paragraph 12)

11. countertransference (paragraph 14)

12. paranoid ideation (paragraph 21)

Questions

13. In paragraph 5, the authors describe the first patient's reluctance to seek care from a local psychiatrist. What is your opinion on the decision to conduct therapy by long-distance telephone with this patient?

14. In your opinion, are there advantages to planning telephone sessions with structure, setting a regular fee structure (see paragraph 5), and having the patient initiate the calls (see paragraph 6). Explain.

15. With the first patient, the psychiatrist offered "support" and "reassurance." Are there other forms of treatment that might have assisted this patient? Explain.

16. The second patient developed conditioned nausea and vomiting. Are there any methods of treatment that might be especially effective in treating this condition?

17. The psychiatrist apparently learned after the fact that the second patient had felt a sense of alienation during the telephone sessions. (See paragraph 14.) Are there any steps that the psychiatrist might have taken to relieve this problem if he/she had known about it? Explain.

18. Rate the article on the seven criteria described in the introduction to this book on a scale from 5 (highest quality) through 1 (lowest quality). Be prepared to explain your ratings.

Criterion 1: The demographics of the case are described: _____

Criterion 2: The condition(s) and behavior(s) that necessitated treatment are described in detail: _____

Criterion 3: The method of treatment is described in sufficient detail so that it can be replicated without additional information: _____

Criterion 4: A rationale is provided for the method of treatment selected: _____

Criterion 5: The client's improvement, if any, is clearly documented: _____

Criterion 6: Follow-up information on the client's improvement, if any, is presented: _____

Criterion 7: The study is appropriate for publication in a journal: _____

Notes:

Case 32

The Longing for Nurturance: A Case of Factitious Cancer*

Marc D. Feldman
Hill Crest Hospital

Rodrigo Escalona
Duke University Medical Center

(1) Factitious disorder with physical symptoms is characterized by the intentional production or feigning of physical dysfunction. The symptoms derive from the individual's psychological need to assume the "sick" or "patient" role. Unlike malingerers, persons with factitious disorders lack readily recognized incentives for their behavior, such as avoiding work or military duty, obtaining drugs or financial compensation, or securing better living conditions.[1]

(2) In this report, we present a variation of factitious disorder in which, for 2 years, a patient maintained the illusion of having terminal cancer. Through her factitious cancer, the patient elicited nurturance and allayed her feelings of abandonment, establishing a social network based almost entirely on an invalid diagnosis. A review of the literature reveals only two other cases of feigned cancer, with neither patient continuing the deception for more than several weeks.[2]

Case Report

(3) Ms. A, a 35-year-old single corporate secretary, presented emergently for psychiatric evaluation with the chief complaint of overwhelming anxiety and dysphoria "because I've been acting like a compulsive liar." Her distress followed the confrontation by the leader of an oncological support group who, although the patient had claimed for 2 years to have terminal breast cancer, had discovered that she had never actually had cancer at all. The patient tearfully recalled that she began to tell coworkers that she had just been diagnosed with breast cancer shortly after her fiancé ended their engagement. She had added that the cancer had already metastasized and that the prognosis was exceedingly grim, modeling her symptoms on the genuine cancer of an acquaintance. Having felt abandoned and betrayed by her fiancé, the patient consciously hoped that the claim of a terminal illness would elicit sympathy and solicitude; indeed, she experienced an immediate out-pouring of warmth and concern. Ms. A was immensely gratified by the response and enrolled in a cancer support group, ostensibly to gain the support of other patients and to explore her feelings about her cancer. Through the group, she rapidly established a network of close friends, even though making friends had been difficult for her in the past. In order to maintain the ruse of cancer, she shaved her head and wore a wig to mimic chemotherapy-induced alopecia. She also forced weight loss through dieting and increasingly refused social invitations because of fears that her vigilance to the deception would falter and that she would appear "too well." At one point, when the patient suspected that others were becoming too complacent about her alleged plight, she mobilized renewed nurturance by fabricating the story that her grandfather had been severely injured in a fire.

(4) The discovery that the cancer was feigned occurred only when a fortuitous review of the patient's medical chart disclosed that she had never seen the oncologist who she claimed had been treating her. When confronted, the patient promptly acknowledged the deception. She agreed to inform her employer the next day

---

Psychosomatics, 32, 1991, pp. 226-228. Copyright 1991 by The Academy of Psychosomatic Medicine. Reprinted with permission.

and was summarily fired. Distraught and remorseful, she then sought psychiatric evaluation and agreed to admission for a diagnostic assessment and treatment. There was no history of previous psychiatric contacts.

(5) From the start of the hospitalization, the patient appeared frank and forthcoming with staff members and other patients about the events of the previous 2 years. She was "relieved" that the "exhausting" pretense had ended, felt profoundly guilty about having misled others, and participated eagerly in individual and group psychotherapies. Her food intake initially was poor "because every time I pick up a fork, I still keep thinking: 'A person with cancer shouldn't be able to eat this.'" Psychological testing confirmed the clinical impression of major depression and mixed (borderline, histrionic, and dependent) personality disorder; there was no suggestion of psychotic thought processes. Trials of trazodone (Desyrel) and alprazolam (Xanax) were initiated. After a few days, the patient reported a definite decrease in her anxiety and dysphoria, and an increase in her appetite became evident. Following 4 weeks of excellent psychotherapeutic progress, the patient was discharged, voicing her resolve "not to lie anymore. It creates more problems than it solves." Having alienated most of her former friends and coworkers, she elected to move in with a friend in another state who now knew of her false claims of cancer, to obtain a new job there, and to pursue outpatient psychotherapy and psychotropic medication management.

Discussion

(6) As noted, reported cases of simulated cancer have been rare. By feigning cancer, Ms. A appears to have fulfilled the criteria for factitious disorder with physical symptoms. The diagnosis of malingering appears inaccurate since no easily recognizable motives other than assumption of the sick role could be elicited during thorough inpatient and outpatient assessments. Similarly, the volition and control underlying her simulation are incompatible with the diagnosis of conversion disorder; in conversion, the alteration in physical functioning is prompted by unconscious factors and is not intentional.[3]

(7) It is remarkable that Ms. A was able to maintain the ruse for 2 years and that an oncological group therapist and numerous patients with genuine cancer were misled. Lande[4] has suggested that caregivers attempt to approach patients with empathy and trust and thus may never even consider the possibility that an individual could be feigning a serious illness. Likewise, patients in Ms. A's group tried to offer each other unconditional support; obviously, an accusation that Ms. A's cancer might be fake would have been incompatible with that aim. Since Ms. A's goals (sympathy and nurturance) were intangible, detection of the factitious nature of her illness was made more difficult than if she had been pursuing medications or disability funding. In retrospect, some of Ms. A's coworkers acknowledged having been surprised by her consistently excellent job performance and relatively healthy appearance; however, though such subtle, nonverbal "leakage"[4] of her true health status may have occurred, the coworkers did not wish to disparage her and potentially embarrass themselves by questioning the veracity of her diagnosis.

(8) Unlike most individuals presenting with factitious disorders,[1] Ms. A readily accepted the confrontation that her allegations of a serious illness were false, attempted to remedy the situation at her workplace, and earnestly sought a diagnostic assessment and treatment. Direct confrontation was also effective in the two cases of feigned cancer reported by D'Andrea.[2] In accepting hospitalization, Ms. A may have been aware that the ward environment could provide a replacement support system and new, albeit psychiatric, diagnoses; yet, she showed little tendency to regress or misuse her new diagnoses as verification that she still merited special attention. Instead, she was relieved that she could proceed with her life, no longer burdened by the need to maintain the illusion of cancer. She also chose to reestablish herself after discharge in a new setting in which she would not be exposed to the likely animosity of those she had misled.

(9) The economic and interpersonal costs of factitious disorders can be minimized only through timely recognition.[5] This report illustrates that, for some patients, loneliness and isolation may lead them well beyond direct requests for support, even to the intricate enactment of a terminal illness.

References

1. American Psychiatric Association: *Diagnostic and Statistical Manual of Mental Disorders, 3rd Edition, Revised.* Washington, DC, American Psychiatric Association, 1987, pp 315-320, 360

2. D'Andrea VJ: Cancer pathomimicry: a report of three cases. *J Clin Psychiatry* 39:233-240, 1978

3. Nadelson T: The Munchausen spectrum: borderline character features. *Gen Hosp Psychiatry* 1:11-17, 1979

4. Lande RG: Malingering. *J Am Osteopath Assoc* 89:483-488, 1989

5. Eisendrath SJ: Factitious disorder with physical symptoms, in *Treatments of Psychiatric Disorders.* Edited by Karasu TB. Washington, DC, American Psychiatric Association, 1989, pp 2159-2164

Terms for Discussion

1. factitious disorder (throughout article)

2. malingerer (paragraphs 1 and 6)

3. major depression (paragraph 5)

4. mixed (borderline, histrionic, and dependent) personality (paragraph 5)

5. psychotic thought processes (paragraph 5)

6. anxiety (paragraph 5)

7. dysphoria (paragraph 5)

8. psychotropic medication (paragraph 5)

9. conversion disorder (paragraph 6)

Questions

10. Do you agree with the authors that a diagnosis of malingering is inappropriate in this case? (See paragraphs 1 and 6). Explain.

11. Do you agree that "it is remarkable that Ms. A was able to maintain the ruse for 2 years"? (See paragraph 7.) Explain.

12. Speculate on why a client might feign a terminal illness in order to obtain emotional support rather than directly requesting emotional support. (See paragraph 9.)

13. What is your prognosis for Ms. A during the course of her continuing psychotherapy and psychotropic medication management? Explain.

14. Rate the article on the seven criteria described in the introduction to this book on a scale from 5 (highest quality) through 1 (lowest quality). Be prepared to explain your ratings.

Criterion 1: The demographics of the case are described: _____

Criterion 2: The condition(s) and behavior(s) that necessitated treatment are described in detail: _____

Criterion 3: The method of treatment is described in sufficient detail so that it can be replicated without additional information: _____

Criterion 4: A rationale is provided for the method of treatment selected: _____

Criterion 5: The client's improvement, if any, is clearly documented: _____

Criterion 6: Follow-up information on the client's improvement, if any, is presented: _____

Criterion 7: The study is appropriate for publication in a journal: _____

Case 33

Eight Cases of Patients with Unfounded Fear of AIDS

Klaus A. Vuorio
Erkki Äärelä
Ville Lehtinen
Turku University Central Hospital, Finland

ABSTRACT: This article describes eight cases of patients treated at the Psychiatric Department of the University Central Hospital of Turku (UCHT) Finland who all had as a common feature an unfounded fear of AIDS. Three of the patients committed suicide and one of them had overt suicidal tendencies. An unfounded fear of AIDS may be a sign of psychiatric disturbance with increased suicidal risk. Increased fear of AIDS seems to have correlation with media and counselling services. Owing to the fact that these patients primarily seek medical help from other fields of medicine than psychiatry, they are a new problem especially for general hospital psychiatry.

(1) AIDS is a previously unknown disease for which no cure is as yet known. It is characterized by its association with sexual behavior patterns and also by its stigmatization as a disease of sexual minorities and intravenous drug abusers. The disease has been a subject of enormous publicity, some objective and informative, but much of it both alarmist and confusing. Even in those without the infection, the special features of AIDS may cause fear and uncertainty, which are manifested as psychiatric conditions [1-3].

(2) Several kinds of disorders have been described in patients who are afraid that they have acquired AIDS. These conditions include serious depression, somatization disorders, hypochondria, adjustment disorders, and various psychoses [4-6]. The unfounded fear of sexually transmitted disease (especially syphilis), which was earlier relatively common, has been considered to have similar features as unfounded fear of AIDS [7], although opinions to the contrary have also been presented [8]. Those resemblances seem to indicate an epidemiological association between the occurrence of patients with fear of disease and the prevalence of the disease itself. The frequency of patients with fear of disease seems to grow when the frequency of patients with the disease increases. A recent case report also emphasizes the suicidal risk in patients with negative HIV-antibody test and fear of AIDS [9]. The article reports three cases with unfounded fear of AIDS who committed suicide and also gives some recommendations for decreasing AIDS-related suicides [9].

(3) Our experience with these patients seems to indicate that fear of AIDS may lead a susceptible person to suicide regardless of whether or not he is at high risk because of his way of living. No accurate information is available on the suicidal rate associated with unfounded fear of HIV infection. The specific aim of this study is to describe the possible suicidal risk associated with unfounded fear of AIDS which, in our experience, seems to be markedly heightened. There seems to be a strong connection between the intensive media coverage during the period in question, concerning AIDS and HIV infection and the increased number of patients with unfounded fear of AIDS in our clinic. We also discuss the implications of these cases on recommendable policies towards publicity among professional people.

---

*Reprinted from *The International Journal of Psychiatry in Medicine*, 20, 1990, pp. 405-411. Copyright 1990 by Baywood Publishing Company Inc. Reprinted with permission.

Own Cases

(4) This study was carried out on the cases of eight patients with unfounded fear of AIDS evaluated and treated at the Psychiatric Department of the University Central Hospital of Turku (UCHT) in 1986. The department is located in a large general hospital and consists of a fourteen-bed crisis intervention unit and an outpatient department giving consultation-liaison services to the somatic departments of the hospital. During the year 1986, the total number of patients treated in the psychiatric department of UCHT was 1031 (inpatients, 168; outpatients, 863).

(4) During the same year in the catchment area of UCHT (population, approximately 400,000), there was only one patient diagnosed with AIDS and six patients were tested as HIV positive. During the same period in the whole of Finland, there were seventeen patients diagnosed with AIDS and 133 patients tested as HIV positive. The estimation of the frequency of unfounded fear of AIDS in the general population on the basis of our case reports is impossible because the patient material of our clinic is selected in many ways.

(5) A summary of the cases is presented in Table 1. None of the patients had acquired HIV infection, which was shown by the repeated HIV antibody tests. None of the patients could be considered to be at any risk for HIV infection. All patients were medically healthy; none of them had a history of previous or present serious general disease. None had a history of earlier psychiatric hospital admissions. As for sex or age, they did not differ from the general patient material of the clinic.

(6) Four of our eight patients were evaluated as neurotically disturbed, one suffered from a more severe borderline disorder, and three could be considered as psychotic. The evaluation was made according to the criteria of DSM III. Three of the patients committed suicide; one had overt suicidal tendencies but she did not, however, commit suicide. All patients showing suicidal tendencies were severely disturbed. The three patients who committed suicide were all male. Case reports are presented of the three patients who committed suicide.

Case Reports

Patient C. D.
(7) Patient C. D. was a thirty-nine year-old married, childless caretaker, who was referred for psychiatric consultation because of attempted suicide.

(8) About a month before his suicide attempt, he had suddenly begun to fear that he had acquired AIDS. He sought help at an AIDS support center, where his HIV antibody test was found negative. However, his fear was unabated and he sought attention at a health center. From there he was referred to a private psychiatrist who prescribed him psychotropic medication (perfenazine 4mg b.i.d.) and referred him to the psychiatric clinic. Before the referral form arrived at the clinic, he attempted suicide with the prescribed drugs. While being treated for this in the internal clinic, he was evaluated by a psychiatrist.

(9) In the consultation interview he believed that he had acquired HIV infection five years earlier from an extramarital sexual contact. He now believed that all female staff in his work place had been infected by him, although he had had no sexual contact with them. He thought that he was contaminated and a contagious threat to the whole community. He was found severely psychotic with paranoid delusions, depression, suicidal, and in need of a closed psychiatric ward.

(10) Before transfer to the psychiatric hospital, the patient committed suicide by jumping out of the window.

Patient G. H.
(11) Patient G. H. was a forty-three year-old teacher, who came to a general practitioner with a six-month history of depression, paranoid thinking, and fear of AIDS.

(12) The initial symptoms consisted of malaise, insomnia, and lack of concentration at work. He began to suspect that he was suffering from AIDS contracted from extramarital sexual contacts of which he had had many; the last of them five years ago. Ten years earlier, after a casual sexual contact he felt anxiety about a possible syphilis infection. The anxiety disappeared after tests had proved negative. At the time of the onset of the fear of AIDS, his wife had been in the hospital and he suspected that she was infected by him. At the same time, he began to suspect that he was considered to be a homosexual and that this was being reported by the local newspaper.

(13) He sought medical advice from a general practitioner who found his HIV antibody test negative and placed him on psychotropic drugs (oxazepam 15-30mg t.i.d.). When this treatment did not have an adequate effect on his symptoms, he was admitted as an emergency to the psychiatric department. He was found to suffer from severe depression with paranoid features. The psychotropic medication was changed to perfenazine 4mg t.i.d. and amitriptyline 25mg t.i.d. After a treatment period of one week, he committed suicide by jumping

Table 1. A Summary of Cases with Unfounded Fear of AIDS

Case	Sex	Age	Psychiatric Diagnosis DSM III	Former Risk Behavior	Duration of Disorder (Months)	Suicidal Tendencies
A. B.	F	36	Atypical anxiety disorder–300.0	None	6	None
C. D.	M	39	Major depression–296.24	None	1	Suicide
E.F.	F	37	Atypical psychosis–298.90	None	1	Suicidal thoughts
G.H.	F	43	Major depression–296.24	None	6	Suicide
I.J.	F	28	Adjustment disorder with anxious mood–309.24	None	2	None
K.L.	F	48	Adjustment disorder with anxious mood–309.24	None	2	None
M.N.	M	29	Adjustment disorder with atypical features–309.90	None	2	None
O.P.	M	29	Acute paranoid disorder—298.30 Borderline personality disorder—301.83	Single contact with a foreign woman	10	Suicide

out of the window on the ward.

Patient O. P.
(14) Patient O. P. was a twenty-nine year-old married electrician with two children. He was referred to the psychiatric unit by a general practitioner for fear of AIDS and for anxiety.

(15) His symptoms had started two months earlier after he had had sexual contact with a foreign woman while on a holiday abroad. Afterwards, he began to feel anxious about HIV infection and to suffer from anxiety and suicidal thoughts. He was afraid that he might infect his family and abstained from sexual contact with his wife. He kept observing his physical state and noticed symptoms which he felt were compatible with AIDS.

(16) In the light of later discussions, the sexual contact could be regarded as indirect suicidal behavior. The patient knew very well that the prevalence of HIV infection was high in the country where he stayed and he was also otherwise informed about the disease. He had also had a similar episode of fear of AIDS after a casual extramarital sexual contact a few years earlier.

(17) He stayed on the ward several months except for short periods of discharge. On several occasions during this period he attempted suicide with drugs while under alcohol intoxication. He underwent HIV antibody testing by private physicians several times. The result was always negative. Attempts were made to remedy the situation by means of individual and family therapy, without significant success. No signs of psychosis could be found. A diagnosis of serious borderline personality was established according to the criteria of DSM III.

(18) Owing to his repeated requests, a virus isolation test was done. In the two weeks after the blood sample had been taken, he became paranoid and depressive. He made a serious suicide attempt on the ward and was transferred to a closed psychiatric ward of another hospital. A diagnosis of borderline personality disorder and acute, reactive paranoid psychosis was made. He committed suicide by hanging two months later.

Discussion

(19) Our cases show that unfounded fear of AIDS may represent many types and many levels of psychopathology with the result that there may be great variation in their treatment requirements and prognosis. Yet there seems to be a connection between unfounded fear of a sexually transmitted disease, hypochondriasis, depression, and suicidal behavior, an observation previously made by other authors. Unfounded fear of AIDS seems to be not too dissimilar to syphilophobia, of which there exists a long experience. Unfounded fear of syphilis as a sexually transmitted disease is itself an instance of hypochondriasis [10]. The particular association of hypochondriasis with depression is known [11]. There is also some evidence to suggest that there could be a particular association between suicide and hypochondriasis involving sexually transmitted disease [12-14]. These suggestions are observations from the era before AIDS, but the same hypothesis could very likely be applied to AIDS also.

(20) Unfounded fear of AIDS may be a sign of serious psychiatric disturbance and markedly heightened suicidal risk, which should be kept in mind when the patient complains of a fear of AIDS. Usually the patient first seeks medical advice from a general practitioner or a specialist in some other field of medicine than psychiatry and, thus, the psychiatric aspects will involve several specialties. Due to the possible risk of suicide, the physician whom the patient first contacts has a great responsibility not only in judging the situation but also in providing further examinations and treatment for the patient.

(21) The cases presented emphasize the need to discuss the way in which AIDS and HIV infection are dealt with in health education and in mass media. During the period in question, the National Board of Health in Finland organized an advertisement campaign concerning the danger of AIDS. At the same time, the theme was extensively covered in the mass media. The publicity was often one-sided, stressing only the threatful aspects of AIDS. The majority of our cases began to feel their symptoms after the increased media coverage concerning AIDS and HIV infection. A recent report also suggests that increased fear of AIDS has correlation with media and counselling services [15]. The majority of patients who are excessively anxious about HIV infection have been found to have a background of anxiety and fear of destruction that they could have associated also with some other threat. However, from the psychiatric viewpoint it is important to emphasize the need of objectivity of information. Public information which only aims at arousing attention and even fear may cause strong reactions in anxious persons. To put it differently, in the same way as HIV infection has its risk groups, there is in the population a group of individuals who will develop excessive anxiety when exposed to frightening publicity. This may lead these persons to mental breakdown and even suicide.

References

1. M. E. Faulstich, Psychiatric Aspects of AIDS, *American Journal of*

*Psychiatry, 144:*5, pp. 551-556, 1987.

2. W. S. Burton, Psychiatry of HIV Infection, *British Medical Journal, 295,* pp. 228-229, 1987.

3. J. P. Frolkis, AIDS: New Faces for Old Fears, *Postgraduate Medicine, 79*:6, pp. 265-276, 1987.

4. E. V. Valdiserri, Fear of AIDS: Implications for Mental Health Practice with Reference to Ego-Dystonic Homosexuality, *American Journal of Orthopsychiatry, 56*:4, pp. 634-637, 1986.

5. M. Forstein, AIDS Anxiety in the "Worried Well" in *Psychiatric Implications of AIDS,* S. E. Nichols and D. G. Ostrow (eds.), American Psychiatric Press, Inc, 1987.

6. H. J. Poland, D. Hellerstein, and J. Amchin, Impact of AIDS-Related Cases on an Inpatient Therapeutic Milieu, *Hospital Community Psychiatry, 36,* pp. 173-176, 1985.

7. E. Freed AIDophobia (letter) *Medical Journal of Australia, 2,* p. 656, 1983.

8. D. Miller, R. Farmer, and J. Green, Venereophobia: Letter to the Editor, *British Journal of Hospital Medicine, 32*:3, p. 155, 1984.

9. R. Frierson and S. Lippmann, Suicide and AIDS, *Psychosomatics, 29,* pp. 226-231, 1988.

10. A. J. Barsky and G. L. Elerman, Overview: Hypochondriasis, Bodily Complaints, and Somatic Styles, *American Journal of Psychiatry, 140,* pp. 273-283, 1983.

11. R. Kellner, Functional Somatic Symptoms and Hypochondriasis, *Archives of General Psychiatry, 95,* pp. 821-833, 1985.

12. I. David, Letter, *British Medical Journal, 1,* p. 1248, 1961.

13. D. Faull, Letter, *British Medical Journal, 1,* p. 206, 1961.

14. G. G. Thyne, Letter, *British Medical Journal, 1,* p. 1248, 1961.

15. J. Todd, AIDS as a Current Psychopathological Theme: A Report on five Heterosexual Patients, *British Journal of Psychiatry, 154,* pp. 253-255, 1989.

Terms for Discussion

1. depression (paragraphs 2, 9, 11, 13, 18, and 19)

2. somatization disorders (paragraph 2)

3. hypochondria (paragraphs 2 and 19)

4. adjustment disorders (paragraph 2)

5. psychoses (paragraphs 2, 6, and 9)

6. neurotically disturbed (paragraph 6)

7. borderline personality disorder (paragraphs 6, 17, and 18)

8. DSM III (paragraphs 6 and 17)

9. psychotropic medication (paragraphs 8 and 13)

10. paranoid delusions (paragraphs 9, 11, 13, and 18)

11. malaise (paragraph 12)

12. insomnia (paragraph 12)

13. syphilophobia (paragraph 19)

Questions

14. In paragraph 3, the authors suggest "that fear of AIDS may lead a susceptible person to suicide regardless of whether or not he is at high risk." Does this surprise you? Explain.

15. Assuming that G.H. is not a homosexual, do his fears of being exposed as a homosexual surprise you? Explain.

16. Three cases were briefly described in the body of the report. What additional information, if any would you like to have about each one?

17. Would you be interested in an extended case study report on one of the eight cases? If yes, which case? Explain why?

18. With the hindsight that three patients actually committed suicide, what forms of treatment, if any, might have been used to reduce the possibility of suicide?

19. The authors note that, based on their data, it is impossible to estimate the frequency of unfounded fear of AIDS in the population. In your opinion, would a national, scientific survey on this topic be of major benefit to mental health professionals? (See paragraph 4.)

20. Rate the article on the seven criteria described in the introduction to this book on a scale from 5 (highest quality) through 1 (lowest quality). Be prepared to explain your ratings.

Criterion 1: The demographics of the case are described: _____

Criterion 2: The condition(s) and behavior(s) that necessitated treatment are described in detail: _____

Criterion 3: The method of treatment is described in sufficient detail so that it can be replicated without additional information: _____

Criterion 4: A rationale is provided for the method of treatment selected: _____

Criterion 5: The client's improvement, if any, is clearly documented: _____

Criterion 6: Follow-up information on the client's improvement, if any, is presented: _____

Criterion 7: The study is appropriate for publication in a journal: _____

Case 34

Bulimia Nervosa and Acne May be Related: A Case Report*

Madhulika A. Gupta
University of Michigan

Aditya K. Gupta
National Institutes of Health

Charles N. Ellis
University of Michigan

John J. Voorhees
University of Michigan

ABSTRACT: Acne is a very common, often cosmetically disfiguring, cutaneous condition of adolescence that is associated with increased sebaceous gland activity. We present the case of a patient with bulimia who reported that the negative effect of acne on her appearance increased her body image concerns and exacerbated her eating disorder. Improvement of the acne was associated with a significant improvement in her eating disorder. Eating disordered patients may go on restrictive diets in order to control their acne since levels of androgens, which are one of the primary stimulants of sebaceous gland activity, are lower in starvation. As a significant number of adolescents with eating disorders also develop acne, it is important for the clinician to be aware of this previously unreported association between acne and eating disorders, and to evaluate the impact of acne upon the patient's body image and eating behaviour.

(1) Acne is a common cutaneous condition which is associated with an increase in the rate of sebum secretion by the sebaceous glands (1). Acne therefore most often affects the regions of the body that are rich in sebaceous glands such as the face and back, and frequently results in significant disfigurement. Acne has a peak incidence during mid-adolescence (1), a time when sebum secretion increases markedly. Mid-adolescence is also associated with a high incidence of eating disorders (2). It is very likely, therefore, that a significant number of patients who develop an eating disorder during adolescence develop acne around the same time.

(2) Certain psychosocial and physiologic features of acne suggest that, in some instances, acne may exacerbate or perpetuate an eating disorder. Four major features of acne interact with eating disorders: 1. the negative effect of acne upon self-esteem and body image in general (3-6); 2. the association of acne with puberty and the fact that the development of acne is often considered a sign of a person's emerging sexuality, factors which are especially distressful for the patient with an eating disorder who wishes to return to the security of the pre-adolescent years (7,8); 3. the tendency of common folklore to associate certain foods, such as chocolate and fried foods, with acne (1); and 4. the fact that androgens, which play an important role in the pathogenesis of acne, are de-

---

*Reprinted from *Canadian Journal of Psychiatry, 37*, 1, 1992. pp. 58-61. Copyright 1992 by the *Canadian Journal of Psychiatry*. All rights reserved. Reprinted with permission.

creased by starvation and in anorexia nervosa (9-11). In comparison to normal skin, acne-bearing skin produces more 5-alpha-dihydrotestosterone from testosterone (1, 12,13), a reaction which is catalyzed by the enzyme 5-alpha-reductase. 5-alpha dihydrotestosterone is the active tissue androgen in relation to the sebaceous gland (1). Anorexia nervosa has been associated with decreased activity of the 5-alpha-reductase enzyme system (14), and this likely results in decreased levels of 5-alphadihydrotestosterone, decreased stimulation of the sebaceous glands, and possibly improvement of acne.

(3) We present the case of a patient attending the dermatology clinic at the University of Michigan in whom we observed a clinically significant association between bulimia nervosa (2) and acne, over six weeks of drug therapy for acne. As part of a larger study evaluating the psychosomatic correlates of the treatment of facial acne (15), the patient had a clinical psychiatric assessment pretreatment, and after three and six weeks of treatment for her acne with a topical acne therapy (3% erythromycin and 5% benzoyl peroxide gel) for facial acne vulgaris. During these three periods she also completed the Eating Disorder Inventory (EDI) (16) and rated the degree to which her acne was negatively affecting her appearance on a ten point scale. She responded to a question which read as follows: "To what degree is your acne affecting your appearance?" The ten point scale was numbered and divided into ten equal sections where 1 denoted "not at all" and ten denoted "very markedly." The patient underwent a dermatologic assessment by a dermatologist who was unaware of the psychiatric findings. Acne severity was graded on the Cook Scale (17), which is a standard method for grading acne severity.

Case History

(4) This 22 year old woman (height = 5 feet 5 inches; weight = 146 pounds; range of body weight at current height = 130 to 155 pounds) first developed bulimia nervosa (2) at the age of 20. She was bulimic (2) at the time of the initial assessment. She reported bingeing and purging three to four times per week, and otherwise remained on a restrictive diet of about 500 kilocalories per day.

(5) The patient first developed acne when she was 13 years old. The week before her menstrual period she usually experienced an exacerbation of her acne, which would heighten her concerns about her appearance. She also experienced a craving for carbohydrates and was more likely to binge at that time. She would feel very out of control and tended to compulsively self-excoriate and squeeze her acne lesions in an attempt to rid herself of the acne. At other times, when bothered by the effect of acne upon her appearance, she restricted her food intake. The dietary restriction would improve her acne within about one week and temporarily improve her body image.

(6) Before treatment, the patient's acne severity was given a rating of 6 on the Cook Scale (17). A Cook Scale rating of 6 indicates acne lesions of 1 to 2 cm diameter which are easily recognized 2.5 meters away. Subjectively, the patient rated the adverse impact of the acne upon her appearance as an 8 on the ten point scale described above. She responded very well to outpatient acne therapy and had noticed a significant improvement in her acne after one week of therapy. After three weeks she underwent a dermatological evaluation, and her acne severity was given a rating of 2 on the Cook Scale (17). A Cook Scale rating of 2 indicates that the acne lesions are hardly visible from a 2.5 meter distance (17). After six weeks of acne therapy, her acne severity was again given a rating of 2 on the Cook Scale (17). Subjectively, the patient rated the adverse effect of the acne upon her appearance as 1 on the ten point scale noted above, both after three and six weeks of treatment respectively.

(7) The patient reported a significant improvement in her bulimic symptoms after one week of therapy and by the end of six weeks had lost five pounds. The frequency of her bingeing and purging had declined to less than once per week. Since her acne had responded remarkably well after one week of treatment, the patient reported that she did not have the impulse to "control" her appearance by dietary restriction and felt less anxious about eating regular meals. She gained more confidence in social situations as her acne improved and "did not worry about her weight." The improvement in her eating disorder was further facilitated by her realization that she could lose weight by eating regular meals.

(8) The EDI subscale scores pre-treatment and after three and six weeks of treatment respectively were as follows: drive for thinness scores of 12, 7 and 5 respectively; bulimia scores of 6, 4 and 2 respectively; body dissatisfaction scores of 25, 16 and 12 respectively; ineffectiveness scores of 19, 2 and 6 respectively; interpersonal distrust scores of 16, 9 and 13 respectively; interoceptive awareness scores of 13, 5 and 2 respectively; perfectionism scores of 7, 5 and 5 respectively; and maturity fears scores of 2, 1 and 1 respectively.

Discussion

(9) The association between bulimia nervosa and acne appears to be multifaceted. The cosmetic disfigurement

caused by acne exacerbated body image concerns related to weight, and dietary restriction was reported to be associated with an improvement of the acne. The latter factor contributed to exacerbations of the eating disorder.

(10) The EDI profiles are consistent with the clinical findings. Pretreatment, the EDI subscale scores for drive for thinness, bulimia and body dissatisfaction were significantly higher than the norms for female college students (16). The body dissatisfaction subscale score was also well above the norms for eating disordered patients (16). These scores suggest disturbed attitudes and behaviours related to eating and body image (16), and support the presence of an eating disorder in our patient. As the patient experienced a marked improvement in her acne both clinically and subjectively over the course of therapy, she also showed a decline in her drive for thinness, bulimia and body dissatisfaction scores. Of the remaining five subscales of the EDI, the scores for ineffectiveness, interpersonal distrust and interoceptive awareness were above norms for the eating disordered population (16) and again consistent with the clinical psychopathologic findings. Overall, the EDI subscale scores decreased with improvement in the acne, and this parallels our clinical observation. The EDI profiles have been shown to have good test-retest reliability over three weeks (18). The changes in the EDI subscale scores over the course of treatment for acne therefore support the changes observed in the clinical state of the patient over the course of therapy.

(11) Our patient reported that dietary restriction improved her acne. This may be a reflection of the effect of starvation on sebum secretion (9). Some patients may resort to restrictive diets in order to control their acne. Furthermore, an acute exacerbation of acne in a patient with an eating disorder may prove to be a cutaneous sign that the patient is bingeing, a feature of bulimia that is sometimes minimized or denied by some patients. This finding requires further endocrinologic evaluation.

References

1. Cunliffe WJ, Cotterill JA. The acnes, clinical features, pathogenesis and treatment. *Major Problems in Dermatology* 1975; 6:151-172.
2. *Diagnostic and statistical manual of mental disorders, third edition, revised.* Washington DC: American Psychiatric Press, Inc., 1987: 65-71.
3. Shuster S, Fisher GH, Harris E, et al. The effect of skin disease on self image. *Br J Dermatol* 1978; 99 (Suppl 16): 18-19.
4. Panconesi E. Psychosomatic dermatology. In: Panconesi E, ed. *Clinics in dermatology. Stress and skin diseases,* volume 2, number 4. Philadelphia PA: J.B. Lippincott, 1984: 94-179.
5. Tolman EL. Acne and acneiform dermatoses. In: Moschella SL, Hurley HJ, eds. *Dermatology.* Philadelphia PA: W.B. Saunders Company, 1985: 1306-1322.
6. Koblenzer CS. *Psychocutaneous disease.* Orlando FL: Grune and Stratton, 1986: 311-319.
7. Crisp AH. The possible significance of some behavioral correlates of weight and carbohydrate intake. *J Psychosom Res* 1967; 11: 117-131.
8. Crisp AH. *Anorexia nervosa! Let me be.* New York: Grune and Stratton, 1980.
9. Pochi PE, Downing DT, Strauss JS. Sebaceous gland response in man to prolonged total caloric deprivation. *Journal of Invest Dermatol* 1970; 55: 303-309.
10. Buvat J, Lemaire A, Ardaens K, et al. Profil des hormones gonadiques dans 8 cas d'anorexie mentale masculine etudies avant et au cours de la reprise de poids. *Annales d Endocrinologie* (Paris); 1983; 44: 229-234.
11. Wheeler MJ, Crisp AH, Hsu LKG, et al. Reproductive hormone changes during weight gain in male anorectics. *Clin Endocrinol* 1983; 18: 423-429.
12. Sansone G, Reisner RM. Deferential rates of conversion of testosterone to dihydrotestosterone in acne and in normal human skin—a possible pathogenic factor in acne. *J Invest Dermatol* 1971; 56: 366-372.
13. Hay JB, Hodgins MB. Metabolism of androgens by human skin in acne. *Br J Dermatol* 1974; 91: 123-133.
14. Boyar RM, Bradlow HL. Studies of testosterone metabolism in anorexia nervosa. In: Vigersky RA, ed. *Anorexia nervosa.* New York: Raven Press, 1977: 271-276.
15. Gupta MA, Gupta AK, Schork NJ, et al. Psychiatric aspects of the treatment of mild to moderate facial acne: Some preliminary observations. *Int J Dermatol* 1990; 29: 719-721.
16. Garner DM, Olmsted MP, Polivy J. Development and validation of a multidimensional eating disorder inventory of anorexia nervosa and bulimia. *International Journal of Eating Disorders* 1983; 2: 15-34.
17. Cook CH, Centner RL, Michaels SE. An acne grading method using photographic standards. *Arch Dermatol* 1979; 115: 571-575.
18. Wear RW, Pratz O. Test-retest reliability for the eating disorder inventory. *International Journal of Eating Disorders* 1987; 6: 767-769.
19. Sneddon J, Sneddon I. Acne excoriee: A protective device. *Clin Exp Dermatol* 1983; 8: 65-68.
20. Spraker MK. Cutaneous artifactual disease: An appeal for help. *Pediatr Clin North Am* 1983; 30: 659-668.
21. Gupta MA, Gupta AK, Haberman HF. Dermatologic signs in anorexia nervosa and bulimia nervosa. *Arch Dermatol* 1987; 123: 1386-1390.

Terms for Discussion

1. anorexia nervosa (paragraph 2)

2. bulimia nervosa (paragraphs 3, 4, 7, 8, 10, and 11)

3. psychosomatic (paragraph 3)

4. test-retest reliability (paragraph 10)

Questions

5. Does the information in paragraph 1 indicate that acne causes eating disorders or does it only indicate that the two are correlated? Explain.

6. Is the Cook Scale described in sufficient detail for the purposes of this article?

7. In your opinion, are the changes reported in paragraphs 7 and 8 the result of the reduction in the severity of the patient's acne? Could they have been coincidental? Explain.

8. Would a study in which there were experimental and control groups provide more definitive information than the case study reported in this article? Explain.

9. Are there other types of treatment that might have helped reduce this patient's bulimia nervosa? Explain.

10. Rate the article on the seven criteria described in the introduction to this book on a scale from 5 (highest quality) through 1 (lowest quality). Be prepared to explain your ratings.

Criterion 1: The demographics of the case are described: _____

Criterion 2: The condition(s) and behavior(s) that necessitated treatment are described in detail: _____

Criterion 3: The method of treatment is described in sufficient detail so that it can be replicated without additional information: _____

Criterion 4: A rationale is provided for the method of treatment selected: _____

Criterion 5: The client's improvement, if any, is clearly documented: _____

Criterion 6: Follow-up information on the client's improvement, if any, is presented: _____

Criterion 7: The study is appropriate for publication in a journal: _____

Notes:

Notes:

Notes:

Notes:

Notes: